D1622358

Professional PHP4 Multimedia Programming

Allan Kent
Devon H. O'Dell
Andy Chase
Jan Rosa
Sanjay Abraham
Iman S.H. Suyoto
Kapil Apshankar

Wrox Press Ltd ®

Professional PHP4 Multimedia Programming

Published by Wrox Press Ltd,
Arden House, 1102 Warwick Road, Acocks Green,
Birmingham, B27 6BH, UK
Printed in the United States
ISBN 1-86100-764-7

Trademark Acknowledgements

Wrox has endeavored to provide trademark information about all the companies and products mentioned in this book by the appropriate use of capitals. However, Wrox cannot guarantee the accuracy of this information.

Credits

Authors
Allan Kent
Devon H. O'Dell
Andy Chase
Jan Rosa
Sanjay Abraham
Iman S.H. Suyoto
Kapil Apshankar

Additional Material
Dilip Thomas

Technical Reviewers
Matt Anton
Luis Argerich
Chuck Hagenbuch
Basil Simonenko
William Mills
Jonathan Stephens
Jon Bardin
Jan Lehnardt
Kapil Apshankar
David Oehmig
Thomas Weinert
Mark Kronsbein
Safiulla S.M.

Project Manager
Dilip Thomas
Safiulla S.M

Content Architect
Dilip Thomas

Technical Editors
Indu Britto
Nitin Vyas
Girish Sharangpani

Proof Reader
Agnes Wiggers

Index
Michael Brinkman
Bill Johncocks

Production Manager
Liz Toy

Production Coordinator
Rachel Taylor
Pip Wonson

Cover
Dawn Chellingworth

Illustrations
Santosh Haware
Manjiri Karande

Editorial Thanks
Nilesh Parmar

About the Authors

Allan Kent

Allan has been programming seriously for the last 9 years and other than a single blemish when he achieved a Diploma in Cobol programming, is entirely self-taught. He runs his own company where they try to make a living out of making a lot of noise and playing Quake. When that doesn't work they make a lot of noise while doing development and design for an ad agency. Allan lives in Cape Town, South Africa, with his girlfriend and 4 cats.

Devon H. O'Dell

Devon has been designing Internet applications from the time he grappled with writing Perl CGI scripts in 1996. He has since expanded to using PHP, C, Java, Tcl for Internet applications. His PHP projects have included database design, search engines, graphic processors, network monitor interfaces with NMP, and more. He also figured as an author on *Professional PHP4* from Wrox Press. He would like to thank Margriet Homma, family, and friends.

Jan Rosa

Jan Rosa is a medical doctor (although he practices it no more). He runs a professional literature-publishing house and advertising agency along with 2 partners. It is one of the three leading medicine-publishing houses in the Czech Republic. Most of his time is devoted to work. He is responsible for all production/technical stuff and has created most of their Information System in a PHP/MySQL/PDFLib environment. He loves programming and automating real-world tasks. Besides work he likes biking, swimming, skiing, good music, and films.

Andy Chase

Andy Chase has been tinkering with computers and programming since his introduction to LOGO in the third grade. He began using PHP in 2000 while working as a web designer at the ill-fated Stan Lee Media, and soon found himself doing more programming than designing. In 2002, after five years spent living in Los Angeles, Andy escaped to his native New England where he lives with his wife, illustrator Kim Parkhurst. He would like to thank Dilip Thomas and the rest of the Wrox team for their patience and support during the writing and editing process of this book.

Sanjay Abraham

Sanjay Abraham has been a PHP developer since 1995 and continues to be an avid publicity-shunning open source evangelist prophesing his wealth of experience to thousands of programmers around the world. His skill sets include Assembly, C, C++, Java, SQL, PHP, Ruby, Perl, Python, and a proficient knowledge of advanced algorithms and data structures. His technology interests also include XML, Mac OS X, and various other *nix technologies.

Kapil Apshankar

Kapil has three years of experience in knowledge management, i18n, L10n, and manufacturing domains. He works as a team leader for a major software corporation in India. Currently he is working with Web Services in all their forms to devise ways and means to take this nascent technology to its limits. His other interests include Linux, networking, and distributed computing. When not dabbling with computers, he can be seen playing the harmonica or drawing pencil portraits.

Table of Contents

Preface   **1**

Chapter 1: PHP Multimedia Installation   **13**

  Ming   **14**

  GD   **16**

  ImageMagick   **18**

  PDF   **20**
    FDF   22

  Summary   **23**

Chapter 2: PHP Refresher   **25**

  Tag Styles   **25**

  Comments   **26**

  Data Types   **26**

  Assigning Variables   **34**

  Constants   **35**

  Operators   **36**

  Control Structures   **42**
    Conditional Structures   43
    Loops   44

  Functions   **46**

  Object-Oriented Programming   **49**
    Functional vs. OO Programs   50
    Objects and Classes   51
    Members   51
    Methods   52
    Constructor   52
    Instances   53
    Calling Instance Methods   54
    Inheritance   55

  Summary   **68**

Table of Contents

Chapter 3: Ming Fundamentals   **71**

  The Ming Library   **72**

  Ming Objects   **74**
    Fundamentals   75
    Drawing   79
    Text   88
    Animation   92
    Interaction   100

  Summary   **102**

Chapter 4: Ming with ActionScript   **105**

  What is ActionScript?   **105**

  Ming with ActionScript   **106**

  Writing ActionScript   **107**
    Data Types   108
    Variable Declaration   111
    Arrays   120
    Operators   121
    Conditions   122
    Loops   122

  Programming in ActionScript   **123**

  Summary   **140**

Chapter 5: Manipulating Images with GD   **143**

  The GD Library   **144**
    Getting Started   145
    Editing Images in GD   147
    Overview of Basic Functions   147
      Creating New Images   148
      Saving or Sending Images To the Browser   149
      Colors   153
      Basic Geometry   162
      Text   176
      Working with Existing Images   183
      Copying, Resizing, and Merging   183

  Summary   **190**

Chapter 6: ImageMagick   193

What is ImageMagick?   193

Getting Started   194

ImageMagick Tools   196
Convert   196
Mogrify   197
Identify   197

Using ImageMagick with PHP   198
The ImageMagick Class Library   199
Implementing the Class Library Functions   211

Summary   215

Chapter 7: PDFs with PDFlib   217

PDF   217
The PDFlib Library   218

Getting Started   219

Programming Concepts   222
Scoping System   222
General Code Flow   223
Coordinate Systems   226
Paths – Circles, Rectangles, Lines, and Curves   231
Templates (XObjects)   234
Patterns   236
Text Handling   238
    Font   238
    Encoding   240
    Resource Configuration File   246
    Text Formatting   249
Image Handling   252
PDF Import with PDI   258

Implementing the PDFlib Functions   261

Including PDF in HTML   279

Summary   280

Table of Contents

Chapter 8: FDF – Sending Data To and From PDF Forms   **283**

PDF Forms   **284**

PDF Forms vs. HTML Forms   284

What is FDF?   285

Getting Started   **286**

Enabling FDF Support   287

Enabling the $HTTP_RAW_POST_DATA Variable   289

Adobe Acrobat   289

Using FDF with PHP   **290**

Creating a Basic PDF Form   290

Validating the User Input in a PDF Form   300

The PHP FDF API   304

Creating a Complementary Application To the Basic PDF Form   326

Summary   **330**

Chapter 9: Case Study – Ming Headline Grabber   **333**

Headline Grabber – Application Spec   **333**

General Requirements   334

Application Development   337

Summary   **357**

Chapter 10: Case Study – Using GD on WAP Sites and PDA   **359**

WAP   **359**

WML vs. HTML   360

A Basic WML Deck   361

WAP on the Desktop   361

PDA Web Content – AvantGo   **361**

Delivering Custom Content with PHP   **363**

Determining the User Agent   363

WML/HTML on the Fly   363

HAWHAW   364

Coffee Shop Finder – Application Spec   **366**

General Requirements   366

Tools   367

Usability   368

Components   368

Program Listings   369

Possible Enhancements   **395**

Summary   **396**

Chapter 11: Case Study – Image Gallery   399

Image Gallery – Application Spec   399

Tools   400
Components   401
Program Listings   402
Configuration   402
Administration   404
Front End   411
Features   414

Possible Enhancements   418

Summary   418

Chapter 12: Case Study: PDF Template System   421

HTML vs. PDF Template System   421

PDF Template System – Application Spec   423
General Requirements   423
Program Listing   426

Testing the PDF Template System   456

Possible Enhancements   459

Summary   460

Appendix A: PHP Ming Language Reference   463

Appendix B: PHP GD Language Reference   475

Appendix C: HAWHAW Reference   483

Appendix D: PHP PDF Language Reference   501

Appendix E: PHP FDF Language Reference   513

Appendix F: PHP and ImageMagick Language Reference   517

Appendix G: Color Screenshots Gallery — 531

Ming — 531

Ming with ActionScript — 541

Manipulating Images with GD — 542

ImageMagick — 544

PDFlib — 545

Case Study – Image Gallery — 546

Appendix H: Setting Up Palm Desktop, POSE, and AvantGo on a Windows Desktop — 547

Using POSE and AvantGo to View HAWHAW Pages — 547

Summary — 554

Index — 557

Preface

PHP and Multimedia development are set to take the world of Internet application to a new level of expertise. In this book we seek to bring about a synthesis between these two technologies. This book also offers quick insights into bringing about integration between Multimedia and the PHP APIs.

Introducing PHP

PHP: Hypertext Preprocessor (PHP) is a general-purpose scripting language that is especially suited for web development and can be embedded into HTML. It excels when used to write web-based applications. It can be easily used with almost all the free and commercial web servers, allowing web applications to be portable and operating system-independent. Besides that, PHP code can be combined very easily with HTML to produce web pages without any programming effort. When used as a web server module PHP is faster and more efficient than CGI and also has a very robust engine. Thus the goal of the language is to allow web developers to write dynamically generated pages quickly.

Another very interesting feature of PHP is that one can usually write applications, even complex ones, very fast. If the Perl motto is 'There's More Than One Way to Do It' the PHP motto could be 'There's a Faster Way to Do It'. PHP provides a lot of extensions and built-in functions for very specific tasks that would require a hard-to-find library or a lot of code in other languages.

PHP's multimedia extension libraries provide wonderful ways of completing tasks that would otherwise be impossible to achieve using PHP alone. These extensions allow developers to handle such tasks as scripting Flash movies, creating images on the fly, creating dynamic WAP and WML pages, and the creation of PDF files.

Further, with PHP we have the freedom to choose our operating system and a web server. We also have the choice of using procedural programming, OOP, or a mixture of both. Although not every standard OOP feature is realized in the current version of PHP, many code libraries and large applications (including the PEAR library) are developed entirely using the OOP paradigm.

All these advantages make PHP the scripting language of choice for:

- **Web site programming and web applications**
  This is the most traditional and main target field for PHP. We need three things to make this work. The PHP parser (CGI or server module), a web server, and a web browser. Firstly we need to run the web server with a connected PHP installation. Then we can access the PHP program output with a web browser, viewing the PHP page through the server. The scripts can be used to collect form data, generate dynamic page content, or send and receive cookies. This diagram depicts the typical interaction between a browser, web server, and the PHP engine:

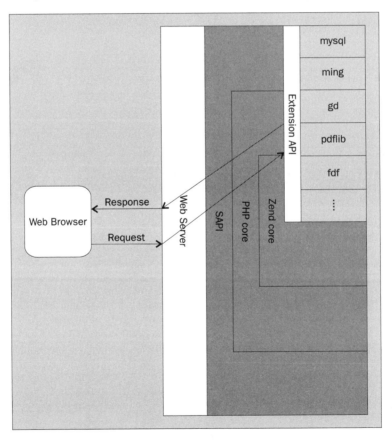

- **Command-line scripting**
  We can run a PHP script without a server or browser. In this case we only need the PHP parser. This type of usage is ideal for scripts regularly executed using **Cron** (for UNIX) or the **Task Scheduler** (for Windows). These scripts can be used for simple text processing tasks. Also, used in this way, PHP competes with scripting languages like Perl or Python.

❑ **Client-side GUI applications**
PHP is not yet the very best language to write windowing applications, but if we need to use some advanced PHP features in our client-side applications, then PHP-GTK is the best choice. We also have the ability to write cross-platform applications this way. PHP-GTK is an extension to PHP; it is not available in the main distribution.

PHP has had a fairly consistent growth rate of 6.5% per month since the summer of 2000 and in May 2002 PHP was running on a whopping 9,059,850 domains and 1,188,121 IP Addresses. For the first time, an open-source scripting solution had passed Microsoft's proprietary Active Server Pages (ASP) scripting language to claim the top spot on the Netcraft survey. This of course excludes the large number of Intranet sites which use PHP, and which would not have been included in these statistics.

PHP4

PHP started off as a quick Perl hack written by Rasmus Lerdorf in 1994. The next couple of years saw it evolve into PHP/FI, which started to get a lot of users. Things started flying when Zeev Suraski and Andi Gutmans came along with a new parser in the summer of 1997, leading to PHP3. This parser defined the syntax and semantics used in both versions 3 and 4.

PHP has been architecturally overhauled since version 3. As a general yardstick, PHP4 is more efficient, more reliable, and much, much faster than PHP3. The performance of PHP4 especially comes into its own for larger and more complex scripts.

Here is a list of the most important changes in PHP4:

❑ **The scripting engine has been redesigned**
The Zend engine was rewritten from the ground up to use an efficient 'Compile-Then-Execute' paradigm, instead of the 'Execute-While-Parsing' model employed in PHP3.

❑ **PHP Extensions**
The function modules now referred to as the PHP extensions, have become self-contained. By self-contained, we mean that most of the binaries (in case of Windows) and the sourcecode (in case of UNIX) are included in the PHP download for a particular platform. Hence we do not have to separately download the extensions every now and then.

❑ **PHP includes the SAPI web server abstraction layer**
This greatly simplifies the task of adding native support for new web servers. SAPI also leads to enhanced stability and support for multi-threaded web servers. SAPI currently has server implementations for Apache, Roxen, Java (servlet), ISAPI (Microsoft IIS, and soon Zeus), AOLserver, and CGI.

The following figure presents PHP4's architecture. The top border of the figure represents the programmer's interface (meaning all except for the web server):

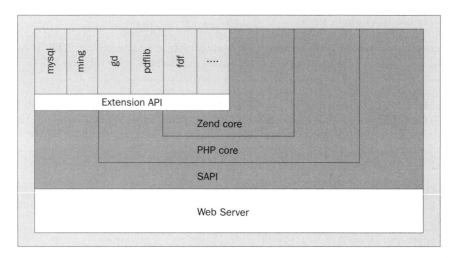

All of PHP's functions are part of one of the layers with a vertical arm in the architecture figure. Most functions such as MySQL support are provided by an extension. These extensions can be linked into PHP at compile time or built, as dynamically loadable extensions, to be loaded on demand.

These are the most important features of PHP4 from the point of view of this book:

❏ **OOP support**
PHP4 provides extended functionality and new features for OOP and building classes and objects. This encompasses nesting of objects and arrays, reference counting, and run-time type information for classes.

❏ **Object-overloading support**
The object-overloading syntax feature allows third-party OO libraries to use the OO notation of PHP4 for accessing their functionality. A COM module that makes use of this feature has already been implemented.

In the chapters that follow, we will discuss both the features and advantages of OOP integration with PHP's multimedia techniques.

Introducing Multimedia

In an age where presentation is paramount and often determines the fate of a web site, we as developers have a rich palette of technologies to choose from. Long gone are the days when we had to make do with HTML. In future, advanced multimedia techniques will make it possible to deliver best-of-breed content to our users with technologies like Flash, PDF, and image manipulation algorithms. In the long run, a successful web site will be one that holistically embraces these technologies.

PHP and Multimedia

PHP includes features that allow us to send back multimedia file types, like images, PDF files, and even Flash movies (using Ming), generated at run-time to the clients. This book covers a wealth of information relating to some of the most popular PHP4 extension libraries, specifically the ones that can be used to create, modify, or deliver multimedia content:

❑ Ming

❑ GD

❑ ImageMagick

❑ PDF

❑ FDF

We will go into the specifics of each of these libraries in the rest of the chapters in the book.

Who Is This Book for?

The target audience for this book broadly falls into three categories:

❑ Intermediate to expert PHP developers who are looking to extend their knowledge further and want detailed information about every aspect of the library; this book will provide a rare source of this information for them.

❑ PHP developers who are happy with their current knowledge, but want immediate knowledge of a specific extension library and its use in the real world, can use this book as the first port of call for that information.

❑ Lastly, we believe that this book will be of use to PHP developers interested in researching the capabilities of PHP when weighing up server-side languages for a potential project.

What You Will Learn

The main strength of this book is that it is unique. Not only does it cover information found in few, if any, other books available; it is also the only book dedicated to PHP4's multimedia extension libraries.

In addition to this, the book is unique in that it is something of a design book for programmers. While it's not going to teach the fundamentals of graphic design, this book will allow developers to use their programming skills to create graphics dynamically, allowing them to broaden their horizons.

The fact that each extension library has its own section in the book helps to focus the reader, and once they are done with the book as a learning tool, it can be used as a handy reference guide to the respective objects, functions, and techniques presented. Each library will be fully covered with numerous examples and case studies that implement many of them.

In addition to all this, the book not only covers how to use the relevant extension libraries from PHP, but it also gives detailed instructions on installing and configuring them. This will also give readers the knowledge to install a lot of other extension libraries for PHP, not just the ones covered in the book.

Book Roadmap

This book contains no fewer than 8 chapters, 4 case studies, and 8 reference appendices.

Let's take a quick rundown:

Part I – Introductory Section

❑ *Chapter 1* briefly discusses the multimedia libraries covered in the book and also provides material on installing the individual extension libraries – Ming, GD, ImageMagick, PDFLib, and FDF.

❑ *Chapter 2* surveys the PHP language features and capabilities. This chapter will serve admirably as a refresher/foundation for PHP programming skills both for developers with established PHP programming skills and the ones who are at the beginning level.

Part II – The Extension Libraries

❑ *Chapter 3* serves as a beginning tutorial to Ming, right from the definition of what Ming is to adding dynamicity to movies using the PHP and Ming interface functions. It will also take a tour through some elements of creating Flash movies, including Flash fundamentals, drawing, text, animation, and interaction.

❑ *Chapter 4* will take the knowledge assimilated from the preceding three chapters – PHP and OOP concepts from Chapters 1 and 2 to put the reader on track to grapple with ActionScript, and the Ming concepts from Chapter 3 –and enable the reader to take this further by adding interactivity to existing dynamic movies.

❑ *Chapter 5* focuses on using PHP and the GD library to create and manipulate graphics for web and mobile phone-based applications.

❑ *Chapter 6* focuses on ImageMagick, which is a collection of tools to modify and gather data about images, and also an API to functions that perform those tasks. In this chapter, we will cover some of the tools distributed with the ImageMagick distribution, how to use these tools, and create a class library that interfaces with these tools.

❑ *Chapter 7* focuses on PDF and creating PDF documents with the help of the PDFlib extension. We will see how to create a PDF document on disk or in memory, lay out text, graphics, and pictures, define and use colors, and place rotated/scaled/skewed objects on a page. Finally we will present an example where we will see how to create PDF documents using an object-oriented approach.

❑ *Chapter 8* complements the previous chapter and presents us with the possibility of populating PDF documents with data and dynamically customizing them using FDF. In this chapter, we will cover what PDF Forms and Form Data Formats are, and how PHP fits into the picture. We will also cover issues that we need to consider while creating PDF Forms – creating PDF files with PHP, utilizing JavaScript to validate the PDF Forms, and using the FDF Toolkit and PHP's API reference for FDF.

Part III – Case Study Solutions

❑ *Chapter 9* will take the knowledge that we have gained from Chapters 3 and 4 of the PHP/Ming module, and see how to use it in creating a useful application. We will not only hone these skills, but also examine the process and thinking behind creating the application. Understanding the structure of a Flash movie is as important as knowing the tools used to create the movie. The application that we will be building is a simple **Headline Grabber**.

❑ *Chapter 10* puts to practical use PHP's image manipulation capabilities to automate the preparation of a single-source image for deployment on more than one platform. In this case study we'll use the GD image functions that we learned in Chapter 5 to automatically generate images optimized for a mobile web **Coffee Shop Finder** application.

❑ *Chapter 11* builds upon Chapter 6 and demonstrates how to design a fully functional **Image Gallery** using the ImageMagick class library that we discussed in Chapter 6. This gallery will be able to select images from a file system or from a MySQL database.

❑ *Chapter 12* puts to practical use the concepts from Chapter 7 to create a general purpose **PDF Template System** that can be used in connection with almost any web application. It will be able to produce PDF documents filled with dynamic content.

Part IV – Reference

❑ *Appendix A* is a listing of the methods available with the 13 classes in PHP/Ming. This will act as a quick function reference to Chapter 3.

❑ *Appendix B* is a listing of the basic GD functions, their return values, and description. This will act as a quick function reference to Chapter 5.

❑ *Appendix C* is a listing of the available PHP HAWHAW functions, their return values, and description. This will act as a quick function reference to Chapter 10.

❑ *Appendix D* is a listing of the basic PDF functions, their return values, and description. This will act as a quick function reference to Chapter 7.

❑ *Appendix E* is a listing of the basic FDF functions, their return values, and description. This will act as a quick function reference to Chapter 8.

❑ *Appendix F* is a listing of the basic ImageMagick functions, their return values, and description. This will act as a quick function reference to Chapter 6.

❑ *Appendix G* showcases some of the more the important color screenshots from all the 12 chapters in the book.

❑ *Appendix H* details the POSE installation procedure used in Chapter 10.

Conventions

To help you get the most from the text and keep track of what's happening, we've used a number of conventions throughout the book.

For instance:

> **These boxes hold important, not-to-be-forgotten information, which is directly relevant to the surrounding text.**

While the background style is used for asides to the current discussion.

As for styles in the text:

❑   When we introduce them, we **highlight** important words

❑   We show keyboard strokes like this: *Ctrl-K*

❑   We show filenames and code within the text like so: `<element>`

❑   Text on user interfaces and URLs are shown as: Menu

We present code in two different ways:

```
In our code examples, the code foreground style shows new, important,
  pertinent code
while code background shows code that is less important in the present
  context or has been seen before.
```

Customer Support

We always value hearing from our readers and we want to know what you think about this book: what you liked, what you didn't like, and what you think we can do better next time. You can send us your comments, either by returning the reply card in the back of the book, or by e-mail to feedback@wrox.com. Please be sure to mention the book title in your message.

How To Download the Sample Code

When you visit the Wrox site, http://www.wrox.com/, simply locate the title through our Search facility or by using one of the title lists. Click on Download in the Code column or on Download Code on the book's detail page.

The files that are available for download from our site have been archived using WinZip. When you have saved the attachments to a folder on your hard drive, you need to extract the files using a decompression program such as WinZip or PKUnzip. When you extract the files, the code is usually extracted into chapter folders. When you start the extraction process, ensure your software (WinZip and PKUnzip, for example) is set to use folder names.

Errata

We've made every effort to make sure that there are no errors in the text or in the code. However, no one is perfect and mistakes do occur. If you find an error in one of our books, like a spelling mistake or faulty piece of code, we would be very grateful for your feedback. By sending in errata you may save other readers hours of frustration, and of course, you will be helping us provide even higher quality information. Simply e-mail the information to support@wrox.com; your information will be checked and if appropriate, posted to the errata page for that title or used in subsequent editions of the book.

To find errata on the web site, go to http://www.wrox.com/, and simply locate the title through our Advanced Search or title list. Click on the Book Errata link, which is below the cover graphic on the book's detail page.

E-Mail Support

If you wish to directly query a problem in the book with an expert who knows the book in detail then e-mail support@wrox.com. A typical e-mail should include the following things:

- ❏ The **title of the book, last four digits of the ISBN**, and **page number** of the problem in the Subject field.
- ❏ Your **name, contact information**, and the **problem** in the body of the message.

We won't send you junk mail. We need the details to save your time and ours. When you send an e-mail message, it will go through the following chain of support:

- ❏ Customer Support – Your message will be delivered to our customer support, and they will be the first people to read it. They have files on most frequently asked questions and will answer anything general about the book or the web site immediately.
- ❏ Editorial – Deeper queries are forwarded to the technical editor responsible for that book. They have experience with the programming language or a particular product, and are able to answer detailed technical questions on the subject.
- ❏ The Authors – Finally, in the unlikely event that the technical editor cannot answer your problem, they will forward the request to the author. We do try to protect the authors from any distractions to their writing; however, we are quite happy to forward specific requests to them. All Wrox authors help with the support on their books. They will e-mail the customer and the editor with their response, and again all readers should benefit.

The Wrox support process can only offer help on issues directly pertinent to the content of our published title. Answer to questions that fall outside the scope of normal book support may be obtained through the community lists of our http://p2p.wrox.com/ forum.

p2p.wrox.com

For author and peer discussion, join the P2P mailing lists. Our unique system provides **Programmer to Programmer**™ contact on mailing lists, forums, and newsgroups, all in addition to our one-to-one e-mail support system. If you post a query to P2P, you can be confident that many Wrox authors and other industry experts on our mailing lists are examining it. At p2p.wrox.com you will find a number of different lists to help you, not only while you read this book, but also as you develop your applications.

To subscribe to a mailing list just follow these steps:

1. Go to http://p2p.wrox.com/

2. Choose the appropriate category from the left menu bar

3. Click on the mailing list you wish to join

4. Follow the instructions to subscribe and fill in your e-mail address and password

5. Reply to the confirmation e-mail you receive

6. Use the subscription manager to join more lists and set your e-mail preferences

> **This book has a dedicated mailing list – php_multimedia, which you can find at http://www.p2p.wrox.com/php/.**

1

PHP Multimedia Installation

PHP extension libraries provide us with methods of producing and writing content that we would be unable to accomplish with PHP's built-in functions. PHP comes with over 75 extensions to the core language – these extensions allow developers to handle such diverse tasks as scripting Flash movies with Ming, creating images with the GD library, creating dynamic WAP and WML pages with HAWHAW, and creating PDF files with PDFlib.

This chapter briefly discusses the Multimedia libraries, covered in this book, that provide extensions to PHPs core language and details the installation of each of the libraries for both UNIX and Windows platforms.

Installing the Extension Libraries

With the exception of ImageMagick, all the other four extensions are included with the PHP distribution. In the unlikely event that they are not available, we can get them from their respective web sites.

Installing on Windows Systems

Windows users have two options:

- ❑ Compile the sourcecode to procure the application extensions of the libraries. However this path is rarely, if ever, followed.

- ❑ The precompiled binary distributions of PHP include the application extension files required for GD, Ming, FDF, and PDFlib. We only need to uncomment the appropriate lines from the php.ini file to make them a part of PHP, like this:

```
extension=php_fdf.dll
;extension=php_filepro.dll
extension=php_gd.dll
;extension=php_gettext.dll
;extension=php_hyperwave.dll
;extension=php_iconv.dll
;extension=php_ifx.dll
;extension=php_iisfunc.dll
;extension=php_imap.dll
;extension=php_ingres.dll
;extension=php_interbase.dll
;extension=php_java.dll
;extension=php_ldap.dll
;extension=php_mbstring.dll
;extension=php_mcrypt.dll
;extension=php_mhash.dll
extension=php_ming.dll
;extension=php_mssql.dll
;extension=php_oci8.dll
;extension=php_openssl.dll
;extension=php_oracle.dll
extension=php_pdf.dll
```

Installing on UNIX Systems

In most cases the binaries for UNIX are not distributed on the PHP site. Therefore, we have to download the sourcecode and compile it ourselves. Once compiled, the procedure is similar – the .so files need to be included or uncommented from the php.ini file.

Ming

Ming is an open-source library that allows us to create SWF Flash movies. Ming supports most Flash 5 features including shapes, gradients, bitmaps (PNG and JPEG), morphs (shape tweens), text, buttons, actions, sprites (movie clips), MP3 streaming, and color transforms. At the time of writing, Ming cannot support sound events.

Ming offers a number of advantages over the existing PHP/LibSWF module. We can use Ming anywhere we can compile the code, whereas LibSWF is closed-source and only available for a few platforms (Windows is not one of them). Ming provides some insulation from the mundane details of the SWF file format, wrapping the movie elements in PHP objects.

The Ming home page is at http://www.opaque.net/ming/.

Now we will look at installing the binaries on a Windows system and compiling from source on a UNIX system.

Windows Installation

On Windows the Ming library is available as php_ming.dll. In the php.ini file, uncomment the corresponding extension and restart the server.

UNIX Installation

The Ming source distribution is available from the SourceForge.net web site at
http://prdownloads.sourceforge.net/ming/ming-0.2a.tgz?download.

Once we have the distribution, we can:

1. Unpack the archive:

```
cd ming-<version>
```

2. Compile:

```
make
make install
```

This will build `libming.so` and install it into the `/usr/lib/` folder, and copy `ming.h` into the `/usr/include/` folder.

3. Edit the PREFIX= line in the Makefile to change the installation directory:

```
CC= gcc -g -pg -a
CC= gcc -05
CC= gcc -g -Wall

PREFIX= /usr/local
PREFIX= /usr

LIBDIR= ${PREFIX}/lib
INCLUDEDIR= ${PREFIX}/include

all: dynamic #static
```

4. There are two ways we can include Ming support with PHP:

❑ Build Ming into PHP:

```
mkdir <phpdir>/ext/ming
cp php_ext/* <phpdir>/ext/ming
cd <phpdir>
./buildconf
./configure --with-ming
```

❑ Include Ming as a PHP module:
Uncompress `php_ming.so.gz` and copy it to the PHP modules directory. Then add `extension=php_ming.so` to the `php.ini` file, or include `dl('php_ming.so');` at the head of all of PHP/Ming scripts.

To build our own PHP module, we should get the Ming source, run `make static` in the top-level Ming directory. Then move to the `php_ext` directory, and run `make php_min.so`.

Testing the Installation

On both the platforms, once the library is installed, running the `phpinfo()` function in a script will result in a page that shows that our PHP distribution is now enabled with Ming support:

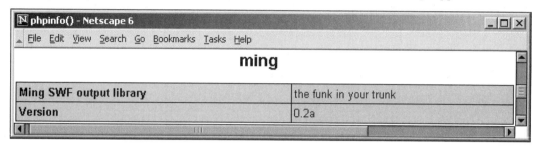

GD

GD is an ANSI C library used for the dynamic creation of images. GD creates PNG and JPEG images, among other formats. Do note that GD does not create GIF images, owing to some licensing issues.

The GD home page is at http://www.boutell.com/gd.

Now we will look at installing the binaries on a Windows system and compiling from source on a UNIX system.

Windows Installation

On Windows, we can load the extension, by uncommenting the appropriate extension in the `php.ini` file, or using the `dl()` function to allow dynamic loading.

The DLLs for PHP extensions are prefixed with `php_` in PHP 4 (`php3_` in PHP 3) and are normally stored in the `./extensions` directory in the PHP distribution. All we have to do is make sure the line in the `php.ini` file which specifies where the extensions can be found, points to the `./extensions` directory.

A common practice is to copy the bundled DLLs from the `extensions` folder of the PHP distribution to our Windows PATH:

- ❑   `c:\windows\system` for Windows 9x/Me
- ❑   `c:\winnt\system32` for Windows NT/2000
- ❑   `c:\windows\system32` for Windows XP

While moving the files to the `windows` or `winnt` directory may not break the extension loading, it may slow it down as the server will need to make at least 2 disk reads (one for the include file, and then another to search the first path in the PATH environment variable). We could try this out in case we are looking out for performance tweaking and tuning.

UNIX Installation

We can get GD 2.0.1 from http://www.boutell.com/gd/. Apart from lots of bug fixes that have come about in GD 2, it also includes support for true color images and alpha channels. This is a very strong motivation for using GD 2 in our own applications.

Once we download the `.tar.gz` file we can get down to installing it:

1. `Ensure that libpeg and libpng are installed.`

2. Unzip the library and move to the GD directory:

```
tar zxvf gd-2.0.1.tar.gz
cd gd-2.0.1
```

3. Edit the Makefile and change the LIBS line to be:

```
LIBS=libgd.a -lpng -lz -ljpeg -lfreetype -lm
```

The Makefile is usually found in the root of the GD directory.

4. Compile the GD library:

```
make libgd.a
```

We don't need to do a `make install`.

5. Include GD support in our PHP distribution, using these flags:

```
--with-gd=/home/<we>/gd-2.0.1
--with-freetype-dir=/usr
--enable-gd-native-ttf
--enable-gd-imgstrttf
--with-jpeg-dir=/usr
--with-png-dir=/usr
--with-zlib
```

Testing the Installation

On both the platforms, once the library is installed, running the `phpinfo()` function in a script will result in a page that shows that our PHP distribution is now enabled with GD support:

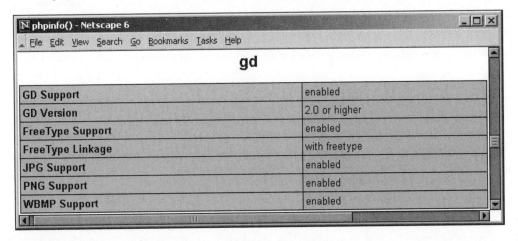

ImageMagick

ImageMagick is a collection of tools to modify and gather data about images, and also an API to functions that perform those tasks, written by the ImageMagick Studio. It allows reading, writing, and manipulating an image in different image formats (over 68 major formats) including popular formats like TIFF, JPEG, PNG, PDF, PhotoCD, and GIF.

With ImageMagick we can create images dynamically, making it suitable for web applications. We can also resize, rotate, sharpen, color reduce, or add special effects to an image and save our completed work in the same or different image format. Further, image processing operations are available from the command line.

ImageMagick support is available in PHP from PECL, the PEAR repository for extensions. For more information refer to http://pear.php.net/manual/en/pecl.imagick.php.

The tools inside the ImageMagick toolkit are written to be very small and efficient. Using these programs within our PHP scripts should not put a strain of any kind on our server; however, a busy site will have lots of spawning and dying convert, mogrify, and identify processes in action. The time needed for task switching on a large number of threads can be significant and can be detrimental to system performance. In such scenarios, it would be worthwhile to avoid using ImageMagick too freely.

We can access ImageMagick functions directly from the command line using the ImageMagick tools – Convert, Mogrify, and Identify. We can then use the display program to interactively manipulate our images or animate an image sequence from a graphical panel. The display is a machine/architecture-independent image processing and display program; the image can be displayed as the background image of any window.

The display determines the hardware capabilities of the client. If the number of unique colors in an image is less than or equal to the number the workstation can support, the image is directly displayed. Otherwise the number of colors in the image is first reduced to match the color resolution of the workstation before it is displayed.

This means that a continuous-tone 24-bits/pixel image can display on an 8-bit pseudo-color device or monochrome device. In most instances the reduced color image closely resembles the original. Alternatively, a monochrome or pseudo-color image sequence can display on a continuous-tone 24-bits/pixels device.

Now we will look at installing the binaries on a Windows system and compiling from source on a UNIX system.

Windows Installation

To install the ImageMagick full package on Windows including the command-line binaries, follow these steps.

❑ Unzip the contents of `ImageMagick.zip` into a directory on the local filesystem

❑ Set the `MAGICK_HOME` variable to point to this path and ensure this directory has been added to your system path – this is easiest done by right-clicking
My Computer->Properties->Advanced->Environment Variables.

Windows 2000 and above include a built-in utility called `convert.exe` that is used to convert a FAT32 partition to NTFS. If we get an error about 'Must specify a filesystem' when trying to convert images, it means that Windows is finding its own version of `convert.exe` before it finds the ImageMagick version. There are three ways around this:

- ❑ Ensure that the ImageMagick directory is before the `WINNT\system32` directory in the system path
- ❑ Rename the Windows version of `convert` to something like `fsconvert.exe`
- ❑ Rename the ImageMagick `convert.exe` to something like `iconvert.exe` or `imageconvert.exe`.

UNIX Installation

The ImageMagick distribution is available at ftp://ftp.planetmirror.com/pub/ImageMagick/ (UNIX) and http://www.dylanbeattie.net/magick/downloads.html (Windows binaries).

Once we have the distribution we can:

1. Unpack the archive:

```
gzip -dc ImageMagick-5.2.2.tar.gz | tar xvf
```

2. Move to the ImageMagick directory and configure:

```
./configure
```

To configure with our choice of compiler, compilation flags, or libraries, we can give `configure` the initial values for variables by setting them in the environment, using a Bourne-compatible shell on the command line:

```
CC=c89 CFLAGS=-O2 LIBS=-lposix ./configure
```

and for systems that have the env program:

```
env CPPFLAGS=-I/usr/local/include LDFLAGS=-s ./configure
```

The env program displays the environment settings on the machine.

3. Compile:

```
make install
```

By default, this will install the package's files in the `/usr/local/bin` directory, the `/usr/local/man` directory, and so on. To specify an installation prefix other than `/usr/local`, include `--prefix=PATH` during configure. Also, `configure` can usually find the X include and library files automatically, but if it doesn't, we can use the configure options `--x-includes=DIR` and `--x-libraries=DIR` to specify their locations. Execute `configure -help` to see the entire configuration options.

Testing the Installation

To test whether our installation was successful or not, open the Command Prompt and type the following command:

```
C:\>Identify logo:
```

to see this output:

PDF

PDF uses the PDFlib library to create PDF files in PHP dynamically. PDFlib is freely available for download at http://www.pdflib.com/pdflib/index.html, but requires purchasing a license for commercial use. Further, JPEG and TIFF libraries are required to compile this extension.

The binary distribution includes both PDFlib and PDF Import Library (PDI), but it generates a watermark across the PDF pages, which can be disabled with a license key. The source distribution does not have a watermark and it also does not include the PDI library.

PDFlib is available for download at http://www.pdflib.com.

Windows Installation

On Windows the PDFlib library is available as php_pdf.dll. Uncommenting the corresponding extension in the php.ini file and restarting the server will be all that we need to do, to enable PDF support with our PHP distribution.

UNIX Installation

The PDFlib binary and source distributions are available from http://www.pdflib.com. If we want to use PDI we must use the binary distribution, since PDI is not available in source form. The PDFlib sourcecode package contains C sourcecode, support files for all language bindings except .NET and COM, the PDFlib reference manual and other documentation, as well as samples for all supported languages. All platform-specific flavors of the main package have the same contents, but differ in line end conventions for text files, as well as compression and packaging method.

Using the loadable module (DSO) is the recommended way of using PDFlib with PHP:

1. We must first ensure that PDFlib support is not precompiled into our PHP version. If our PHP already includes PDFlib support (this is the case for versions of PHP distributed with many UNIX distributions) we must rebuild PHP with the -with-pdflib=no configure option.

2. The PDFlib loadable module is present in the bind/php/ directory of the PDFlib binary distribution; for Linux this is libpdf_php.so, while for other UNIX systems we can use libpdf_php.* with the appropriate shared library suffix.

3. Place the PDFlib loadable module in the directory specified in the php.ini variable extension_dir.

4. Make sure that `php.ini` must includes the lines `safe_mode=Off` and `enable_dl=On`.

At times, we might get an error message similar to the following:

> Your PHP version number does not match that of the PDFlib module:
> Warning: pdf: Unable to initialize module
> Module compiled with debug=0, thread-safety=1 module API=20001214
> PHP compiled with debug=0, thread-safety=1 module API=20001222

In this case, it is best to rebuild PHP with PDFlib support:

1. Configure, make, and install PDFlib:

```
./configure --enabled-shared-pdflib
make
make install
```

Now PDFlib is installed in the /usr/local/lib directory.

2. Configure PHP:

```
./configure --with-pdflib=/usr/local
make
make install
```

3. Update the system library by inserting `/usr/local/lib` in `/etc/ld.so.conf`, then run:

```
/sbin/ldconfig
```

4. Restart Apache:

```
apachectl restart
```

Testing the Installation

On both the platforms, once the library is installed, running the `phpinfo()` function in a script will result in a page that shows that our PHP distribution is now enabled with PDF support:

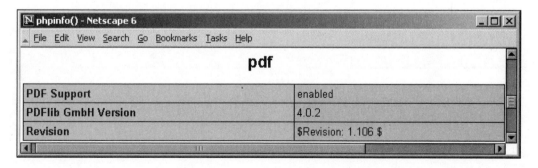

FDF

Forms Data Format (FDF) is a format for handling forms within PDF documents. Adobe Acrobat allows developers to create electronic forms. FDF is the file format used for Acrobat Forms and is used when submitting Form data to a server, receiving a response, and incorporating it back into a Form. For more information refer to http://partners.adobe.com/asn/developer/acrosdk/forms.html.

We will look at installing the binaries on a Windows system and compiling from source on a UNIX system.

Windows Installation

We don't have to download the FDF toolkit from the Adobe web site if we have installed PHP using the Windows binary zip package. But if we have installed PHP on our Windows system using a precompiled binary in the form of a Windows installer, then we cannot use the FDF feature, as this does not support any external extensions. So there is no point in downloading the FDF toolkit in this case. If we have to work with FDF we will have to install PHP manually. Also, we need to configure our web server for the extension application mapping. Once we uncomment the FDF extension in the php.ini file and restart our web server, this extension will be loaded for use by the PHP engine.

On Windows the FDF library is available as php_fdf.dll. Uncommenting the corresponding extension in the php.ini file and restarting the server will be all that we need to do, to enable FDF support with our PHP distribution.

UNIX Installation

On UNIX, all we have to do is compile PHP with this option:

```
--with-fdftk[=DIR]
```

• If there are any problems in configuring PHP with fdftk support, check whether the header file FdfTk.h and the libFdfTk.so library are in fdftk-dir/include and fdftk-dir/lib, respectively. This will not be the case if we just unpack the FdfTk distribution.

Testing the Installation

On both the platforms, once this library is installed, running the phpinfo() function in a script should produce the following result:

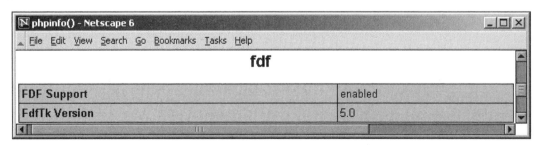

Summary

In the course of this chapter we worked around a couple of facts:

❑ PHP excels as a language that allows web developers to write dynamically generated pages quickly

❑ Multimedia techniques make it possible to deliver the best-of-breed content to our users using technologies like Ming, Flash, GD, PDF, image manipulation algorithms, and so on

❑ PHP includes extension libraries that allow us to create, modify, and deliver Multimedia content which will be generated at run time to the clients

We discussed the most popular of PHP's extension libraries that include Multimedia functionality – Ming, GD, ImageMagick, PDFlib, and FDF and then detailed instructions on how to get these libraries working with Windows and UNIX systems.

This chapter will thus serve as a foundation to get started with the rest of the material in this book. We hope you like the book and enjoy using it as much as we enjoyed writing it.

2

PHP Refresher

This chapter presents an overview of the basic syntax and control structures of the PHP language. It is a must-read for those who do not have a completely confident PHP programming experience. Even for others this chapter is recommended as a reference for the basic techniques of object-oriented programming before diving into programming with the extension libraries – Ming, Ming with ActionScript, GD, ImageMagick, PDFlib, and FDF.

PHP programs can be executed either by a web server or by a console program. These programs are stored in standard text files normally with a .php extension. However we can configure the file extension to anything we like, by editing the web server's configuration file. For example, if we want to save PHP files on an Apache web server with a .phpmm extension, then we should edit the httpd.conf file to recognize that extension:

```
AddType application/x-httpd-php .phpmm
```

The other common extensions are .php3 and .phtml, both of which are now deprecated.

Tag Styles

In the context of a web page, PHP sits embedded within the surrounding markup, which is probably but not necessarily HTML or XHTML. PHP allows for four different tag types to distinguish it from the rest of the markup:

Tag Syntax	Tag Type
`<? ... ?>`	Short tags
	This is best for use with SGML processing instructions
`<?php ... ?>`	XML tags
	This is best for use with XML processing instructions
`<% ... %>`	ASP-style tags
	This is best for use with editors that understand ASP tags but not PHP tags. This is not recommended, particularly on Windows development servers where ASP is also being run.
`<script language="php"> ... </script>`	HTML editor-friendly script-style tags

We will be using the XML-style tags throughout this book since this is the recommendation in most of the coding standards for PHP. However, one can choose the type of tag one wants to use by enabling that specific type under the `Language Options` section in the `php.ini` configuration file.

Comments

PHP uses C-style comments (as do Java and JavaScript) as well as Perl-style comments (as does Tcl):

```php
<?php

# This is an example of PHP's Perl-style comment

/* This is an example of PHP's
   C-style multi-line comment */

// This is an example of PHP's C++-style comment
?>
```

Use of Perl/shell-style comments (#) is discouraged.

Data Types

Variables can be used to store some data – a variable is like a label that refers to a value. In PHP, all variables are represented by the use of a dollar sign ($) preceding the variable name. A variable name in PHP can be a combination of alpha characters, digits 0-9, and the underscore (_) character. In a variable name, the first character cannot be a digit and no character can be a space. PHP's variables, like Perl's, are loosely typed. The data type of a variable is determined by the first value assigned to it.

There are eight distinct primitive variable types that can be used with PHP for storing data. The eight types are divided into three categories – scalar, compound, and special types.

The scalar types include:

- ❏ Integer
- ❏ Double
- ❏ String
- ❏ Boolean

The compound types include:

- ❏ Arrays
- ❏ Objects

And the special types include:

- ❏ Resources
- ❏ NULL

We will look at each of these in detail later on in this section.

gettype() and settype() Functions

We will review a few built-in functions to test the type of the PHP variables and also look at casting data types.

gettype()

We can use the gettype() function to return the type that PHP has assigned to a variable:

```php
<?php

$variable = "This is a string";
print (gettype($variable));
?>
```

This will print out string.

settype()

The settype() function can be used to explicitly set the type:

```php
<?php

$variable = 1;
print (gettype ($variable));
settype ($variable, string);
print (gettype ($variable));
?>
```

This will print out integer on the first test using gettype() and string on the second test. This is because we explicitly used the settype() function after the first test.

Casting

PHP also has casting operators, which allow us to tell PHP to treat a value of one type as if it were another type. Casting is done by surrounding the desired type in parentheses, and applying it to any expression. The code and the embedded comments below illustrate how casting works:

```php
<?php

$value1 = 7.1;
$value2 = "58.1 avg";
$value3 = 8;

$var1 = (integer) $value1;                  // assigns 7
print (gettype($var1)."<br>\n");            // prints "integer"

$var2 = (string) $value1;                   // assigns "7.1"
print (gettype($var2)."<br>\n");            // prints "string"

$var3 = (object) $value3;       // $var3 becomes an object with 1 attribute
print ($var3->scalar."<br>\n"); // the attribute is 'scalar'. prints 8
?>
```

Types of Casting

PHP allows values to be cast to the following types:

❑   int or integer

❑   bool or boolean

❑   float, double, OR real

❑   string

❑   array

❑   object

Casting from one type to another can give unusual results when the source or destination type is non-scalar. Therefore, we should use undefined type casts with caution.

Scalar Types

A scalar data type is so called because it's used to hold a single item of data. This could be a number, a sentence, a single word or character, or another item appropriate to the scalar variable type that contains it.

The four scalar types are:

❑   Integer

❑   Floating point a.k.a double

❑ String

❑ Boolean

Integer

Integer values can be specified in decimal, octal, or hexadecimal format, optionally preceded by a + or sign. Integers beginning with a leading zero (0) are interpreted as octal. Integers beginning with a leading zero followed by an x (0x) are interpreted as hexadecimal.

Also, all integers in PHP are 32 bits long, and all integers are signed. Therefore the range is from -2,147,483,646 to 2,147,483,647.

If we specify a number beyond the bounds of an integer, or perform an operation that results in a number that is beyond the bound of an integer, it will be represented as a **float**. In case of division, if both the numerator and denominator are integers, and the result comes out as an integer, then the return value will be an integer; otherwise the return value will be a float.

We can use the is_int() function (or its is_integer() alias to test whether a value is an integer:

```
if (is_int($a)) {
    // $a is an integer
}
```

Floating Point

Floating point number is also known as float, double, or real number. The exact size is platform-dependent though a precision of roughly 14 decimal places is common. This conforms to the 64-bit IEEE format. It is important to note that in some cases the floating point arithmetic in PHP is not as precise as one might like. To perform high-precision calculations, we should use the appropriate mathematical functions available in the language.

> **PHP provides a library of arbitrary precision math functions (the bc* family) that are useful for these situations. For more information refer to the online PHP language manual available at http://www.php.net/manual/en/ref.bc.php.**

A typical float declaration looks like this:

```
$float_variable = 3.1415;
```

We can use the ceil() function to round up a floating point number:

```
$six = ceil(5.3);       // $six = 6.0;
$ten = ceil(9.999);     // $ten = 10.0;
```

We can use the floor() function to round down a floating point number:

```
$five = floor(5.3);     // $five = 5.0;
$seven = floor(7.999);  // $seven = 7.0;
```

String

String variables are very easy to use in PHP, and there is a wide range of built-in functions to help us manipulate them. A typical declaration looks like this:

```
$string_variable = "Jon Doe is a Professional writer";
```

This is an example of using double quotes to specify a string literal – this is the most common method. However, PHP tries to expand any variables it sees within double-quoted strings. This code:

```
$writing_style = "professional";
$string_variable = "Jon Doe is a $writing_style writer";
print ($string_variable);
```

will print:

Jon Doe is a professional writer

There are a number of escape characters that PHP will recognize in double-quoted strings. Here is a list of the most commonly used ones:

Sequence	Meaning
\n	Linefeed
\r	Carriage return
\t	Horizontal tab
\\	Backslash
\$	Dollar sign
\'	Single quote
\"	Double quote

We can specify string literals with single quotes. However, in this case, PHP does not recognize the above escape characters, and it will not try to expand variables. This example:

```
$writing_style = "professional";
$string_variable = 'Jon Doe is a $writing_style writer\n';
print ($string_variable);
```

will output:

Jon Doe is a professional writer\n.

There is a third method of creating string literals called **heredoc syntax**. It is useful when we have multiple-line strings, and employ the <<< notation. When creating the quotation, we provide an identifier after the <<<, then the string, and finally the same identifier to close. For example:

```
$str = <<<EOQ
    This is a multi-line string.
    Note that I don't have to escape any "quotes" here.
EOQ;
```

As with double-quoted strings, variables found in heredoc statements are expanded. In this code sample, the variable $str would have the value 'Getting, there!':

```
$foo = "there!";
$str = <<<EOQ
Getting, $foo
EOQ;
```

There are two very important and potentially problematic issues that must always be remembered when using heredoc syntax:

❑ The closing identifier must begin in the first column of the line it is on. It may not be indented with spaces or tabs.

❑ After the closing semicolon, there can be no other characters on the same line except for the linefeed (\n) character. This can cause problems when using Windows-based editors, as Windows uses the sequence \r\n as a line terminator, which might make the code fail. Many of these editors have an option that lets us set the line terminator character. If this option is available, then telling it to use UNIX-style terminators should fix the problem.

> **The semicolon at the end of the closing identifier of heredoc is optional, but it is good practice to use it for consistency with the rest of the PHP code.**

Boolean

Boolean variables can have one of the two values: TRUE or FALSE. Like all keywords in the PHP languages, these are case-insensitive. A typical declaration would look like:

```
$boolean_variable = TRUE;
```

It is generally the convention to use all uppercase letters, hence we will be using uppercase throughout the book.

Compound Types

The compound types allow us to store more complicated things than a single item of data. Arrays let us store groups of items, and objects are used to group data and the functions that operate on that data.

PHP allows two compound types:

❑ **Array** – Arrays let us store groups of items

❑ **Object** – Objects are used to group data and the functions that operate on that data

Array

Arrays are an important part of the PHP language. They are in reality optimized ordered maps in PHP. This means that they can be used as real arrays, hashes, dictionaries, lists, and so on interchangeably, without any real work on the part of the programmer. It is one of the things that make development in PHP so much faster than in languages such as C.

A new array can be created with the `array()` construct. Note that it is, in fact, a true language construct, though it looks just like a function. An array will contain a certain number of comma-separated 'key => value' pairs, where `key` is either a non-negative integer or a string, and `value` can be anything. Note that negative integers are allowed but are to be discouraged, simply because they can be confusing to handle. As with most languages, the preferred way of doing things is to begin the index of the array with 0 and go up by one for each index after that.

Here is an example array declaration:

```
$arr_variable = array(0 => 'Person', 'name' => 'jon', 'height' => 'tall');
```

We can also specify arrays using square bracket syntax. The above sample, with square bracket declaration, looks like this:

```
$arr_variable[0] = 'Person';
$arr_variable['name'] = 'Jon';
$arr_variable['height'] = 'tall';
```

If `$arr_variable` doesn't exist yet, then it is created with the first declaration. Note that unlike in Perl, both arrays and scalar variables are designated with the dollar sign (`$`).

We can use the empty bracket (`[]`) syntax to push new values into an array. When this syntax is employed, PHP will put the assigned value into the array corresponding to an integer key. Taking the current maximum integer index, and adding one to it determines this integer. If there are no existing integer indices then 0 is used. This means that the above example is equivalent to:

```
$arr_variable[] = 'Person';
$arr_variable['name'] = 'Jon';
$arr_variable['height'] = 'tall';
```

Likewise, the following code snippet:

```
$news_sites[] = "fingertips.com";
$news_sites[] = "wemakenews.com";
$news_sites[] = "flashnews.net";
```

is functionally identical to:

```
$design_sites[0] = "fingertips.com";
$design_sites[1] = "wemakenews.com";
$design_sites[2] = "flashnews.net";
```

Arrays are very versatile and flexible in PHP. We often make use of multidimensional arrays that use compound square brackets notation, as in C and other languages. A sample declaration for a multidimensional array looks like this:

```
$compound_array['person']['name'] = "Missileman";
$compound_array['person']['occupation'] = "president";
$compound_array['dog']['name'] = "Lassie";
$compound_array['dog']['occupation'] = "none";
```

This could also be declared using the array() construct as follows:

```
$compund_array =
    array('person' => array('name' => 'kalam', 'occupation' => 'president'),
          'dog' => array('name' => 'Lassie', 'occupation' => 'none'));
```

Objects

Objects are another compound type used in PHP. They are instances of classes that group properties and methods together. A simple class declaration looks like this:

```
class SimpleClass
{
    var $mReturn;
    function ShowReturn($str)
    {
        return $this->$mReturn;
    }
} // End class SimpleClass
```

In this example, variable $mReturn is of type object.

Special Types

PHP 4 also provides two special types:

❑ Resources

❑ NULL

Resources

Resources are created and handled by particular PHP functions, and hold a reference to some external resource (such as a database connection). In earlier versions of PHP, resources were primarily relevant because they sometimes had to be freed manually when no longer in use.

However, since PHP4, this is no longer an issue as there is a built-in garbage collector that takes care of these issues. The garbage collector may clear out the resource before the page is done executing if the resource is no longer needed. This issue is never a problem in a web-based development environment, but can be relevant when we are using something like PHP-GTK to write programs.

The exception to this is the case of persistent database connections that are left available for future use if employed.

A complete list of resource types is available at http://www.zend.com/manual/resource.php.

NULL

The case insensitive NULL type represents a variable that has no value. Introduced with PHP4, this type has only one possible value, that is, NULL.

This is different from the value 0, FALSE, or the empty string " ". In each of these cases, there is a value in question. The value 0 is an integer, the value FALSE is a Boolean, and " " is a string with length zero.

A NULL means that the variable has no value whatsoever. Therefore, the following two snippets are checking for different things:

```
if ($value == FALSE) {
    // execute code
}

if ($value == NULL) {
    //execute code
}
```

The first if statement is checking to see if $value has the Boolean value FALSE. The second is checking to see if $value has any value assigned at all.

Assigning Variables

Variables can be assigned by value or by reference.

Assigning Variables By Value

Typically, in PHP, new variables are assigned by value. Consider the following snippet:

```
$name = 'Jon';
$second_name = $name;
```

The variables $name and $second_name would both hold the value Jon. However, subsequently changing the value of $second_name would have no effect on $name. This means that it is possible to make many copies of a particular value that are essentially photocopies of each other. But once the copy is made, its value is entirely independent of the orginal variable's value – they are all identical, but they are distinct from each other.

Assigning Variables By Reference

Although the standard assignment mechanism in PHP assigns variables by value, it is possible to assign variables by reference using the & syntax as follows:

```
$name = 'Jon';
$second_name = &$name;
```

Essentially, assigning a value by reference creates a pointer to the data in question. Here, $second_name and $name are effectively synonyms for the same data. Changing the value of $name would change the value of $second_name and vice versa.

Variable Variables

A powerful but arguably underused aspect of PHP is the ability to assign variable variables. A variable variable takes the value of one variable, and uses that as the name for a new variable.

Let us examine the following snippet:

```
$name = 'krypton_kooker';
$$name = 'programmer';
```

Here, we create two separate variables. The first is $name which has the value krypton_kooker, while the second is a variable named $krypton_kooker with the value programmer.

This can give us some powerful options as a developer. However, it also gives us the ability to write code that is quite hard to follow, so, when we use these, it is best to include plenty of comments explaining precisely what is going on.

Constants

Constants can be either numbers or string literals. For example, 'rookie' is a string constant; '45' and '3.59' are numeric constants. Constants can be used in expressions either singly or in combination with other constants, variables, or function calls returning strings or numbers, as appropriate. Constant identifiers can also be defined in a way similar to C, using the PHP define() function.

Below is an example code for defining a constant:

```
<?php

$rate = 12.5;        // This not truly a constant, since $rate can be changed

define("RATE", 12.5); // Now a constant called RATE has been defined
?>
```

Note that once a constant has been assigned, any attempt to change its value will result in an error. Also, by convention, constants are written using uppercase variables.

Operators

Expressions require operators and operands (parameters). PHP operations can be applied to numbers or strings. As would be expected, PHP has the basic mathematical operations of +, -, *, /, as well as modulus (%), increment (++), decrement (--), and string concatenation (.) operators. There is no exponent operator (**), but there is a pow(base,power) function. These, along with other operators are discussed below.

String Operators

Two strings are concatenated by joining them into a single string. PHP has two string operators to do this:

❑   The concatenation operator which requires a left and right argument surrounding a period symbol

❑   The concatenating assignment operator which appends the argument on the right side to the argument on the left side

Here is an example:

```
<?php

//using the concatenation operator
$avg = 39.4;
print "The avg is $avg<br />\n";    //note that <br /> is
                                    //HTML 4.01-compliant although <br> isn't

//using the concatenating assignment operator
$name = "rookie cat";
$msg  = "My name is ";
$msg .= $name;          //concatenates $msg to the end of the current value
                        //of $msg, and assigns the result,
                        //"My name is rookie cat", to $msg. This operation
                        //is the equivalent of: $msg = $msg.$name;

?>
```

Note that the example concatenates three values in the print statement, two of which are already strings. The value of $avg, which is a double, is converted into the string "39.4" during the string concatenation operation. Note that the data type of $avg does not change.

Arithmetic Operators

The four basic mathematical operations (+, -, *, /) are available, along with the % and post- and pre-increment (++) and decrement (--) operators.

The arithmetic operators are summarized in the table below:

Operator	Name	Usage	Meaning
+	add	$A + $B	Add two operands
-	subtract	$A - $B	Subtract a second operand from a first
*	multiply	$A * $B	Multiply two operands
/	divide	$A / $B	Divide a first operand by a second
%	modulus	$A % $B	Returns the integer remainder when integer A is divided by integer B (the base)
++	post-increment	$A++	Add one to A after evaluating A in some expression
++	pre-increment	++$A	Add one to A before evaluating A in some expression
--	post-decrement	$A--	Subtract one from A after evaluating A in some expression
--	pre-decrement	--$A	Subtract one from A before evaluating A in some expression

The term operand in the table refers to any numeric value, expression, or variable.

Comparison Operators

PHP4 includes the standard arithmetic operators, as well as a new equality operator. The term operand in the table below refers to any logical value, expression, or variable (that is, TRUE or FALSE), unless otherwise noted:

Operator	Name	Usage	Meaning
==	equal	$A == $B	Compares the value of two operands and evaluates to TRUE if they are both TRUE.
===	identical	$A === $B	Compares the 'complete identity' of two operands. If they have the same value and are of the same data type (not just logical), the expression evaluates to TRUE.
!=, <>	not equal	$A != $B $A <> $B	Compares two operands to see if their values are NOT equal. If so, then the expression is TRUE.
<	less than	$A < $B	If A is less than B, then the expression is TRUE.

Table continued on following page

Operator	Name	Usage	Meaning
>	greater than	$A > $B	If A is greater than B, then the expression is TRUE.
<=	less than or equal	$A <= $B	If A is less than or equal to B, then the expression is TRUE.
>=	greater than or equal	$A >= $B	If A is greater than or equal to B, then the expression is TRUE.
?	ternary	($A)? $B : $C	If expression A evaluates to TRUE, assign value B. Otherwise, assign value C.

Logical Operators

The standard logical operators are available:

Operator	Name	Usage	Meaning
!	not	!$A	Negates a TRUE/FALSE value
&&, and	and	$A && $B	Checks for the truth of both operands
||, or	or	$A || $B	Checks for the truth of at least one of two operands
Xor	xor	$A xor $B	Checks for the truth of either one operand or the other; not both

Reference Operator

The reference operator (&) allows you to pass variables by reference, or to call functions dynamically through a variable. Passing a variable by reference to a function means that the function accesses the actual global variable instead of using a copy. For function-heavy code, this method reduces memory requirements.

One use of being able to call functions dynamically is for web applications in which we want a different set of menu options to appear for different users. Then we can dynamically decide which function needs to be called instead of having to hard code a function call. This can also make for hard-to-read and hard-to-maintain code if we're not careful. It's best used sparingly.

Passing Arguments to a Function By Reference

Here is an example that demonstrates passing arguments to a function by reference:

```php
<?php

function increment1($x)
{
```

```
    return ++$x;
}

function increment2(&$x)
{
    return ++$x;
}

$i=10;
print ("\$i = $i<br />");
print ("increment1(\$i) =" . increment1($i) . "<br />");
print ("\$i = $i<br />");
print ("increment2(\$i) =" . increment2($i) . "<br />");
print ("\$i = $i<br />");
?>
```

the output of which is:

```
$i = 10
increment1($i) =11
$i = 10
increment2($i) =11
$i = 11
```

> **To pass arguments to a function by reference, either the function definition or the function call can have the reference.**

Calling a Function By Reference

Here is an example that demonstrates calling a function dynamically (by reference):

```
<?php

// Calling functions by reference
function Add($x,$y)
{
    $add = $x + $y;
    return $add;
}

function Subtract($x,$y)
{
    $sub = $x - $y;
    return $sub;
}

$func = "Add";
$val = $func(3.5, 4.4);        // Calls add()
print ("value is $val<br>\n");
?>
```

Bitwise Operators

These are operators that allow us to manipulate specific bits within integers. They look somewhat analogous to the logical operators we have already seen. In practice, these are rarely used in PHP programming, since they are typically more complicated to think about than other operators. The reward for this complication is that they are very fast.

> *If truly blinding speed is a requirement, then we should probably question whether or not PHP is the correct language for our application in the first place. A compiled language like C might suit our needs better.*

The bitwise operators are summarized in the table below:

Operator	Name	Usage	Meaning
&	and	$A & $B	Compares bits from A and B that are in the same position. For each pair of bits (A$_i$, B$_i$) that are both 1 (on), the resulting bit in that position is also 1. Otherwise the resulting bit is 0.
|	or	$A | $B	Bit pairs where at least one bit is 1 cause the resulting bit to be 1.
~	not	~A	Bits that are 1 changed to zero in the result, and vice-versa.
^	xor	$A ^ $B	Bit pairs must be either (1,0) or (0,1) to set the resulting bit to 1. Otherwise the resulting bit is 0.
<<	shift left	$A << $B	The bits of $A are shifted left by $B bits. The bits on the right that are shifted, are replaced by zero. Effectively, this operation multiplies integer value $A by 2 to the power of $B.
>>	shift right	$A >> $B	The bits of $A are shifted right by $B bits. The bits on the left that are shifted, are replaced by zero. Effectively, this operation divides integer value $A by 2 to the power of $B.

Assignment Operators

PHP has a full complement of assignment operators. The table below illustrates a few of them:

Operator	Name	Usage	Meaning
+=	plus equals	$A += $B	Equivalent to $A = $A + $B
-=	minus equals	$A -= $B	Equivalent to $A = $A - $B
/=	divide equals	$A /= $B	Equivalent to $A = $A / $B
*=	multiply equals	$A *= $B	Equivalent to $A = $A * $B

Operator	Name	Usage	Meaning
%=	mod equals	$A %= $B	Equivalent to $A = $A % $B
.=	concatenate equals	$A .= $B	Equivalent to $A = $A . $B

Miscellaneous Operators

Other operators in PHP that will come in handy in later examples are:

❑ Array operators: []
For example, $arr[0] accesses the first element in array $arr.

❑ Variable variable operator: $$
Evaluates a string var's value and creates a new variable with that as the name. For example, if $varname = "width", and $$varname = 5, then PHP creates a variable called $width and assigns it the value 5. This feature is handy for creating parsers, personalized menus, and other constructs.

❑ Execution operator: `` (two backticks)
For example, $output = `ls - al`; will attempt to execute the contents of the backticks as a shell command.

❑ Class instantiation operator: new
For example, $tweety = new Bird("tweety", "yellow", "talks"); creates a new object Bird.

❑ Object member access operator: ->
For example, $tweety->height = "3 inches";

❑ Error control operator: @
For example, $state = @$cache[$key]; will not issue a notice if the index $key doesn't exist

Operator Precedence

PHP expressions are typically evaluated from left to right, with operator precedence applied if necessary. Operator precedence is shown in the table below, from highest to lowest. All operators in a given row are of the same precedence, and evaluated in order from left to right, if two or more of them occur simultaneously in an expression:

Operator(s)	Notes
new	Instantiation of a new object
[]	Array index operator
!, ~, ++, --, (int), (double), (string), (array), (object), @	The operators in brackets are all type-casting operators. @ is the error control operator
*, /, %	Multiply, divide, modulus
+, -	Add, subtract

Table continued on following page

Operator(s)	Notes
`<<`, `>>`	Left shift, right shift
`<`, `<=`, `>`, `>=`	Less than, less than or equal, greater than, greater than or equal
`==`, `!=`, `===`, `!==`	Equal, not equal, identical, not identical
`&`	Reference
`^`	Bitwise xor
`|`	Bitwise or
`&&`	Logical and
`||`	Logical or
`?:`	Ternary
`=`, `+=`, `-=`, `*=`, `/=`, `.=`, `%=`, `&=`, `|=`, `^=`, `~=`, `<<=`, `>>=`	Full set of assignment operators
`print`	Print function/statement
`and`	Logical and
`xor`	Logical xor
`or`	Logical or
`.`	String concatenation

> The general rule of thumb, if you cannot remember the precedence rules, is to use parentheses around groups of operations. This always takes precedence over any other operators.

Control Structures

A PHP program is a collection of statements. We can tell the program which statements to execute with the use of conditional control structures. We can also tell the program to perform a series of repetitive steps over and over based on some condition. We will look at both of these techniques in this section. Before we start, we need just a moment to review code blocks.

A **code block** is a group of statements enclosed by opening and closing curly braces ({ }). PHP will execute the statements within the braces as one group. They are most often used in conjunction with control structures, because this allows executing a group of statements, possibly many times, based on some kind of test. We will see this in use right away.

Conditional Structures

Conditional structures such as if and switch allow different blocks of code to be executed depending on the circumstances at the time of the execution.

if

```
if (expression) {
    statement;
}
```

The if statement is the simplest conditional structure. This allows us to execute a certain piece of code based on a test. Here, expression must provide a Boolean value to the if statement.

Here is an example:

```
if ("Wrox" == $name) {
    print ("\$name equals $name\n");
    print ("All done!\n");
}
```

Here, two lines would be printed out if the variable $a held the value Wrox. However, we might want to be able to tell the program to do something different if the name was not Wrox. This is where the else structure comes into play:

```
if ("Wrox" == $name) {
    print ("\$name equals $name\n");
    print ("All done!\n");
}
else {
    print ("\$name is not Wrox\n");
    print ("All done!\n");
}
```

This gives us a fair amount of control. However, what happens if we want to check to see if the name is either Wrox or FriendsofEd, and act accordingly? There are several ways we could do this, here we can use the elseif control structure:

```
if ("Wrox" == $name) {
    print ("\$name equals $name\n");
    print ("All done!\n");
}
elseif ("FriendsofEd == $name) {
    print ("\$name equals $name\n");
    print ("All done!\n");
}
else {
    print ("\$name is not Wrox or FriendsofEd");
    print ("All done!\n");
}
```

We can include as many elseif statements as necessary in the if...elseif...else sequences. This lets us test for a variety of different things.

switch

There may be situations where we need to test some variable for a variety of different values; in this case we might be better served by using the **switch** control structure. Then the above example would look like this:

```
switch ($name) {

case "Wrox":
    print ("\$name equals Wrox\n");
    print ("All done!\n");
    break;

case "FriendsofEd":
    print ("\$name = FriendsofEd\n");
    print ("All done!\n");
    break;

default:
    print ("\$name is not Wrox or FriendsofED\n");
    print ("All done!\n)";
}
```

We may use as many case blocks as we like; just be sure to add break at the end of each one. Otherwise PHP will continue to cascade down each test until it finds either a break or a default block to execute. The **default block** is a special one that will always execute if PHP makes it that far into the switch statement.

Note that we do not need to put multiple statements inside curly braces when using switch. PHP regards everything between a case and its corresponding break, or between default and end of the switch block (}), as a block, and will execute all the statements it finds.

Logically speaking, if...elseif...else structures and switch...case...default structures are identical. Anything we can accomplish with one, we should be able to do with the other. We should choose our structure based on what we are comfortable with, and what will produce the most legible code.

Loops

Loops allow a block of code to execute a given number of times, or until a certain condition is met. They are often used for tasks like accessing records from a database query, reading lines from a file, or traversing the elements of an array. There are four types of loop in PHP: while, do ... while, for, and foreach.

While

```
while (expression) {
    statement;
}
```

while can help us perform specific actions many times over, very easily. Again, expression must provide a Boolean to the while structure. Here is an example:

```
$i = 1;
while ($i <= 10) {
    print ("\$i equals $i\n");
    $i++;
}
```

This will print out:

```
$i equals 1
$i equals 2
...
$i equals 10
```

Note that we had to increment the variable within the code block. Otherwise, we would have had an infinite loop situation. The variable $i would have kept the value 1, so the expression $i <= 10 would never have become FALSE.

do...while

```
do {
    statement;
} while (expression);
```

Closely related to while is the do...while structure. It works the same way, except that the Boolean expression is checked at the end of the loop iteration.

This means that with a do...while loop, we are always guaranteed that the statement will be executed at least once. The above example could be written using this structure, like so:

```
$i = 1;
do {
    print ("\$i equals $i\n");
    $i++;
} while ($i < 10);
```

Note that the same potential problem with an infinite loop exists as described for the while loop.

for

```
for (expression1; expression2; expression3) {
    statements;
}
```

Although while and do...while are very useful, the most common kind of loop used is the for loop. It is also the most complex control structure in PHP, though it behaves just like its counterparts in other languages.

When the loop iterates for the first time, expression1 is evaluated unconditionally. At every iteration of the loop, expression2 is evaluated as Boolean. If it returns TRUE then the loop continues and the statement is executed. Of course, statement could be a group of statements nested in a code block. Finally, after the loop iterates each time, expression3 is executed. The above example would look like this using a for loop:

```
for ($i = 1; $i <= 10; $i++) {
    print ("\$i equals $i\n");
}
```

foreach

```
foreach (array_expression as $value) statement;
foreach (array_expression as $key => $value) statement;
```

The special **foreach** operator is designed specifically to help us handle arrays in the simplest way possible. There are two syntaxes for the operator, the second being a minor (but useful) extension of the first:

❑ foreach (array_expression as $value) statement;
This syntax simply loops through all the values of the array, and puts the current one in the $value variable for use in the statement.

❑ foreach (array_expression as $key => $value) statement;
In this syntax, the array key is also put in the $key value. If the array has a string key in a particular slot, then that is used. Otherwise, the integer index is used.

A subtle but important note is that the foreach operator works on a copy of the array_expression, not the array itself. The internal array pointer is always set to the first element, so we do not need to use PHP's reset() function before putting the array into the operator.

Here is a simple example demonstrating the use of foreach:

```
$person['name'] = "Veliath Punter";
$person['height'] = "Six foot Five"
$person['genre'] = "Punk Rock";

foreach ($person as $key => $value) {
    print "$key is $value\n";                    // this will output:
                                                 // name is Veliath Punter
                                                 // height is Six foot Five
                                                 // genre is Punk Rock

}
```

Functions

PHP has a huge wealth of built-in functions that are a part of the language. A great deal of our time as a PHP programmer will be spent writing functions to handle various tasks.

User-Defined Functions

```
function FunctionName($arg_1, $arg_2, ..., $arg_n)
{
    statement1;
    statement2;
    ...
}
```

Any valid PHP code can be put into the code block, including other functions or classes (we will look at them in a moment). Also, any number of arguments can be used for $arg_1, $arg_2, and so on and these arguments can be any type the programmer wishes. However, PHP does not support **function overloading**.

> **Function overloading means that several functions have the same name, but will behave differently depending on the number or type of the arguments supplied to them. As mentioned, the workaround in PHP is to have the same function behave differently, depending on its argument list.**

Typically, the arguments are passed to the function by value once the function has been defined. This means that, in the usual case, PHP is working on a copy of the variable that we give to the function:

```
$foo = 2;
function AddTwo($num)
{
    $num += 2;
}
AddTwo($foo);
```

In this snippet, running the AddTwo() function on $foo does nothing. The value of $foo is not changed. However, we may explicitly pass variables by reference using the reference syntax on the argument. Consider this:

```
$foo = 2;
function AddTwo($num)
{
    $num += 2;
}
AddTwo(&$foo);
```

Here, $foo will now have the value of 4, once AddTwo() has been run on it.

At this point, we have not arrived at a very good solution for implementing our AddTwo() function for two reasons:

❑ If the PHP configuration allow_call_time_pass_reference is set to Off in the php.ini file, this will generate an error message. Since this particular configuration grants a speed increase, it is common to find this setup.

❑   The programmer must remember to always pass the argument by reference, or else it won't work as expected. Fortunately, PHP has a way around this as well. If we employ the reference syntax when we define the function, PHP will always force the argument to be passed by reference regardless of whether or not the programmer remembers to do it.

With this in mind, we modify our snippet to:

```
$foo = 2;
function AddTwo(&$num)
{
    $num += 2;
}
AddTwo($foo);
```

Again, $foo has the value 4 as expected. But we don't have to pass the argument by reference anymore, since we defined the function to always use a reference.

In all of the above examples, the variable $num is scoped locally to the function. This means that it will not interfere with a $num variable that has been defined globally and is used elsewhere. Also, $num can be used as an argument when defining other functions with no problems.

A last but important issue regarding functions is the ability to define functions with **default variables** for their arguments. Assigning variables to constant values when defining the function does this. For example:

```
function PersonFunction($age , $name = "Jon Doe")
{
    // statements
}
```

Having done this, we can call the function with one or two arguments. If we leave the second one out, the function will simply assume that $name is Jon Doe. However, if we do supply the second argument then whatever we put in will override the default value.

The only thing to keep in mind is that PHP requires all arguments with default values to be stacked to the right of the argument list. The script will not execute otherwise.

Returning Values

Often, we will want to manipulate data that we give to a function and return our results. This is accomplished by the optional return keyword in PHP:

```
function DoubleNumber($num)
{
    return 2 * $num;
}
// will output 6
print (DoubleNumber(3));
```

We can return any of the primitive variable types, including arrays. Also, a function may be able to return more than one type of value, as in the following example:

```
function Divide($a, $b)
{
    if (0 == $b) {
        return FALSE;
    }
    return $a / b;
}
```

Here, the function will return the value of $a divided by $b (which will be an integer or a float), unless $b is zero. In that case, it will return the Boolean value FALSE. This makes PHP more flexible than strictly typed languages where functions can only return one type of value, and we have to declare that type when we define the function.

It is also possible to return a reference from a PHP function, but we must use the reference operator & when we define the function and assign its return value to a variable:

```
function &ReturnReference()
{
    return $ReferenceVar;
}
$SomeReference = &ReturnReference();
```

Variable Functions

In a way analogous to PHP's variable variables, we can create and use variable functions. This is accomplished by putting parentheses after a variable. When PHP sees these, it looks for a function with the appropriate name to execute:

```
function PrintHello()
{
    return "Hello!\n";
}

$FunctionVar = 'PrintHello';
print ($FunctionVar());        // prints Hello!
```

There is a very wide range of functionality that we can get out of user-defined functions in PHP. This is particularly powerful when used in conjunction with PHP's system of classes and objects, which we will cover in the section after next.

Object-Oriented Programming

Before we start with a technical definition of classes and objects, we should talk for a moment about a more basic issue, the difference between procedural and object-oriented programming (OOP).

Functional vs. OO Programs

The simple examples we have seen so far in this chapter are all procedural. That is to say, there was data, and we manipulated that data with various routines or functions. Sometimes these were functions provided by the language, and sometimes we had written them ourselves. In any case, the important thing to recognize is that the data held in the different variables we saw, was not in any way connected with or associated to the functions that acted on them. We start with some data, manipulate it in some way, do something with the results, and then the script ends. This is what the term **functional programming** means.

This is a perfectly reasonable top-level approach to writing programs. However, as programs get larger, we may find that it has some drawbacks. Firstly, we may end up doing the same types of thing over and over. Second, it is possible that we will have a great many functions and variables all over, and we will want to find a good way to help organize them. Finally, we may want to associate functions and the data they manipulate more closely. When this happens, we should code in an **OO** style.

So what makes OOP different from functional programming? When we code an application with functions, we create programs that are code-centric, applications that call function by function consecutively. The data is first sent as the input, the function does the actual transformation, and then it returns the corresponding output. OOP takes the opposite approach since it is data-centric.

Here is an illustration showing the two paradigms:

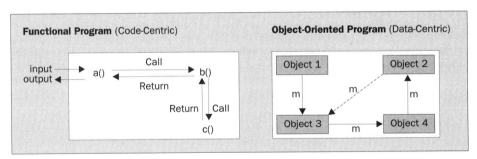

As we can see from the above diagram, input enters the function a (), which then calls the function b() using the output of a (). Function b () then calls c () using the output of b (). Then c () returns its output to b () which then returns its output to a (). Function a () finally produces the program output. Function a () would be the main function of a typical C program. In the object-oriented model, objects request the services of others, easily seen when Object 1 requests the service of Object 3. Object 3 in turn requests the service of Object 4 and so on, until Object 1 receives a reply from Object 3 of the end result, tracing backwards.

What's happening is that each object uses the services provided by the others within the program to receive information so it can do its own work, that is, make its own decisions based on asking other objects for information. The passing of these messages is the flow of the program in itself, the data and the methods or the functionality of the object are contained in one central location.

The difference between the two paradigms is that objects contain all the data and behavior that should exist together while the data and functions are clearly separated in the functional paradigm. This makes OO code very easy to trace during maintenance and increases the modularity of the project.

Now, this doesn't mean that procedural programs aren't maintainable, because they can be. It just requires a lot more thinking and organization on the architect's part to ensure that everything is located in the proper location. Also we should ensure that there is no global variables being manipulated in many of the project files if any should exist. The best thing about OOP is that we just make the objects senseful, follow some guidelines, and things should be pretty organized. With more complex applications, the use of special patterns can strengthen the design of the systems so we can reap added benefits.

Objects and Classes

OO programs consist of objects. So unlike having functions act on primitives or data structures, objects provide the functionality and behavior for the application. For example, we can have a `Form` object that represents an HTML form on a web page. Inside this form we might have various buttons, text fields, and radio options, which are all modeled as objects as well. To define what these objects are, what they consist of, and what actions they can do, we use the concept of a **class** that defines all these criteria to PHP. To reiterate, a class provides the programmatic definition of the objects that we use in our applications in the same way that a `struct` defines a data structure in C. Let's first talk about classes in more detail.

A class defines a concept or idea that we want to use in the program. For instance, if we want to model the idea of keeping the user's session, we can maintain this information in a `Session` object (or sometimes it can be called `SessionManager`). Classes can model things that are tangible, like forms, sockets, and database connections, and things that are less tangible like proxies, handlers, or listeners. The most important concept is that the class represents a single idea. Usually, classes like `MyEntireProgram` and `TheWorldIsInsideOfMe` do not provide great functionality and should be avoided. This usually indicates the class is doing too many things and can probably be split up into several smaller classes. A general rule is that classes should 'do one thing and do it well'.

Now that we know what classes should do, it's time to talk about what they really consist of. Classes must consist of data (the object's members and components) and code (the functionality it provides) called **methods**. This means that a class that is missing one of these things is not really a class, but rather a group of functions or a data structure. If we do not pair the code and data that belong together, there is high probability that our class has been incorrectly defined. Now let's take a look at the components of a class.

> *For more information on class and object functions within PHP, check out* http://www.php.net/manual/en/ref.classobj.php.

Members

These are elements, which we intend the class to contain. For instance, forms contain buttons, text fields, and combo boxes. These items would be considered members of the `Form` class. As with any class, the members might be intangible things like a `DataValidator` for client-server regular expression validation. The members can also be primitive data types like integers, floats, and strings. For instance, the form's `name` and the `action` can also be members of the `Form` class.

Methods

Methods provide the behavior we expect a particular object to perform. For instance, continuing with our current example, forms provide the ability to validate themselves, populate the fields with data from a data store such as a database, process the form to add it to a database or send an e-mail. These methods describe exactly what we intend the forms to do. We wouldn't expect a form to be able to drive a car or do our homework for instance. Although this might sound funny at first, it's true – many programmers simply put methods where they don't belong and this is something that should be avoided.

Constructor

A constructor is responsible for initializing the object's ready state. What this means is that if there are any members (objects or primitive types) that need to be initialized for the methods to work properly, this code usually goes into the class constructor. For instance, we can use the constructor to add all the form elements to the form and specify the regular expression constraints on each form item. One thing to note is that PHP's objects can only have one constructor. This is because PHP does not support a concept called **overloading**. Another thing to note is that it must not return a value.

Here is an example of a Form class. It's not a complete example because the intention is to identify and show the various concepts that we've just learned about:

```php
<?php

class Form
{
```

Here we define a class called Form. Everything within the curly braces is considered to be a method, member, or a constructor of the class. Notice that the class name is capitalized. This is generally the style that is used throughout PHP classes to distinguish them from other items in the language; it has been adopted from Java:

```php
    var $name;
    var $elements;
```

Here we define several member variables that are objects or other primitive type variables that this class contains. The $name field stores the name of the form while the $elements member actually contains all the objects that get displayed on the form. It is generally considered good practice to add the members at the top of the class rather than anywhere else, just as in a functional program. This provides a good reference for maintenance later on:

```php
    function Form($name = "The Form")
    {
        $this->name = $name;
        $this->elements = array();
        // add the elements to the form
    }
```

Here is the class's constructor. To define the constructor properly, it must have the same name as the class itself. So in this case, the constructor's name is also Form. This is actually one reason why the class name has a capital letter, so it makes it very easy to distinguish the constructor from the rest of the methods.

The form's name is assigned the value 'The Form' if one is not provided and the elements member was assigned an empty array. Later, we will look at adding objects to this array. The $this keyword is rather unique to OO programs. Think of $this as a variable that points to the object that we are currently writing. Therefore, when we say $this->name, we are referring to the Form object's name variable that we defined above.

The $this keyword allows PHP to distinguish between any local variables and variables (members) that are contained within the object. So the line $this->name = $name is assigning the value of the argument to the object's name member. Although in other languages, the $this keyword is optional and is used to clear up naming conflicts and their associated delays, the PHP interpreter did not adopt this feature for increased speed. This might take a little while to get used to, but with practice and the motivation to avoid interpretation errors the usefulness of this syntax becomes apparent.

Here is an example:

```
    function Validate()
    {
        $boolean = TRUE;
        foreach ($this->elements as $element) {
            // check all the elements and set $boolean to FALSE if
            // any errors occur
        }
        return $boolean;
    }

    function Process()
    {
        // put the data in the elements into the database
    }

    function Populate()
    {
        // populate the elements
    }
} //End of class Form
?>
```

These are the object's functions, or rather the methods it provides. Note that these look exactly as they do in a procedural program, except for that they are contained within the class { } block. This signifies that they belong to this class; if another part of the program needs to use these functions, they must go through the object first.

Instances

Now that we defined our Form class, we use the following code to define and create a variable that is of the type Form:

```
$form = new Form("My quick form");
```

Here we use the new operator to create a new Form object. When an object has been created using the new operator, it is said that the object has been **instantiated**. It can also be said that the object is called an **instance** of the Form class. A good analogy between instances and classes is that the blueprints and prototypes for a single car can be called a class while all the cars that are on the road that were built using that particular blueprint can be called instances.

Remember our discussion on constructors? That is what we are calling here, passing the name of the form so that the internal name member can be initialized. With PHP's loosely typed variable concept, we don't have to specify the object's type when we create an object. Constructors always allocate the memory for the object. This is actually done automatically, so once we write the constructor for an object that initializes the members, PHP will do this for us.

Calling Instance Methods

Since the object is created into the $form variable, we can freely use the methods provided by the object. For instance, we can call the Validate() method to validate the form using the following code:

```
if ($form->validate()) {
    print ("The form was validated successfully.");
}
```

In this example, we use the -> operator to call the Validate() method that belongs to the $form object. Notice that it takes no parameters. This is one of the benefits of object-oriented programs. Since each object knows and is associated with its member variables, it doesn't need to have any parameters. This serves several benefits. For one, the programmer using the object doesn't need to know how those elements were coded. The internal data is 'hidden' away from the programmer.

The second benefit is that the implementation could have used other objects to store the elements rather than an array. As far as the calling code knows, the object hasn't changed. This makes each object very abstract and provides a nice candy-like interface. It also improves the maintainability of the system. Lastly, this cleans up the code a lot as well. Since each call to the $form object doesn't need to supply rudimentary data every time a method is invoked, this makes our code much cleaner and simplifies our statements greatly.

How This Works

For those that are interested in the 'how', the interpreter adds some information before the code is executed. Within PHP, the engine keeps track of which methods belong to which class, but it doesn't actually tie the members to the object itself. Naturally, like any procedural language, it maintains a data structure that is also linked with the class name. Each time the method is invoked, the object's variable is automatically supplied to it. So in this case, the call is modified to:

```
if ($form->Validate($form)) {
    print ("The form was validated successfully.");
}
```

This passes the object back into itself so that the method can access the members of the object that are not declared as local variables. This enables each method to share the same members. So in the class code itself, the $form parameter actually gets transformed into the $this object. Here is the transformation:

```
function Validate($this)
{
    $boolean = TRUE;

    foreach ($this->elements as $element) {
```

```
        // check all the elements and set $boolean to FALSE if
        // any errors occur
    }

    return $boolean;
}
```

Since the PHP engine automatically puts the $this variable as the first argument to the Validate() method, it is more easily seen why $this->elements actually exists and why it is done that way (passing the object back into itself). This also provides an explanation about how the object's members in the $this object do not collide with any local variables or function arguments. Remember that the $this parameter is done automatically – so we don't have to define this variable for our methods. In some languages like Python, we actually have to do this. PHP has made this easy for us so we can think of our object's members as being contained within the class definition rather than being closer to the implementation of the interpreter.

Inheritance

Now that the Form class has been defined, we need to define a class for the buttons, text fields, and other form controls that we would like to add to the form. Since PHP does not supply a type for this, we need to define our own class. These classes that we are about to look into have been taken from the eXtremePHP Form Framework (http://www.extremephp.org/). Since the Form Framework actually uses several classes (around 30), some of the classes have been combined and shortened for this example. Therefore, the example is meant to demonstrate OO code clearly rather than present the most refactored solution.

Now, one way to create text fields and submit buttons would be to create different classes that represent each form control and provide the necessary functionality for each one. Although this can work, it's not the best solution. When we think of HTML form controls, most people think of them as being very similar. Generally, the name of the tag and some of the attributes that are assigned represent the only difference between controls, but each control has a name, a value, might have a regular expression constraint, and can display or convert itself into HTML.

To express these commonalities among all form controls that need to be placed inside the Form object, we first make a FormControl class. Later, when we need a very specific control that puts a text field on the screen or creates a submit button, we can create classes called TextField and SubmitButton, which are called **subclasses**. These classes are said to **inherit** functionality from the FormControl class, meaning they have all the members and methods of that class. FormControl is also said to be the **parent**, **base**, or **superclass** to the TextField and SubmitButton classes.

We can define a new subclass for each type of FormControl by only specifying specific information. Since TextField and other subclasses all **extend** from FormControl, they will possess all the existing functionality from the FormControl – which allows for software reuse. The way this works logically is this – if a TextField is a FormControl, then it should posses all the state and behavior of a FormControl. Notice that the converse is not necessarily true since a FormControl may not contain all the functionality and members of a TextField. This is because a TextField might have additional settings to adjust the field's width, which may not be available to all FormControl objects.

The ability to extend a class by subclassing is the core idea of OO programming. By creating trees of objects, we are able to reuse code, and later we'll see how this makes our programs more generic and easier to work with and maintain.

The Parent Class – FormControl

Here is the code for the FormControl class:

```php
<?php

// FormControl.class.php

define("NO_VALUE", md5("novalue"));
define("NEWLINE", "\n");
```

Here we provide several constants that are used by the other classes. The NO_VALUE constant is the value that is used to specify that a form control does not contain any value. Since NULL values are hard to maintain and keep state across HTML, it is sensible to use a value that means nothing:

```php
class FormControl
{
    var $name;
    var $value;
```

Here we provide two member variables for the name and value of the form. The name provides the unique server-side name that is automatically added to the global variables array and is used when getting the value. The value will be contained within this variable if it is set:

```php
function FormControl($name, $value = NO_VALUE)
{
    $this->SetName($name);
    $this->SetValue($value);
}
```

Our constructor initializes the FormControl with a name and there is an optional parameter to specify the value. Usually when we create a new form and we do not wish to populate it with data, we want to provide just a name. In the case where we want the form control to be initialized to a value before it is displayed to the screen, we can use the second parameter $value. To initialize these values, we use the setName() and setValue() methods. These are usually referred to as **setter** methods and contain assignment code. In some cases, we might also want to have rules defined so that the data maintains its integrity:

```php
function setName($name)
{
    $this->name = $name;
}

function getName()
{
    return $this->name;
}
```

There is also the concept of a **getter** method that returns the value of a member that is in the object. In the above code, we define a setter and getter for the name member. This allows clients that use the object to be able to manipulate and get the object's name. Instead of saying getter and setter all the time, for a pair, we could say that these two methods are both **data accessor methods**:

```
function SetValue($value)
{
    if ($value == NO_VALUE) {
        global ${$this->name};

        if (!isset(${$this->name})) ${$this->name} = '';
        $this->value = ${$this->name};
    } else {
        $this->value = $value;
    }
}

function GetValue()
{
    return $this->value;
}
```

As with the name member, there is also a getter and setter for the value member. The setValue() method is actually more complicated in that it must handle the special case of the NO_VALUE constant. If the NO_VALUE constant was passed into this function, we check to see if a variable already exists with the FormControl's name. If it does, we can automatically set the value of this form element to that variable. If not, we just make the element contain the empty string. This allows FormControl to maintain state as it was when submitted, and it can be very helpful when the form is not validated correctly. This saves the programmer a great deal of time checking the global values and setting them within the value attribute of the HTML code. The class now does this automatically:

```
function SetConstraint(&$validator, $regex, $errorMessage)
{
    $validator->setConstraint($this->getName(), $regex,
                              $this->getValue(), $errorMessage );
}
```

The SetConstraint() method provides an easy way to add a regular expression check of this form control to an eXtremePHP DataValidator object, $validator. This component is much like the Matcher object in Java or .NET. For the simplicity of this example, we will assume that the $validator object has a method called SetConstraint() as well, and it contains the code to a list of constraints:

```
function Validate()
{
    return $validator->Validate();
}
```

Once the constraints have been added, they may be also verified using a similar Validate() method:

```
// template method that calls abstract methods.
function ToHtml()
{
    return $this->GetHeaderHtml() . $this->getFooterHtml();
```

```
    }

    // abstract
    function GetHeaderHtml() {}

    // abstract
    function GetFooterHtml() {}
```

The next set of functions provides the base mechanism for displaying the HTML for the `FormControl` component. `ToHtml()` is meant to receive the entire HTML document. In some cases, we might only want to view the header or footer of the HTML, so we can use `GetHeaderHtml()` or `GetFooterHtml()` respectively.

Even though these functions do not provide any functionality, this is actually where the meat of the class is. These methods were left blank intentionally so that they can be redefined in the subclasses of `FormControl`. For instance, a `TextField` has its own HTML that it would like to display as compared to a `SubmitButton`. By **overriding** these methods (as shown in the next class file), we can provide very specific functionality to each subclass of `FormControl`. We'll take a closer look at overriding methods later on in more detail.

The `ToHtml()` method is actually very powerful in that all subclasses will contain this method. Since every class that inherits `FormControl` will contain the `GetHeaderHtml()` and `GetFooterHtml()` methods, `ToHtml()` makes sure that every class won't need to bother with creating a duplicate `ToHtml()` method. This **templates** the header and footer methods and the implementer of the subclasses is expected to fill them in.

How do we know when we have to fill them in? Usually in a language that supports full object orientation like Java, there is a concept called **abstract** methods that forces any subclasses to implement the methods before the class is compiled. Since the compiler tool will not successfully compile a class where the implementer didn't override the methods, it will be impossible to use this in a program. This is extremely helpful since objects are well defined in this way and we can guarantee that all the methods in the parent class will work in the subclasses.

However, PHP does not contain this feature so it is up to the designer to indicate that these classes are indeed abstract. This is usually done with an empty body ({ }) for the method. A comment just above the method will also help clarify the intentions of the programmer:

```
    function Display()
    {
        print ($this->ToHtml());
    }

    function DisplayHeader()
    {
        print ($this->GetHeaderHtml());
    }

    function DisplayFooter()
    {
        print ($this->GetFooterHtml());
```

```
        }
    }
?>
```

The last methods simply make it a bit easier to display the HTML to the screen: they have been separated to make it easy to put the HTML into a string. This can be useful if we'd like to insert it into a database or an e-mail message. If we had tied the HTML generation to the `Display*()` methods, some applications may have been very difficult to write.

The Subclasses

The next file shows how to implement a new subclass, `TextField`, as a subclass of `FormControl`:

```php
<?php

// TextField.class.php

require_once './FormControl.class.php';

class TextField extends FormControl
{
```

Here, we use the `extends` keyword to tell PHP that the `TextField` class inherits from the `FormControl` class. As mentioned before, this means that all the members and methods from the `FormControl` class are now available to this class as well:

```php
    function TextField($name, $value = NO_VALUE)
    {
        FormControl::FormControl($name, $value);
    }
```

Since all `FormControl` objects were expected to have a `name` and `value`, we can use the parent class's constructor to initialize the incoming members rather than rewriting the code again. To do this, we use the class-method call operator to reference the parent function. This is achieved by calling the class name with two colons, followed by the method name we would like to call. Generally, it works like this:

```php
ClassName::MethodName();
```

So in our example, we use `FormControl` to replace `ClassName` and we use the same name for the `MethodName()` because we'd like to call the constructor. By passing the arguments again to the parent method, we can be assured that the `name` and `value` members will be set to this object when it is instantiated. This is a huge benefit to programmers because as long as we know the parent class is bug-free, we can be assured that any subclasses will be dealing with error-free code. Thus, this can save a great deal of time when debugging applications:

```php
    function GetHeaderHtml()
    {
        return '<input type="text" ' .
                'name="' . $this->name . '" ' .
                'value="' . $this->value . '">';
```

```
    }

    function GetFooterHtml()
    {
        return '</input>' . NEWLINE;
    }
}
?>
```

Remember those two abstract methods GetFooterHtml() and GetHeaderHtml()? Well, it's our job to implement the code for those in the TextField class. In this case, we simply return the <input> tag to create a text field in the browser using HTML. Notice the use of $this->name and $this->value. These fields have been inherited from the FormControl superclass, and as such, they are available to use in our code above. As mentioned before, we need not redefine the ToHtml() method because it has been made to call these overridden methods automatically.

More On Overriding Methods

So how does the parser know which method to call – the one in the superclass or the subclass? Whenever a subclass defines a method that has been previously defined in its parent, it is overriding its behavior. Now, in the previous case, there was no behavior provided by the superclass because the method was blank. In other examples, however, there are times when we may want to override a method that does have an implementation, because its current implementation does not suit the more specific object. Consider three classes where Baby is a subtype of Parent and Parent is a subtype of GrandParent, and take this code for example:

```
$babyObject = new Baby("");
$babyObject->SayHello();
```

When an instance of the Baby subtype is created and the SayHello() method is called, the PHP interpreter will first look to see if the method is defined in $babyObject class. If it is, it will execute the code within that method. In this case, if the SayHello() method overrides the one in a superclass, the PHP interpreter skips the superclass entirely.

If no method is defined by SayHello() within the Baby() interface, PHP will then go to the Parent class of $babyObject and will attempt to execute the same method using the parent's implementation. If this method is defined in the Parent class, PHP will begin executing its code and PHP will commence as normal. If in turn the method wasn't found in the Parent class, PHP will search the parent class of each current class until there are no parent classes left. At this time PHP will display an error message saying the following:

```
Fatal error: Call to undefined function: SayHello() in
/websites/babytest.php on line X
```

The Remaining Subclasses – SubmitButton and HiddenField

As we make more FormControl objects, we can appreciate how fast it can be to develop various form components. For demonstration purposes, the next two files will be the SubmitButton class and the HiddenField class which we will use in the following example. Here is the SubmitButton class code:

```php
<?php

// SubmitButton.class.php

require_once './FormControl.class.php';

class SubmitButton extends FormControl
{

    function SubmitButton($value)
    {
        FormControl::FormControl('submit', $value);
    }

    function GetHeaderHtml()
    {
        return '<input type="submit" ' .
               'name="' . $this->name . '" ' .
               'value="' . $this->value . '">';
    }

    function GetFooterHtml()
    {
        return '</input>' . NEWLINE;
    }
}
?>
```

Similarly, the code for the HiddenField class that models a hidden value for HTML forms can be written like this:

```php
<?php

// HiddenField.class.php

require_once './FormControl.class.php';

class HiddenField extends FormControl
{

    function HiddenField($name, $value = NO_VALUE)
    {
        FormControl::FormControl($name, $value);
    }

    function GetHeaderHtml()
    {
        return '<input type="hidden" ' .
               'name="' . $this->name . '" ' .
               'value="' . $this->value . '">';
    }

    function GetFooterHtml()
```

```
    {
        return '</input>' . NEWLINE;
    }
}
?>
```

Creating the Form Class

Now that we have created various form controls to be placed onto our Form class, let's take another look how we might build it:

```php
<?php

// Form.class.php

require_once './TextField.class.php';
require_once './HiddenField.class.php';
require_once './SubmitButton.class.php';
require_once './Vector.class.php';
```

To use the classes we developed earlier, we need to include them in the main Form class. The Vector class is a utility class that was taken right out of the eXtremePHP library. It operates very similar to the way Vector objects behave in Java. For those who haven't used Java, a Vector is basically a scalable array. We don't have to worry about indexes and boundaries as the object takes care of all of this information for us. In fact, we won't even realize that it's an array and we'll think of it as a List of objects.

A Vector provides a very consistent way to iterate over the data contained within the array. Called an Iterator, it is analogous to Java Enumeration or C++'s Iterator. This allows us to traverse all the items within the Vector. If we decide to change the Vector into another class that supports Iterator objects, we won't actually have to change any of the traversal code because it supports the same interface. This is very powerful since program maintenance is reduced.

We now define two Vector objects that we will use in our Form. One Vector object, $formControls, will store a list of form controls that we developed earlier. Since PHP variables are loosely typed, it is actually possible to have the first position of the Vector contain a TextField object while the second position contains a SubmitButton object, and so on. This is very useful as we can group all these objects together in a generic fashion:

```php
class Form
{
    var $formControls;
    var $parameters;
```

The $parameters Vector will store the name/value pairs for this Form. In this case we also could have used a Dictionary object or even a HashMap, which resembles an associative array, but again for demonstration purposes this will suffice:

```php
function Form($name, $action, $method = "post")
{
    $this->formControls = new Vector();
```

```
        $this->parameters   = new Vector();

        $this->SetParameter('name', $name);
        $this->SetParameter('action', $action);
        $this->SetParameter('method', $method);
    }
```

Our constructor takes in the name of the form, the PHP page which will process the form when it is submitted, and a $method parameter that can either be POST or GET. This is the same information that would be supplied on an HTML <form> tag. Since the constructor is responsible for putting the object into an unvarying state, we must create new instances of the Vector objects that we defined above. We can use the SetParameter() instance method to set up all the properties that were passed into the constructor.

We now define the data accessor methods GetParameter() and SetParameters() for the <form> tag. In both cases $name and $value are strings. Vector objects have a Set() method where they can not only add a new item to the list, but also set it at a defined index. In this case, we use $name for the index and place the contents of $value at this position. Later we can use the get() method on the $parameters Vector object to retrieve the value at this position as well:

```
    function SetParameter($name, $value)
    {
        $this->parameters->Set($name, $value);
    }

    function GetParameter($name)
    {
        return $this->parameters->Get($name);
    }
```

To make the interface simpler for someone who would like to define several other parameters other than the ones defined in the constructor, there is a SetParameters() method that is intended to take in an associative array and then add each name/value pair within the array to the parameter list:

```
    function SetParameters(&$parameters)
    {
        foreach ($parameters as $name => $value) {
            $this->SetParameter($name, $value);
        }
    }
```

To complete the functionality of parameters, we have a method that easily constructs the HTML code for the parameter list that is meant to be appended to the beginning of an HTML element. Every Vector object has ToArray() that converts its contents back into an associative array. This is helpful when we need to retrieve both the indices (the parameter names) and the values:

```
    function ConstructParameterHtml()
    {
        $parameterString = '';
```

```
    foreach ($this->parameters->ToArray() as $name => $value) {
        $parameterString .= ' ' . $name . '="' .
                            $value . '"';
    }

    return $parameterString;
}
```

After traversing the entire list, we should end up with a string like this "name1=value1", "name2=value2", and so on. Generally, besides the toArray() call, there is nothing very interesting here.

Finally we define an Add() method so we can add controls to the form. The argument $control expects any instance of the FormControl class. Because we can take any instance, we don't have to say AddTextField() or AddSubmitButton() like in a procedural program. We can simply instantiate the class and then pass it into the Add() method:

```
function Add($control)
{
    if (get_class($control) == 'submitbutton') {
        $submitName = $this->GetParameter('name') .
                      ucfirst($control->getName());

        $this->Add(new HiddenField( $submitName, $control->GetValue()));
    }

    $this->formControls->Add( $control );
}
```

So what if we really do want to know the type of an object? Well, PHP has a function called get_class() that takes in any object and the function will return a string containing the class name. Since all class and function names are case-insensitive, the function will return the entire string in lowercase letters.

In the eXtremePHP framework, there is a special check to see if a SubmitButton instance is being passed to the function, so we can use the get_class() function to check the instance type of the object dynamically and add a hidden field with the same name with a capital first letter to the form when this happens. Although for our example, we don't really use the hidden field for anything, the eXtremePHP framework requires a field to be defined to do some fancy tricks and to generally make programming forms much easier and more reusable.

The lesson learned here is that we can check the types of objects in our code and execute extra code for various conditions:

```
function GetHeaderHtml()
{
    return $this->GetTagHeader('form') . NEWLINE;
}

function GetFooterHtml()
{
```

```
        return $this->GetTagFooter('form') . NEWLINE;
    }

    function GetTagHeader($tagName)
    {
        return "<$tagName" . $this->ConstructParameterHtml() . '>';
    }

    function GetTagFooter($tagName)
    {
        return "</$tagName>";
    }
```

As with the FormControl, the Form object itself can also get the header and footer HTML. We use some helper methods to generate the HTML more easily. Notice that the GetTagHeader() method uses the ConstructParameterHtml() method defined earlier. This method places the string containing the generated attributes right after the tag name. In this case, our form options defined in the constructor will be placed after the <form> tag as they should be:

```
    function GetContainedTagsHtml()
    {
        $html = '';

        for ($i = $this->CreateIterator(); !$i->isDone(); $i->next()) {
            $control = $iterator->GetCurrent();
            $html .= $control->ToHtml();
        }

        return $html;
    }
```

Since Form objects can contain other FormControl objects, it is also required that we generate the entire HTML for each control. The result needs to go in between the <form> and </form> tags. The general strategy here is that we create an Iterator on the $formControls member variable (remember, it's a Vector object), and we can traverse all the Form elements as they were added to the Vector. The call to:

```
    $html .= $control->ToHtml();
```

is actually very interesting. The ToHtml() method returns the HTML markup for the TextField or the SubmitButton class. Remember that the Vector object can contain a whole bunch of different FormControl instances. PHP is actually smart enough to call the correct code for each of these controls, regardless of what it is. So when a TextField object is the next object in the iteration, the PHP interpreter will execute the GetHeaderHtml() and GetFooterHtml() of the TextField class.

This method calling on a group of similar objects is called **polymorphism**. So regardless of what the object is, since PHP knows all FormControl instances have a ToHtml() method, it will execute the proper code for each control relieving the programmer from having to decide which method to call. This greatly improves the maintainability of the application since if any new FormControl objects are added, we will not need to modify much of our current code.

How Polymorphism Works

Since the code doesn't specify which code to execute, how does PHP know which method to call? To answer this question, let's look how we might do something like this in a procedural program:

```
if ($control->type == TEXT_FIELD) {
    DisplayTextField($control);
} elseif() {
    DisplaySubmitButton($control);
    ...
}
```

As with most procedural programs, we define data structures for complicated types. In this case $control is a record containing the name, value, and so on, of the form control. By testing its type against various constants, we can determine which method to call to draw the correct component. So if it's a text field, it should call DisplayTextField(). Likewise, if it's a submit button, the code should execute DisplaySubmitButton() and so on. So where is this code in our OO program?

This is what makes OO programs very different from procedural ones. Recall that all FormControl objects contain a ToHtml() method and that any subclass of FormControl will also contain this method. So when we iterate through the Vector and call the ToHtml() method on each FormControl, we are guaranteed that each control can deliver this method and return the appropriate HTML for the form control. So how does PHP know which one to call? Let's assume the Vector contains the following values:

```
["formControls"]=> &object(vector)(2) {
    ["collection"]=> array(4) {
        [0]=> object(textfield)(3) {
            ["name"]=> string(4) "name"
            ["value"]=> string(3) "Hey"
        }
        [1]=> object(textfield)(3) {
            ["name"]=> string(5) "stuff"
            ["value"]=> string(3) "You"
        }
        [2]=> object(hiddenfield)(3) {
            ["name"]=> string(12) "Submit"
            ["value"]=> string(6) "submit"
        }
        [3]=> object(submitbutton)(3) {
            ["name"]=> string(6) "submit"
            ["value"]=> string(6) "submit"
        }
    }
    ["size"]=> int(4)
```

Upon the first iteration of the Vector, the call to $i->GetCurrent(); will return the TextField object at index 0. Once a call to ToHtml() has been made, the PHP interpreter finds that a ToHtml() method is found in the base class, FormControl (as explained in the section about overriding methods). Let's take a look at the code for the ToHtml() method once more:

```
function ToHtml()
{
    return $this->GetHeaderHtml() . $this->GetFooterHtml();
}
```

As PHP executes this code, it comes across `$this->GetHeaderHtml()` first and decides that it has to execute this code. So what is `$this` really referring to? In this case, `$this` is still an instance of the `TextField` class, even though we are currently executing code from the `FormControl` class. So now that it has to call `GetHeaderHtml()` from the current `TextField` object, it checks to see if the method exists. As we already know, it does perform this check and the function returns the `<input>` HTML code for the text field. The same process happens for the `GetFooterHtml()` as well and both results are concatenated together and the result is returned to the caller.

Back To the Form Class

Now that we have all three HTML methods defined, we can create the `Form` class's `ToHtml()` method as shown below:

```
function ToHtml()
{
    return $this->GetHeaderHtml() .
            $this->GetContainedTagsHtml() .
            $this->GetFooterHtml();
}
```

As with the form controls, the `Form` needs to be able to display itself. So we defined a `Display()` method for this purpose:

```
function Display()
{
    print ($this->ToHtml());
}
}
```

Using the Form

In this application, we are going to create a form with two text fields and a submit button. When the form is submitted, the application will simply type out the contents of the two boxes to the screen. Now that all our classes have been written, we can start to build an application at the problem-domain level. This generally means that we can work with objects that make sense to the problem. This is much like building structures with Lego blocks. Generally, this turns out to be really simple, so let's look at the code:

```
$form = new Form("MyForm", $_SERVER["PHP_SELF"]);
$form->Add(new TextField('name'));
$form->Add(new TextField('stuff'));
$form->Add(new SubmitButton('submit'));
$form->Display();
```

Here we create a new instance of the Form object. We give it any random name (in this case, PHP_SELF) to tell PHP to use this script to process the form when it has been submitted. At this time, all the internal vectors are initialized so the object's services are ready to be used. So in this case, we add several form controls using the Add() method of the $form object. But creating new instances and passing them to Add(), we are placing the controls onto the form. Lastly, we can invoke the Display() method which displays the generated HTML to the screen. Simple enough:

```
if (isset($_REQUEST['submit'])) {
    print ("You have typed in '" . $_REQUEST['name'] .
            "' into the first box and ");
    print ("'" . $_REQUEST['stuff'] . "' into the second box");
}
?>
```

Assuming the form has been submitted with the words 'Jon Doe' and 'Some Stuff', the display of the application would look like this:

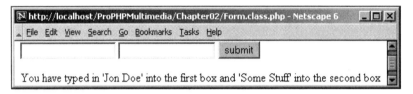

In this section, we have learnt the essential concepts of programming OO code using PHP. Although there are many more concepts we need to learn, this should provide us with a good footing to start with as well as utilize OO capabilities within our applications.

Summary

This chapter has been a brief refresher on the PHP language.

First we looked at the basic PHP syntax. Then we saw how we can create variables and skimmed through the different types. Later we considered constants. We also looked at the most commonly used operators.

Then we turned our attention to the structures that form the building block of any successful application:

❏ The conditional statements if and switch are used to test a condition and execute different blocks of code depending on the results.

❏ The loops while, do ... while, for, and foreach allow repetitive behavior. The foreach loop is specifically designed for traversing the elements of an array.

❏ Functions are reusable units of code that can be invoked as necessary to perform specific tasks. They make code more modular and maintainable.

Then we looked at OOP, which is essential for PHP to survive as the web platform of tomorrow. We talked about how it differs from procedural programming and discussed its benefits – increased reusability and maintainability. We learned that objects contain methods, members, and a constructor and that they become instantiated in our program with PHP's operators.

The aspects of OOP that PHP supports make it possible to create large and complex applications in a full OOP framework. It is interesting to note that some of the most popular PHP-based libraries out there, such as PHPLib and PEAR, are implemented as OOP classes.

There is an enormous amount of functionality built into the APIs that are available. In particular, it is always a good idea to read through the references for string manipulation functions, array manipulation functions, regular expressions, and file or directory access functions.

For a detailed treatment of the basics of PHP programming, refer to *Beginning PHP4* (*ISBN 1-861003-73-0*) and *Professional PHP4* (*ISBN 1-861006-91-8*) from *Wrox Press*. The most up-to-date information is always available on the official PHP web site at http://www.php.net/.

3

Ming Fundamentals

Ming is a library that provides functionality for making SWF Flash movies. There are interfaces to the Ming Library available for a number of programming languages, one of which is PHP. PHP with Ming gives developers tremendous power over dynamic creation of Flash without a lot of expense. The learning curve is small, especially if we are familiar with Macromedia Flash, as efforts were made to preserve the functionality.

Just as PHP is used to generate dynamic HTML content, Ming is used to generate Flash content on the fly. On-the-fly Flash content is used in large sites for:

❑   Dynamic-content banners

❑   Ticker-style scrolling headlines

❑   Random-challenge games

❑   Online CAD
    Lego's web site, https://club.lego.com/build/brickbuilder.asp, has something similar, where one can play with Lego sets online

❑   Web radio
    Here MP3s are streamed dynamically via an SWF interface. For more information refer http://www.teleferique.org/stations/Erational/jargon/

In the course of this chapter we will discuss Ming programming in detail. We will start with a discussion on the fundamentals of Ming programming and then take a look at how we can add basic shapes to our movie. We will also see how to add text and textboxes, and animation to our movie. Finally we will introduce the concept of adding interaction to our movie but will discuss it in detail in the next chapter.

Let's see why we would want to use Ming and how we can get it up and running.

The Ming Library

Before Ming was created, the LibSWF library was used to generate dynamic Flash content. However, LibSWF is not commonly used anymore for several reasons:

❑ It is closed source

❑ It does not support ActionScript

❑ It does not have a port for Windows users, and with no sourcecode available, there was little chance of someone writing one

❑ It is no longer actively developed

Ming, on the other hand, is open source and is available for Windows. It is licensed as an open-source library under the terms of the GNU Lesser General Public License (LGPL), written by the Free Software Foundation, Inc. The complete LGPL license can be found at http://www.gnu.org/copyleft/lesser.txt.

Ming was introduced into PHP in version 4.05, replacing the previously supported module, LibSWF. Created by Dave Hayden, the Ming library is written in C. It comes from a project to support Flash with a variety of scripting languages, with an eye toward PHP in particular.

The library is easy to use and deploy and integrates nicely into any PHP script. The Ming functions are structured intuitively for both Flash and PHP developers. With Ming and PHP, not only can we give our site the desired panache, but we can also enjoy reduced overhead and cost compared with deploying other Flash solutions. For more information refer to http://ming.sourceforge.net.

The latest version of Ming outputs Flash version 5 SWF files, and supports the new version of ActionScript (version 5). Almost all the features that we can incorporate in a Flash movie are available through the PHP/Ming interface: shapes, gradients, bitmaps in the form of JPEG and PNG, shape tweens (changing the shape of an object), text fields, buttons, actions, movie clips, color transforms, and MP3 streaming.

> **MP3 streaming means taking an existing MP3 file and streaming its content out via an SWF file. However, we cannot add events that allow us to attach sounds to a button so that, for example, when we put the mouse over the button, it plays the sound to our movie. At the time of writing, this feature is missing from PHP/Ming.**

Getting Started

Let's look at the easiest way to get Ming working on UNIX and Windows systems.

Refer to Chapter 1 for detailed installation instructions.

Enabling Ming on UNIX

If we are using a UNIX system then we will need to configure PHP with Ming and recompile. The latest version of PHP (4.2.1) comes with the Ming wrappers included as an extension, so there is no need to download Ming from the web. Here are the commands that we will need to configure PHP with Ming:

```
tar zvf php-4.2.1.tar.gz
cd php-4.2.1
./buildconf
./configure -with-ming
make
make install
```

If Ming is to be installed as a dynamic module, we will need to enable it by adding this line to the top of our PHP scripts:

```
dl(' php_ming.so');
```

Enabling Ming on Windows

If we are using a Windows machine, the latest version of PHP is distributed with the PHP/Ming module. It is not enabled by default, but we can enable it by uncommenting the line:

```
;extension=php_ming.dll
```

in our php.ini file. Besides this we must also specify the correct path to our modules using the extension_dir directive in our php.ini file.

We can also manually load the Ming DLL in each script we want to use it in, using PHP's dl() function by adding this line to the top of our PHP scripts:

```
dl(' php_ming.dll');
```

Cross-Platform Scripts

To determine which operating system the script is running on, we can check the first few letters of the constant variable PHP_OS. If they are 'WIN', we know we're running on Windows. Otherwise, it's pretty safe to assume we are on a Unix-based platform.

To determine whether or not the Ming extension is already loaded (in the case of a UNIX server where it has been compiled into PHP), we can use the extension_loaded() function. When we put it all together, we get a snippet of code that will check if Ming is already loaded; if it is not, load the correct version for the current operating system:

```php
<?php

if(!extension_loaded('ming')) {
    if(strtoupper(substr(PHP_OS,0,3)) == 'WIN') {
        dl('php_ming.dll');
    } else {
        dl('php_ming.so');
    }
}
?>
```

Testing the Installation

To ensure that Ming support is enabled with the PHP installation, we will run the `phpinfo()` script:

```php
<?php

if(!extension_loaded('ming')) {
    if(strtoupper(substr(PHP_OS,0,3)) == 'WIN') {
        dl('php_ming.dll');
    } else {
        dl('php_ming.so');
    }
}

phpinfo();
?>
```

When viewed in a web browser, `phpinfo.php` will show a list of all the features that have been compiled into PHP on the server. If our installation is successful, we will see this:

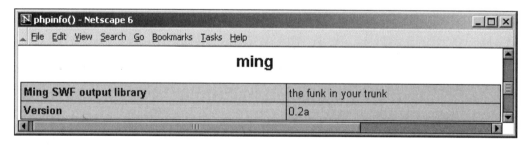

Ming Objects

PHP/Ming includes thirteen classes. Let us take a quick look at the classes and the type of tasks they perform:

Class	Description	Task
SWFMovie	Creates a Flash SWF Movie	Fundamentals
SWFShape	Creates a geometric shape	Drawing
SWFFill	Provides a method for transforming gradient and bitmap fills for shapes	Drawing
SWFGradient	Creates a gradient object which can be used as a fill for a shape	Drawing
SWFBitmap	Allows us to include JPEG or PNG images in our movie	Drawing
SWFFont	Holds fontface information	Text
SWFText	Displays a string of text	Text

Class	Description	Task
SWFTextField	Creates a text input area	Text
SWFDisplayItem	Provides abstractions to many other Flash objects	Animation
SWFSprite	Creates a movie clip	Animation
SWFMorph	Allows us to create a morph, or a shape tween between two shape objects	Animation
SWFButton	Creates buttons through which we can interact with the movie	Interaction
SWFAction	Creates an ActionScript object to provide interaction with the movie	Interaction

We will work through each of the five sections along with the classes and discuss where and how they can be used.

Fundamentals

Before detailing the class, we need to talk about something that will play an integral part in every example we see in the rest of the chapter, and more importantly, in every movie that we make with Ming – color.

Color

Normally we express colors by names, such as 'blue', 'tan', or 'teal'. However, when we work with color in a computer programming language we have to express color by a system of numbers. A common way of doing this is the RGB system.

Any color, ranging from black to white, can be created using the RGB system by combining different amounts of red, green, and blue. Each of the values of red, green, and blue can range from 0 to 255. On one end of the spectrum we have black, the absence of color, created with a value of 0 for all three, while on the other end we have white, created with values of 255 for all three.

Please refer to *Fig.3.1 – RGB Color System Representation* in *Appendix G* to see the representation of the RGB color system.

PHP/Ming creates color in the same way. When a PHP/Ming function requires us to specify a color, we will do so by specifying the individual values for red, green, and blue. For example, if we want to create a pure red, we will set R=255, G=0, and B=0. Also, PHP/Ming allows us to specify an alpha value for our color, which represents the level of transparency. This value also ranges from 0 (opaque) to 255 (completely transparent).

SWFMovie

The SWFMovie class is arguably the most important class when it comes to creating SWF movies with Ming. On instantiating, this class creates a top-level object that holds all the shapes, buttons, and text items that we will add to our movie.

Here is a code snippet that creates a `SWFMovie` object:

```
$movie = new SWFMovie();
```

`$movie` now contains an instance of the `SWFMovie` class. We can now call any of the `SWFMovie` methods using the syntax:

```
$movie->method();
```

Of course `method()` is just an example of how the syntax works, it's not one of the actual methods!

Let us discuss the actual methods. The `SWFMovie` class has ten methods. We shall not list all of them here, but we will deal with them in the course of this chapter.

Refer to Appendix A for a detailed method reference list.

To start with, let's look at three methods that deal with the initial setup of the movie.

setDimension()

The `setDimension()` method allows us to specify the size that our movie will display on the screen. The method takes two arguments, width and height. These are integer values and specify the width and height of the movie in pixels.

This code snippet sets the movie size to 400 pixels wide by 300 pixels high:

```
$movie->setDimension(400,300);
```

The dimensions that we set become important when we start placing objects in the movie. By specifying the dimensions for the movie, we are stipulating the size of the stage on which we will be working. If we draw a shape onto the stage at a point that is beyond either the width or the height of the movie, then that shape will not be visible when we see the movie.

It is worth noting at this point that there are two ways for us to see our SWF movie. We can see it using the stand-alone Flash player or in our web browser. If we see the movie in a web browser, the SWF will scale it to fill our browser window. In this case setting the dimensions of the `SWFMovie` will not appear to have had any effect. When we create our first SWF movie, we will see how to embed our SWF movie in an HTML web page so that the movie dimensions are retained.

setRate()

A Flash movie is actually a set of frames, through which the Flash player plays. By slightly altering the shape on subsequent frames we can create the illusion of animation in the Flash movie. We will discuss animation in more detail towards the end of the chapter, but for now let's talk about the rate of the movie. The rate is a measure of how fast the movie plays through the frames in the movie. This rate is specified as Frames Per Second (fps). Therefore if we have a movie with a rate of 10 fps, and we want our movie length to be a full minute, then we must make sure our movie contains 600 frames (60 seconds x 10 frames per second = 600 frames).

This code snippet sets the rate of the movie to 10 fps:

```
$movie->setRate(10);
```

setBackground()

Before we start placing objects on the movie, we need to set the background color of the movie using the `setBackground()` method. The method takes 3 arguments – values of the red, green, and blue components respectively. As we discussed in the section on color, each of these values can range from 0 to 255 and by combining equal values of red and green we can create pure yellow color.

This code snippet sets the background color of our Flash movie to yellow:

```
$movie->setBackground(255,255,0);
```

With the code that we have seen so far, we can create a new Flash movie, and set the size, rate, and background:

```php
<?php

$movie = new SWFMovie();
$movie->setDimension(400,300);
$movie->setRate(12);
$movie->setBackground(255,255,0);
?>
```

However if we run this script nothing will happen. This is because we have not output the movie to the browser yet. We do that with the `output()` method.

output()

Before sending any output to the browser, we must tell the browser the correct MIME type of the file it is receiving; in the case of a Flash movie it is `application/x-shockwave-flash`. A browser will normally use the extension of the filename to determine the type of file it is receiving, and display it accordingly. Since we are creating our SWF movie from a PHP script, the filename of the script, and therefore the SWF movie, has an extension of `.php` and not `.swf`. Hence, we first send the `Content-type` header to explicitly tell the browser what type of file to expect and then output the file.

Here is the code snippet to output the SWF movie to the browser:

```php
header("Content-type:application/x-shockwave-flash");
$movie->output();
```

That's all we need to display our first Flash movie:

```php
<?php

// script: SWFMovie.php

if(!extension_loaded('ming')) {
    if(strtoupper(substr(PHP_OS,0,3)) == 'WIN') {
        dl('php_ming.dll');
    } else {
        dl('php_ming.so');
    }
```

```
    }

    $movie = new SWFMovie();

    $movie->setDimension(400,300);
    $movie->setRate(12);
    $movie->setBackground(255,255,0);

    header("Content-type:application/x-shockwave-flash");

    $movie->output();
    ?>
```

To see the resulting image refer to *Fig 3.2 – SWFMovie* in *Appendix G.*

As we can see, the yellow SWF movie has stretched to fill the entire browser window, though we had specified the dimensions. There are two ways by which we can alter this behavior:

❑   Embed the SWF movie in an output page

❑   Use the save() method

Here is the HTML code to embed the SWF movie output inside an HTML page:

```
<html>
  <body>
    <h1>Chapter 3: Ming</h1>
    <p>
      <object classid="clsid:D27CDB6E-AE6D-11cf-96B8-444553540000"
                      codebase="http://active.macromedia.com/flash2/
                      cabs/swflash.cab#version=4,0,0,0" id="objects"
                      width="400" height="300">
        <param name="movie" value="SWFMovie.php">
        <embed src="SWFMovie.php" width="400" height="300"
                      type="application/x-shockwave-flash"
                      pluginspace="http://www.macromedia.com/shockwave/
                      download/index.cgi?P1_Prod_Version=ShockwaveFlash">
      </object>
    </p>
  </body>
</html>
```

The <object> tag specifies that we are embedding a Flash object and the <param> tag specifies the PHP script that is creating our movie. We also use the <embed> tag specifying the src as the PHP script. When we save the above script as an HTML file (ming.html) and run it, we will see our movie as per the specified dimensions.

To see the resulting image refer to *Fig 3.3 – SWFMovie-HTML* in *Appendix G.*

save()

The `SWFMovie` class has another method of outputting the SWF movie. The `save()` method saves the SWF movie stream to a file on disk. To use this method, we must alter the line:

```
$movie->output();
```

to:

```
$movie->save("ming.swf");
```

Since we are now saving the SWF movie stream to a file called `ming.swf` and not sending it to a web browser, we can remove the line that sends the `Content-type` header.

Now if we run our SWFMovie script, a new file `ming.swf` is created in the same directory as the PHP script. If we open this file with the stand-alone Flash player, it will show the effect of having set the movie dimensions with the `setdimension()` method.

To see the resulting image refer to *Fig 3.4 – SWFMovie-Flash* in *Appendix G*.

> *If our web server is so configured that it does not allow scripts to write to the directory we are running the script from, then this will not work. We must refer to the appropriate web server documentation for more information on setting up a directory, which the web server can write to.*

Now that we have created the basic shell of a Flash movie, let's add some content.

Drawing

Let us discuss the classes of this group, which deal with drawing and placing objects on our movie.

SWFShape

This class represents geometrical shapes, like lines, triangles, rectangles, circles, and ellipses. At its most basic we can use an instance of this class to draw lines and curves on our movie.

Once we master the methods for drawing arbitrary lines and curves, we can look at how we can join them together and create shapes. The basic steps involved in drawing a line or curve are:

- ❑ Create an instance of the `SWFShape` class
- ❑ Set the line style of the pen
- ❑ Draw the line or curve

Instantiating SWFShape

`SWFShape` objects are created like this:

```
$shape = new SWFShape();
```

Setting the Line Style

The line style is basically the width, color, and transparency of the line that we will be drawing. We will set these with a single method – `setLine()`.

`setLine()` takes 5 arguments – width of the line in pixels, the red, green, and blue components of the color (each ranging from 0 to 255), and the alpha value of the line (also ranging from 0 to 255).

This code snippet sets a red-colored, 2 pixel-wide transparent line style of the SWFShape object:

```
$shape->setLine(2,255,0,0,255);
```

Drawing Straight Lines

When drawing shapes in our movie, we need to think of our movie stage as a canvas the size of which was defined with the `setDimension()` method. The (x, y) coordinates of the top left-hand corner of the movie are (0,0). The coordinates increase as we move across and down the canvas. Drawing on our movie is just like drawing on a piece of paper. We have a 'pen' that we can move to any point on the page and from that point draw a line.

There are two methods for drawing lines on our canvas:

- ❑ **drawLine()**
  This method draws a line from the current pen position to a point (x, y) pixels away from the current position

- ❑ **drawLineTo()**
  This method draws a line from the current pen position to the point (x, y) on the canvas

The following two diagrams show the difference between the two methods. In both cases the starting point is x=40, y=20 and the line is drawn to a point x=140, y=100:

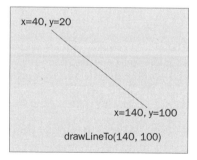
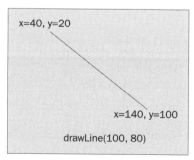

In the first image, `drawLineTo()` is drawing to a specific point, while in the second image `drawLine()` is using an offset from the starting point to draw the line.

In a similar way the methods `movePen()` and `movePenTo()` allow us to move the pen position on the canvas.

In this example, we draw a horizontal and vertical line intersecting the center of our movie. First, we will define some constants for the movie. We will use them to set the movie dimensions and the extents of our stage. Since the x and y coordinates begin at (0,0), we must subtract 1 from the width and height to get the rightmost and bottom positions of the stage:

```php
<?php

//script: SWFShapeLine.php

if(!extension_loaded('ming')) {
    if(strtoupper(substr(PHP_OS,0,3)) == 'WIN') {
        dl('php_ming.dll');
    } else {
        dl('php_ming.so');
    }
}

define("MOVIE_DIM_X",400);
define("MOVIE_DIM_Y",300);
define("MAX_X",MOVIE_DIM_X-1);
define("MAX_Y",MOVIE_DIM_Y-1);
```

Then we create a new SWFMovie object and set the dimensions and the background color:

```php
$movie=New SWFMovie();
$movie->setBackground(255,255,0);
$movie->setDimension(MOVIE_DIM_X,MOVIE_DIM_Y);
```

We also create a new SWFShape object and set the line style to 10 pixels wide with red color:

```php
$horiz_line=New SWFShape();
$horiz_line->setLine(10,255,0,0);
```

Then we move the pen to a position where x=0 and y is half the height of the movie:

```php
$horiz_line->movePenTo(0,MAX_Y/2);
```

and draw the line from the current position to the far right edge of the movie, maintaining the y position. This will give us a red horizontal line:

```php
$horiz_line->drawLineTo(MAX_X,MAX_Y/2);
```

The vertical line works in the same way, except we draw from the top (y=0) to the bottom (y=MAX_Y) along an x value that is half the width of the movie:

```php
$vert_line=New SWFShape();
$vert_line->setLine(10,255,0,0);
$vert_line->movePenTo(MAX_X/2,0);
$vert_line->drawLine(0,MAX_Y);
```

Something that we have not spoken about yet is the add() method of the SWFMovie class. Any object that we create has to be added to our movie. We have created $vert_line and $horiz_line but unless we add them to our movie, they will not be displayed. The add() method takes a single argument of the object we want to add, in this case the instances of SWFShape that we have created – $horiz_line and $vert_line:

```php
$movie->add($horiz_line);
$movie->add($vert_line);
```

Finally we specify the Content-type and output the movie:

```
header("Content-type:application/x-shockwave-flash");
$movie->output();
?>
```

We will save this script as SWFShapeLine.php.

Let us also alter the following lines in our ming.html file:

```
<param name="movie" value=" SWFShapeLine php">
<embed src=" SWFShapeLine.php" width="400" height="300">
```

to reflect the name of the new PHP script. When we run this script we will see a vertical and a horizontal line intersecting at the center of our movie.

To see the resulting image refer to *Fig 3.5 – SWFMovieLine* in *Appendix G.*

Drawing Curves

Besides straight lines, we can also draw curves, using:

❑ **drawCurveTo()**
This method accepts four integer arguments – control_x, control_y, anchor_x, and anchor_y. It draws a curve from the current pen position to the coordinate (control_x, control_y) using (anchor_x, anchor_y) as an anchor point. The following illustration shows this:

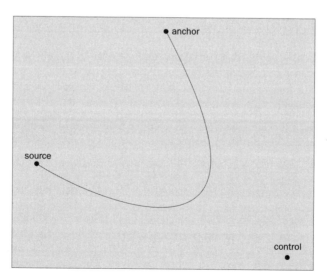

❑ **drawCurve()**
This method has four integer arguments – dcontrol_x, dcontrol_y, danchor_x, and danchor_y, where dcontrol_x and dcontrol_y give the position of the control point with respect to the current pen position and danchor_x and danchor_y give the position of the anchor point with respect to the current pen position.

It's the same concept as `drawLine()` and `drawLineTo()` – `drawCurve()` draws in relative space while `drawCurveTo()` draws with respect to absolute coordinates.

Let's take a look at an example. We will draw a line from the bottom left-hand corner of the stage to the bottom right-hand corner of the stage, arching the line up towards the top of the stage. Here is the initial part of the code where we create a new movie object and set its background and dimensions:

```php
<?php

//script: SWFShapeCurve.php

if(!extension_loaded('ming')) {
    if(strtoupper(substr(PHP_OS,0,3)) == 'WIN') {
        dl('php_ming.dll');
    } else {
        dl('php_ming.so');
    }
}

define("MOVIE_DIM_X",400);
define("MOVIE_DIM_Y",300);
define("MAX_X",MOVIE_DIM_X-1);
define("MAX_Y",MOVIE_DIM_Y-1);

$movie=New SWFMovie();
$movie->setBackground(255,255,0);
$movie->setDimension(MOVIE_DIM_X,MOVIE_DIM_Y);
```

We'll use a blue line, 10 pixels wide:

```php
$curve=New SWFShape();
$curve->setLine(10,0,0,255);
```

and move the pen to the start position – the bottom left-hand corner of the stage:

```php
$curve->movePenTo(0,MAX_Y);
```

Now we draw the curve. The first 2 arguments are the x and y values of the control point of the curve, we'll make that the top-most point in the middle of the movie: $x = MAX\_X/2$, $y = 0$. The anchor point is the bottom right-hand corner of the stage: $x = MAX\_X$, $y = MAX\_Y$:

```php
$curve->drawCurveTo(MAX_X/2,0,MAX_X,MAX_Y);
```

Finally, we add the curve to the movie and output it:

```php
$movie->add($curve);

header("Content-type:application/x-shockwave-flash");
$movie->output();
?>
```

To see the resulting curve on the browser refer to *Fig 3.6 – SWFShapeCurve* in *Appendix G*.

We can produce various shapes by drawing lines and curves and joining them. However, when we deal with shapes we generally want them to be filled in too. This brings us to the SWFFill class.

SWFFill

SWFShape has a method addFill() that returns an SWFFill object.

This can then be used by the setLeftFill() and setRightFill() methods of SWFShape:

- ❑   setLeftFill() – This method sets the fill raster color on the left-hand edge of the shape's outline. We would use this if we are drawing the shape in a counter-clockwise direction.

- ❑   setRightFill() – This method sets the fill raster color on the right-hand side of our shape outline. We would use this if we are drawing our shape in a clockwise direction.

Whether we use setLeftFill() or setRightFill() depends on whether we are drawing our shape in a clockwise or counter-clockwise direction.

Let us discuss an example where we draw a diamond in the middle of the movie. We start by creating the SWFMovie object:

```php
<?php

//script: SWFFill.php

if(!extension_loaded('ming')) {
    if(strtoupper(substr(PHP_OS,0,3)) == 'WIN') {
        dl('php_ming.dll');
    } else {
        dl('php_ming.so');
    }
}

define("MOVIE_DIM_X",400);
define("MOVIE_DIM_Y",300);
define("MAX_X",MOVIE_DIM_X-1);
define("MAX_Y",MOVIE_DIM_Y-1);

$movie=New SWFMovie();
$movie->setBackground(255,255,0);
$movie->setDimension(MOVIE_DIM_X,MOVIE_DIM_Y);
```

We specify a blue, 10 pixel wide line style and then create a SWFFill object ($filler) of pure green. We then set the right fill of the shape to our new SWFFill object:

```php
$diamond=New SWFShape();
$diamond->setLine(10,0,0,255);
$filler = $diamond->addFill(0,255,0);
$diamond->setRightFill($filler);
```

Because we have used `setRightFill()` we will draw the shape in a clockwise direction:

```
$diamond->movePenTo(MAX_X/2,MAX_Y/4);
$diamond->drawLine(MAX_X/4,MAX_Y/4);
$diamond->drawLine(-MAX_X/4,MAX_Y/4);
$diamond->drawLine(-MAX_X/4,-MAX_Y/4);
$diamond->drawLine(MAX_X/4,-MAX_Y/4);
```

Finally, we add the diamond to the movie and output it:

```
$movie->add($diamond);

header("Content-type:application/x-shockwave-flash");
$movie->output();
?>
```

To see the resulting diamond at the center of our movie, refer to *Fig 3.7 – SWFFill* in *Appendix G*.

SWFGradient

The `SWFGradient` class creates an object with which we can create a gradient fill. Once we have created and set up the gradient we will use the `SWFGradient` object as the argument to the `addFill()` method of `SWFShape` to create the `SWFFill` object.

We will set up the `SWFGradient` object using:

❏ **addEntry()**
   This method takes 5 arguments – a ratio value between 0 and 1 that specifies where in the gradient the color occurs, the red, green, and blue color values, and an optional fifth argument that specifies the alpha value.

Here is the initial part of the script:

```
<?php

//script: SWFGradient.php

if(!extension_loaded('ming')) {
    if(strtoupper(substr(PHP_OS,0,3)) == 'WIN') {
        dl('php_ming.dll');
    } else {
        dl('php_ming.so');
    }
}

define("MOVIE_DIM_X",400);
define("MOVIE_DIM_Y",300);
define("MAX_X",MOVIE_DIM_X-1);
define("MAX_Y",MOVIE_DIM_Y-1);

$movie=New SWFMovie();
$movie->setBackground(255,255,0);
$movie->setDimension(MOVIE_DIM_X,MOVIE_DIM_Y);

$rect = New SWFShape();
$rect->setLine(10,0,0,0);
```

Next we create a new SWFGradient object:

```
$gradient = new SWFGradient();
```

We add 2 entries to it – the first red, and the second blue; therefore our gradient will be from red to blue:

```
$gradient->addEntry(0.0, 255,0,0);
$gradient->addEntry(1.0,0,0,255);
```

This time when we create the SWFFill object with the addFill() method, instead of passing the method RGB values, we pass the SWFGradient object we created, with the additional argument of SWFFILL_RADIAL_GRADIENT. This specifies that our gradient is a radial gradient. If we leave the argument out, the gradient will be a linear gradient:

```
$filler = $rect->addFill($gradient,SWFFILL_RADIAL_GRADIENT);
```

We set the right fill of the shape and draw the shape to the same size as that of the movie:

```
$rect->setRightFill($filler);
$rect->movePenTo(0,0);
$rect->drawLineTo(MAX_X,0);
$rect->drawLineTo(MAX_X,MAX_Y);
$rect->drawLineTo(0,MAX_Y);
$rect->drawLineTo(0,0);
```

We add the shape to our movie and output it to the browser:

```
$movie->add($rect);

header("Content-type:application/x-shockwave-flash");
$movie->output();
?>
```

To see the resulting color gradient in the movie, refer to *Fig 3.8 – SWFGradient* in *Appendix G*. The center of the radial fill will appear to be centered on the top-left corner of the movie.

SWFBitmap

We've seen how to fill an object with a solid color and a gradient. It is also possible to fill an object using a bitmap, by creating a new SWFBitmap object and passing the data of the bitmap to it.

The bitmap can either be a DBL (Define Bits Lossless) file or a non-progressive JPEG file:

- ❏ A DBL file is either a GIF or a PNG that has been converted using a utility gif2dbl or png2dbl that comes with Ming. This utility is available with the Ming distribution.

- ❏ A non-progressive, or baseline JPEG, is stored as a single top-to-bottom scan of the image. Most graphics programs will allow us to save our JPEG as a baseline JPEG. This is unlike a progressive JPEG that stores the image in a series of scans of improving quality – the first scan will gives a very low quality image, the second will improve the quality, and so on. As the image loads we will quickly get an image of poor quality, which will improve as the rest of the image downloads.

  More information on baseline JPEGs can be found at http://www.faqs.org/faqs/jpeg-faq/part1/section-11.html.

Let's take a look at an example:

```php
<?php

//script:SWFBitmap.php

if(!extension_loaded('ming')) {
    if(strtoupper(substr(PHP_OS,0,3)) == 'WIN') {
        dl('php_ming.dll');
    } else {
        dl('php_ming.so');
    }
}

define("MOVIE_DIM_X",400);
define("MOVIE_DIM_Y",300);
define("MAX_X",MOVIE_DIM_X-1);
define("MAX_Y",MOVIE_DIM_Y-1);

$movie=New SWFMovie();
$movie->setBackground(255,255,0);
$movie->setDimension(MOVIE_DIM_X,MOVIE_DIM_Y);

$rect = New SWFShape();
$rect->setLine(10,0,0,0);
```

We open the JPEG file and read all the data of the JPEG into a variable $data. $data is then passed as the argument to the SWFBitmap constructor:

```php
$fp = fopen("smiley.jpg","rb");
$data = fread($fp,filesize("smiley.jpg"));
$bitmap = new SWFBitmap($data);
```

Then we create $filler with the addFill() method with the SWFFILL_TILED_BITMAP parameter which will give a tiled image of our JPEG file:

```php
$filler = $rect->addFill($bitmap,SWFFILL_TILED_BITMAP);
```

This is the final part of the code:

```php
$rect->setRightFill($filler);
$rect->movePenTo(0,0);
$rect->drawLineTo(MAX_X,0);
$rect->drawLineTo(MAX_X,MAX_Y);
$rect->drawLineTo(0,MAX_Y);
$rect->drawLineTo(0,0);

$movie->add($rect);

header("Content-type:application/x-shockwave-flash");
$movie->output();
?>
```

To see the resulting smiley face tiled across our movie, refer to *Fig 3.9 – SWFBitmap* in *Appendix G*.

> **Since Ming is under constant development we often find conflicting information on how to do certain things.**
>
> **The** SWFBitmap **class is a good example of this. The documentation at http://ming.sourceforge.net/docs/swfbitmap.php?mode=php for the class gives an example similar to the one given above. However, on http://www.php.net/manual/en/function.swfbitmap.php, the function reference says that we can give the filename as a string to the** SWFBitmap **constructor.**
>
> **The PHP 4.2.1, Ming 0.2a versions use the syntax as described above and on the Ming web site.**

Text

There are two ways to add text to our movies – the SWFText class creates a piece of text on the movie, while the SWFTextField creates a text field on the movie that allows the user to enter their own text.

Unfortunately the text support for Windows is not as stable as it is on UNIX machines. We will discuss the possibilities of text layout on Windows machines in a later section.

SWFFont

Before creating a SWFText or SWFTextField object, we first need to create a SWFFont object. The SWFFont object defines the fontface that will be used for the text object. When creating the SWFFont object we need to pass the fontface we want to use as an argument to it.

Here is a code snippet that defines the Arial.fdb font:

```
$arial= new SWFFont("arial.fdb");
```

The easiest fonts to use are the browser-defined fonts, the definitions of which are provided by the Flash movie player. These fonts are **_serif**, **_sans**, and **_typewriter**. Further, these are the only fonts that work on Windows.

Another option is to use an FDB (Font Definition Block) file for the fontface. An FDB file contains the full definition for a font. FDB files are created by running the **makefdb** Ming utility on an SWT Generator Template file. SWT files are created in Macromedia Flash by saving the Flash movie as a template.

Unfortunately, if we are using the standard PHP Windows distribution from http://www.php.net, then we can currently only make use of the browser-defined fonts. Loading an FDB file will cause the web server to hang. Therefore, while working on Windows, depending on the distribution and version of PHP and Ming that we are using, our results will vary when using FDB files with the SWFFont class.

SWFText

As the name suggests, the SWFText class allows us to add text to our movie. An instance is easy to create and requires no arguments:

```
$wrox = new SWFText();
```

Once we have created our text object we can start setting it up using its member functions. The first thing to do is to set the font that the text object must use. We will do this by creating the SWFFont object to define the font and set it with the setFont() method:

```
$font = new SWFFont("arial.fdb");
$wrox = new SWFText();
$wrox->setFont($font);
```

Once we have set the font, we can set the color, size, and position of the text. To set the color, we use the setColor() method, which includes 3 arguments specifying the red, green, and blue values, and an optional fourth parameter specifying the alpha value:

```
$wrox->setColor(255,255,255);
```

The size is set with the setHeight() method. The value that we pass here is the height of the font in pixels. This height is from the top of the ascender to the bottom of the descender of the font:

```
$wrox->setHeight(200);
```

The ascender is that part of the font, in lowercase letters, that rises up. The descender is the part that drops below the imaginary line that the font appears to be standing on, like this. This is best explained in this diagram:

We can then position the text object using the moveTo() method. The x and y position that we pass to this method positions the lower left-hand corner of the font at that coordinate:

```
$wrox->moveTo(0,200);
```

Now that we have decided where and how we want our text to appear, we just have to add the actual text string to the text object. We use the addString() method:

```
$wrox->addString("text to add");
```

Then as usual we add the object to the movie and output it.

Here is the full code:

```
<?php

//script: SWFText.php
```

```
if(!extension_loaded('ming')) {
    if(strtoupper(substr(PHP_OS,0,3)) == 'WIN') {
        dl('php_ming.dll');
    } else {
        dl('php_ming.so');
    }
}

define("MOVIE_DIM_X",400);
define("MOVIE_DIM_Y",300);
define("MAX_X",MOVIE_DIM_X-1);
define("MAX_Y",MOVIE_DIM_Y-1);
define("WROX","Wrox");

$arial=New SWFFont("arial.fdb");

$wrox=New SWFText();
$wrox->setFont($arial);
$wrox->setColor(255,255,255);
$wrox->setHeight(150);
$wrox->moveTo(0,200);
$wrox->addString(WROX);

$movie=New SWFMovie();
$movie->setBackground(255,0,0);
$movie->setDimension(MOVIE_DIM_X,MOVIE_DIM_Y);

$movie->add($wrox);

header("Content-type:application/x-shockwave-flash");
$movie->output();
?>
```

To see the resulting image refer to *Fig 3.10 – SWFText* in *Appendix G*.

The SWFText class is not stable on Windows and hence Windows users may not be able to run the above script. However, the SWFTextField class works fine on Windows and with a little tweaking we can simulate the SWFText class with SWFTextField. We will see how to do this when we cover the SWFDisplayItem class in the *Animation* section. But first let us get acquainted with the SWFTextField class.

SWFTextField

The SWFTextfield class provides a way for us to gather user input. In this chapter we will only be looking at what is involved in creating a text field. We will discuss how to use the information that the user has entered in our text field in Chapter 4.

This class is very easy to use. When creating the object we can pass an optional argument to the constructor that specifies how the textbox should behave. Here is a listing:

Optional Parameter	Description
SWFTEXTFIELD_DRAWBOX	The text field will have an outline
SWFTEXTFIELD_HASLENGTH	The text field will restrict the number of characters
SWFTEXTFIELD_HTML	Allows HTML markup
SWFTEXTFIELD_MULTILINE	Creates a multi-line text field
SWFTEXTFIELD_NOEDIT	This text field is not editable
SWFTEXTFIELD_NOSELECT	The user cannot select any text in the field
SWFTEXTFIELD_PASSWORD	The text is obscured by a password character (*)
SWFTEXTFIELD_WORDWRAP	The text will wrap inside the text field

If we wish to use more than one of these flags we can do so by combining them with a bitwise OR.

Let us discuss an example:

```php
<?php

//script:SWFTextField1.php

if(!extension_loaded('ming')) {
    if(strtoupper(substr(PHP_OS,0,3)) == 'WIN') {
        dl('php_ming.dll');
    } else {
        dl('php_ming.so');
    }
}

define("MOVIE_DIM_X",400);
define("MOVIE_DIM_Y",300);
define("MAX_X",MOVIE_DIM_X-1);
define("MAX_Y",MOVIE_DIM_Y-1);
define("WROX","Wrox");
$movie=New SWFMovie();
$movie->setBackground(255,0,0);
$movie->setDimension(MOVIE_DIM_X,MOVIE_DIM_Y);
```

Now we create our font object. Since this is a textbox we don't want to use a fancy font:

```php
$sans=New SWFFont("_sans");
```

We also create the new SWFTextField object – we pass SWFTEXTFIELD_PASSWORD and
SWFTEXTFIELD_DRAWBOX combined using a bitwise OR operator. (Our textbox will have a border and
any text in the box will be masked by * characters):

```php
$wrox=New SWFTextField(SWFTEXTFIELD_PASSWORD|SWFTEXTFIELD_DRAWBOX);
```

We also set the font, height, and the color and add the string:

```
$wrox->setFont($sans);
$wrox->setHeight(50);
$wrox->setColor(0,0,0);
$wrox->addString(WROX);
```

Finally, we add our object and output it to the browser with the appropriate header:

```
$movie->add($wrox);

header("Content-type:application/x-shockwave-flash");
$movie->output();
?>
```

To see the resulting image refer to *Fig 3.11 – SWFTextField1* in *Appendix G*.

Unfortunately the `SWFTextField` class does not have a method to position it on the stage, but we will see how we can do this in the next section.

Animation

In order to animate something on the screen we must do two things. The first thing we need to do is add an element of time to the movie and the second thing is to change the shapes around. If everything stayed in the same place it would be a pretty boring animation! We have already seen how we can position text objects with the `moveTo()` method, and we have also seen how, by specifying a starting location for our pen while drawing `SWFShape` objects, we can make it appear as if we have placed the `SWFShape` in a specific place on the stage. In this section we will discuss it in detail.

SWFDisplayItem

In the same way that the `addFill()` method of the `SWFShape` class returns a `SWFFill` object, the `add()` method of the `SWFMovie` class returns a `SWFDisplayItem` object. Until now we have used the `add()` method in the following way:

```
$movie->add($text);
```

But `add()` method returns a `SWFDisplayItem` object, so we should really be writing the line as:

```
$texthandle = $movie->add($text);
```

`$texthandle` is now a `SWFDisplayItem` object and we can use any of the `SWFDisplayItem` methods to manipulate the object. These methods include moving, rotating, and scaling.

Let's see how these methods work. We'll use a simplified version of the script we wrote earlier to draw the green and blue diamond:

```
<?php

//script: SWFDisplayItem1.php

if(!extension_loaded('ming')) {
    if(strtoupper(substr(PHP_OS,0,3)) == 'WIN') {
```

```
        dl('php_ming.dll');
    } else {
        dl('php_ming.so');
    }
}

$movie=New SWFMovie();
$movie->setBackground(255,255,0);
$movie->setDimension(400,300);

$diamond=New SWFShape();
$diamond->setLine(10,0,0,255);
$filler = $diamond->addFill(0,255,0);
$diamond->setRightFill($filler);

$diamond->movePenTo(100,0);
$diamond->drawLineTo(200,75);
$diamond->drawLineTo(100,150);
$diamond->drawLineTo(0,75);
$diamond->drawLineTo(100,0);

$diamondhandle = $movie->add($diamond);

header("Content-type:application/x-shockwave-flash");
$movie->output();
?>
```

Here, we have removed all the define statements, drawn the diamond in the top left-hand corner, and returned the SWFDisplayItem into the $diamondhandle variable.

To see the resulting image refer to *Fig 3.12 – SWFDisplayItem1* in *Appendix G*.

Now let's start doing something with the object. The first thing that we can do is move the object about on the stage. The **move()** and **moveTo()** methods of the SWFDisplayItem class provide this functionality and work in exactly the same way as the movePen() and movePenTo() methods of the SWFShape class.

We will move our object down and a bit to the right, by adding the following line of code:

```
$diamondhandle->moveTo(10,150);
```

We can also rotate the object through 45 degrees using the **rotate()** method. This method rotates the object by the specified number of degrees in a counterclockwise direction from the horizontal axis. We achieve this by adding the following line of code:

```
$diamondhandle->rotate(45);
```

Here is the full script:

```
<?php

/script: SWFDisplayItem2.php

if(!extension_loaded('ming')) {
    if(strtoupper(substr(PHP_OS,0,3)) == 'WIN') {
```

```
                dl('php_ming.dll');
        } else {
                dl('php_ming.so');
        }
}

$movie=New SWFMovie();
$movie->setBackground(255,255,0);
$movie->setDimension(400,300);

$diamond=New SWFShape();
$diamond->setLine(10,0,0,255);
$filler = $diamond->addFill(0,255,0);
$diamond->setRightFill($filler);

$diamond->movePenTo(100,0);
$diamond->drawLineTo(200,75);
$diamond->drawLineTo(100,150);
$diamond->drawLineTo(0,75);
$diamond->drawLineTo(100,0);

$diamondhandle = $movie->add($diamond);
$diamondhandle->moveTo(10,150);
$diamondhandle->rotate(45);

header("Content-type:application/x-shockwave-flash");
$movie->output();
?>
```

To see the resulting image refer to *Fig 3.13 – SWFDisplayItem2* in *Appendix G.*

Let's take a detailed look at how the shape was rotated. Any shape has a rectangular bounding box, and rotation happens around the top left-hand corner of this bounding box:

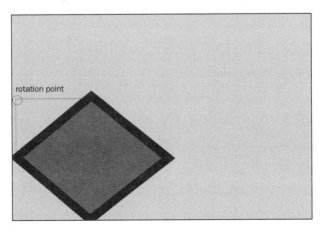

As the shape rotates the bounding box rotates with it:

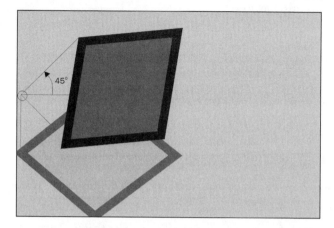

Changing the size of the shape is a matter of using the **scale()** method. The method takes two arguments – a scaling of the x value and a scaling of the y value. The value we use scales the object from its current size. To square the size of the shape we would use a value of 2 for both the x and y scale by adding the following line of code to the previous script (just before sending the header information):

```
$diamondhandle->scale(2,2);
```

Here is the complete script:

```php
<?php

//script: SWFDisplayItem3.php

if(!extension_loaded('ming')) {
    if(strtoupper(substr(PHP_OS,0,3)) == 'WIN') {
        dl('php_ming.dll');
    } else {
        dl('php_ming.so');
    }
}

$movie=New SWFMovie();
$movie->setBackground(255,255,0);
$movie->setDimension(400,300);

$diamond=New SWFShape();
$diamond->setLine(10,0,0,255);
$filler = $diamond->addFill(0,255,0);
$diamond->setRightFill($filler);

$diamond->movePenTo(100,0);
$diamond->drawLineTo(200,75);
$diamond->drawLineTo(100,150);
```

```
$diamond->drawLineTo(0,75);
$diamond->drawLineTo(100,0);

$diamondhandle = $movie->add($diamond);
$diamondhandle->moveTo(10,150);
$diamondhandle->rotate(45);
$diamondhandle->scale(2,2);

header("Content-type:application/x-shockwave-flash");
$movie->output();
?>
```

To see the resulting image refer to *Fig 3.14 – SWFDisplayItem3* in *Appendix G*.

Now that we have seen how we can change the shape, let's do this over a period of time to achieve the effect of animation.

We do this by adding extra frames to our movie. The movies that we have made up to this point have all been a single frame, but in order to allow animation we need to put some more frames in. We do this with the **nextFrame()** method.

We will modify the script in the previous example, to rotate and scale the diamond up and down over a period of time:

```
<?php

//script:animation.php

if(!extension_loaded('ming')) {
    if(strtoupper(substr(PHP_OS,0,3)) == 'WIN') {
        dl('php_ming.dll');
    } else {
        dl('php_ming.so');
    }
}

$movie=New SWFMovie();
$movie->setBackground(255,255,0);
$movie->setDimension(400,300);

$diamond=New SWFShape();
$diamond->setLine(10,0,0,255);
$filler = $diamond->addFill(0,255,0);
$diamond->setRightFill($filler);

$diamond->movePenTo(100,0);
$diamond->drawLineTo(200,75);
$diamond->drawLineTo(100,150);
$diamond->drawLineTo(0,75);
$diamond->drawLineTo(100,0);

$diamondhandle = $movie->add($diamond);
```

```
$diamondhandle->moveTo(0,100);
$movie->nextFrame();
$diamondhandle->rotate(15);
$diamondhandle->scale(1.5,1.5);
$movie->nextFrame();
$diamondhandle->rotate(15);
$diamondhandle->scale(2,2);
$movie->nextFrame();
$diamondhandle->rotate(-15);
$diamondhandle->scale(.75,.75);
$movie->nextFrame();
```

```
header("Content-type:application/x-shockwave-flash");
$movie->output();
?>
```

To see the resulting image refer to *Fig 3.15 – Animation* in *Appendix G*.

The Flash player will loop through all the frames in the movie and then start again from the beginning. In Chapter 4 we will look at how to control the Flash player.

Revisiting SWFTextField

We had mentioned earlier that Windows users would be able to fake a SWFText object with the SWFTextField class and the SWFDisplayItem object! Let's see how we can do that.

First, pass some flags – SWFTEXTFIELD_HTML, SWFTEXTFIELD_NOEDIT, SWFTEXTFIELD_NOSELECT – to the SWFTextField constructor. This will create a textbox which can neither be edited nor be selected. Also, we have specified that it can take HTML markup.

Then, we can use the setHeight() method of the SWFTextField to set the size of the font in the text field. When we add the string to the text field, we can include HTML markup in the string to provide bold or italic features to our font.

The SWFTextField object does not have a moveTo() method like the SWFText object, but now that we know all about the SWFDisplayItem object, we can simply use its moveTo() method.

Here is the script:

```php
<?php

//script:SWFTextField2.php

if(!extension_loaded('ming')) {
    if(strtoupper(substr(PHP_OS,0,3)) == 'WIN') {
        dl('php_ming.dll');
    } else {
        dl('php_ming.so');
    }
}

$sans=New SWFFont("_sans");
```

```
$wrox=New
SWFTextField(SWFTEXTFIELD_HTML|SWFTEXTFIELD_NOEDIT|SWFTEXTFIELD_NOSELECT);

$wrox->setFont($sans);
$wrox->setHeight(150);
$wrox->setColor(0,0,255);
$wrox->addString("<b><i>Wrox</i></b>");

$movie=New SWFMovie();
$movie->setBackground(255,255,0);
$movie->setDimension(400,300);
$texthandle = $movie->add($wrox);
$texthandle->moveTo(10,100);

header("Content-type:application/x-shockwave-flash");
$movie->output();
?>
```

To see the resulting image refer to *Fig 3.16 – SWFTextField2* in *Appendix G*.

SWFSprite

The SWFSprite class creates a movie clip. This lets us create objects that have their own independent timelines. Just like we can add objects to the main SWFMovie, we can add objects to SWFSprite objects. The SWFSprite has a special feature in that it is the only object that we can manipulate using ActionScript – we shall discuss this in detail in Chapter 4.

SWFMorph

The SWFMorph class provides a mechanism by which we can morph one shape into another. In Macromedia Flash, this is known as a **shape tween**.

The SWFMorph class includes two methods – getShape1() and getShape2(), which return SWFShape objects that correspond to the start and end shapes of the tween. Tweening is achieved by using an SWFDisplayItem method called setRatio() which specifies the ratio of the tweening of the morph.

We start by creating a new movie:

```
<?php

//script:SWFMorph.php

if(!extension_loaded('ming')) {
    if(strtoupper(substr(PHP_OS,0,3)) == 'WIN') {
        dl('php_ming.dll');
    } else {
        dl('php_ming.so');
    }
}

$movie=New SWFMovie();
$movie->setBackground(255,255,0);
$movie->setDimension(400,300);
```

and set the rate to 3 so that we can watch the tween happen slowly:

```
$movie->setRate(3);
```

We also create a new SWFMorph object and set the start shape by using the getShape1() method, which returns a SWFShape object:

```
$morph = new SWFMorph();
$diamond = $morph->getShape1();
```

We proceed to define the diamond:

```
$diamond->setLine(10,0,0,255);
$filler = $diamond->addFill(255,0,0);
$diamond->setLeftFill($filler);
$diamond->movePenTo(100,0);
$diamond->drawLineTo(200,75);
$diamond->drawLineTo(100,150);
$diamond->drawLineTo(0,75);
$diamond->drawLineTo(100,0);
```

Once we finish defining the diamond shape, we can specify the target shape of the tween, using the getShape2() method. We draw a different colored square in a different place on the stage:

```
$square = $morph->getShape2();
$square->setLine(10,0,0,255);
$filler = $square->addFill(0,0,255);
$square->setLeftFill($filler);
$square->movePenTo(300,0);
$square->drawLineTo(380,0);
$square->drawLineTo(380,80);
$square->drawLineTo(300,80);
$square->drawLineTo(300,0);
```

We also add the morph to the stage and move it to the middle left-hand side of the stage:

```
$morphhandle = $movie->add($morph);
$morphhandle->moveTo(0,100);
```

Now we can start the actual tween:

```
for ($i = 0.0; $i <= 1.0; $i+=0.1) {
    $morphhandle->setRatio($i);
    $movie->nextFrame();
}
```

Here we are using a loop to count $i up from 0 to 1. Each time we go through the loop we use setRatio() to set the ratio of the SWFMorph to $i and add a new frame to the movie. This has the effect of creating an 11 frame morph from the diamond to the square.

Finally, we send the appropriate headers and output our movie to the browser:

```
header("Content-type:application/x-shockwave-flash");
$movie->output();
?>
```

To see the resulting image refer to *Fig 3.17 – SWFMorph* in *Appendix G*.

Interaction

In this section we will discuss how to provide interaction to our movie by creating buttons.

SWFButton

We create a button in Ming with the SWFButton class. Once we have created the button, all we need to do is add SWFShape objects for each of the states of the button. These states are:

State	Description
SWFBUTTON_UP	This is the normal state of the button
SWFBUTTON_OVER	This is the state when the mouse is hovering over the button
SWFBUTTON_DOWN	This is the state when the user clicks the button
SWFBUTTON_HIT	This state is never displayed but describes the shape of the button that responds to the previous 3 events

Let us talk detail the SWF_BUTTON_HIT state a little more. The shape that we define as the SWFBUTTON_HIT state is the area of the button that will react to the mouse. Typically for a button we would want the HIT state to be the same shape as the rest of the button, but if we want to have a button that has a smaller active area than the area of the entire button that changed, then we use a smaller HIT state.

To define the shapes we use the addShape() method and pass two arguments to it – the SWFShape object to add as the shape, and the flag that specifies which state of the button we are working with.

Let us build an example. We start by defining the sizes of the movie and buttons. This will make it easier when we are creating the button shapes:

```
<?php

//script:SWFButton.php

if(!extension_loaded('ming')) {
    if(strtoupper(substr(PHP_OS,0,3)) == 'WIN') {
        dl('php_ming.dll');
    } else {
        dl('php_ming.so');
    }
}
```

```
define("MOVIE_DIM_X",400);
define("MOVIE_DIM_Y",300);
define("MAX_X",MOVIE_DIM_X-1);
define("MAX_Y",MOVIE_DIM_Y-1);
define("BUTTON_WIDTH",100);
define("BUTTON_HEIGHT",50);
define("BUTTON_X",(MAX_X-BUTTON_WIDTH)/2);
define("BUTTON_Y",(MAX_Y-BUTTON_HEIGHT)/2);
```

We store our SWFShape objects in an associative array:

```
$shape["over"]=New SWFShape();
$shape["over"]->setLine(1,255,255,0);
$shape["over"]->setRightFill(160,160,160);
$shape["over"]->movePenTo(0,0);
$shape["over"]->drawLine(BUTTON_WIDTH,0);
$shape["over"]->drawLine(0,BUTTON_HEIGHT);
$shape["over"]->drawLine(-BUTTON_WIDTH,0);
$shape["over"]->drawLine(0,-BUTTON_HEIGHT);

$shape["up"]=New SWFShape();
$shape["up"]->setLine(1,255,255,0);
$shape["up"]->setRightFill(0,255,0);
$shape["up"]->movePenTo(0,0);
$shape["up"]->drawLine(BUTTON_WIDTH,0);
$shape["up"]->drawLine(0,BUTTON_HEIGHT);
$shape["up"]->drawLine(-BUTTON_WIDTH,0);
$shape["up"]->drawLine(0,-BUTTON_HEIGHT);

$shape["down"]=New SWFShape();
$shape["down"]->setLine(1,255,255,0);
$shape["down"]->setRightFill(128,0,0);
$shape["down"]->movePenTo(0,0);
$shape["down"]->drawLine(BUTTON_WIDTH,0);
$shape["down"]->drawLine(0,BUTTON_HEIGHT);
$shape["down"]->drawLine(-BUTTON_WIDTH,0);
$shape["down"]->drawLine(0,-BUTTON_HEIGHT);
```

Once we have created all our shapes, we can create the button and then add the shapes to the button using the addShape() method. We will use the 'up' state of the button for both the SWFBUTTON_UP and SWFBUTTON_HIT states. Do remember that the SWFBUTTON_HIT state is not displayed:

```
$button = new SWFButton();
$button->addShape($shape["up"],SWFBUTTON_UP|SWFBUTTON_HIT);
$button->addShape($shape["down"],SWFBUTTON_DOWN);
$button->addShape($shape["over"],SWFBUTTON_OVER);
$button->addShape($shape["up"],SWFBUTTON_UP|SWFBUTTON_HIT);
```

Finally, we create the movie, add the button, and output it to the browser:

```
$movie=New SWFMovie();
$movie->setBackground(0,0,255);
$movie->setDimension(MOVIE_DIM_X,MOVIE_DIM_Y);

$movie->add($button);

header("Content-type:application/x-shockwave-flash");
$movie->output();
?>
```

To see the resulting images refer to *Fig 3.18 – SWFButton* in *Appendix G*.

SWFAction

Actions in Flash terminology are script commands that perform operations. We can use the SWFAction class to add a further level of interactivity to our buttons and movies by adding scripts that will run when the user clicks on a button. The script that runs in this scenario is called ActionScript. Chapter 4 is dedicated to ActionScript and using it with Ming and we will discuss SWFAction in that chapter.

Summary

During the course of this chapter we learned

- ❏ What Ming is
- ❏ How to get it running on our computer
- ❏ How to use the various classes of Ming
- ❏ The basic elements of movie making in the following sections:
  - ❏ Flash fundamentals
  - ❏ Drawing
  - ❏ Text
  - ❏ Animation
  - ❏ Interaction

By now we have a good idea of how to go about creating a basic Flash movie with PHP/Ming. We can add shapes and text to our movie and design basic animation scripts too.

We will continue our discussion by looking at the interaction features of PHP/Ming movies in the next chapter.

Since Ming is constantly evolving, we must keep checking the Ming web site (http://ming.sourceforge.net). Any changes to the syntax or operation of the Ming classes and functions will be documented there with the new version release notes and will help us in writing better scripts and designing better movies.

4

Ming with ActionScript

In the first two chapters we had a refresher in basic PHP programming skills. In the third chapter we learned how to create SWF movies using the Ming library; we looked at the various functions that are available to us for creating and tweening shapes in Flash movies. The PHP/Ming skills that we have acquired will allow us to create our own Flash movies, with content that could change from user to user. Now let us discuss how to add interactivity to those movies using ActionScript.

In this chapter we will cover:

- ❑ What is ActionScript
- ❑ Data types and variable declaration in ActionScript
- ❑ How to use ActionScript with the PHP/Ming extension
- ❑ Programming in ActionScript

What is ActionScript?

ActionScript is an object-oriented programming (OOP) language designed specifically for web site animation. It is a tool within **Flash** itself that allows adding true interactivity to a Flash movie. It allows everything from dynamically loading sprites inside a movie to dynamically moving and sizing movie clips.

A Flash movie is made up of a **timeline** that is played through by a **Flash Player** – from the first frame to the final frame of the timeline. ActionScript allows us to alter the way in which the movie plays through the timeline. It allows us to dynamically start or stop the timeline or dynamically load or unload objects onto our timeline. Thus, it allows the user to have control of the movie. With ActionScript we can also modify objects in our movie, load XML data from servers, and load other Flash movies too.

A full description of the features available in ActionScript is available at http://www.macromedia.com/support/flash/action_scripts_dict.html.

Versions of ActionScript

ActionScript is a refined version of the scripting language introduced in Flash 3. The Flash 3 ActionScript was not supported in Ming and while the ActionScript that was available to us with Flash version 4 was powerful in its own right, programmers from an object-oriented (OO) background found it lacking in many regards. The language lacked many of the constructs that programmers were familiar with, and while this did not impede the Flash programmers, it did make it more difficult to use. For example, Flash 4 did not have arrays and these had to be emulated using a series of escalating variable names (`client01`, `client02`, `client03`, and so on). Assigning variables was also tricky – variable names had to be enclosed in double quotes, unless we were assigning the contents of that variable to another variable.

It is for these reasons that the ActionScript language that we have available for use with Flash version 5 has been completely rewritten, and is now an OO language. Flash 5 defines the new set of conventions, syntax, and features that are included in ActionScript, which makes it very similar to JavaScript. Additionally, it also has full XML capabilities, and can load data from the server while the movie is playing.

Since the language closely conforms to the ECMA-262 specification, it is in many regards now almost indistinguishable from JavaScript. The ECMA (European Computers Manufacturers Association) specification can be found at ftp://ftp.ecma.ch/ecma-st/Ecma-262.pdf.

Further, the language constructs of ActionScript are quite similar to that of PHP programming.

Ming with ActionScript

The PHP/Ming extension supports both versions of ActionScript. By default it will expect any ActionScript that we write to be in Version 5 format, but if we have to use Flash version 4 ActionScript we can tell PHP/Ming to expect this, and it will handle the actions accordingly. But it makes more sense to carry OO skills over into the work that we do with the PHP/Ming extension. For this reason we will concentrate on ActionScript version 5.

Chapter 2 has an introduction to the concepts and programming methods involved with writing OO code.

Of course nothing is without its drawbacks, and the PHP/Ming extension has some of these as well. The PHP documentation (http://www.php.net/manual/en/ref.ming.php) clearly states that the extension is experimental and that the behavior of it may change at any moment. Not that this should stop us from using it – as long as we are aware of this fact, and check the CHANGES file in the Ming distribution before updating our PHP/Ming installation. Of course, when working with something that is described as 'experimental' we should expect to find things that don't work as expected or even at all, as we saw in Chapter 3 with the SWFFont and SWFText classes.

Writing ActionScript

This section will quickly run us through the things we need to keep in mind while creating our movie, and more importantly, while adding ActionScript to it.

When we think of a Flash movie it helps to think of it in 3 dimensions – time, depth, and dot notation.

Time is measured as a function of the number of frames on the timeline, and the frame rate of the movie. As we saw in Chapter 3, the frame rate is the number of frames that are displayed per second and is set using the setRate() function. Therefore, a movie with a length of 60 frames and a frame rate of 30 will run for 2 seconds.

This is how we would set the rate of a movie to 20 frames per second:

```php
<?php
$m = new SWFMovie();
$m->setRate(20);
...
?>
```

This main timeline has a special name within JavaScript and is called _root.

This is all in theory of course because if a computer or a Flash Player is not capable of rendering a movie at the rate that we have specified, it will slow down to a rate that it can. We don't have to worry too much about it though – the Flash 5 player is capable of displaying a much higher frame rate than the previous Flash 3 and 4 players, and this will only become an issue with high frame rates (in the region of 30 to 120 fps).

The second dimension in the Flash movie is **depth**. In PHP/Ming we achieve depth by using the swf_placeobject() function. In Macromedia Flash, we achieve depth by adding extra layers to the Flash movie and creating our objects on these new layers. We will cover this in detail towards the end of the chapter when we start working through some examples.

The third dimension is the ability that we have within Flash to nest objects inside one another. For example, not all movies have to exist on the main timeline of our movie, we can have movies that exist within movies and each of these movies will have their own individual timelines. Suddenly the picture we have in our minds of our movie's architecture has taken on a new level of complexity, one that would be tricky to control if we didn't have ActionScript to help us.

We navigate this hierarchy of objects within ActionScript by using the **dot notation**.

This is similar to the dot notation method of accessing properties of objects that lie deep within the hierarchy, used in JavaScript's' HTML Document Object Model (DOM Level 0). For example, if we had a form on our page named clientinfo that contained a textbox named firstname, we could access the text that the user entered into the textbox with this snippet of JavaScript:

```
Document.clientinfo.firstname.value
```

In ActionScript we would use the same notation to reference objects and their properties that have been embedded within other objects. To use this feature, we have to give names to the objects that we add to our movie with the `setName()` function.

The examples in the last section of this chapter will illustrate how we use this concept within our Flash movies.

The ActionScript that we add to our movies is event-driven. There will be some sort of trigger (event) that will cause a behavior/effect (action). Any ActionScript that we write has to be triggered by an event of some sort. These events can be anything – from the user moving the mouse over a button, to our movie reaching a particular frame, while the action can be anything that we can do with ActionScript.

Now that we have a better picture in our mind about what we can do, let us look at the tools that we will be using:

- Data types
- Variable declarations
- Arrays
- Operators
- Conditional Statements
- Loops

Data Types

A data type specifies the kind of information that a variable can hold.

One major difference between Flash 4 and Flash 5 ActionScript is that in Flash 5 we have 'typed' data. Flash 4 was not picky in its handling of data stored in variables. We could quite easily write code that took a string variable containing the name of a movie clip on our timeline, and use that variable to refer to the movie clip. In Flash 5, ActionScript we have to use variables of the appropriate data types. We cannot use a string to declare the name of our movie clip; we will have to use the Movieclip data type. Being forced to stick to a single data type for a variable helps prevent errors in our code and will make it a lot easier to come back and alter our code at a later date.

The data types that we can use are:

- String
- Number
- Boolean
- MovieClip
- Object

String

A string is a series of individual characters – it is any value enclosed within quotes. For example:

```
strAppName = "PHP/Ming";
```

Number

This data type stores a numeric value that we can perform mathematical operations on. For example:

```
numPosition = 3;
```

The number is a double precision, floating point number.

Boolean

A variable of `Boolean` type can contain either `TRUE` or `FALSE`, For example:

```
boolComplete = FALSE;
```

MovieClip

This data type allows us to store a movie clip object. Let us understand this data type by means of an example:

```php
<?php

//script: movieclip.php

if(!extension_loaded ('ming')) {
    if(strtoupper(substr(PHP_OS,0,3)) == 'WIN') {
        dl('php_ming.dll');
    } else {
        dl('php_ming.so');
    }
}

$movie = new SWFMovie();
$movie->setRate(2);
$movie->setBackground(0,0,0);

$round = new SWFShape();
$round->setLine(20,255,255,255);
$round->movePenTo(0,0);
$round->drawLineTo(1,1);

$sprite = new SWFSprite();
$handle = $sprite->add($round);
$sprite->nextFrame();
$handle = $movie->add($sprite);
$handle->moveTo(50,50);
$movie->nextFrame();
$handle->move(0,10);
$movie->nextFrame();

$handle->setName("moon");

header('Content-type: application/x-shockwave-flash');

$movie->output();
?>
```

The output of the above code will be a bouncing ball:

In this example we created our main timeline, that is, we created a basic shape, and then a sprite (movie). Next, we added the shape to the sprite and then the sprite to the movie. Finally, we made it move about a bit in the movie, and also gave a name (moon) to the movie.

As mentioned earlier, we can use the dot notation to access nested movie clips, as this one. We have added our white bouncing ball (moon) to our main timeline (_root), we would therefore address it as:

```
_root.moon
```

Now we create a variable and store this in it, like this:

```
movMoon = _root.moon;
```

We can access that movie clip's properties directly through the variable. Therefore, both _root.moon.y, and _movMoon._y are valid ways of accessing the y position (the vertical positioning) of the movie clip containing the white ball.

Object

This data type is used for storing objects that we create within our code. An object is a collection of named properties and their values. We can create generic objects in ActionScript by using the new Object constructor, like this:

```
startPoint = new Object;
```

Then, we can add properties to that object by simply specifying them, like this:

```
startPoint.x = 100;
startPoint.y = 67;
```

or by using the object initializer ({}):

```
startPoint = { x: 100, y: 67 };
```

By using our own functions in ActionScript we can create custom objects within Flash, like this:

```
function MkPoint(theX, theY)
{
    This.x = theX;
    This.y = theY;
}
startPoint = new mkPoint(100,67);
```

At this point we now have a new object in our Flash movie called startPoint. It has two properties, x and y – startPoint.x has a value of 100 while startPoint.y a value of 67.

For more information about memory requirement for the data types refer to the ActionScript coding standards document at http://www.macromedia.com/desdev/mx/flash/whitepapers/actionscript_standards.pdf.

Variable Declaration

Now that we know what kinds of data we can work with, let's look at how we can assign these values to variables.

ActionScript

We can use a line of ActionScript to initialize a variable of a certain type and assign data to it. This is the most common way of declaring variables in Flash. We saw examples of how to do this in the previous section and we will use this technique many times in the rest of this chapter and in Chapter 9.

TextField

We can create a **textbox** in Flash that allows the user to input some data, for example, a name or an e-mail address. We can specify that the contents of that textbox are available to us in the rest of our movie as a variable. We can then easily take this value and with the help of ActionScript, use it in some way within the rest of our movie.

In PHP/Ming we add the textbox using the SWFTextField class (detailed in Chapter 3). The only difference here is that, when we add our text field, we must make sure that we give it a name using the setName() function. This name will then be exposed as a variable with the same name within that movie clip's timeline.

In this code snippet:

```
$textField->setName("clientname");
```

we have a textbox named clientname. If we add this textbox to our timeline we would have a variable called clientname available to us. We will discuss this concept further in the *Putting It Into Practice – SWFAction* section.

Loading External Variables

ActionScript has a function called loadVariables() which allows us to use a URL as an external data source and grab data into variables from there. The variables can be from a flat text file or be generated by a PHP script.

In the function:

```
loadVariables (url ,location [, variables]);
```

url is the absolute or relative URL where the variables are located, location is a level or target to receive the variables, and the third optional argument is the method (POST or GET) for obtaining these variables.

The format of the data in the target file must be in the standard MIME format:

```
application/x-www-urlformencoded
```

HTML

The fourth way of adding variables to our Flash movie is by using HTML. A Flash movie is embedded in an HTML page using an `<object>` tag. Within the `<object>` and `</object>` tags we add an `<embed>` tag to actually embed the movie itself.

We can add a URL-encoded string at the end of the movie URL, and these values will be passed through to the Flash movie. To ensure browser-independency we have to add the URL-encoded string in the `<embed>` tag:

```
<embed src='movie.swf?publisher=WROX'>
```

and in the `<param>` tag:

```
<param name='movie value'=movie.swf?publisher=WROX'>
```

Putting It Into Practice with SWFAction

Before we go further it's best to refresh what we have covered so far, and put it to use within Flash. To do this we will take the example of the bouncing white dot that we created earlier, and see how we can include some ActionScript within it to make it a little more interesting. In order to do this we have to know how to add ActionScript, and we do that by using the SWFAction class. It takes a single argument and that argument is a string that contains an ActionScript command.

SWFAction is best explained by way of an example.

Using SWFTextField and setName()

In order to demonstrate how to create variables using ActionScript and textboxes, we will add a single textbox to our movie and then use ActionScript to update the contents of the textbox with the properties of our white bouncing ball. We will look into the entire movie creation process and the reasons behind this, as it is important that we understand how to nest objects within Flash as well.

To begin with we create the main movie and set its frame rate to 2. Since we are going to dynamically update the screen, we want to give ourselves a chance to see the values that we are updating:

```php
<?php

//script: textbox.php

if(!extension_loaded('ming')) {
    if(strtoupper(substr(PHP_OS,0,3)) == 'WIN') {
        dl('php_ming.dll');
    } else {
        dl('php_ming.so');
    }
}

$movie = new SWFMovie();
$movie->setRate(2);
```

Set the background color of the movie to black:

```
$movie->setBackground(0,0,0);
```

Create a new SWFShape, setting the line style to white with a 20 pixel width. Then draw the line for 1 pixel to create the round shape:

```
$round =new SWFShape();
$round->setLine(20,0xff,0xff,0xff);
$round->movePenTo(0,0);
$round->drawLineTo(1,1);
```

Next, create a movie clip by instantiating SWFSprite and add the round dot to it. We also add a single frame to this movie clip:

```
$sprite = new SWFSprite();
$sprite->add($round);
$sprite->nextFrame();
```

The reason that we are adding the shape to a movie clip and not just adding the shape directly into our main timeline is because of the way Flash works. When we spoke about variables we said that MovieClip was one of the data types that we could have within ActionScript. This was not an arbitrary decision on the part of Macromedia. Movie clips are special in Flash and more important to us as they are the only things within Flash that we can animate with ActionScript.

In the Animation section of Chapter 3, we have seen that we can move these shapes around by placing them in different places on the stage as we move along our timeline, but this is not ActionScript at work.

In order to access the properties of our movie clips we have to name them. We add the movie clip with the add() function and give it the name setName(), on our main timeline. We then move the sprite to a position on the stage:

```
$handle = $movie->add($sprite);
$handle->setName("moon");

$handle->moveTo(50,50);
```

Here we create a textbox. To keep the example as simple as possible and to use it on both UNIX and Windows machines, we shall use one of the browser-defined fonts: _serif, _sans, or _typewriter:

```
$font = new SWFFont("_sans");
```

Chapter 3 details the issues involved in using FDB font resources on Windows systems.

We feed SWFTextField the SWFTEXTFIELD_DRAWBOX argument so that it will draw a line around the outside of the box, this way we can see where the textbox is (on the stage):

```
$text = new SWFTextField(SWFTEXTFIELD_DRAWBOX );
```

We set the bounds of the textbox to 20 pixels wide by 15 pixels high, and the font to the font resource created earlier:

```
$text->setBounds(20,15);
$text->setFont($font);
$text->setColor(0xff, 0, 0);
```

The next step here is to set the name of the textbox to display:

```
$text->setName("display");
```

If we now add this textbox to our main timeline, we would have a variable called display available to us. One thing worth mentioning here is that the variable we create for our textbox works both ways. With SWFTextField we can expose the contents as a variable. Also, we can alter the contents of the text box by altering the contents of the variable.

One of the drawbacks of the current implementation of PHP/Ming is that the SWFTextField class does not have the moveTo() member function. This means that we do not have an easy way of specifying where on our stage we want the textbox to appear. We will work around this problem by placing our textbox inside the movie clip, and then add that movie clip to the timeline.

Here we create the new sprite and then add the text resource to it, adding a single frame to the movie clip, so that we can actually see its contents:

```
$container = new SWFSprite();
$container->add($text);
$container->nextFrame();
```

We then add this new movie clip to our main timeline:

```
$handle2 = $movie->add($container);
```

As mentioned earlier, by giving a name to the SWFTextField object textbox, we would expose the contents of that textbox, as a variable of the same name, to that movie clip's timeline. Here we have added the textbox to a movie clip, and added that movie clip to our main timeline, so the variable display is exposed to this new ($container) movie clip's timeline. In order to access it we should be able to refer to it in our ActionScript. We do this by using the dot notation. We know that the top level is _root and the variable that we created from our textbox is called display, but in order to put the two together we will need to give this container movie clip a name, so let's call it container:

```
$handle2->setName("container");
$handle2->moveTo(100,100);
```

We can now access the textbox with the full path: _root.container.display.

Now that all the bits and pieces have been added to our main stage, we can start building some time into our main timeline by adding frames. Before we begin though, we need to add some top-level ActionScript that declares some variables.

Currently we've got two movie clips on our timeline: _root.moon and _root.container. If we are going to write a lot of code to access these movie clips, it's quickly going to become tedious to type the whole name every time. If we can declare a variable that contains a movie clip, why not use this to shorten the name?

We can use SWFAction to do just this:

```
$a = new SWFAction("movMoon = _root.moon;");
$movie->add($a);
```

Our first line creates a new action, and the argument passed to SWFAction is a text string containing the ActionScript we want to run. The text string is a line to create a variable called movMoon that contains the _root.moon movie clip. Notice that we have two semicolons on this line. The first one inside the quotes is the termination of the line of ActionScript; the second one is the termination of our PHP line. We then add the action to our movie.

We can condense these two lines into one for convenience, so let's create another variable for our second movie clip:

```
$movie->add(new SWFAction("movCont = _root.container;"));
```

Our next step is to move along to the next frame and add some ActionScript to update the display variable. We will use the text box to display the vertical position (_y value) of our movie clip.

Movie clips have a number of properties that we can programmatically get and set from ActionScript, and one of these is the _y value of the movie.

We update the variable display, which is inside the container movie clip (on our root timeline) with the value of the vertical position of the movie clip (moon) on the root timeline:

```
$movie->nextFrame();
$movie->add(new SWFAction("_root.container.display = _root.moon._y;"));
$handle->move(0,10);
$movie->nextFrame();
```

Earlier we created variables for these two movie clips, so let's use them instead. The movie clip that contains our textbox is stored in a variable called movCont, and the movie clip that contains the white dot is called movMoon. We can set the display variable inside movCont to the _y value of movMoon, with this line of ActionScript:

```
movCont.display = movMoon._y;
```

Let us write the next line:

```
$movie->add(new SWFAction("movCont.display = movMoon._y;"));
```

This is a useful shortcut to save us some typing when we start nesting movie clips within movie clips.

Finally, we write the header and output the movie:

```
header('Content-type: application/x-shockwave-flash');
$movie->output();
?>
```

Our movie will have two frames, like this:

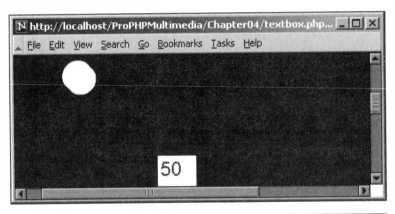

Using loadVariables()

Now that we have seen how to use variables in ActionScript through the use of textboxes, let's change our example and show how we can create variables from an external source.

First create a PHP file called vars.php, and save it in the same folder on our web server, as the scripts we're writing for this chapter. We write the current time in MIME URL-encoded format.

```
<?php
print ("timeNow=".strftime("%H:%M:%S",time()));
?>
```

If we run the script on its own we will see this:

timeNow=18:45:03

Now, we will create a PHP script to generate the SWF Movie:

```php
<?php

//script: timeclip.php

if(!extension_loaded('ming')) {
    if(strtoupper(substr(PHP_OS,0,3)) == 'WIN') {
        dl('php_ming.dll');
    } else {
        dl('php_ming.so');
    }
}

$movie = new SWFMovie();
$movie->setRate(2);
$movie->setBackground(0xfff,0xfff,0xfff);

$font = new SWFFont("_sans");
$text = new SWFTextField(SWFTEXTFIELD_DRAWBOX );
$text->setBounds(100,15);
$text->setFont($font);
$text->setColor(0xff, 0, 0);
$text->setName("display");

$container = new SWFSprite();
$container->add($text);
$container->nextFrame();

$handle = $movie->add($container);
$handle->setName("container");
$handle->moveTo(10,10);

$movie->nextFrame();
$movie->nextFrame();
```

We add two frames to the movie, and on the second frame we add some ActionScript. The first line uses the loadVariables() function to load the variables generated by vars.php onto the root timeline:

```php
$movie->add(new SWFAction("loadVariables('vars.php','_root');"));
```

Once this line has completed we will have a variable timeNow on the main timeline that contains the current time. We can then use the technique we already know to update the textbox:

```php
$movie->add(new SWFAction("_root.container.display = _root.timeNow;"));

header('Content-type: application/x-shockwave-flash');
$movie->output();
?>
```

Here is the output:

```
18:45:03
```

Bear in mind though that hammering our web server for the current time every second is not the sort of thing that we will want to do in the real world. Also, the variables are only filled with data as soon as the vars.php script returns the value. If we are running this over a slow connection then we may have to wait a little while for the time to appear for the first time.

Using <embed>

Let's quickly take a look at an example of creating a variable inside our Flash movie using the <param> and <embed> tag in our HTML page.

To begin with we will need to create an HTML page that embeds our Flash movie in it:

```html
<html>
  <body>
    <object classid="clsid:D27CDB6E-AE6D-11cf-96B8-444553540000"
                    codebase="http://download.macromedia.com/pub/shockwave/
                    cabs/flash/swflash.cab#version=5,0,0,0" width="300"
                    height="200" id="varexternal">

        <param name="movie" value="varexternal.php">
        <param name="quality" value="high">
        <param name="bgcolor" value="#FFFFFF">

        <embed src="varexternal.php" quality="high" bgcolor="#FFFFFF"
                    width="300"  height="200" id="varexternal" type=
                    "application/x-shockwave-flash" pluginspage=
                    "http://www.macromedia.com/go/getflashplayer">
        </embed>
      </object>
    <body>
<html>
```

So, our HTML file will be embedding the Flash movie at the URL varexternal.php into our page:

```php
<?php

//script: varexternal.php

if(!extension_loaded('ming')) {
    if(strtoupper(substr(PHP_OS,0,3)) == 'WIN') {
        dl('php_ming.dll');
    } else {
        dl('php_ming.so');
    }
}
```

```
$movie = new SWFMovie();
$movie->setRate(10);
$movie->setBackground(255,255,255);

$f = new SWFFont("_sans");
$t = new SWFTextField();
$t->setBounds(50,15);
$t->setFont($f);
$t->setColor(0xff, 0, 0);
$t->setName("publisher");

$movie->add($t);
$movie->add(new SWFAction("stop();"));

$movie->nextFrame();

header('Content-type: application/x-shockwave-flash');
$movie->output();
?>
```

In our PHP/Ming script we have set the name of the textbox to `publisher`. If we run the HTML script, the browser will display a blank white page. To send through the variable we want, alter the tags in the HTML document, by changing the `<param>` tag from:

```
value="varexternal.php"
```

to:

```
value="varexternal.php?publisher=WROX"
```

and the `<embed>` tag from:

```
src="varexternal.php"
```

to:

```
src="varexternal.php?publisher=WROX"
```

Here is the modified `embed.html` document, which will create a variable (`publisher`) with a value `Wrox` in our Flash movie:

```
<html>
  <body>
    <object classid="clsid:D27CDB6E-AE6D-11cf-96B8-444553540000"
                codebase="http://download.macromedia.com/pub/shockwave
                /cabs/flash/swflash.cab#version=5,0,0,0"  width="300"
                height="200" id="varexternal">
```

```
            <param name="movie" value="varexternal.php?publisher=WROX">
            <param name="quality" value="high">
            <param name="bgcolor" value="#FFFFFF">

            <embed src="varexternal.php?publisher=WROX" quality="high"
                   bgcolor="#FFFFFF"  width="300"  height="200"
                   id="varexternal" type="application/x-shockwave-flash"
                   pluginspage="http://www.macromedia.com/go/getflashplayer">
            </embed>

       </object>
     </body>
   </html>
```

This is the output of the script:

Since we called our textbox the same name as the variable we are passing through from the HTML, we don't need to add any ActionScript to update the textbox – the Flash player does that automatically for us.

Before we look at more complex examples we need to get acquainted with a few more elements of the ActionScript language.

Arrays

Arrays were added to ActionScript in Flash version 5. In Flash 4 we had to emulate arrays by using multiple variables – not an elegant way of working.

In ActionScript we work with arrays, like this:

```
theMonths = Array();
theMonths[0] = 'January';
theMonths[1] = 'February';
```

An array in ActionScript is also an object, so it has a number of member properties and functions that come in handy while writing ActionScript. The property that we will use the most is the `length` property:

```
numOfMonths = theMonths.length;
```

In PHP we use the `count()` *function to return the number of elements in our array. In JavaScript it's the property of the* `array` *object.*

The ActionScript dictionary at the Macromedia Flash Support Center
(http://www.macromedia.com/support/flash/action_scripts/actionscript_dictionary/)
explains the member functions that we have available to work with. Many of these member functions
like `Array.pop`, `Array.push`, and `Array.reverse` work in the same way as the PHP's array
functions like `array_pop`, `array_push`, and `array_reverse`.

Operators

The numeric operators:

Numeric	Function	Description
+	Addition	`TheTotal = theSubTotal + theTax;` If one of the operands is a string, a string concatenation will occur (see next section).
-	Subtraction	`MySalary = myGross - theTax;`
*	Multiplication	`SecondsRemaining = minutesRemaining * 60;`
/	Division	`MyShare = totalAmount / numPeople;`
%	Modulus	`IsOdd = theNumber % 2;` If `theNumber` is odd, `isOdd` will be 1 (remainder of division), otherwise `isOdd` will be 0
++	Increment	`TheMonth++;`
--	Decrement	`TheMonth--;`

The string operator:

String	Function	Description
+	Concatenation	`FullName = firstName + ' ' + lastName;`

The logical operators:

Logical	Function	Description
&&	Logical And	Returns TRUE if both are true
||	Logical Or	Returns TRUE if either one is true
!	Logical Not	Returns the opposite – TRUE becomes FALSE

The comparison operators:

Comparison	Function	Description
>	Greater than.	All of the comparison operators compare two expressions and returns TRUE if the comparison holds true. `10 > 5; //true`
<	Less than	`10 < 5; //false`
>=	Greater than or equal to	`10 >= 5; // true`
<=	Less than or equal to	`5 <= 5; //true`

Conditions

ActionScript supports the `if` condition:

```
if (condition) {
    // if the condition is true
} else {
    // if the condition is false
}
```

Loops

ActionScript supports the `while`, `do while`, `for`, and `for in` loops:

Loop	Syntax	Result

while	`theCount = 0;`
	
	 `while (theCount < 10) {`
	    `// perform action`
	    `theCount++;`
	 `}`
		The condition is checked before any action is performed

do while	`theCount = 0;`
	
	 `do {`
	    `// perform action`
	    `theCount++;`
	 `} while (theCount < 10);`
		The action is always performed once and then the condition is checked after the action

Loop	Syntax	Result
for	```for (I=0;I<10;I++) { // perform action }```	The for loop maintains its own internal counter. In the while and do while loops we are responsible for updating the values that are being tested in the condition – failure to do so will result in an endless loop
for in	```TheTask = new Object(); TheTask.publisher = 'WROX'; TheTask.name = 'PHP Multimedia'; for (items in theTask) { // perform action }```	The for in loop loops through all of the items in a object. In our example we create a new object and then give it two properties. The for in loop will loop through each of the properties of our object. Each of the individual properties can be accessed inside the loop with theTask[item]

We have now covered all we need to know, to start creating some more advanced PHP/Ming examples with ActionScript.

Programming in ActionScript

In the previous sections we've seen what ActionScript is all about. We looked at the basics of the ActionScript language and how we can add ActionScript to the PHP/Ming movie. Since ActionScript is the language used to interact with a Flash movie, it stands to reason that by using ActionScript we should be able to programmatically alter anything that we can add to a Flash movie. The next few examples will open up the possibilities that are available to us with Flash and ActionScript.

Eye Candy

In this example we create a PHP/Ming movie that outputs random dots on the screen.

Normally when creating a Flash movie, or in fact creating any application, we would first spend some time planning how we are going to achieve our goal. In this case we do not yet have all the knowledge that we need about the ActionScript language. Hence for this example we will talk through it, explaining the reasoning for it as we go along.

To start with, let's create a container HTML file (randomdots.html) for our movie:

```
<html>
  <body>
    <object classid="clsid:D27CDB6E-AE6D-11cf-96B8-444553540000"
                codebase=http://download.macromedia.com/pub/
                shockwave/cabs/flash/swflash.cab#version=5,0,0,0
                width="400" height="400" id="random">
      <param name="movie" value="randomdots1.php">
      <param name="quality" value="high">
```

```
            <param name="bgcolor" value="#FFFFFF">
            <embed src="randomdots1.php" quality="high" bgcolor="#FFFFFF"
                   width="400" height="400" id="random" type="application/
                   x-shockwave-flash"pluginspage=
                   "http://www.macromedia.com/go/getflashplayer">
        </embed>
    </object>
  </body>
</html>
```

Next, we will create the movie and set a frame rate. Since we want dots to flash on the screen we're setting the rate to 24 frames per second. Also, we set the background to white:

```
<?php

//script: randomdots1.php

if(!extension_loaded('ming')) {
    if(strtoupper(substr(PHP_OS,0,3)) == 'WIN') {
        dl('php_ming.dll');
    } else {
        dl('php_ming.so');
    }
}

$movie = new SWFMovie();
$movie->setRate(24);
$movie->setBackground(255,255,255);
```

The next thing we need to do is to actually create the shape that we want to display on the screen, in this case a circle. The SWFShape object does not have a function for creating a circle, so we will simulate it by using drawCurveTo().

DrawCurveTo() draws from our current pen position to a target position.

We will also specify an anchor position; the line is distorted towards this anchor point. What we're going to do is set quite a large pen size and then draw 4 small connecting arcs that will together form a filled circle. To do this we write a small function:

```
function MkPCircle($shape, $radius, $cX, $cY)
{
    $shape->movePenTo($cX-$radius,$cY);
    $shape->drawCurveTo($cX-$radius, $cY-$radius, $cX, $cY-$radius);
    $shape->drawCurveTo($cX+$radius, $cY-$radius, $cX+$radius, $cY);
    $shape->drawCurveTo($cX+$radius, $cY+$radius, $cX, $cY+$radius);
    $shape->drawCurveTo($cX-$radius, $cY+$radius, $cX-$radius, $cY);
}
```

The function takes 4 arguments – the resource handle of the SWFShape we are drawing on, the radius of the circle in pixels, the center, and the x and y coordinates of the circle. We then use the center point and the radius to determine the anchor and end points of the curve.

This is best explained with a diagram:

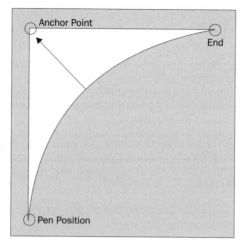

For the first curve we move our pen $radius pixels to the left, then draw to a point $radius pixels above the center point, using a point $radius pixels to the left and $radius pixels above the center point, as the anchor point. This closely approximates a quarter of a circle. The other 3 arcs are drawn in a similar fashion. We will call the function MkPCircle as it's a pseudo-circle and not a real one.

We create a new SWFShape and set the pen to 20 pixels wide, and we'll draw the line in gray. We pass the resource handle to the SWFShape, circle radius, and center points of the circle through to the MkPCircle function:

```
$ball = new SWFShape();
$ball->setLine(20,192,192,192);
MkPCircle($ball, 10, 0, 0);
```

The next step would be to add our SWFShape to the main movie timeline, but remember we want to add more of these dots on-the-fly with ActionScript. If we add the SWFShape to the timeline it will exist there simply as a shape, and we won't be able to do anything more with it. So let's see how to achieve our objective.

duplicateMovieClip()

ActionScript has a method called duplicateMovieClip() which allows us to generate the flashing dots on the screen. This is the syntax of the function:

```
duplicateMovieClip(target, newname, depth);
```

where target is the name of the movie clip that we want to duplicate, newname is the name we are going to give to the new movie clip, and depth is the level at which we load the new movie clip.

Therefore, what we need to do is add our shape to a SWFSprite object, and then add that to the main movie timeline. $sprite is our new SWFSprite object and to this we add the resource handle to our SWFShape object, $ball. Because this is a movie clip it will loop around endlessly unless we tell it otherwise. Since nothing is actually happening on the movie clip and all we are doing is displaying a dot, it's not going to influence our machine in any noticeable way, but it doesn't hurt to get into the habit of good programming practice. Hence, we add a stop() ActionScript command onto the frame of our sprite.

Let's continue with the script:

```
$sprite = new SWFSprite();
$handle = $sprite->add($ball);
$sprite->add(new SWFAction("stop();"));
$sprite->nextFrame();
```

Now we have everything that we need to start working on the main timeline. Let's add the sprite to the main timeline. The duplicateMovieClip() function that we will be using later requires that we name our movie clips. So, after we have added the sprite to the main timeline, we give it the name, orig. This movie clip will be our master movie clip that we will duplicate to form all other clips:

```
$handle = $movie->add($sprite);
$handle->setName("orig");
```

Since we don't really want to see the original one, we move it to the top left of the stage, and set its _alpha value to 0. _alpha affects the transparency of the object. An _alpha of 100 is completely opaque and 0 is completely transparent.

```
$handle->moveto(0,0);
$movie->add(new SWFAction("_root.orig._alpha = 0;"));
```

We mentioned at the beginning of the chapter that Flash had multiple layers for us to work in, and this is what we mean by the level. When we add a new movie clip we should always load it on its own layer or level. Also, we must give the movie clip a unique name on the stage, and we will do this by maintaining an internal counter within our movie, and then using the value of this counter as part of the movie name; this way our movie name will always be unique. We'll call this counter movCount and we can initialize it by adding a new action to the main timeline:

movCount will begin with a value of 1, and we can then use this counter to dynamically create the movie name and set its depth:

```
$movie->add(new SWFAction("movCount++;"));
$movie->nextFrame();
```

Now, _root.orig is the name of the original movie clip that we loaded earlier. We will name the duplicate as newDot plus the value of movCount (newDot+movCount), and the third argument is the level at which we load the movie (this is also movCount):

```
$movie->add(new SWFAction
          ("duplicateMovieClip(_root.orig,'newDot'+movCount,movCount);"));
```

Before we go any further let us look into a possible problem that we will very soon have. How do we reference this duplicated movie clip within ActionScript? Well, we know that it is newDot plus some number, so let's use a line of ActionScript like this:

```
$movie->add(new SWFAction("_root.newDot+movCount+._x = random(400);"));
```

If we tried to run the script with this line (along with the header information) we would get the following error from PHP:

Fatal error: _root.newDot+ ^ Line 1: Reason: 'parse error' in c:\program files\apache group\apache\htdocs\prophpmultimedia\chapter_04\randomdots.php on line 45

ActionScript provides us with a way to get around this problem, and the solution is the eval() function.

eval()

eval() takes a string that can contain the name of a variable, a property or a movie clip, and returns the value of that variable, property, or movie clip.

We saw earlier how we could store an entire movie clip in a variable, so using these two bits of information we could pass a string that is made up of the movie clip's name (newDot) plus its unique number (movCount) to eval(), and store the return value in a variable:

```
$movie->add(new SWFAction("currMovie = eval('newDot'+movCount);"));
```

After this line of ActionScript the variable currMovie now contains the new movie clip that we just created with duplicateMovieClip().

Since we have that now, let's place our new movie clip somewhere randomly on the stage, and set its _alpha value to a random value as well.

> *Flash version 4 had a random() function that took a single number as an argument and returned a random number between 0 and 1 less than the value specified in the argument. Although this function still works in Flash version 5 it has been deprecated, hence it's recommended to use Math.random() instead.*

Math.random() returns a random number between 0 and 1. We can then multiply this value by the maximum possible value we wish to have to return our random number. Let's now place and display our movie:

```
$movie->add(new SWFAction("currMovie._x = Math.random()*400;"));
$movie->add(new SWFAction("currMovie._y = Math.random()*400;"));
$movie->add(new SWFAction("currMovie._alpha = Math.random()*100;"));
```

All that we need to do is add a frame to our main timeline, send out the header, and output the SWF movie:

```
$movie->nextFrame();
header('Content-type: application/x-shockwave-flash');
$movie->output();
?>
```

And this is the output:

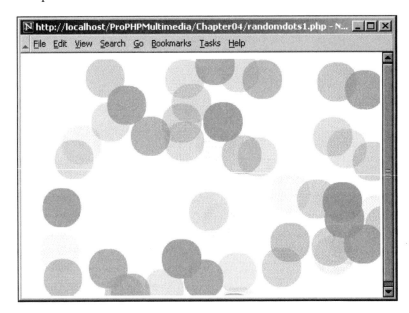

This is not very exciting, and it starts looking even less exciting after some time:

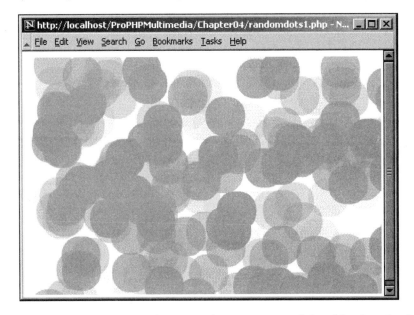

So we have two issues to address – the dots must change in size and the older dots should be removed.

The first issue is quick and easy to implement. Movie clips have two properties _xScale and _yScale that determine the x and y scale of the movie clip. The _xScale property resizes the movie clip horizontally and the _yScale property resizes it vertically. Hence after the line:

```
$movie->add(new SWFAction("currMovie._alpha = Math.random()*100;"));
```

we must add:

```
$movie->add(new SWFAction("theScale = Math.random()*500;"));
$movie->add(new SWFAction("currMovie._xScale = theScale;"));
$movie->add(new SWFAction("currMovie._yScale = theScale;"));
```

Because we want both the x and y scale to be the same, we first create a variable in ActionScript to store the scale, and then assign that scale to both the _xScale and _yScale.

To handle the removing of older dots, we have to use an ActionScript function called removeMovieClip().

removeMovieClip()

removeMovieClip() takes a movie clip as a single argument and this movie clip is then removed from the timeline. Since we want to keep at least some of the dots on the screen at one time we'll put this statement inside the if structure. If we have more that 10 movies on the stage, then we will remove the oldest one. After the line:

```
$movie->add(new SWFAction("currMovie._yScale = theScale;"));
```

we will add:

```
$movie->add(new SWFAction(" if (movCount > 10) { toGo = eval('newDot'+(movCount-
10)); removeMovieClip(toGo); } "));
```

If the number of movies (movCount) is greater than 10 then we will use eval() to create a variable called toGo that stores the movie clip that has to be removed. We find it by subtracting 10 from movCount, and then adding that value to the end of the string newDot – we then feed that string to eval() to return the movie clip variable. And then we simply feed the variable toGo to the removeMovieClip() function and we're in business.

Here is the full script:

```
<?php

//script: randomdots2.php

if(!extension_loaded('ming')) {
    if(strtoupper(substr(PHP_OS,0,3)) == 'WIN') {
        dl('php_ming.dll');
    } else {
        dl('php_ming.so');
    }
}

$movie = new SWFMovie();
$movie->setRate(24);
```

```
$movie->setBackground(255,255,255);

function MkPCircle($shape, $radius, $cX, $cY)
{
    $shape->movePenTo($cX-$radius,$cY);
    $shape->drawCurveTo($cX-$radius, $cY-$radius, $cX, $cY-$radius);
    $shape->drawCurveTo($cX+$radius, $cY-$radius, $cX+$radius, $cY);
    $shape->drawCurveTo($cX+$radius, $cY+$radius, $cX, $cY+$radius);
    $shape->drawCurveTo($cX-$radius, $cY+$radius, $cX-$radius, $cY);
}

$ball = new SWFShape();
$ball->setLine(20,192,192,192);
MkPCircle($ball, 10, 0, 0);

$sprite = new SWFSprite();
$handle = $sprite->add($ball);
$sprite->add(new SWFAction("stop();"));
$sprite->nextFrame();

$handle = $movie->add($sprite);
$handle->setName("orig");

$handle->moveto(0,0);
$movie->add(new SWFAction("_root.orig._alpha = 0;"));

$movie->add(new SWFAction("movCount++;"));
$movie->nextframe();

$movie->add(new SWFAction


("duplicateMovieClip(_root.orig,'newDot'+movCount,movCount);"));

$movie->add(new SWFAction("currMovie = eval('newDot'+movCount);"));

$movie->add(new SWFAction("currMovie._x = Math.random()*400;"));
$movie->add(new SWFAction("currMovie._y = Math.random()*400;"));
$movie->add(new SWFAction("currMovie._alpha = Math.random()*100;"));

//different sizes
$movie->add(new SWFAction("theScale = Math.random()*500;"));
$movie->add(new SWFAction("currMovie._xScale = theScale;"));
$movie->add(new SWFAction("currMovie._yScale = theScale;"));

//removing older dots
$movie->add(new SWFAction(" if (movCount > 10) { toGo = eval('newDot'+(movCount-
10)); removeMovieClip(toGo); } "));

$movie->nextFrame();

header('Content-type: application/x-shockwave-flash');
$movie->output();
?>
```

When we change our `randomdots.html` file to point to the new script and run it, we get following output:

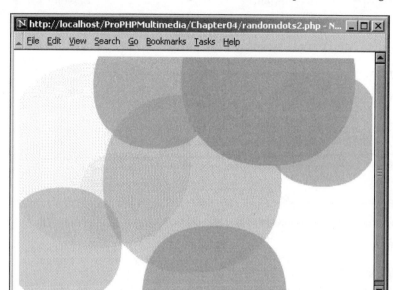

Gray is all well and good, but let's get a bit of color into this screen. To do that we need to talk about two new objects that we can use in ActionScript, the `Color` and `ColorTransform` objects.

Color and ColorTransform

The `Color` object allows us to set and retrieve RGB information about a movie clip. `Color` objects are always associated with a movie clip, and the name of the movie clip is passed to the constructor object. If we wanted to create a new `Color` object for the movie clip that was named `myMovie`, we would use the following line of ActionScript:

```
myColor = new Color(myMovie);
```

We could now set the color of the movie clip by passing to the `setRGB()` member function, a hexadecimal representation of the RGB that we wish the movie clip to have.

Here is a code snippet:

```
myColor.setRGB(0xff9933);
```

One of the member functions of the `Color` object is the `setTransform()` method. This takes a single argument of a `ColorTransform` object and applies it to the movie clip that our `Color` object is associated with. We then create a `ColorTransform` object with the `Object` constructor:

```
myColorTransform = new Object();
```

The `ColorTransform` object has 8 properties:

Property	Description	Possible Values
`ra`	Percentage of the red component	-100 to 100
`rb`	Offset for the red component	-255 to 255
`ga`	Percentage for the green component	-100 to 100
`gb`	Offset for the green component	-255 to 255
`ba`	Percentage for the blue component	-100 to 100
`bb`	Offset for the blue component	-255 to 255
`aa`	Percentage alpha, or opacity	-100 to 100
`ab`	Offset for the alpha	-255 to 255

The percentage signifies the percentage of red, green, or blue in the color makeup. The offset determines the influence of that color. 0 is no influence, 255 is full influence and -255 for reversed influence.

Each of these properties can be set by using ActionScript. Here is a code snippet:

```
myColorTransform.ra = 100;
```

Once we have set all the properties we pass it to the setTransform() method:

```
myColor.setTransform(myColorTransform);
```

What this means is that we can take our previous example, and expand it to change the color of the dots that are flashing on the screen. Since we can change the alpha value of the movie clip by using the ColorTransform objects we can leave out the line that sets the _alpha property of the movie clip and simply use ColorTransform object. To do this, we must replace the following line from the previous example;

```
$movie->add(new SWFAction("currMovie._alpha = Math.random()*100;"));
```

with the following block of code:

```
$movie->add(new SWFAction("theColor = new Color(currMovie);"));
$movie->add(new SWFAction("theColorTransform = new Object();"));
$movie->add(new SWFAction("theColorTransform.ra = Math.random()*100;"));
$movie->add(new SWFAction("theColorTransform.rb = 0;"));
$movie->add(new SWFAction("theColorTransform.ga = Math.random()*100;"));
$movie->add(new SWFAction("theColorTransform.gb = 0;"));
$movie->add(new SWFAction("theColorTransform.ba = Math.random()*100;"));
$movie->add(new SWFAction("theColorTransform.bb = 0;"));
$movie->add(new SWFAction("theColorTransform.aa = Math.random()*100;"));
$movie->add(new SWFAction("theColorTransform.ab = 0;"));
$movie->add(new SWFAction("theColor.setTransform(theColorTransForm);"));
```

The first line creates a Color object called theColor and associates it with the currMovie movie clip. We then set the red, blue, and green component to a random percentage and the offset to 0. We also do that for the green and blue components. We also set the alpha component to a random percentage, with an offset of 0. Finally, we apply the color transform to the color object.

We will save this script as `randomdots3.php` and on executing it we will see colored dots. To see the resulting image refer to *Fig.4.1 – randomdots3.php* in *Appendix G*.

Let's also change the line:

```
$movie->add(new SWFAction(" if (movCount > 10) { toGo = eval('newDot'+(movCount-
10)); removeMovieClip(toGo); } "));
```

to:

```
$movie->add(new SWFAction(" if (movCount > 50) { toGo = eval('newDot'+(movCount-
50)); removeMovieClip(toGo); } "));
```

to see some more dots on the screen at one time.

To see the resulting image refer to *Fig.4.2 – randomdots4.php* in *Appendix G* to see the screenshot.

We have covered a lot in this example. We started with the dynamic loading of movie clips through the `duplicateMovieClip()` and `removeMovieClip()` functions and went on to discuss the use of the `eval()` function, and finally looked at transforming movie clips with the `Color` object.

A Simple Clock

To illustrate how we can rotate objects with ActionScript we'll use PHP/Ming to write a simple code which displays an analog clock.

First, we will create a movie, set the frame rate, and the background:

```
<?php
//script: clock.php

if(!extension_loaded('ming')) {
    if(strtoupper(substr(PHP_OS,0,3)) == 'WIN') {
        dl('php_ming.dll');
    } else {
        dl('php_ming.so');
    }
}

$movie = new SWFMovie();
$movie->setRate(20);
$movie->setBackground(255,255,255);
```

Since we will be rotating the object on-the-fly with ActionScript, we will have to create a movie clip for each of the hands of our clock.

For the second hand we'll make a single pixel black line. We will then draw the line down for 40 pixels:

```
$line = new SWFShape();
$line->setLine(1,0,0,0);
$line->movePenTo(0,0);
$line->drawLine(0,40);
```

After we have created an `SWFSprite` instance we can add the shape to it. We also add the `stop()` action and a single frame:

```
$secHand = new SWFSprite();
$handle = $secHand->add($line);
$secHand->add(new SWFAction("stop();"));
$secHand->nextFrame();
```

We can do the same for the minute and hour hands, but altering their appearance slightly so that we can tell them apart:

```
//minute hand
$line = new SWFShape();
$line->setLine(2,100,100,100);
$line->movePenTo(0,0);
$line->drawLine(0,40);

$minHand = new SWFSprite();
$handle = $minHand->add($line);
$minHand->add(new SWFAction("stop();"));
$minHand->nextFrame();

//second hand
$line = new SWFShape();
$line->setLine(4,192,192,192);

$line->movePenTo(0,0);
$line->drawLine(0,30);

$hrHand = new SWFSprite();
$handle = $hrHand->add($line);
$hrHand->add(new SWFAction("stop();"));
$hrHand->nextFrame();
```

The next step is to add these sprites to our main timeline, assign names to them on the timeline, and move them all to the same place. After all, we want the clock's hands to rotate around the same point:

```
$handle = $movie->add($hrHand);
$handle->setName("hHand");
$handle->moveto(100,100);
$handle = $movie->add($minHand);
$handle->setName("mHand");
$handle->moveto(100,100);
$handle = $movie->add($secHand);
$handle->setName("sHand");
$handle->moveto(100,100);
$movie->nextframe();
```

Now that everything is in place let's start thinking about how we are going to actually rotate these movie clips, and more importantly where we are going to rotate them. Rotating them is easy – the movie clip has a property called _rotation that specifies in degrees, how far the movie clip is to be rotated around. To do this we need to know the current hour, minutes, and seconds.

One way of finding the time is by using the `loadVariables()` function, but we don't want to hammer our web server. The best option is to use one of ActionScript's built-in objects – **Date**. The `Date` object has member functions that allow us to quickly retrieve the current date and time (date and time on the user's machine). The following two lines create the `Date` object and retrieve the current hour value:

```
$movie->add(new SWFAction("theNow = new Date();"));
$movie->add(new SWFAction("theHours = theNow.getHours();"));
```

Now we need to decide how far we need to rotate the hour hand. It's a vertical line and when we rotate it by setting the value of the movie clips `_rotation` property it will rotate in a clockwise direction around its topmost point.

Presently, we have all the hands pointing down to six o'clock. There are 12 hours around the face of a clock, so each hour will be 30 degrees (360 degrees / 12). We multiply the value returned by the `getHours()` function by 30 to get the number of degrees by which we should rotate the hand. But it's already pointing to 6, so let's add 180 degrees to make sure any degrees we rotate will be measured from 12 o'clock. Since we're adding 180 degrees onto a variable amount, we might exceed 360 degrees. Just to be neat, let's take the modulus 360 of the number of degrees, so that we remain within a 360-degree rotation:

```
$movie->add(new SWFAction("theRotation = (((theHours * 30)+180)%360);"));
$movie->add(new SWFAction("_root.hHand._rotation = theRotation;"));
```

Also, there are 60 minutes and 60 seconds around the face of a clock, so for each minute or second we need to rotate the hand 6 degrees:

```
$movie->add(new SWFAction("theMinutes = theNow.getMinutes();"));
$movie->add(new SWFAction("theRotation = (((theMinutes * 6)+180)%360);"));
$movie->add(new SWFAction("_root.mHand._rotation = theRotation;"));
$movie->add(new SWFAction("theSeconds = theNow.getSeconds();"));
$movie->add(new SWFAction("theRotation = (((theSeconds * 6)+180)%360);"));
$movie->add(new SWFAction("_root.sHand._rotation = theRotation;"));
```

Now that we have moved all the hands to their correct positions we can add a frame to the main movie timeline:

```
$movie->nextframe();

header('Content-type: application/x-shockwave-flash');
$movie->output();
?>
```

Here is the output:

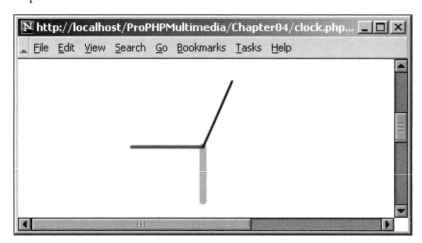

This example moves the hour hand in jumps from one hour mark to the next – if the time was 2 minutes before an hour, our hour hand would still be looking a bit strange pointing at the previous hour mark. If we want to use this as a real working clock we'd need to write a bit of code that moved the hour hand proportionately between hour marks as the minute hand progressed.

Let's quickly take a look at how to do this. We know that the hour hand needs to move proportionately between two hour positions. We already have the information that we need in the form of the minutes. The proportion would be the number of minutes, divided by 60. All we need to do is progress the hour hand by the correct number of degrees. Since we have 30 degrees to an hour, after the line:

```
$movie->add(new SWFAction("_root.sHand._rotation = theRotation;"));
```

we must add the following line of code:

```
$movie->add(new SWFAction("_root.hHand._rotation += (theMinutes/60) * 30;"));
```

Now that we know the basic functionality of a clock, we can spice it up by adding a dial or making nicer looking hands.

Sending Variables from Flash

We have seen how to get variables into our PHP/Ming movie by using the loadVariables() function, but how do we send variables out of the movie? We could use PHP/Ming to create a funky form, but what do we do when the user clicks on Submit? No, we don't have any function called sendVariables(). Once again we will use the loadVariables() function.

> ActionScript has a function called getURL(), which will also allow us to call a URL, but in some cases Flash Player will launch a web browser window for the specified URL. This is messy, as we don't want to open up unnecessary browser windows on the client machine, and more importantly from a security point of view, we may not want others to see the script that we are calling and what variables we are sending through.

`loadVariables()` allows us to load variables onto the main timeline by calling a URL. We can call our PHP form-processing script with the variables MIME encoded in the URL, and our PHP script can then process them. If our script was updating a database, validating the form contents, or sending an e-mail we could then return a success or error code to our Flash movie – thereby adding the possibility of some error checking to our Flash movie – depending on the return code, we can either display a different movie, or prompt the user to fill in the form, again.

To see how this works we'll create a simple movie with two textboxes and a button. The first textbox will be where we fill in our e-mail address; the second textbox will display the results:

```php
<?php

//script: button.php

if(!extension_loaded('ming')) {
    if(strtoupper(substr(PHP_OS,0,3)) == 'WIN') {
        dl('php_ming.dll');
    } else {
        dl('php_ming.so');
    }
}

$movie = new SWFMovie();
$movie->setRate(20);
$movie->setBackground(255,255,255);

$font = new SWFFont("_sans");

$textEmail = new SWFTextField(SWFTEXTFIELD_DRAWBOX );
$textEmail->setBounds(200,15);
$textEmail->setFont($font);
$textEmail->setColor(0xff, 0, 0);
$textEmail->setName("email");

$textResult = new SWFTextField(SWFTEXTFIELD_DRAWBOX );
$textResult->setBounds(200,15);
$textResult->setFont($font);
$textResult->setColor(0xff, 0, 0);
$textResult->setName("results");
```

As we can see, we have created our main movie, a font identifier, and two textboxes. We name the first textbox `email` and the other `results`. By naming them like this their contents will be exposed, and they can be manipulated through variables having the same names as the textboxes.

We are going to need a button, so let's first create the shapes for the states of the button that we want to display. For brevity we'll use the same shape for the **over**, **down**, and **hit** states of the button:

```php
$buttonA = new SWFShape();
$buttonA->setLine(1,0,255,0);
$buttonA->setRightFill(0,255,0);
$buttonA->movePenTo(0,0);
$buttonA->drawLine(20,0);
$buttonA->drawLine(0,15);
$buttonA->drawLine(-20,0);
$buttonA->drawLine(0,-15);
```

```
$buttonB = new SWFShape();
$buttonB->setLine(1,0,0,255);
$buttonB->setRightFill(0,0,255);
$buttonB->movePenTo(0,0);
$buttonB->drawLine(20,0);
$buttonB->drawLine(0,15);
$buttonB->drawLine(-20,0);
$buttonB->drawLine(0,-15);
$button = new SWFButton();
$button->addShape($buttonA,SWFBUTTON_UP);
$button->addShape($buttonB,SWFBUTTON_HIT|SWFBUTTON_DOWN|SWFBUTTON_OVER);
```

Note that the hit state is not a visible state of the button, it merely specifies the shape of the hittable area of the button.

Now we need to attach an action to the button. Our action is going to use the `loadVariables()` function to call a PHP script to process the contents of our e-mail textbox. A Flash form is not like an HTML form – the form elements are not automatically passed through to the form handler script as variables, so we will have to manually build the query string, and append it to the URL we call in the `loadVariables()` function. The information we want to pass through to the script is the contents of the `_root.email` textbox, so the URL we should call, written in ActionScript, is `'processform.php?email='+_root.email`.

This is the complete line in PHP/Ming:

```
$button->addAction(new SWFAction ("loadVariables
        ('processform.php?email='+_root.email,_root);"), SWFBUTTON_MOUSEUP);
```

The `processform.php` form can now return a success, or an error message in a URL-encoded string and these variables will be available to us on the main timeline.

Let's take a look at the `processform.php` script. We know from the ActionScript line above that we will be getting a single variable $email. For the sake of this example we won't do any processing of the string we get, just return a set of variables. In the real world we may store the e-mail address in a database or send an e-mail to the specified address:

```
<?php
print ("formResult=1&resMessage=It+worked+-+you+sent+". $_REQUEST["email"]);
?>
```

> It is important for us to discuss the above script with respect to the `register_globals` variables. It is advisable not to write our scripts so that they require `register_globals` to be turned on, since using global form variables can easily lead to security problems. In PHP, since version 4.2 the `register_globals` feature is turned off by default. The `processform.php` script works with `register_globals` turned off.
>
> However, when using older versions of PHP we should use the following line of code in the `processform.php` script:
>
> `print ("formResult=1&resMessage=It+worked+-+you+sent+".$email);`

After the script has run we would expect to have two new variables in the main timeline:

❑   formResult will be equal to 1

❑   resMessage will be set to "It worked - you sent+" + the contents of the $email variable

All that remains for us to do is write something that will handle the returned variables, and put the movie together. The way to do this is to create an empty sprite on the movie that loops around endlessly testing the value of that variable:

```
$chkRes = new SWFSprite();
$chkRes->nextFrame();
$chkRes->add(new SWFAction("if (_root.formResult==1) { _root.results =
_root.resMessage; } else { _root.results = 'no result'; }"));
$chkRes->nextFrame();

$movie->add($chkRes);
$textEmail = $movie->add($textEmail);
$textEmail->moveTo(30,20);
$textResult = $movie->add($textResult);
$textResult->moveTo(30,50);
$button = $movie->add($button);
$button->moveTo(30,80);
$movie->add(new SWFAction("formResult = 0;"));
$movie->add(new SWFAction("stop();"));
$movie->nextFrame();

header('Content-type: application/x-shockwave-flash');
$movie->output();
?>
```

When we run our script we will see this:

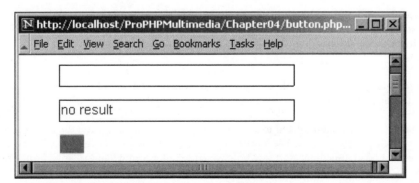

There are two textboxes. The first one is empty, and this is where we have to enter the e-mail address. The second box shows no result. It would keep displaying 'no result' unless we click the button.

When we enter the e-mail address and put the mouse on the button we would see the button's color change:

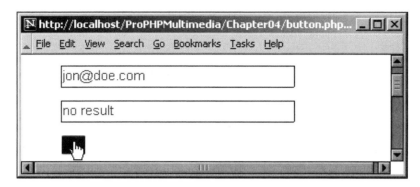

On clicking the submit button, we would see the following:

Summary

We have covered a fair amount of information within this chapter. Let's refresh what we have done.

We discussed ActionScript and how it relates to the PHP/Ming module and we briefly explained how we could use it. Since the basic constructs of the ActionScript language are similar to PHP we took a quick tour through the language and looked at a few examples of how we could set variables in our Flash movie.

We discussed data types and variable declaration in considerable detail and discussed a few examples to understand the basic concepts.

We then went on to more complicated examples to explain and demonstrate the use of some native ActionScript functions and objects. We learned how to use the duplicateMovieClip() and removeMovieClip() functions, and saw how we could alter a movie clips' appearance by using the Color and ColorTransform objects. We also saw how we could alter the size, location, rotation, and opacity of a movie clip by using ActionScript to set properties of the movie clip. The Date object allowed us to obtain date and time information from the machine that the movie clip was playing on, and finally we saw how we could send variables out of our Flash movie, with the loadVariables() function.

In Chapter 9 we will be putting all of these techniques into practice when we look at a case study that dissects and inspects the workings of a Headline Grabber written with PHP/Ming.

Manipulating Images with GD

In the first two chapters we refreshed our basic programming skills. In Chapter 3 we looked at the fundamentals of Ming and built on them to create dynamic SWF movies using the PHP and Ming interface functions. In Chapter 4 we took those skills further to add interactivity to those movies using Ming and ActionScript. In this chapter we'll see how PHP and the GD library can be used to create and manipulate graphics for web- and mobile phone-based applications.

Graphics are an important component of most web sites, yet one that usually falls under the jurisdiction of a web or graphic designer. Some of the most common tasks performed in getting graphics ready for a web site include resizing photographs, making buttons, and making text titles with decorative fonts – dry, repetitive tasks that are just begging for an automated solution.

Image editing programs like Adobe Photoshop and The GIMP (GNU Image Manipulation Program) include automated features of their own, but if a graphic's ultimate destination is a web server, then why not create all those graphics right there and cut out the middleman? Rather than opening all those source .PSD (Photoshop) files, changing foreground and background colors, switching fonts, and wading through the 'Save For Web' dialog every time the marketing department changes their mind over the look of the site, one can alter graphics on the fly with PHP.

PHP has built-in functions to handle image generation, using the GD graphics library.

After reading this chapter, we will be able to use PHP and GD to:

- ❑   Create new images
- ❑   Draw simple shapes
- ❑   Manipulate image color information

- ❏ Add text to images
- ❏ Open existing images
- ❏ Crop and resize images

Armed with these basic drawing and manipulation tools, a whole range of possibilities will open up to us. We could use GD to generate charts and graphs from user data, or use PHP-generated images to display mathematical formulae and foreign-language text not supported by the browser's standard fonts. We can use PHP and GD to generate title graphics and buttons that fit with our web site's overall look, and easily update our site graphics on demand. We could even import our dynamically-generated JPEGs into MING projects using the MING `SWFBitmap()` function.

In Chapter 9, we will see how we can use PHP and GD to generate browser-specific images on the fly for handheld and WAP applications.

The GD Library

GD is a C programming library that provides functionality for creating and manipulating JPEG (JFIF-compliant), PNG (Portable Network Graphics), and WBMP (BMP format for WAP devices) graphics. PHP provides an interface to the GD library, letting us take advantage of many powerful functions for creating and editing images within our scripts.

Does GD Support GIF?

The answer is 'Yes and No'. Earlier versions of PHP and GD included full support for the GIF format, but in 1999 Unisys – the company that holds US patent 4,558,302 for the LZW compression scheme used by the GIF format – declared a change in their previously relaxed licensing practices. Unisys announced that a written license agreement is required for any use of the LZW compression scheme, including any software for displaying or editing GIF images, even freeware applications like GD. Even if Boutell.Com, Inc. decided to obtain a license to include LZW functionality in the GD library, that license probably wouldn't extend to any software we develop that uses GD to manipulate GIF images. With the continued free use of the GIF format uncertain, the switch to PNG was made in version 1.6 of the GD library.

Older versions of GD with GIF support can still be found on the Web with a little bit of searching, as can independent efforts at incorporating GIF support into newer versions of GD and PHP.

PNG is capable of creating transparent, indexed-color graphics with small file sizes like GIF, but it is not hampered by any of the licensing complications associated with the GIF format.

> **Indexed-color refers to the way the image stores its color information. In an indexed-color graphic, up to 256 different colors are stored in an 'index', and each pixel in that image is limited to using one of those 256 colors. This limited palette is a drawback when it comes to storing photographs or artwork with many different colors and smooth gradients, but if we need to create graphics with crisp text or flat-colored, geometric shapes then indexed-color is the way to go. By using only a few colors for text and geometric graphics we can keep our file sizes to an absolute minimum, which has the dual benefit of using less bandwidth while downloading quickly in the user's browser.**

Unisys' policy change caused a lot of consternation in 1999 when PNG support was still limited, but there's no reason not to use PNG nowadays. Furthermore, PNG is widely supported in the latest versions of browsers like Netscape, Mozilla, Konqueror, and IE.

Refer to http://www.faqs.org/faqs/compression-faq/part2/section-1.html for a neat introduction to the mechanics of the LZW compression scheme.

Getting Started

GD is freely available from Boutell.Com, Inc. (http://www.boutell.com/gd/).

Refer to Chapter 1 for detailed installation instructions.

Enabling GD On UNIX

Precompiled versions of GD are included in most major Linux distributions, but we may need to recompile PHP with the `--with-gd` option to enable image generation in PHP.

It is also possible to compile GD as a dynamically loadable module named `gd.so` on UNIX systems by compiling PHP with the `--with-gd=shared` option. If GD is installed as a dynamic module we will need to enable it by adding this line to the top of our PHP scripts:

```
dl('gd.so');
```

Enabling GD On Windows

PHP extensions exist as separate DLL files in the standard Windows distribution of PHP. This means that we need to manually load the GD DLL in each script we want to use it in, using PHP's `dl` function. The Windows distribution of PHP comes with two GD DLLs – `php_gd.dll` (which contains support for GD 1.6.2) and `php_gd2.dll` (which contains support for GD 2.0.1). For the examples in this chapter we'll be using `php_gd2.dll`, which can be enabled by adding this line to the top of our PHP scripts:

```
dl('php_gd2.dll');
```

Cross-Platform Scripts

One of the nice features about PHP is that scripts written on a UNIX system will often run on Windows systems and vice versa. In this case, however, we can't always be sure whether GD will be compiled statically into PHP, or whether it needs to be loaded as a `.so` file or a `.dll` file. If we want to ensure that our scripts will run on both UNIX and Windows systems, we need to check two things at the top of each script – which operating system (OS) the script is running on and, if that OS is Linux, whether or not GD needs to be loaded using the `dl` function.

To determine which operating system the script is running on, we can check the first few letters of the constant variable `PHP_OS`. If they are `'WIN'`, we know we're running on Windows. Otherwise, it's pretty safe to assume we are on a Unix-based platform.

To determine whether or not the GD extension is already loaded (in the case of a UNIX server where it has been compiled into PHP), we can use the `extension_loaded()` function. When we put it all together, we get a snippet of code that will check to see if GD is already loaded and, if it is not, load the correct version for the current operating system:

```php
<?php

if(!extension_loaded('gd')) {
    if(strtoupper(substr(PHP_OS,0,3)) == 'WIN') {
        dl('php_gd2.dll');
    } else {
        dl('gd.so');
    }
}
?>
```

Testing the Installation

To ensure that GD support is enabled with the PHP installation, use the `phpinfo()` script, including our new GD detection script first:

```php
<?php

if(!extension_loaded('gd')) {
    if(strtoupper(substr(PHP_OS,0,3)) == 'WIN') {
        dl('php_gd2.dll');
    } else {
        dl('gd.so');
    }
}

phpinfo();

?>
```

When viewed in a web browser, `phpinfo.php` will get a detailed list of all the features that have been compiled into PHP on the server. Look for a section labelled **gd**, as shown:

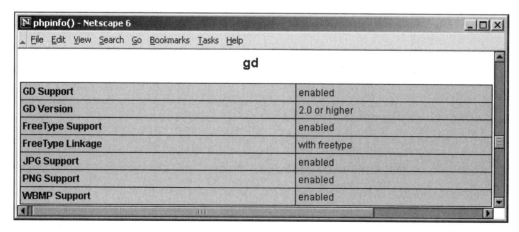

GD Support	enabled
GD Version	2.0 or higher
FreeType Support	enabled
FreeType Linkage	with freetype
JPG Support	enabled
PNG Support	enabled
WBMP Support	enabled

Editing Images in GD

When creating or editing an image with the GD functions, we are actually creating an 'image resource' variable and manipulating it with other variables and GD functions. After the script finishes working with that image resource, the image can be written to the filesystem or sent directly to a web browser.

Editing images with a GUI program like Photoshop or GIMP is slightly different from treating the images as PHP variables.

Editing Images in a GUI

When we open an image in Photoshop, the program opens a new window, reads the image data from the file on the hard drive, and puts a copy of that data into the window. Now we have a whole set of tools that can be used to draw lines, crop, resize, or add text to the image. Any changes we make in that window do not affect the original image unless we tell Photoshop to write over it; we can preserve the original and save a copy of the modified image somewhere else. When we are done editing the image, we close the window so that Photoshop can free up the memory it was using.

Editing Images in PHP

When we open an image with GD, PHP reads the data from the file on the hard drive and puts a copy of that data into a variable, referred to as an **image handler** in the PHP documentation. Now we have a whole set of GD functions that we can apply to that image handler to crop, resize, or add text. Anything we do to that image handler won't affect the original image file unless we tell PHP to write over the original file; we can preserve the original and create a new image file from the modified image handler, or send it directly to the browser. When we are done working with the image handler, we destroy it so that PHP can free up the memory it was using.

Overview of Basic Functions

Although the GD extension provides more than 90 PHP functions for working with images, we don't need to know nearly that many to begin writing useful scripts. In this section we will detail the functions that we need to get started.

The functions detailed in this chapter have been grouped together by the types of tasks they perform:

- ❑ Creating new images
- ❑ Saving or sending images to the browser
- ❑ Colors
- ❑ Basic geometry
- ❑ Text
- ❑ Working with existing images

> **The code examples in this chapter are perfectly functional, but if you plan to adapt any of these scripts into your own productions, you'll probably want to add some error handling for things like missing files and fonts. For more information on error handling, refer to *Professional PHP4* from *Wrox Press* (*ISBN 1-861006-91-8*).**

Creating New Images

The first thing we need to do when editing an image with GD is to create an image resource. We have a couple of choices when creating an image from scratch:

❑   ImageCreate()

❑   ImageCreateTrueColor()

There are also functions for creating new GD image resources from existing image files, which we'll look at in the *Working with Existing Images* section.

ImageCreate()

```
resource ImageCreate (int width, int height);
```

ImageCreate() creates an empty image, where width is the number of pixels across, and height is the number of pixels tall. The image will use an indexed-color palette, which means we are limited to 256 colors.

In web design, remember that indexed-color images are ideal for flat-color images with simple geometric shapes and/or text; the fewer the colors and the simpler the lines and shapes, the less information there is to store in the palette, and the smaller the resulting image.

As mentioned earlier in the chapter, GD doesn't support the GIF file format. We can output our finished images as 8-bit PNGs instead. PNGs produced from GD image resources created with the ImageCreate() function will automatically use indexed-color.

> We can also output indexed-color GD images as JPEGs, but JPEGs don't handle large, flat areas of color or detailed text well when compressed. So we are likely to wind up with a file that's very large compared to its PNG counterpart, or very blotchy.

ImageCreateTrueColor()

```
resource ImageCreateTrueColor (int width, int height);
```

ImageCreateTrueColor() behaves exactly the same as ImageCreate(), but the resulting image is true-color instead of indexed-color.

> True-color graphics contain much more color information than their indexed-color counterparts, which results in the ability for an image to display literally millions of colors.

The obvious benefit is that we are not limited to a mere 256 colors, making this function perfect for working with photographs or other colorful subjects.

The tradeoff is that all that extra color information results in larger file sizes, and we also lose the ability to use some of the handier GD color functions that let us manipulate colors on a pixel-by-pixel level, like:

- ❑ ImageColorsTotal() – Returns the number of colors in the specified image's palette.

- ❑ ImageColorAt() – Returns the index of the color of the pixel at the specified location in the image.

- ❑ ImageColorSet() – Sets the specified index in the palette to the specified color. This is useful for creating flood-fill-like effects in paletted images without the overhead of performing the actual flood-fill.

- ❑ ImageColorsForIndex() – Returns an associative array with red, green, and blue keys that contain the appropriate values for the specified color index.

PNGs created from GD image resources with the ImageCreateTrueColor() function will be true-color images.

Saving or Sending Images To the Browser

Once we're finished editing the image, we'll want to save it to the disk, or send it straight to the browser depending on its purpose. If we are using PHP to resize an entire directory of image files for later use, we would save the newly resized images somewhere on the server. On the other hand, if we're using PHP to generate live statistical graphs we would want to send the image data straight to the user.

In case we're going to send the image to the browser, the first thing we need to do is to send an HTTP header containing the image's MIME type so that the browser knows what to do with the image data; otherwise the end user is likely to wind up with a screen full of gobbledygook if they attempt to view the script directly, or a broken/missing image if they attempt to use the script as the SRC attribute of an HTML image tag. Usually a broken image icon means that a file is missing, but in this case it indicates that the image data being produced by the script is corrupt.

The next piece of information we need to know is the format we're going to send the image in. We have three choices – JPEG, PNG, or WBMP. The respective MIME types for these three formats are image/jpeg, image/png, and image/wbmp.

The HTTP Content-type header tells the browser what to do with the image data, and we can send it using PHP's header() function.

The three GD functions for saving or sending images are:

- ❑ ImagePng()
- ❑ ImageJpeg()
- ❑ ImageWbmp()

ImagePng()

```
int ImagePng(resource image [, string [filename]);
```

ImagePng() attempts to save a copy of image, as filename, on the local disk. If the filename is not set, ImagePng() sends the image data directly to STDOUT.

In PHP, STDOUT is usually the user's web browser.

This example sends a PNG image to the browser:

```php
<?php

if(!extension_loaded('gd')) {
    if(strtoupper(substr(PHP_OS,0,3)) == 'WIN') {
        dl('php_gd2.dll');
    } else {
        dl('gd.so');
    }
}

// Create a new image resource
$im = ImageCreate(100,100);

// Define the background color
$white = ImageColorAllocate($im, 255, 255, 255);

// Define the foreground color
$black = ImageColorAllocate($im, 0, 0, 0);

// Draw a square using the ImageRectangle() function
ImageRectangle($im, 10, 10, 90, 90, $black);

/* Send a copy to the browser using the header() function:
(Our image is a PNG, so the MIME type will be image/png) */

header("Content-type: image/png");

// Finally, output the image data
ImagePng($im);

// Destroy the image resource to conserve memory
ImageDestroy($im);
?>
```

This is how the script looks when it is run from the browser:

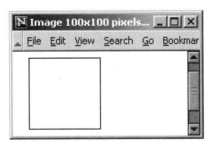

ImageJpeg()

```
int ImageJpeg(resource image [, string [filename], int [quality]]);
```

ImageJpeg() works just the same as ImagePng() but it takes the optional third parameter quality, which specifies how much or how little compression we want to apply to the image.

If quality is set to 100, no compression will be applied to the image. If quality is set to 0, maximum compression will be applied (and the result will probably be very ugly, indeed!). If quality is not set the function uses the Independent JPEG Group default, which is about 75.

It may take some experimentation to find the quality setting that works best for us; the higher the quality, the better the JPEG will look – but the larger the file will be! Conversely, we can get small file sizes with a low quality setting but the image may become so blotchy that it would be worth putting up with the extra few kilobytes from a higher quality setting.

This example saves a JPEG to disk:

```php
<?php

if(!extension_loaded('gd')) {
    if(strtoupper(substr(PHP_OS,0,3)) == 'WIN') {
        dl('php_gd2.dll');
    } else {
        dl('gd.so');
    }
}

// Create a new image resource
$im = ImageCreate(100,100);

// Define the background color
$white = ImageColorAllocate($im, 255, 255, 255);

// Define the foreground color
$black = ImageColorAllocate($im, 0, 0, 0);

// Draw a square
ImageRectangle($im, 10, 10, 90, 90, $black);

/* Save this image as a file named "square.jpg" in the /tmp
 directory, at 80% quality */

ImageJpeg($im,"./tmp/square.jpg",80);

// Destroy the image resource to conserve memory
ImageDestroy($im);
?>
```

ImageWbmp()

```
int ImageWbmp(resource image, [string filename [, int foreground]]);
```

ImageWbmp() works just like ImagePng() and ImageJpeg(), but outputs the image in WBMP format for use on WAP devices.

ImageWbmp() also takes a third foreground color parameter. foreground should be a GD color resource, and since WBMP graphics only have two colors our choice is limited to black or white. Normally the foreground parameter defaults to black when omitted, but on some platforms omitting foreground may generate a PHP warning message. The image will be successfully created, but if the image is being sent directly to a WAP device it will be corrupted by the error message text. To suppress this error, we simply use PHP's @ error control operator in front of the call to ImageWbmp():

```php
<?php

if(!extension_loaded('gd')) {
    if(strtoupper(substr(PHP_OS,0,3)) == 'WIN') {
        dl('php_gd2.dll');
    } else {
        dl('gd.so');
    }
}

// Create a small rectangle and save it to disk:

// Create a new image resource
$im = ImageCreate(72,48);

// Define the background color:
$white = ImageColorAllocate($im, 255, 255, 255);

// Define the foreground color:
$black = ImageColorAllocate($im, 0, 0, 0);

// Draw a rectangle
ImageRectangle($im, 6, 6, 66, 42, $black);

$filename = 'rectangle.wbmp';

@ImageWbmp($im,$filename);

// Destroy the image resource to conserve memory
ImageDestroy($im);

/* Since WAP browsers won't render a WBMP image by itself, we'll send a simple WML
deck that displays our new rectangle. First we need to send the right content
header:
*/
header('Content-type: text/vnd.wap.wml');

print <<<END

<?xml version="1.0"?>

<!DOCTYPE wml PUBLIC "-//WAPFORUM//DTD WML 1.1//EN"
"http://www.wapforum.org/DTD/wml_1.1.xml">

<wml>
  <card title="My WBMP">
    <p>
      <img src="$filename" alt="A Rectangle"/>
    </p>
  </card>
</wml>
END;

?>
```

This is the image on a WAP browser:

Refer to Chapter 9 for more information on creating and viewing WML.

Colors

Colors are handled by the GD functions in much the same way as the image resources they belong to. When working with colors, it is important to remember whether we created the image with ImageCreate() or with ImageCreateTrueColor(), because that will affect which of the color functions we are able to use on the image.

These are the basic functions related to color:

- ❑ ImageColorAllocate()
- ❑ ImageFill()
- ❑ ImageColorTransparent()
- ❑ ImageTrueColorToPalette()
- ❑ ImageColorsTotal()
- ❑ ImageColorAt()
- ❑ ImageColorsForIndex()
- ❑ ImageColorSet()

ImageColorAllocate ( )

```
int ImageColorAllocate(resource image, int red, int green, int blue);
```

ImageColorAllocate() returns a color with RGB components – red, green, and blue, where the values for R, G, and B are between 0 and 255. This function must be called to create each color that is to be used in the image (image).

> *This is similar to a web page or Cascading Style Sheet (CSS), where colors are defined by hexadecimal strings composed of the color's separate red, green, and blue values. We don't need to convert anything into hexadecimal in ImageColorAllocate(), though.*

If we are more comfortable working with hexadecimal color values, we can use a combination of PHP's substr (substring) and hexdec (hexadecimal to decimal) functions. For example, we would use substr to split a string like '#FF9933' (a bright orange) into its R, G, and B components 'FF', '99', and '33'. From there we would just use hexdec to convert those components into their decimal equivalents – 255, 153, and 51.

Before defining a color variable, we need an image resource to associate it with. Let's say we have an image resource named $image, and we want to define a few colors to work with: .

```
$image = ImageCreate(100,100);

$white = ImageColorAllocate($image, 255, 255, 255);
$black = ImageColorAllocate($image, 0, 0, 0);
$red   = ImageColorAllocate($image, 204, 0, 0);
```

After defining $white, $black, and $red with our $image resource, we'll be able to use them in any GD function we apply to $image that takes a color parameter.

One handy feature of ImageColorAllocate() is that the first color we define for a new image resource automatically becomes the background color of that image. Since $white was the first color in the example above, it was automatically used as the background color.

To make $black the image background color, we would just move it to the top of the list, like this:

```
$black = ImageColorAllocate($im, 0, 0, 0);
$white = ImageColorAllocate($im, 255, 255, 255);
$red   = ImageColorAllocate($im, 204, 0, 0);
```

Remember, we can only allocate 256 colors if we're working with an indexed-color image!

ImageFill()

```
void ImageFill(resource image, int x, int y, int color);
```

ImageFill() does a flood fill using color, starting at the coordinate (x, y). The x and y coordinates passed to this function don't really affect its outcome; the entire image will be filled with the specified color no matter what coordinates we start at.

ImageColorTransparent()

```
void ImageColorTransparent(resource image, int color);
```

To output the final image in a format that supports transparency (like PNG), we can use ImageColorTransparent() which will set color as the transparent color for the image.

The GD functions can use the transparent color the same way they would any other color, but any line or shape drawn with it becomes transparent, almost as though we were erasing through to the browser background.

For example, let's say we have a script that draws a red circle on top of a black square. If we use this script to generate an image on a web page with a striped blue background, it will still have a red circle on a black square, all on top of the striped blue background called stripes.png.

If we use ImageColorTransparent() to set the red color used to draw the circle as transparent, the image will show up in the browser as a black square with a circular hole in the middle, where the striped blue background shows through. Let's look at both on one page:

```php
<?php

if(!extension_loaded('gd')) {
    if(strtoupper(substr(PHP_OS,0,3)) == 'WIN') {
        dl('php_gd2.dll');
    } else {
        dl('gd.so');
    }
}

//Create a new image:
$im = ImageCreate(128,128);

//Define black and red colors:
$black = ImageColorAllocate($im, 0, 0, 0);
$red = ImageColorAllocate($im, 204, 0, 0);

//Draw a red circle in the center of the image:
ImageFilledArc($im, 64, 64, 110, 110, 0, 360, $red, IMAGE_ARC_PIE);

//Save a PNG copy to disk:
ImagePng($im,"redcircle.png");

//Now set $red as the transparent color:
ImageColorTransparent($im, $red);

//Save another PNG copy to disk:
ImagePng($im,"transparentcircle.png");

//Make a simple HTML page displaying both images
?>

<html>
  <head>
    <title>ImageColorTransparent</title>
  </head>

  <body background="stripes.png">
    <div>
      <img src="redcircle.png">  
      <img src="transparentcircle.png">
    </div>
  </body>
</html>
```

To see what shows up on our browser refer to *Fig 5.1 – ImageColorTransparent* in *Appendix G*.

ImageTrueColorToPalette()

```
void ImageTrueColorToPalette(resource image, bool dither, int colors);
```

`ImageTrueColorToPalette()` takes a true-color image resource (created from a JPEG or 24-bit PNG, for example) and converts it into an indexed-color image. If `dither` is set to `TRUE`, dithering will be used to improve color approximation. `colors` is the number of colors the resulting palette should contain; 256 is the maximum.

If we convert a nice, true-color JPEG photo into an indexed-color image, the decline in quality will be very noticeable; in most cases we probably won't want to use this function.

Here's an example of a true-color image converted to an indexed-color image using `ImageTrueColorToPalette()`:

```php
<?php

if(!extension_loaded('gd')) {
    if(strtoupper(substr(PHP_OS,0,3)) == 'WIN') {
        dl('php_gd2.dll');
    } else {
        dl('gd.so');
    }
}

/* Convert a true-color image into two indexed-color images:
   one dithered and one undithered: */

/* Set up the file names we want to use for our images: */

//Our source image
$source_image = 'truecolortopalette_before.jpg';

//The dithered image
$dithered_image = 'truecolortopalette_dithered.png';

//The undithered image
$undithered_image = 'truecolortopalette_undithered.png';

/* Create an image resource from the true-color original: */
$im = ImageCreateFromJpeg($source_image);

/* Now use ImageTrueColorToPalette() to convert the image to indexed-color
   Use 'true' to tell the function to dither the resulting image. */

ImageTrueColorToPalette($im, true, 256);

/* Save the dithered image to disk: */

ImagePng($im,$dithered_image);

/* Destroy the image resource: */
ImageDestroy($im);

/* Create another image resource from the orignal; this time we'll make
   an undithered, indexed-color image: */
$im = ImageCreateFromJpeg($source_image);

/* Use ImageTrueColorToPalette() with 'FALSE' to prevent dithering: */
ImageTrueColorToPalette($im, FALSE, 256);

/* Save the undithered image to disk: */
ImagePng($im,$undithered_image);

/* Destroy the image resource: */
ImageDestroy($im);

/* Now we'll create an XHTML page with a table for side-by side comparison: */

print <<<END
```

```
<?xml version="1.0" encoding="iso-8559-1"?>

<!DOCTYPE html PUBLIC "-//W3C//DTD XHTML 1.0 Strict//EN" "xhtml1-strict.dtd">

<html>
  <head>
    <title>ImageTrueColorToPalette</title>
  </head>

  <body>
    <div style="text-align:center">
      <table style="margin-left:auto; margin-right:auto; width:90%">

        <tr>
          <td style="text-align:center; vertical-align:bottom">
            <img src="$source_image" alt="Before"/>
          </td>
          <td style="text-align:center; vertical-align:bottom">
            <img src="$dithered_image" alt="After - Dithered"/>
          </td>
          <td style="text-align:center; vertical-align:bottom">
            <img src="$undithered_image" alt="After - No Dither"/>
          </td>
        </tr>

        <tr>
          <td style="text-align:center; vertical-align:top">
            Original true-color image
          </td>
          <td style="text-align:center; vertical-align:top">
            Indexed-color (dithered)
          </td>
          <td style="text-align:center; vertical-align:top">
            Indexed-color (no dither)
          </td>
        </tr>

      </table>
    </div>
  </body>
</html>
END;
?>
```

This is the ouput on the browser:

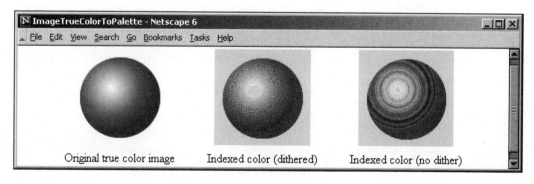

ImageColorsTotal()

```
int ImageColorsTotal(resource image);
```

`ImageColorsTotal()` returns the total number of colors in the palette of `image`. This function only works on indexed-color images.

```php
<?php

if(!extension_loaded('gd')) {
    if(strtoupper(substr(PHP_OS,0,3)) == 'WIN') {
        dl('php_gd2.dll');
    } else {
        dl('gd.so');
    }
}

//Create an indexed-color Image
$im = ImageCreate(150,150);

//Allocate a color for the background:
$gray = ImageColorAllocate($im, 153, 153, 153);

//Allocate an array of colors
$colors = array();

$colors['white']  = ImageColorAllocate($im, 255, 255, 255);
$colors['black']  = ImageColorAllocate($im, 0, 0, 0);
$colors['red']    = ImageColorAllocate($im, 204, 0 ,0);
$colors['orange'] = ImageColorAllocate($im, 255, 153, 0);
$colors['yellow'] = ImageColorAllocate($im, 255, 255, 0);
$colors['green']  = ImageColorAllocate($im, 0, 255, 0);
$colors['blue']   = ImageColorAllocate($im, 0, 0 ,204);
$colors['purple'] = ImageColorAllocate($im, 102, 0, 204);

/* Now we'll display each color in our $colors array: */

// Define the 'y' position for the first color name
$y = 10;

foreach(array_keys($colors) as $colorname) {

    //Write the color's name to the image in its own color
    ImageString($im, 5, 10, $y, $colorname, $colors[$colorname]);

    //Increase the value of 'y' so each image appears below the last:
    $y = $y + 15;
}

//Save a copy of the image to the disk:
ImagePng($im,'imagecolorstotal.png');

//Determine the total number of colors:
$totalcolors = ImageColorsTotal($im);
```

```
//Display the image, and a message about the number of colors used:
print ("<img src='imagecolorstotal.png'><br>");

print ("There are $totalcolors colors in this image.");

//Destroy the image:
ImageDestroy($im);
?>
```

If we refer to *Fig 5.2 – ImageColorsTotal* in *Appendix G* we see that `ImageColorsTotal()` correctly counts the 8 colors in the `$colors` array, and the gray background color.

ImageColorAt()

```
int ImageColorAt(resource image, int x, int y);
```

This is another function that only works on true-color images. `ImageColorAt()` returns the index of the color of the pixel at (x, y) in `image`.

The index can be used in conjunction with `ImageColorsForIndex()` to retrieve the exact RGB value for a specific pixel.

For instance, say we have a 320 x 240 pixel photo called `motel.jpg` and we want to determine the color of the sky, so we can use it as an accent throughout our page. The spot we want to sample is right in the middle of the sky and an inch down, at the x, y coordinates 159, 71:

Here's how we can find the RGB value of that pixel:

```
<?php

if(!extension_loaded('gd')) {
    if(strtoupper(substr(PHP_OS,0,3)) == 'WIN') {
        dl('php_gd2.dll');
    } else {
        dl('gd.so');
```

```
    }
}

/* Create an image resource from 'motel.jpg': */
$im = ImageCreateFromJpeg('motel.jpg');

/* Images created from JPEGs with GD2 are automatically created
   as true-color images, but in order to use ImageColorAt() we need
   an indexed-color image: */

ImageTrueColorToPalette($im,true,256);

/* Now we can get the index of the color at (159,71): */

$x = 159;
$y = 71;

$colorindex = ImageColorAt($im, $x, $y);

/* Finally, we can get the R,G, and B values of the
   color whose index is '$colorindex': */

$rgb = ImageColorsForIndex($im, $colorindex);

/* $rgb is now an associative array with keys 'red', 'green', and 'blue: */

$red   = $rgb['red'];
$green = $rgb['green'];
$blue = $rgb['blue'];

/* We're now done with our image resource, so we can destroy it: */
ImageDestroy($im);

/* Using the 'sprintf' function, we can format our RGB values into
   HTML-friendly hexadecimal color definitions: */

$htmlcolor = '#' . sprintf("%02X%02X%02X",$red,$green,$blue);

$results = "The RGB value of the pixel at ($x, $y) is <em>$red, $green,
$blue</em>.<br>\n The HTML color is <em>$htmlcolor</em>";

/* Make a simple HTML page using the selected color as the background, and
   print the '$results' string on it in both white and black: */

print <<<END

<html>
  <head>
    <title>Results:</title>
  </head>

  <body style='background-color:$htmlcolor'>
    <div style='color:#FFFFFF'>$results</div>
```

```
          <hr>
        <div style='color:#000000'>$results</div>
      </body>
    </html>

  END;
  ?>
```

Here's the output in a browser, printed once in black and once in white so we can see which contrasts better:

Of course, we may not always know the dimensions of the photos we are working with or the exact coordinate of the color we want, but we could easily put together a color picker script that would get its $x and $y values from an HTML form using the photo as an image input, like this:

```
<input type='image' src='motel.jpg' name='image'>
```

When clicked, the image will submit the form and pass along the exact coordinate that was clicked in the values image_x and image_y, from there the rest is easy!

ImageColorsForIndex()

```
array ImageColorsForIndex(resource image, int index);
```

The array returned by ImageColorsForIndex() returns an associative array of the red, green, and blue values for the palette color with an index of index.

The array keys are 'red', 'green', and 'blue'.

ImageColorSet()

```
bool ImageColorSet(resource image, int index, int red, int green, int blue);
```

This function will change the index in the palette with the specified color.

Basic Geometry

Now that we have seen how to create an image and lay out a palette, we'll start drawing.

If you ever sat in Math class at school and thought, "I'm never going to need to know this in real life!", you were wrong. GUI graphic editors make drawing lines and shapes easy, because they handle all of the nitty-gritty stuff for us. Drawing a line or a shape in a GUI editor is as simple as clicking the mouse and dragging, but creating graphics programmatically requires a bit more attention to detail.

That being said, drawing basic shapes in GD isn't hard at all. We'll just have to dust off some of those basic geometry skills, jump in, and get our hands dirty.

Coordinates in GD Images

All of the GD line and shape functions take one or more sets of coordinates as parameters.

The coordinate system used within images is an xy-grid (Cartesian coordinate system) wherein movement to the right is movement in the positive x-direction and movement down is movement in the negative-y direction. This is the same coordinate system as is used for CSS positioning and creating HTML image maps.

GD keeps track of coordinates a little bit differently. The pixel at the top left corner of a GD image resource is always the origin, with coordinates of (0, 0). x coordinates are handled the same but, since the left side of the image is always at 0, we'll never use a negative number for x. y coordinates are reversed in GD images; the higher the value of y, the further below the origin it is.

The GD functions for drawing pixels, lines, and shapes are:

- ❏ ImageSetPixel()
- ❏ ImageLine()
- ❏ ImageRectangle()
- ❏ ImageFilledRectangle()
- ❏ ImagePolygon()
- ❏ ImageFilledPolygon()
- ❏ ImageArc()
- ❏ ImageFilledArc()

ImageSetPixel ()

```
void ImageSetPixel(resource image, int x, int y, int color);
```

ImageSetPixel() draws a single pixel at the coordinates (x, y) of color (color) in the image resource (image).

ImageLine ()

```
void ImageLine(resource image, int x1, int y1, int x2, int y2, int color);
```

ImageLine() draws a line from the coordinates (x1, y1) to the coordinates (x2, y2) of the color (color) in the image resource (image).

Let's create a 140 x 100 pixel image, and a color to draw with.

This is the script:

```php
<?php

if(!extension_loaded('gd')) {
    if(strtoupper(substr(PHP_OS,0,3)) == 'WIN') {
        dl('php_gd2.dll');
    } else {
        dl('gd.so');
    }
}

$im = ImageCreate(140,100);

$white= ImageColorAllocate($im,255,255,255);
$black = ImageColorAllocate($im, 0, 0, 0);
```

To draw a black line from the coordinates (10, 10) to the coordinates (120, 90), we would add this line:

```php
ImageLine($im, 10, 10, 120, 90, $black);
```

To send the image to the browser and close the script, add:

```php
header("Content-type: image/png");

ImagePng($im);

ImageDestroy($im);
?>
```

Here's how the line gets drawn in the browser:

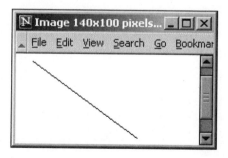

ImageRectangle ()

```
void ImageRectangle(resource image, int x1, int y1, int x2, int y2, int color);
```

ImageRectangle() takes exactly the same parameters as ImageLine(), but instead of drawing a line between (x1, y2) and (x2, y2) it uses the two points to determine the upper-left and lower-right corners of a rectangle:

```php
<?php

if(!extension_loaded('gd')) {
    if(strtoupper(substr(PHP_OS,0,3)) == 'WIN') {
        dl('php_gd2.dll');
    } else {
        dl('gd.so');
    }
}

$im = ImageCreate(140,100);

$yellow = ImageColorAllocate($im, 255, 255, 191);

$black = ImageColorAllocate($im, 0, 0, 0);

/* Draw a black rectangle whose upper left corner is at (20, 10)
 and whose lower right corner is at (120, 60): */

ImageRectangle($im, 20, 10, 120, 60, $black);

header("Content-type: image/png");

ImagePng($im);

ImageDestroy($im);
?>
```

To see how the rectangle is placed in the image, refer to *Fig 5.3 – ImageRectangle* in *Appendix G*.

It's pretty straightforward, but if we need to draw a rectangle we're probably more concerned with its width and height than we are with the exact coordinates of its lower right corner. Let's put together a wrapper function for ImageRectangle() that takes width and height parameters, and calculates x2 and y2 automatically:

```php
<?php

if(!extension_loaded('gd')) {
    if(strtoupper(substr(PHP_OS,0,3)) == 'WIN') {
        dl('php_gd2.dll');
    } else {
        dl('gd.so');
    }
}
function MyRectangle($image, $x1, $y1, $width, $height, $color)
{
    /* Calculate the values for x2 and y2 based on the contents
    of '$width' and $height'. We can do this by simply adding '$width' to
    our starting horizontal point, '$x1', and adding '$height' to our
    starting vertical point, '$y1' */

    $x2 = $x1 + $width;
    $y2 = $y1 + $height;

    /* Now we have all the information we need to call ImageRectangle() */

    ImageRectangle($image, $x1, $y1, $x2, $y2, $color);
}
```

Now that we have a more intuitive way of drawing rectangles, our `MyRectangle()` function lets us say, "I want to draw a `width` pixel by `height` pixel `color` rectangle that starts at (x1, y1)":

```php
$im = ImageCreate(140,100);

$yellow = ImageColorAllocate($im, 255, 255, 191);
$black  = ImageColorAllocate($im, 0, 0, 0);

/* Draw a 100px x 50px black rectangle starting at (20, 10): */

MyRectangle($im, 20, 10, 100, 50, $black);

header("Content-type: image/png");

ImagePng($im);

ImageDestroy($im);
?>
```

ImageFilledRectangle ()

```
void ImageFilledRectangle(resource image, int x1, int y1, int x2, int y2, int
color);
```

`ImageFilledRectangle()` behaves exactly the same as `ImageRectangle()`, but the resulting rectangle drawn to the image is filled solid. Let's adapt our `MyRectangle()` function from above to draw a filled rectangle:

```php
<?php
if(!extension_loaded('gd')) {
    if(strtoupper(substr(PHP_OS,0,3)) == 'WIN') {
        dl('php_gd2.dll');
    } else {
        dl('gd.so');
    }
}

$im = ImageCreate(140,100);

$yellow = ImageColorAllocate($im, 255, 255, 191);
$black  = ImageColorAllocate($im, 0, 0, 0);

function MyFilledRectangle($image, $x1, $y1, $width, $height, $color)
{
    $x2 = $x1 + $width;
    $y2 = $y1 + $height;

    ImageFIlledRectangle($image, $x1, $y1, $x2, $y2, $color);
}

/* Draw a 40 x 80, solid black rectangle at 50, 10: */
```

```
MyFilledRectangle($im, 50, 10, 40, 80, $black);

header("Content-type: image/png");

ImagePng($im);

ImageDestroy($im);
?>
```

This is how the resulting rectangle looks:

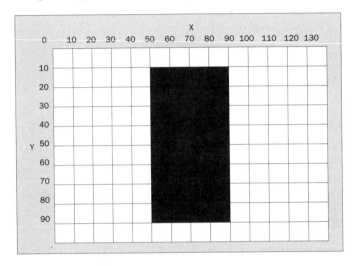

To see the screenshot refer to *Fig 5.4 – ImageFilledRectangle* in *Appendix G*.

ImagePolygon ()

```
void ImagePolygon(resource image, array points, int num_pts, int color);
```

ImagePolygon() takes an array of coordinates (points) and connects each point with lines. num_pts is the total number of vertices contained in the polygon.

To draw a triangle with points at (70, 20), (90, 60), and (50, 60), our $points array would look like this:

```
$points = array(70, 20,
                90, 60,
                50, 60);
```

Calculating the value for num_pts is easy, since the $points array contain two elements (x, y) for every one vertex in the polygon. We can just use the sizeof() function on points and divide the result by two:

```
$vertices = sizeof($pts) / 2;
```

Let's put everything together and draw a parallelogram with vertices at (40, 30), (100, 30), (80, 70), and (20, 70):

```php
<?php

if(!extension_loaded('gd')) {
    if(strtoupper(substr(PHP_OS,0,3)) == 'WIN') {
        dl('php_gd2.dll');
    } else {
        dl('gd.so');
    }
}

$im = ImageCreate(140, 100);

$black = ImageColorAllocate($im, 0, 0, 0);
$white = ImageColorAllocate($im, 255, 255, 255);

ImageFill($im, 0, 0, $white);

$pts = array(40, 30,
             100, 30,
             80, 70,
             20, 70);

$vertices = sizeof($pts) / 2;

ImagePolygon($im, $pts, $vertices, $black);

header("Content-type: image/png");

ImagePng($im);

ImageDestroy($im);
?>
```

Here's the resulting polygon:

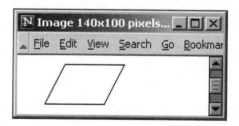

ImageFilledPolygon ()

```
void ImageFilledPolygon(resource image, array points, int num_pts, int color);
```

ImageFilledPolygon() behaves exactly the same as ImagePolygon(), but produces a solid polygon instead of an outline.

Parallelograms are nice, but let's try something with a few more sides:

```php
<?php

if(!extension_loaded('gd')) {
    if(strtoupper(substr(PHP_OS,0,3)) == 'WIN') {
        dl('php_gd2.dll');
    } else {
        dl('gd.so');
    }
}

$im = ImageCreate(140, 100);

$black = ImageColorAllocate($im, 0, 0, 0);

$white = ImageColorAllocate($im, 255, 255, 255);

ImageFill($im, 0, 0, $white);

$pts = array( 70,20,
              90,30,
              100,50,
              90,70,
              70,80,
              50,70,
              40,50,
              50,30
        );

$vertices = sizeof($pts) / 2;

ImageFilledPolygon($im, $pts, $vertices, $black);

header("Content-type: image/png");

ImagePng($im);

ImageDestroy($im);
?>
```

Here's what our filled polygon looks like:

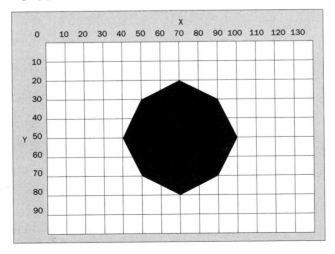

And here is the result on the browser:

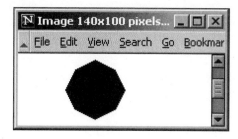

ImageArc ( )

```
void ImageArc(resource image, int center_x, int center_y, int width, int height,
int start, int end, int color);
```

ImageArc() draws an arc width pixels wide and height pixels tall using center_x and center_y as the center point. The resulting arc starts at start degrees and ends at end degrees.

ImageArc() puts 0 degrees at the three o'clock position of the arc, and counts clockwise: 90 degrees is at six o'clock, 180 degrees at nine o'clock, and 270 at twelve o'clock.

The documentation on http://www.php.net says that ImageArc() draws counter-clockwise, but in fact it goes clockwise starting at 0 and going to 270; it goes forward from 3 o'clock past 6 o'clock (90 degrees) and 9 o'clock (180 degrees). This is the case under Linux x86 and Win32.

To draw a 60 pixel x 60 pixel arc from 0 to 210 degrees at the center of a 140 x 100 image named $im, this is what the call to ImageArc() would look like:

```
ImageArc($im, 70, 50, 60, 60, 0, 210, $black);
```

This is the resulting arc:

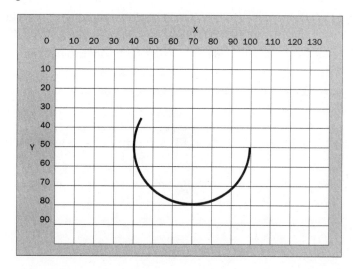

This is the output on a browser:

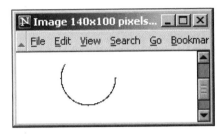

If we give the end parameter a negative number, the function will automatically convert it to a positive number by subtracting it from 360. Therefore,

```
ImageArc($im, 70, 40, 60, 60, 45, -45, $black);
```

is equivalent to:

```
ImageArc($im, 70, 40, 60, 60, 45, 315, $black);
```

Giving the start parameter a negative number produces unpredictable results. If we need to start an arc at a negative number, we can convert it to the equivalent positive angle by subtracting it from 360; so instead of starting our arc at –15, we would start it at 345.

ImageFilledArc()

```
void ImageFilledArc(resource image, int center_x, int center_y, int width, int
height, int start, int end, int color, int style);
```

ImageFilledArc() behaves the same as ImageArc(), but it takes an additional parameter for style, which is a bitwise OR of one or more of the following integer constants:

- ❏ IMG_ARC_PIE – Draws a pie chart-styled, solid wedge with lines connecting the beginning and end points of the arc to its center point.

- ❏ IMG_ARC_CHORD – Draws a triangle connecting the beginning and end points of the arc to its center point.

- ❏ IMG_ARC_NOFILL – Draws the arc without filling it, essentially duplicating the ImageArc() function.

- ❏ IMG_ARC_EDGED – Indicates that the end points of the arc should be connected to its center. Used in combination with IMG_ARC_NOFILL, this style results in an empty outline of the wedge defined by the arc and its center point.

IMG_ARC_PIE and IMG_ARC_CHORD are mutually exclusive; they can't be combined in the same call to ImageFilledArc().

Here is a filled arc from 0 to 135 degrees, with the IMG_ARC_PIE style:

```php
<?php

if(!extension_loaded('gd')) {
    if(strtoupper(substr(PHP_OS,0,3)) == 'WIN') {
        dl('php_gd2.dll');
    } else {
        dl('gd.so');
    }
}

//Create a new image resource
$im = ImageCreate(140,100);

//Allocate Colors
$white = ImageColorAllocate($im, 255,255,255);
$black = ImageColorAllocate($im, 0, 0, 0);

//Draw the Filled Arc
ImageFilledArc($im, 70, 50, 50, 50, 0, 135, $black, IMG_ARC_PIE);

//Send it to the browser
header("Content-type: image/png");

ImagePng($im);

// Destroy the image resource:
ImageDestroy($im);
?>
```

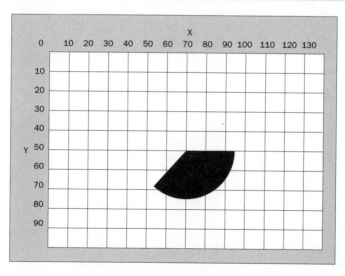

Here is the output on a browser:

With the `IMG_ARC_CHORD` style:

```
ImageFilledArc($im, 70, 50, 50, 50, 0, 135, $black, IMG_ARC_CHORD);
```

the arc looks like this:

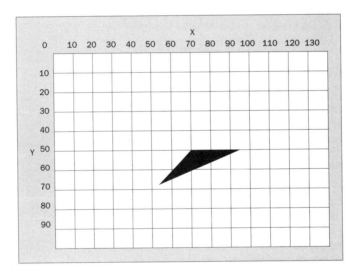

Using the `IMG_ARC_NOFILL` style results in a simple line:

```
ImageFilledArc($im, 70, 50, 50, 50, 0, 135, $black, IMG_ARC_NOFILL);
```

like this:

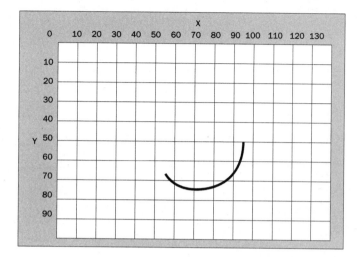

Combining `IMG_ARC_NOFILL` and `IMG_ARC_EDGED` with the bitwise `OR` operator (`|`) produces an empty wedge:

```
ImageFilledArc($im, 70, 50, 50, 50, 0, 135, $black, IMG_ARC_NOFILL |
IMG_ARC_EDGED);
```

like this:

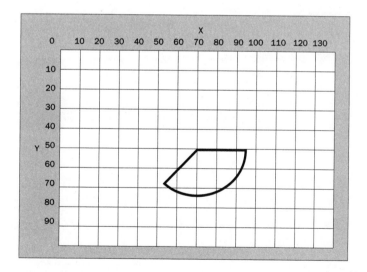

Creating Ellipses

One thing that is conspicuously absent from the list of geometric drawing functions is a function for creating solid and outline ellipses. Such a feature is planned for future releases of the GD library, but in the meantime we can create ellipses with `ImageArc()` and `ImageFilledArc()`. Just use a start value of 0 and an end value of 360, and our arcs will end right where they started, effectively forming an ellipse.

Here is the code for an outlined ellipse:

```php
<?php

if(!extension_loaded('gd')) {
    if(strtoupper(substr(PHP_OS,0,3)) == 'WIN') {
        dl('php_gd2.dll');
    } else {
        dl('gd.so');
    }
}

//Create a new image resource:
$im = ImageCreate(140,100);

//Allocate Colors
$white = ImageColorAllocate($im, 255,255,255);
$black = ImageColorAllocate($im, 0, 0, 0);

//Draw the ellipse
ImageArc($im, 70, 50, 50, 80, 0, 360, $black);

//Send it to the browser
header("Content-type: image/png");

ImagePng($im);
//Destroy the image resource:
ImageDestroy($im);
?>
```

This is how the resulting ellipse looks:

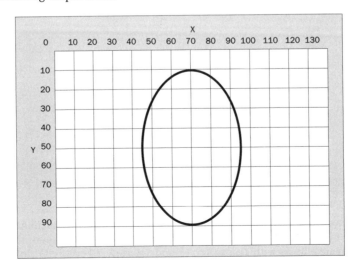

This is the output on a Netscape browser:

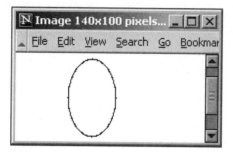

Here is the code for a filled ellipse:

```php
<?php

if(!extension_loaded('gd')) {
    if(strtoupper(substr(PHP_OS,0,3)) == 'WIN') {
        dl('php_gd2.dll');
    } else {
        dl('gd.so');
    }
}

//Create a new image resource:
$im = ImageCreate(140,100);

//Allocate colors:
$white = ImageColorAllocate($im, 255,255,255);
$black = ImageColorAllocate($im, 0, 0, 0);

//Draw the filled ellipse:
ImageFilledArc($im, 70, 50, 80, 50, 0, 360, $black, IMG_ARC_PIE);

//Send it to the browser:
header("Content-type: image/png");

ImagePng($im);

//Destroy the image resource:
ImageDestroy($im);
?>
```

and this is the output:

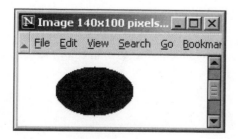

Text

A picture full of lines, arcs, rectangles, and ellipses may be worth a thousand words, but in some cases a picture with words too is worth even more.

There are times during web design when we have to make endless revisions to buttons and header graphics containing text. Inevitably somebody wants the text to be made larger or smaller, or changed into a different color, or changed into a different font altogether. On a big site, that would mean a lot of graphics to update, and a lot of time spent in Photoshop updating text graphics one by one.

With the GD text functions, it's possible to make changes in the size, color, and typeface of the site's graphics from a central script, and have all the graphics on the site updated instantly. Once you try it, you'll wonder how you ever got through all those tedious site updates without going crazy.

These are the main functions that help to add text to the images:

❑   ImageString()

❑   ImageTTFText()

❑   ImageTTFBBox()

> **On UNIX machines, FreeType needs to be installed to use the `ImageTTFText()` and `ImageTTFBBox()` functions.**

ImageString()

```
void ImageString(resource image, int font, int x, int y, string text, int color);
```

ImageString() writes the text contained in text to image using color at the coordinates (x, y) where x is the beginning of the text and y is the top of the text (not the baseline.)

If we give font a value of 1 to 5, the function uses a built-in font. This is especially well suited for small labels and captions, since the built-in fonts are both small and easy to read. font can also be the identifier of a user-defined bitmap font, but for most applications it'll probably be easier to use the ImageTTFText() function. ImageTTFText() allows to use TrueType Fonts (TTF), and does anti-aliasing to boot.

ImageTTFText()

```
array ImageTTFText (resource image, int size, int angle, int x, int y, int color,
string fontfile, string text);
```

ImageTTFText() draws the contents of text in the image identified by image, starting at the coordinates x, y (top left is 0, 0), at an angle (angle) in color (color), using the TrueType font file identified by fontfile.

At the time of writing, there is a bug in `php_gd2.dll`, in the current distribution of PHP (4.2) for Windows. The bug causes `ImageTTFText()` to fail with a 'Could not find/open font' error even if the font file exists. While we can still use `ImageTTFtext()` with `php_gd.dll`, this means that we won't be able to use `ImageTTFString()` in conjunction with true-color images. `ImageTTFText()` works normally with GD 2.0.1 and PHP 4.2 for UNIX.

Depending on the version of GD library that PHP is using, when `fontfile` does not begin with a leading /, `.ttf` will be appended to the filename and the library will attempt to search for that filename along a library-defined font path.

The coordinates given by x, y will define the basepoint of the first character (roughly the lower-left corner of the character). This is different from the `ImageString()`, where x, y define the upper-right corner of the first character.

`angle` is in degrees, with 0 degrees being left-to-right reading text (3 o'clock direction), and higher values representing a counter-clockwise rotation (that is, a value of 90 would result in bottom-to-top reading text). Also, the text string (`text`) may include UTF-8 character sequences (of the form: `&#123;`) to access characters in a font beyond the first 255.

Text added to an image resource with `ImageTTFText()` is anti-aliased by default. If we want to disable anti-aliasing, use the negative of the desired color (that is, `-$red` instead of `$red`).

`ImageTTFText()` returns an array with 8 elements representing four points making the bounding box of the text:

Index of the Array	Description
0	Lower-left corner, x position
1	Lower-left corner, y position
2	Lower-right corner, x position
3	Lower-right corner, y position
4	Upper-right corner, x position
5	Upper-right corner, y position
6	Upper-left corner, x position
7	Upper-left corner, y position

The order of the points is lower-left, lower-right, upper-right, and upper-left. The points are relative to the text regardless of the angle, so 'upper-left' means in the top left-hand corner when we see the text horizontally.

Now, let's use `ImageTTFText()` to draw a simple string. Let's say we have a font called 'Bullpen' in our home directory, whose filename is `bullpen_.ttf`. We will use this font to write some 48-point text in black on a gray, 320 x 240 pixel image:

```php
<?php

if(!extension_loaded('gd')) {
    if(strtoupper(substr(PHP_OS,0,3)) == 'WIN') {
        dl('php_gd.dll');
    } else {
        dl('gd.so');
    }
}

//Create an image resource:
$im = ImageCreate(320, 240);

//Define our colors - gray first, since that's our background color:
$gray = ImageColorAllocate($im, 153, 153, 153);
$black = ImageColorAllocate($im, 0, 0, 0);

//Define other variables for the ImageTTFText function:
$size = 48;
$angle = 0;
$x = 90;
$y = 135;
$fontfile = "bullpen_.ttf";
$text = "Foo.";

//Write text to the image:
ImageTTFText($im, $size, $angle, $x, $y, $black, $fontfile, $text);

//Send the image to the browser:
header("Content-type: image/png");

ImagePng($im);

//Destroy the image resource:
ImageDestroy($im);
?>
```

This is the image the script sends to the browser:

Now let's look into embossing some text. While we may not be able to replace our entire favourite Photoshop filters with PHP and GD just yet, with planning we can achieve some nice effects in our images.

The previous example is a good start, but it's pretty flat. By adding a highlight color and doing some careful overlapping with `ImageTTFText()`, we get a nice embossed effect on our text. Let's put the text at a 10 degree angle, too:

```php
<?php

if(!extension_loaded('gd')) {
    if(strtoupper(substr(PHP_OS,0,3)) == 'WIN') {
        dl('php_gd.dll');
    } else {
        dl('gd.so');
    }
}

//Create an image resource:
$im = ImageCreate(320, 240);

//Define our colors - gray first, since that's our background color:
$gray = ImageColorAllocate($im, 153, 153, 153);
$black = ImageColorAllocate($im, 0, 0, 0);
$white = ImageColorAllocate($im, 255, 255, 255);

//Define other variables for the ImageTTFText function:
$size = 48;
$angle = 10;
$x = 90;
$y = 135;
$fontfile = "bullpen_.ttf";
$text = "Foo.";

/* Step 1: Use black to create the shaded edge of the text.
   Offset $x and $y by 1 to make a thin, crisp edge
   below and to the right of the final text: */

ImageTTFText($im, $size, $angle, $x + 1, $y + 1, $black, $fontfile, $text);

/* Step 2: Use white to create the highlighted edge of the text.
   Offset $x and $y by -1 to make a thin, crisp edge
   above and to the left of the final text: */

ImageTTFText($im, $size, $angle, $x - 1, $y - 1, $white, $fontfile, $text);

/* Step 3: Use gray, the background color, to write the string on
   top of the last two; the black and white areas suddenly look
   like they are raised: */

ImageTTFText($im, $size, $angle, $x, $y, $gray, $fontfile, $text);

//Send the image to the browser:
header("Content-type: image/png");

ImagePng($im);

//Destroy the image resource:
ImageDestroy($im);
?>
```

This is what the embossed, angled text looks like:

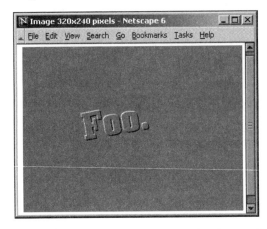

We could also use this technique with rectangles, ellipses, and polygons for simple buttons. Further, by switching the positions of the white and black strings we would get a relief effect.

ImageTTFBBox()

```
array ImageTTFBBox(int size, int angle, string fontfile, string text);
```

ImageTTFBBox() returns an array of coordinates indicating the bounding box for the string text, drawn in the font (fontfile) with a point size (size) at an angle (angle).

This is extremely helpful information if we want to make sure a line of text will fit in an existing image, or if we want to know how big we need to make a new text graphic.

The array returned by ImageTTFBBox() contains four sets of coordinates, indicating the four corners of the bounding box. These are the indexes of the array and the points they represent:

Index of the Array	Description
0	Lower-left corner, x position
1	Lower-left corner, y position
2	Lower-right corner, x position
3	Lower-right corner, y position
4	Upper-right corner, x position
5	Upper-right corner, y position
6	Upper-left corner, x position
7	Upper-left corner, y position

For instance, if we wanted to find the bounding box of the text from our first ImageTTFText() example above, we could write a script like this:

```php
<?php

if(!extension_loaded('gd')) {
    if(strtoupper(substr(PHP_OS,0,3)) == 'WIN') {
        dl('php_gd.dll');
    } else {
        dl('gd.so');
    }
}

$size = 48;
$angle = 0;
$fontfile = "bullpen_.ttf";
$text = "Foo.";

$bbox = ImageTTFBbox($size, $angle, $fontfile, $text);

print ("Upper left: (" . $bbox[6] . ", " . $bbox[7] . ")<br>\n");
print ("Upper right: (" . $bbox[4] . ", " . $bbox[5] . ")<br>\n");
print ("Lower left: (" . $bbox[0] . ", " . $bbox[1] . ")<br>\n");
print ("Lower right: (" . $bbox[2] . ", " . $bbox[3] . ")<br>\n");

?>
```

The results will vary from font to font, but they should look something like this:

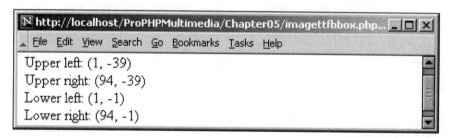

Note the negative y coordinates. This is because `ImageTTFBBox()` returns coordinates relative to the font baseline. To determine the actual width and height of the bounding box, we need to take the absolute value of the difference between opposite corners of the box. We can do this using just the upper-left and lower-right corner information. Let's add this to our script:

```php
/* Determine the bounding box width using the
   upper-left and lower-right x values: */

$width = abs($bbox[6] - $bbox[2]);

/* Determine the bounding box height using the
   upper-left and lower-right y values: */

$height = abs($bbox[7] - $bbox[3]);

print ("Bounding Box is $width pixels wide and $height pixels tall.<br>\n");
```

Now that we know how big to make our text image, we need to know where to position the text in the image using `ImageTTFText()`. Because the y coordinate passed to `ImageTTFText()` indicates the baseline of the font, we'll subtract the absolute value of the lower-right corner's y position from the bounding box height:

```
$baseline = $height - abs($bbox[3]);
```

Now we have all the information we need to create a new image with the exact dimensions for our text:

```
$im = ImageCreate($width, $height);

$gray = ImageColorAllocate($im, 153, 153, 153);

$black = ImageColorAllocate($im, 0, 0, 0);

ImageTTFText($im, $size, $angle, 0, $baseline, $black, $fontfile, $text);

ImagePng($im, "my_image.png");

print ("<img src='my_image.png' width='$width' height='$height'>");
```

If we load our final script in a browser, we should see something like this:

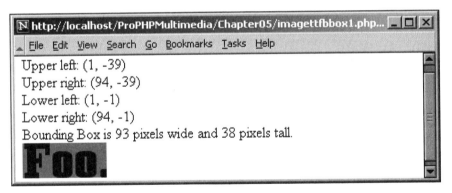

That's just the beginning of the useful things one can do with `ImageTTFBBox()`. We could modify the script further to add a few pixels of padding around the text, and use `ImageLine()` to draw highlights and shadows on the top-left and bottom-right edges of the image respectively, effectively turning it into a button. We could add a customizable visitor counter to our page that would take parameters passed on the query string from the IMG tag's `src` parameter.

Even if we didn't want to use GD to generate title graphics on the fly, we could easily create a PHP script to generate dozens or even hundreds of titles from a database and write them to disk, saving us all kinds of time spent using the Photoshop Text tool. The best part is that we can set our site's text graphics up so that we can change the entire look of the site just by switching font files or color definitions in a single script.

Working with Existing Images

So far we've seen how PHP's GD functions let us create empty images and fill them with lines, shapes, and text. By themselves these are very useful features, but one of the other things we'll probably want to do with GD is make changes to existing images; we can get a lot of basic stuff done with GD that we would have otherwise done by hand using a photo editor.

ImageCreateFromJpeg()

```
resource ImageCreateFromJpeg(string filename);
```

ImageCreateFromJpeg() returns a GD image resource containing the image data from the JPEG file located at filename. If PHP can't open the image, the function returns FALSE.

ImageCreateFromPng()

```
resource ImageCreateFromPng(string filename);
```

ImageCreateFromPng() returns a GD image resource containing the image data from the PNG file located at filename.

Copying, Resizing, and Merging

Now that we've got a copy of our JPEG or PNG file opened as a GD image resource, what can we do with it?

Another task that was once dreaded drudgework for web designers is cropping and/or resizing large numbers of images to prepare them for deployment on the web site. PHP can take care of these things for us right on the server, and it will save us the extra steps of uploading and downloading all the images we want to change.

These are the functions we'll use to copy, resize, and merge images:

- ❑ ImageCopy()
- ❑ ImageCopyResized()
- ❑ ImageCopyResampled()
- ❑ ImageCopyMerge()

ImageCopy()

```
void ImageCopy(resource destination_image, resource source_image, int
destination_x, int destination_y, int source_x, int source_y, int source_width,
int source_height);
```

The copying functions look a little bit confusing at first because they take so many parameters, but they're easy once we get the hang of it.

For example, let's say we have two images – frame.jpg and motel.jpg:

These are the `ImageCopy()` resources:

frame.jpg	motel.jpg

Let's copy `motel.jpg` onto `frame.jpg`. The first thing we have to do is create image resources for the two files:

```php
<?php

if(!extension_loaded('gd')) {
    if(strtoupper(substr(PHP_OS,0,3)) == 'WIN') {
        dl('php_gd2.dll');
    } else {
        dl('gd.so');
    }
}

$frame = ImageCreateFromJpeg("frame.jpg");

$content = ImageCreateFromJpeg("motel.jpg");
```

Now we're ready to use `ImageCopy()` to copy the image in `$content` into `$frame`. Because both images are exactly the same size, we'll want to crop our motel photo so that it doesn't overlap the frame. The frame is 10 pixels wide, which means we need to trim a total of 20 pixels from the height and width of the photo, and position it 10 pixels over and 10 pixels down when we copy it into the frame.

Here's a breakdown of the coordinates we need to pass to `ImageCopy()`:

- ❑ destination_image: `$frame` is our destination resource.
- ❑ source_image: `$content` is our source resource.
- ❑ destination_x: since the frame is 10 pixels wide, we want to position the source image 10 pixels from the left edge of the destination image. Therefore, destination_x = 10.
- ❑ destination_y: since the frame is 10 pixels wide, we want to position the source image 10 pixels from the top edge of the destination image. Therefore, destination_y = 10.
- ❑ source_x: we want to crop the source image to fit exactly inside the frame, so we'll start copying at the same position as destination_x. Therefore, source_x = 10.
- ❑ source_y: we want to crop the source image to fit exactly inside the frame, so we'll start copying at the same position as destination_y. Therefore, source_y = 10.

- ❏ source_width: since the frame occupies 10 pixels on both the left and right sides of the destination image, we need to trim 20 pixels total from the width of the source image. The original image is 320 pixels wide, so source_width = 320 – 20, or 300.

- ❏ source_height: since the frame occupies 10 pixels on both the top and bottom sides of the destination image, we need to trim 20 pixels total from the height of the source image. The original image is 240 pixels tall, so source_height = 240 – 20, or 220.

Let's call ImageCopy():

```
ImageCopy($frame, $content, 10, 10, 10, 10, 300, 220);
```

$frame should now contain the cropped image from $content. Let's save a copy and close the script:

```
ImageJpeg($frame,"framed_motel.jpg");
?>
```

If we open framed_motel.jpg we should see our nicely framed photo:

ImageCopyResized()

```
void ImageCopyResized(resource destination_image, resource source_image, int
destination_x, int destination_y, int source_x, int source_y, int
destination_width, int destination_height, int source_width, int source_height);
```

ImageCopyResized() is similar to ImageCopy(), with the addition of two more parameters, destination_width and destination_height. This allows us to take a large section from the source_image and shrink it to fit in a smaller destination_image.

For example, we can take the framed_motel.jpg image we created with ImageCopy() and resize it to create a thumbnail version:

```
<?php

if(!extension_loaded('gd')) {
    if(strtoupper(substr(PHP_OS,0,3)) == 'WIN') {
        dl('php_gd2.dll');
    } else {
        dl('gd.so');
    }
}
```

```
/* Set the width (in pixels) for the smaller version - we will calculate
   the smaller version height based on the dimensions of the source image
*/
$smallwidth = 200;

/* Create an image resource from the source graphic, framed_motel.php */

$im = ImageCreateFromJpeg('framed_motel.jpg');

/* Get the source image dimensions */

$srcwidth = ImagesX($im);
$srcheight = ImagesY($im);

/* By dividing our smaller version width by the source image width,
   we will have the correct proportion for the smaller version height: */

$proportion = $smallwidth / $srcwidth;
$smallheight = round($srcheight * $proportion);

/* Now we can create a new image resource for the smaller version: */

$small = ImageCreateTrueColor($smallwidth, $smallheight);

/* Finally, we can copy the contents of $im into $small
   and resize it at the same time: */

ImageCopyResized($small, $im, 0, 0, 0, 0, $smallwidth, $smallheight, $srcwidth,
$srcheight);

/* Save a copy to the disk: */
ImageJpeg($small, "framed_motel_small.jpg");

/* Destroy the image resources */
ImageDestroy($im);
ImageDestroy($small);
?>
```

Here's what `framed_motel_small.jpg` will look like:

The resized image gets a little bit choppy along the diagonal lines. Fortunately, GD 2 provides an improved function with the exact same syntax, `ImageCopyResampled()`.

ImageCopyResampled()

> **This function only works with GD version 2.0.1 or later.**

```
void ImageCopyResampled(resource destination_image, resource source_image, int
destination_x, int destination_y, int source_x, int source_y, int
destination_width, int destination_height, int source_width, int source_height);
```

ImageCopyResampled() behaves like ImageCopyResized, but it provides much smoother results. For instance, take our code example from ImageCopyResized() and replace the line:

```
ImageCopyResized($small, $im, 0, 0, 0, 0, $smallwidth, $smallheight, $srcwidth,
$srcheight);
```

with this line:

```
ImageCopyResampled($small, $im, 0, 0, 0, 0, $smallwidth, $smallheight, $srcwidth,
$srcheight);
```

Save the change, and rerun the script; you should notice a definite improvement in the quality of framed_motel_small.jpg.

Here are the two different images produced by ImageCopyResized() and ImageCopyResampled(), side by side:

ImageCopyResized()	**ImageCopyResampled()**

So why would we ever want to use ImageCopyResized() when ImageCopyResampled() produces better results? Speed is one reason; because ImageCopyResampled() uses a more complex algorithm to resize image data, it can take longer to complete than ImageCopyResized(). This isn't a big deal if we are only resizing a dozen images here and there, but if one is planning on processing hundreds or thousands of images it will probably begin to show.

For thumbnails below a certain size, we may also find that we can get away with using ImageCopyResized() – if our web site is going to be generating a lot of thumbnails on the fly, this can help lighten the load on the server's CPU.

> There is a known bug in this function – it ignores the `source_x` and `source_y` parameters, effectively setting them both to 0 and forcing us to always copy from the upper left corner of the source image. This isn't a problem if we're using `ImageCopyResampled()` for simple tasks like creating thumbnails, but if we need to copy a specific portion of the source image, we would be better off with the `ImageCopyResized()` function.

ImageCopyMerge()

```
void ImageCopyMerge(resource dest_img, resource resource_img, int dest_x, int
dest_y, int src_x, int src_y, int src_width, int src_height, int percent);
```

`ImageCopyMerge()` behaves just like `ImageCopy()` with the exception of the additional parameter `percent`, which indicates the opacity to use for `resource_img` when merging it with `dest_img`. A value of 100 means that the resource image will be completely opaque (making the function identical to `ImageCopy()`), and a value of 0 will make the resource image completely transparent.

This function would be useful for creating a **watermark** image that can be used as a decorative page background without interfering with the text on top of it. Let's turn `motel.jpg` into a watermark by merging it with a completely white image:

```php
<?php

if(!extension_loaded('gd')) {
    if(strtoupper(substr(PHP_OS,0,3)) == 'WIN') {
        dl('php_gd2.dll');
    } else {
        dl('gd.so');
    }
}

//Create an image from motel.jpg
$motel = ImageCreateFromJpeg("motel.jpg");

/* Find out how many pixels tall and wide $motel is
  so we can create a new image the same size*/

$width = imagesx($motel);
$height = imagesy($motel);

/* Create the all-white image which we will merge
  with motel.jpg: */

$watermark = ImageCreateTrueColor($width,$height);

/* Create white color resource */
$white = ImageColorAllocate($watermark, 255, 255, 255);
```

```
/* Fill the background with $white */
ImageFill($watermark, 0, 0, $white);

/* Now use ImageCopyMerge() to merge $motel with $watermark.
   Use a low value (10) for opacity, which means that
   most of the white background will show through: */

ImageCopyMerge($watermark, $motel, 0, 0, 0, 0, $width, $height, 10);

header("Content-type: image/jpeg");

ImageJpeg($watermark);

//Destroy the image resource:
ImageDestroy($im);
?>
```

To see the resulting image refer to *Fig 5.5 – ImageCopyMerge* in *Appendix G*.

This resulting image can be used as the background for a web page, like this:

```
<html>
  <head>
    <title>Motels of the San Fernando Valley</title>

      <style>
        body{
            padding:0px;
            margin:0px;
            background-image:url("watermark.jpg");
            background-repeat:repeat-y;
            background-position:0px -25px;
            background-color:#DDEFFF;
            color:#000000;
        }

        div,p,h1,li{
            font-family:arial,helvetica;
        }

        li{
            padding-bottom:.5em;
        }

        h1{
            background-color:#003366;
            color:#FFFFFF;
            width:100%
        }
```

```
      </style>

  </head>

  <body>
    <h1>Motels of the San Fernando Valley</h1>
    <ul>
      <li><strong>Pink Motel</strong> - San Fernando Road, Sun Valley</li>
      <li><strong>Flamingo Motel</strong> - Lankershim Blvd, North Hollywood</li>
      <li><strong>Ritz Motel</strong> - Lankershim Blvd, North Hollywood</li>
      <li><strong>Park Motel</strong> - Ventura Boulevard, Studio City</li>
      <li><strong>Sportsmen's Lodge</strong> - Ventura Boulevard, Studio City</li>
      <li><strong>Heritage Motel</strong> - Ventura Boulevard, Sherman Oaks</li>
      <li><strong>Starlight Cottage</strong> - Sepulveda Boulevard, Van Nuys</li>
    </ul>
  </body>
</html>
```

To see how the output looks refer to *Fig 5.6 – Motels of the San Fernando Valley*, in *Appendix G*.

Summary

In this chapter we looked at how the GD library provides PHP with a powerful set of functions that allow us to:

- ❏   Create new indexed- and true-color images

- ❏   Send images to the browser on the fly, or save them to disk for later use

- ❏   Define colors for drawing onto an image, and retrieve color information from existing images

- ❏   Draw basic lines and geometric shapes including rectangles, polygons, arcs, and ellipses

- ❏   Add true-type text to images

- ❏   Copy, crop, resize, and merge existing images

Two of the most highly touted features in PHP are that it is versatile and easy to learn. As we start delving into the more specialized extensions like the GD functions, one really begins to get a sense of how powerful PHP really is. If you're still adjusting to the idea of creating images, drawing on them, writing on them, copying, resizing, or merging them, and then saving them to disk without actually seeing the changes as you make them, just remember the 'easy to learn' part, and keep playing with it.

Of all PHP's capabilities, image manipulation is one of the most interesting to experiment with. Feedback is highly visual and immediate, which will help to make learning that much faster. Once you've set up your first site using GD for generating title graphics and thumbnails, you'll never go back to the desktop.

6

ImageMagick

In the first two chapters we refreshed our PHP programming skills. We then went on to look at how we could create dynamic Flash content using Ming and how we could add interactivity to our Flash movies using ActionScript. During the course of these chapters we saw how we could use the basic drawing methods of Ming to draw simple shapes. We also saw how we could incorporate existing images within our Flash content. But what happens if we have an existing image that we want to modify? This is where **ImageMagick** comes in.

What is ImageMagick?

Written by ImageMagick Studio (http://www.imagemagick.org), ImageMagick is a collection of tools to modify and gather data about images, and also an API to functions that perform those tasks. It allows manipulation of over a hundred different image and document formats and at the same time allows us to apply complex transformations and filters to images.

Though ImageMagick can work with a large variety of document formats, since we are working in a web environment, we will focus only on JPEG (Joint Photographic Experts Group) and PNG (Portable Network Graphics) formats.

In this chapter will focus on ImageMagick tools that allow us to manipulate web images – **Convert** (converts images in different formats), **Mogrify** (transforms images), and **Identify** (identifies the format and characteristics of an image).

In this chapter, we will cover:

- ❏ Installing ImageMagick
- ❏ Some of the tools distributed with the ImageMagick distribution

❑ How to use these tools with PHP

❑ How to create a class library that interfaces with these tools

❑ How to implement the class library functions

Getting Started

ImageMagick can be used on a number of platforms. Besides the usual Windows and UNIX versions, there are binaries available for Macintosh and VMS (Virtual Memory System) operating systems as well. The sourcecode is available for ImageMagick, so if we wish, we can compile it ourselves for our chosen platform. Here we will look at installing from binaries on a Windows system and compiling from source on a UNIX system.

Installing on UNIX

For UNIX we will install ImageMagick from source. Download the latest sourcecode from one of the sites listed on the ImageMagick web site (http://www.imagemagick.org/). Here we will use the `ImageMagick-5.4.6-3.tar.gz` file. All that we need to do is extract, configure, and compile the source. Use the following commands at the system prompt:

1. `tar -zxvf ImageMagick-5.4.6-3.tar.gz`

2. `./configure -prefix=/usr/local`

3. `make`

4. `make install`

The configure program will determine what our system architecture is and what libraries we have installed. The binaries will be installed to `/usr/local/bin`. We can now test that the binaries have installed correctly and that `/usr/local/bin` is in our path by issuing the command:

```
# identify logo:
```

which gives this result:

Installing on Windows

Download the Windows binary distribution (`ImageMagick-win2k.zip`) from one of the sites listed on the ImageMagick web site. Unzip the contents into a folder on the hard drive. It is always better to keep all the utility programs at the same place, for example, `c:\bin\ImageMagick`. Since we want PHP to have access to the ImageMagick tools, we have to add the ImageMagick folder to the `Path` environment variable.

In Windows 2000 or Windows NT, we can alter this variable by right-clicking My Computer, and selecting Properties from the menu, and then selecting the Advanced option. Click the Environment Variables button to bring up the following dialog box:

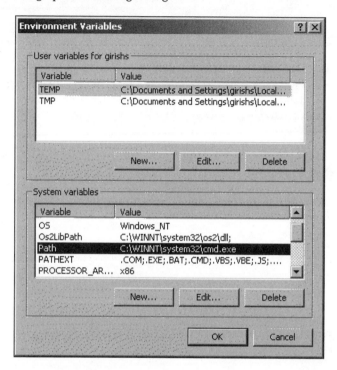

Choose the Path option under System variables, click Edit, and add the full path to ImageMagick and a semicolon to the beginning of the existing value:

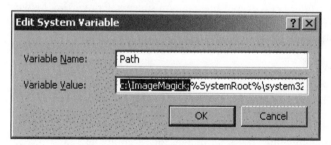

Click OK on all of the open dialogs to accept the change. To test whether our installation was successful or not, open the Command Prompt and type the following command:

```
C:\>Identify logo:
```

to see this output:

> Windows NT has a program called `convert.exe` that converts files to NTFS file systems; since we don't want this tool to run on our images we have added the ImageMagick folder at the beginning of the environmental variable path.

ImageMagick Tools

ImageMagick tools are used to access the ImageMagick functions directly from a command-line prompt. The tools that we will be using in this chapter are:

- ❏ Convert
- ❏ Mogrify
- ❏ Identify

For a full list of the tools available in ImageMagick, refer to http://www.imagemagick.org/www/tools.html.

Convert

The Convert tool converts images from one format to another, while optionally passing the image through filters, and produces no output message on success. Converting between file formats is very straightforward – we just have to specify the input and output filenames. The Convert tool will use the extension of the output file name to determine the output format:

```
Convert glitter.jpg glitter.png
```

The ImageMagick library contains filters that can be used to add sound to images, remove pixel aliasing, add blurs, change image sizes, and even simulate a charcoal drawing.

Suppose we want to change the size of an image, for example, let's say from 320x240 pixels to 160x120 pixels, using this command:

```
convert -geometry "160x120!" -draw "text 0,0 'glitter'"
                         -negate glitter.jpg glitter.png
```

Here, we add text that says `glitter` at point (0,0), and make a negative image, we then change the format again from JPEG to PNG.

The Convert utility has some pretty nifty functions that can be used on our images:

❑ Add a Gaussian blur

❑ Colorize the image

❑ Add comments to it

❑ Crop, emboss, rotate, or sharpen the image

We can even make our own online image manipulation studio application using the Convert utility.

Mogrify

Like Convert, Mogrify also gives no output message if successful. The Mogrify tool works mostly the same way as the Convert tool, the only exception being that Mogrify works on the input image and doesn't save the image to another file. The Mogrify utility can be used to do the same tasks as the Convert utility but without changing the output file type, like this:

```
mogrify -geometry '160x120!' -draw "text 0,0 'glitter'" -negate glitter.jpg
```

It is also possible to change the file format with the Mogrify utility. To do this, we use the `format` option and specify the target format. However, the specified target format should be one of the ImageMagick-supported formats. We will see how we can do this when we create our class later on.

Some of the file formats require additional libraries and support files to be installed before ImageMagick can use them. For example, we will need the **FreeType** software in order to add annotations to images. On Windows machines, where no X server is available, ImageMagick will use **GhostScript** to annotate images.

For more information refer to the listing at http://www.imagemagick.org/www/install.html#extr.

Identify

The Identify tool reads and outputs information about a specified image, and has some options to specify image geometries for images that are raw CMYK, RGB, or GREY values.

Here's an example that shows the usage and the output:

```
Identify -ping cheap.jpg
```

Here is the output:

```
Command Prompt

C:\PHPMultimedia\Chapter06>Identify -ping cheap.jpg
cheap.jpg JPEG 320x240 DirectClass 8-bit 21407b 0.0u 0:01
```

And if we use:

```
$ Identify -verbose -ping cheap.jpg
```

This is the output:

As we can see, using the `-ping` option with `Identify` is more efficient, as it does not read the entire image into memory. Although the load and CPU time taken by this program is already minimal, it is recommended for servers with heavier loads.

Now that we have learned how to use the ImageMagick command-line tools, let's look at how we can use them within our PHP scripts.

Using ImageMagick with PHP

At the time of writing, there is no PHP extension library that interfaces with ImageMagick's API. Therefore, we must execute the small and efficient pre-built programs that come with the ImageMagick distribution. Work has begun on an extension using **PECL** (PHP Extension C Layer), but it is not yet stable enough to be used in a working environment. The extension manual can be found at http://pear.php.net/manual/en/pecl.imagick.php.

Currently, the way that we execute these tools is by calling them directly from the PHP script. There are a number of ways in which we can do this in PHP, but not all of them will work in this case. Remember when we looked at the `Identify` tool – it returned a number of lines detailing the image format. Obviously we would want all of that information to be returned to us. The PHP function that will do this is the `shell_exec()`. It takes a single string argument of the `shell` command to run, and returns the complete output of that command. There is a shortcut for this, known as the execution operator or `backtick`. The `backtick` looks like a single quote, but slants backwards like a backslash.

Let's take a look at an example to illustrate this. Save the following code as `backtick.php`. We will also have to have a JPEG file called `cheap.jpg` in the same folder as the script.

```
<pre>
<?php
    $output = `identify -verbose cheap.jpg`;
    print $output;
?>
</pre>
```

Nothing complicated here – all we're doing is using the backtick operator to execute the command and have the output of the command stored in the $output variable.

This is the output of the script:

```
N Netscape 6                                                        _ □ ×
  File Edit View Search Go Bookmarks Tasks Help
Image: cheap.jpg
  Format: JPEG (Joint Photographic Experts Group JFIF format)
  Geometry: 320x240
  Class: DirectClass
  Type: true color
  Depth: 8 bits-per-pixel component
  Colors: 31664
  Filesize: 21407b
  Interlace: None
  Background Color: white
  Border Color: #dfdfdf
  Matte Color: grey74
  Iterations: 0
  Compression: JPEG
  signature: 4b7b5abb9545ae781e3d67c54480a016f25526a960b1137751c7832caabe108d
  Tainted: False
  User Time: 0.0u
  Elapsed Time: 0:01
```

The ImageMagick Class Library

So far we have seen what we can do with ImageMagick and how we can interface it with PHP. Now we can create a class to interface with the command-line tools. Our class will allow us to easily use the Convert, Identify, and Mogrify tools.

> All the options provided by the Convert, Mogrify, and Identify tools are explained in great detail inside their respective 'man' pages (http://www.imagemagick.org). The options that we will be using in this chapter and in the Case Study that follows later in the book will be explained here though.

Save this file as class.imagemagick.php:

```
<?php

/********************************************************************************/
class.imagemagick.php
```

```
Class library interface to the ImageMagick toolkit accessing
Convert, Identify, and Mogrify
/***********************************************************************/

class ImageMagick
{
```

First, we will set some variables that will help us with basic error handling:

```
var $errorLevel = 0;
var $errorExitLevel = 2;
var $lastError = '';
```

Next, we initialize an array that provides a list of available image file formats for the user to convert to. ImageMagick can recognize and output these document types:

```
var $imageTypeList = array

      ("AVS" => "AVS X image file", "BIE" => "Joint Bi-level
              Image Experts Group file interchange format",
       "BMP" => "Microsoft Windows bitmap image file",
       "BMP24" => "Microsoft Windows 24-bit bitmap image file",
       "CGM" => "Computer Graphics Metafile",
       "DCX" => "ZSoft IBM PC multi-page Paintbrush file",
       "DIB" => "Microsoft Windows bitmap image file",
       "DICOM" => "Medical image file",

       "EPDF" => "Encapsulated Portable Document Format",
       "EPI" => "Adobe Encapsulated PostScript Interchange format",
       "EPS" => "Adobe Encapsulated PostScript file",
       "EPS2" => "Adobe Level II Encapsulated PostScript file",
       "EPSF" => "Adobe Encapsulated PostScript format",
       "EPSI" => "Adobe Encapsulated PostScript Interchange format",
       "EPT" => "Adobe Encapsulated PostScript Interchange
                format with TIFF preview",
       "FAX" => "Group 3",
       "FIG" => "TransFig image format",
       "FITS" => "Flexible Image Transport System",
       "FPX" => "FlashPix Format",
       "GIF" => "CompuServe graphics interchange format; 8-bit color",
       "GIF87" => "CompuServe graphics interchange format;
                   8-bit color (version 87a)",
       "HDF" => "Hierarchical Data Format",
       "HPGL" => "HP-GL plotter language",

       "JBIG" => "Joint Bi-level Image experts Group file interchange
                  format",
       "JPEG" => "Joint Photographic Experts Group JFIF format;
                  compressed 24-bit color",
       "ICO" => "Microsooft icon",
       "LABEL" => "text image",
       "MIFF" => "Magick image file format",
```

```
        "MNG" => "Multiple-image Network Graphics",
        "MONO" => "Bi-level bitmap in least-significant byte (LSB)
            first order",
        "MPEG" => "Motion Picture Experts Group file interchange format",
        "M2V" => "Motion Picture Experts Group file interchange format
                  (version 2)",

        "NETSCAPE" => "Netscape 216 color cube",
        "NULL" => "NULL image",
        "PBM" => "Portable bitmap format (B&W)",
        "PCD" => "Photo CD, maximum resolution of 512x768",
        "PCDS" => "Photo CD. Decode with sRGB color table",
        "PCL" => "Page Control Language",
        "PCX" => "ZSoft IBM PC Paintbrush file",
        "PDF" => "Portable Document Format",
        "PGM" => "Portable graymap format (grayscale)",
        "PICT" => "Apple Macintosh QuickDraw/PICT file",
        "PIX" => "Alias/Wavefront RLE image format",
        "PNG" => "Portable Network Graphics",
        "PNG" => "Portable Network Graphics",
        "PNM" => "Portable anymap",
        "PPM" => "Portable pixmap format (color)",
        "PS" => "Adobe PostScript file",
        "PS2" => "Adobe Level II PostScript file",
        "RAD" => "Radiance image file",
        "RLA" => "Alias/Wavefront image file (read-only)",
        "RLE" => "Utah Run length encoded image file (read-only)",
        "SGI" => "Irix RGB image file",
        "SUN" => "SUN Rasterfile",
        "SVG" => "Scalable Vector Graphics",

        "TGA" => "Truevision Targa image file",
        "TIFF" => "Tagged Image File Format",
        "TIFF32" => "24-bit Tagged Image File Format",
        "TIM" => "PSX TIM file",
        "TTF" => "TrueType font file",
        "UIL" => "X-Motif UIL table",
        "VID" => "Visual Image Directory",
        "VIFF" => "Khoros Visualization image file",
        "XBM" => "X Windows system bitmap, black and white only",
        "XPM" => "X Windows system pixmap file (color)",
        "XWD" => "X Windows system window dump file (color)");
```

The $resizeFlag variable is used to pass different values to Convert and Mogrify, to specify when, or when not to resize the manipulated image by using the -geometry option. When we create a new object, we are going to grab the image properties and store them for our functions to use later:

```
    var $resizeFlag;
```

Let's declare the variables:

```
var $imageBits;
var $imageBytes;
var $imageChannels;
var $imageClass;
var $imageHeight;
var $imageName;
var $imageType;
var $imageWidth;
```

Each of these variables describes the properties of the image initialized when the library is called.

Name	Description
`$imageBits`	Describes the bits per pixel in each image (usually 8 or 16)
`$imageBytes`	Provides the file size of the image
`$imageChannels`	Contains the number of channels in the image
`$imageClass`	Describes the class of the image (can be either `'DirectClass'` or `'PseudoClass'`)
`$imageHeight`	Height of the image (`$imageWidth` provides the image width)
`$imageName`	Stores the name of the image (if specified, when the class is initialized, full path)
`$imageType`	Stores the type of the image (JPEG, or PNG for example)

The `$imageComments` variable is not initialized inside the constructor of the class library (it is not necessary for any of the ImageMagick functions). However, a class variable is reserved since the image comments are part of the image's headers, and are useful when describing an image in the user interface:

```
var $imageComments;
```

If we are working on a machine where we do not have administrative rights and ImageMagick is not in our path, we specify the full path of the folder where we have installed ImageMagick, like this:

```
var $imageMagickPath = 'c:/bin/ImageMagick/';
```

ImageMagick()

Now we can create the ImageMagick constructor function. When we create the object we can pass the filename as an optional argument to the constructor; we will do this in our example:

```
function ImageMagick()
{
```

Test for the number of arguments that have been passed through; if we have only a single argument then we must test to see if the file exists:

```
if (func_num_args() == 1) {
    if (@file_exists(func_get_arg(0))) {
```

If the file exists then we can call ImageProperties(). As we will see later, the ImageProperties() function sets the variables we declared earlier:

```
        $this->ImageProperties(func_get_arg(0));
    } else {
```

If the filename does not exist then we output an error message using the Error() member function:

```
            $filename = func_get_arg(0);
            $this->error
                (2,'Fatal error trying to use file "'.$filename.'": file
                doesn´t exist or has wrong permissions to be accessed');
        }
```

If the class was initialized without passing a filename, then we can continue creating the object, but we will not call the ImageProperties() function. In this case the script creating the ImageMagick object will have to set the $imageName variable and call ImageProperties() function manually:

```
    } elseif(func_num_args() == 0) {
```

If we get any other number of arguments, it means the class has been invoked incorrectly and we generate an error:

```
    } else {
        $this->error
            (2,"Fatal error invoking class  ImageMagick: we may use a
                maximum of one argument (an image filename) when
                invoking this class");
    }
} // ImageMagick()
```

That is it for the ImageMagick constructor function. The next function that we will create is the Error() function.

Error()

This function takes two arguments – the level of the error and the message. Earlier we defined a variable called $errorExitLevel that defined a threshold for the type of error that we can get. With certain errors we would want the script to exit but with minor errors or warnings we would like to continue:

```
function Error($level,$message)
{
    switch ($level) {
    case 2 :
        $this->lastError = "<b>Fatal Error:</b> $message<br />";
        break;
    case 1 :
        $this->lastError = "<b>Warning:</b> $message<br />";
        break;
    default :
        $this->lastError = "<b>Information:</b> $message<br />";
    }
```

The $errorLevel variable holds the current error level of the script. It was initialized to 0 and we want it to be at the highest error level that has been generated. We therefore test to see if the current error level ($level) is higher than $this->errorLevel, then we update $this->errorLevel with $level:

```
if ($this->errorLevel <= $level) {
    print $this->lastError;
    flush();
}
```

If the error level is greater than or equal to the threshold we have defined, then we exit from the script:

```
if ($this->errorExitLevel <= $level) {
    exit;
}
} // Error()
```

ImageProperties()

In the constructor function we called the ImageProperties() member function. It is the first function that we are creating, which will call one of the ImageMagick tools. As mentioned earlier, the Identify tool returns the image properties:

```
function ImageProperties($image)
{
```

Although in the constructor function (ImageMagick()) we tested whether the file existed or not, we also said that if no arguments are passed to it then we would have to manually set the $imageName variable and call the ImageProperties() function. Therefore, there is a possibility that we could call this function without setting the $imageName variable, hence we must test again:

```
if (file_exists($this->imageName)) {
    $this->imageName = $image;
```

We call the Exec() member function to call the program. This function will use a combination of the path to the ImageMagick installation and the command line, like this:

```
$identify = $this->Exec("identify $this->imageName");
```

The output of `Identify` will be parsed using a regular expression match, but before we do that we need to build the pattern:

```
$match = '#'.preg_quote($this->imageName).' (.+)  (\d+)x(\d+)
                              (\w+)  (.+)  (\d+) [b|kb|mb]#';
```

We can then execute the regular expression and store the results in `$matches`:

```
preg_match($match, $identify, $matches);
```

The output from a valid image file parsed with our regular expression will return an array of seven elements. We can now test to see whether we have 7 elements or not:

```
if (sizeOf($matches) != 7) {
     $this->Error(2,"This($this->imageName)is not an image
                 file.");
}
```

We don't have to exit the script here, as the `Error()` function will do that for us. We can now set the member variables to the values returned by `preg_match()`.

```
$this->imageType    = $matches[1];
$this->imageWidth   = $matches[2];
$this->imageHeight  = $matches[3];
$this->imageClass   = $matches[4];
$this->imageBits    = $matches[5];
$this->imageBytes   = $matches[6];
```

We can then clean up any variables that we no longer need:

```
unset($match);
unset($identify);
```

If the file does not exist then we generate an error to that effect:

```
   } else {
       $this->error(2,"File $this->imageName doesn´t exist");
   }
} // ImageProperties()
```

We can now start writing the functions that allow us to modify our images. The first set of functions that we will deal with is the `Convert` functions.

Convert()

We will create a `Convert()` function that acts as a raw interface to the `Convert` tool. Here, we will have to provide all of the options for the `Convert` tool:

```
function Convert($outFile, $options)
{
```

The function will take two arguments – the name of the output file and the options that we will be passing to the `Convert` tool. All we do is build a command line with these arguments and pass them to the `Exec()` member function:

```
$output = $this->Exec("convert $options $this->imageName
                      $outFile");
```

If this is successful, the `Convert` tool will not generate any message. Therefore, we can test the length of `$output` – if it has something in it, then we get an error message:

```
if (strlen($output) > 0) {
    $this->Error(1, "convert probably didn't finish
                    successfully. Convert says: $output");
    return -1;
}

$this->ImageProperties($outFile);
return 0;
} // Convert()
```

The next set of functions that we will write also uses the `Convert` tool, but each function will execute only one set of the more popular options that we can pass to the `Convert` tool. We prefix each of these functions with `C_`.

C_Comment()

The first function will allow us to add a comment to the image file. The comment can be any string, except for some `%[letter]` values that are ImageMagick macros. These values are listed in the table below:

Values	Description
%b	Image file size (in bytes)
%c	If the comment is `V1.jpg` and we `-comment` to `%c v2`, we get `V1.jpg v2`
%d	Directory of image
%e	Filename extension (for example, `lalou.jpg` to `.jpg`)
%f	Filename (for example, `lalou.jpg`)
%h	Image height (for example, `1024`, representing 1024 pixels)
%i	Input filename
%k	Number of unique image colors
%l	Image label
%m	ImageMagick file format type (for example, JPEG, GIF, PNG, and MNG)
%n	Number of scenes
%o	Output filename

Values	Description
%p	Page number (useful for PostScript, PDF documents, and so on)
%q	Quantum depth
%s	Scene number
%t	Prefix of filename (for example, `lalou` from `lalou.jpg`)
%u	Unique temporary filename
%w	Width
%x	x resolution
%y	y resolution
\n	New line
\r	Carriage return

Here is the function:

```
function C_Comment($outFile, $comment)
{
    $this->Convert($outFile, "-comment '$comment'");
} // C_Comment()
```

C_Resize

Another popular action to perform on a file is to resize it. So we pass the new width and height that we want for the image to the function:

```
function C_Resize($outFile, $newWidth, $newHeight)
{
    $this->imageWidth = $newWidth;
    $this->imageHeight = $newHeight;

    $this->Convert($outFile, "-geometry  {$newWidth}x{$newHeight}!");
} // C_Resize()
```

The next set of functions interface with the `Mogrify` tool.

Mogrify()

As we did with the `Convert` tool, we will create a `Mogrify()` function that will act as a raw interface to the `Mogrify` tool, and some functions for the more common options that we can pass to it. Remember the `Mogrify` tool works with the existing image and does not need an output file to be specified:

```
function Mogrify($options)
{
    $output = $this->Exec("mogrify $options $this->imageName");
    if (strlen($output) > 0) {
```

```
                    $this->Error(1,"mogrify probably didn't finish successfully.
                                    Mogrify says: $output<br />");
               return -1;
           }


           return 0;
       } // Mogrify()
```

ChangeFormat()

This function changes the format of the file, for example, this will allow us to convert from a JPEG format to a PNG format. The format will have to be one of the ImageMagick-supported formats:

```
function ChangeFormat($newFormat)
{
    if (isset($this->imageTypeList[strToUpper($newFormat)])) {
            $this->Mogrify("-format $newFormat");
    } else {
        $this->Error(0,"This image format is not supported by
                        ImageMagick");
        return -1;
    }
} // ChangeFormat()
```

If the format is not listed, then we output an error message, which says that the format is not supported.

Resize()

This function will write an interface to resize an image. There are a number of constraints that we can use when resizing an image, and we will have to take these into account. These constraints can be accessed using the $resizeFlag variable. The function will create the options string and then pass that to the Mogrify() member function:

```
function Resize($newWidth, $newHeight)
{
    $this->imageWidth = $newWidth;
    $this->imageHeight = $newHeight;
    $this->Mogrify("-geometry '{$newWidth}x{$newHeight}
                                {$this->resizeFlag}'");
} // Resize()
```

These functions allow us to specify the restraints on the resize. All that they do is set the $resizeFlag member variable, and call the Resize() function.

```
function Resize_F($newWidth, $newHeight)
{
    $this->resizeFlag = "!";
    $this->Resize($newWidth, $newHeight);
} // Resize_F
```

The ! character forces the resize to use the exact dimensions we have specified:

```
function Resize_Gt($newWidth, $newHeight)
{
    $this->resizeFlag = ">";
    $this->Resize($newWidth, $newHeight);
} // Resize_Gt()
```

The > character tells the Resize() to resize the image only if the new size is smaller than the existing size – it will only allow us to make the image smaller:

In the same way the < character will tell the Mogrify tool to only resize the image if the new width and height are larger than the existing width and height:

```
function Resize_Lt($newWidth, $newHeight)
{
    $this->resizeFlag = "<";
    $this->Resize($newWidth, $newHeight);
} // Resize_Lt()
```

The @ character specifies the maximum area in pixels, of an image:

```
function Resize_Max($newWidth, $newHeight)
{
    $this->resizeFlag = "@";
    $this->Resize($newWidth, $newHeight);
} // Resize_Max()
```

By specifying a % sign in the options to the Mogrify tool we tell the tool to expect a percentage as the width and height values, rather than a pixel value:

```
function Resize_P($pWidth, $pHeight)
{
    $this->imageWidth = $this->imageWidth * $pWidth / 100;
    $this->imageHeight = $this->imageHeight * $pHeight / 100;
    $this->resizeFlag = "%";
    $this->resize($this->imageWidth, $this->imageHeight);
} // Resize_P()
```

Identify()

The final set of functions interface with the Identify tool:

```
function Identify($options)
{
    $output = $this->Exec("identify $options $this->imageName");
    return $output;
} // Identify()
```

IdentifyPing()

It is best to specify the -ping as an option to the Identify tool, since the entire file is not read into memory:

```
function IdentifyPing($options)
{
    $output = $this->Exec("identify -ping $options
            $this->imageName");
    return $output;
} // IdentifyPing()
```

IdentifyVerbose()

Specifying -verbose as an option will return a full set of information about the image:

```
function IdentifyVerbose($options)
{
    $output = $this->Exec("identify -verbose $options
            $this->imageName");
    return $output;
} // IdentifyVerbose()
```

When we ask for verbose image information, one piece of information that is returned is the user-specified comments. The next function uses a regular expression to parse the output and return only the comments.

ReadComments()

Here is the function:

```
function ReadComments()
{
    $output = $this->Exec("identify -verbose -ping
            $this->imageName");

    $match = "/comment: (.+?)\n  signature: /s";
    preg_match($match, $output, $matches);

    //We must make sure that we got a valid comment back:
     if (sizeOf($matches) != 2) {
        return $matches[1];
     } else {
        return -1;
     }
} // ReadComments()
```

The final function in our class is the Exec() function.

Exec()

This is the member function that is used to call the actual command line. The single argument of the command line along with its options that we created is appended to the full path to the ImageMagick installation and the results returned to the calling function:

210

```
    function Exec($cmd)
    {
        $command = $this->imageMagickPath.$cmd;
        return `$command`;
    } // Exec()

}//End of class ImageMagick
?>
```

Implementing the Class Library Functions

In this section, we will look at how to implement the class library through several examples in the following code snippets. We will create a simple page that will allow us to dynamically resize an image, change its format, and apply one of several different effect filters to the image.

Save the following code as `imagemagick.php`:

```php
<?php

require_once "class.imagemagick.php";

$path = '';
$ORIGINAL_FILE = "cheap.jpg";
```

First, we check to see whether we have an image name to work with:

```
if (isset($_POST['pName'])) {
```

Here we use the $_POST variable as `register_globals` is turned off by default since PHP 4.1; this means $pName won't work unless we specifically turn `register_globals` on.

Next, we create a new ImageMagick object and pass the filename to it:

```
$iObj = new ImageMagick($path.$_POST['pName']);
```

There are three possible actions that we can perform in this script: resize, convert, and produce effects.

We will first look at resizing the image:

```
if ($_POST['action'] == "resize") {

    $iName = $path.$_POST['tmpName'].'.'.strToLower
            ($iObj->imageType);

    $iObj->C_Resize($iName, $_POST['width'], $_POST['height']);

        if ($_POST['pName'] != $ORIGINAL_FILE)
            unlink($_POST['pName']);
```

Here, first we build a temporary filename based on the `tmpName` form field with an extension of the file type, then we resize the temporary file. Also, if we are not working with the original image then we can delete the previous temporary file.

Next we will look at converting the image:

```
} elseif ($_POST['action'] == "convert") {

    $iObj->ChangeFormat(strToLower($_POST['format']));

    $iName = preg_replace('/^([^\.]+)\.(\w+)$/i',
        '\1.'.strToLower($_POST['format']), $iObj->imageName);

    $iObj->ImageProperties($iName);

    if ($_POST['pName'] != $ORIGINAL_FILE)
        unlink($_POST['pName']);
```

The `Convert` action changes the format of the file. We call our `ChangeFormat()` member function and pass it the format that we want to change to. We also change the file extension to the new type. Once the image has been converted we re-initialize the image properties and again delete the temporary file.

This section of the script adds effects to the image. The effect to add is selected from a select box - **Add** button in our form:

```
} elseif ($_POST['action'] == "effect") {
    $iName = $_POST['tmpName'].strToLower($iObj->imageType);
    $iObj->Convert($iName, $_POST['effect']);

    if ($_POST['pName'] != $ORIGINAL_FILE)
        unlink($_POST['pName']);
}
```

If we have not specified an image name, then we must create the image from our existing base image:

```
} else {
    $iObj = new ImageMagick($ORIGINAL_FILE);
    $iName = $ORIGINAL_FILE;
}

?>
```

Let's now look at the HTML script:

```
<html>

  <head>
    <title>ImageMagick Manipulation Examples</title>
  </head>

  <body bgcolor="#FFFFFF">
    <table width="80%" bgcolor="#000000" border="0"
      cellspacing="1" cellpadding="5">
```

The PHP script is used to display the current image:

```
<tr>
  <td bgcolor="#FFFFFF" colspan="3" align="center">
    <?php
      print ("<img src=\"$iObj->imageName\">");
    ?>
  </td>
</tr>
```

The form lets us resize the image. We will need two input boxes – one for the width and one for the height. We also need to store some values for the temporary filename, the current filename, and the action to perform:

```
<tr>
  <td bgcolor="#FFFFFF" width="33%" align="center">

    <form action="<?php print $PHP_SELF; ?>" method="POST">
    <input type="hidden" name="pName"
           value= "<?php print $iName; ?>">

    <input type="hidden" name="tmpName"
           value= "<?php print uniqid(time()); ?>">

    <input type="hidden" name="action" value="resize">

    <b><u>Resize</u></b><br />

    W: <input type="text" size="4" name="width"> x
    H: <input type="text" size="4" name="height"><p />

    <input type="submit" name="submit" value="Resize"></form>
  </td>
```

Our second form is for changing the format of the image. Again, we need to store the current and temporary filenames, and the action to perform. Instead of input boxes for the width and height, we will build a selection box of the supported file formats:

```
<td bgcolor="#FFFFFF" width="33%" align="center">
  <form action="<?php print $PHP_SELF; ?>" method="POST">

    <input type="hidden" name="pName"
           value= "<?php print $iName; ?>">

    <input type="hidden" name="tmpName"
           value= "<?php print time(); ?>">

    <input type="hidden" name="action" value="convert">

    <b><u>Convert Format</u></b><br />

    <select name="format">
```

```
        <?php
         foreach($iObj->imageTypeList as $cKey=>$cVal) {
            print ("<option value=\"$cKey\"> $cKey ($cVal)</option>");
         }
        ?>

        </select><p /><input type="submit" name="submit" value="Change">
      </form>
    </td>
```

Our third form allows us to apply effects to the image. Our selection box this time contains a list of possible effects that we can apply to the image:

```
    <td bgcolor="#FFFFFF" width="33%" align="center">

      <form action="<?php print $PHP_SELF; ?>" method="POST">

        <input type="hidden" name="pName"
               value= "<?php print $iName ;?>">

        <input type="hidden" name="tmpName"
               value= "<?php print time(); ?>">

        <input type="hidden" name="action" value="effect">

        <b><u>Add Effect</u></b><br />

        <select name="effect">
          <option value="-cycle 16">Cycle Colormap 16 Positions</option>
          <option value="-despeckle">De-speckle image </option>
          <option value="-enhance">Enhance Noisy Image</option>
          <option value="-flip">Vertical Mirror </option>
          <option value="-flop">Horizontal Mirror </option>
          <option value="-monochrome">B&W</option>
          <option value="-negate">Negative</option>
          <option value="-normalize">Normalize Image       </option>
        </select><p />

        <input type="submit" name="submit" value="Add">

      </form>

    </td>

  </tr>

  </table>
 </body>
</html>
```

To see the resulting image, after implementing the class library functions and opening `imagemagick.php` in a browser, refer to *Fig 6.1 – ImageMagick Manipulation Examples* in *Appendix G*.

To see the resulting image, when we apply a negative effect to the image, refer to *Fig 6.2 – ImageMagick Manipulation Examples* in *Appendix G*.

Summary

In this chapter we started by taking a look at what ImageMagick is and what it can do. We looked at how we could get ImageMagick installed on UNIX and Windows machines. Then we discussed the three tools – `Convert`, `Mogrify`, and `Identify` – that we use in the chapter.

We went on to see how we can interface between ImageMagick and PHP – there is currently no extension for ImageMagick, so we had to pass information between ImageMagick and PHP with the `backtick` operator.

Once we had seen how we could do this, we created a class to perform some basic ImageMagick functions and then implemented the class with a simple form-based interface.

For a more realistic example of how to use the class library and the ImageMagick toolkit, refer to Chapter 11 which uses the class library to implement a fully functional Image Gallery application.

7

PDFs with PDFlib

In the preceding chapters we have looked at the extension libraries that allowed us to handle diverse tasks such as scripting Flash movies, creating images on the fly, and so on. In this chapter we will focus on PDF and create PDF documents with the help of the PDFlib extension.

In the course of this chapter, we will cover how to:

- ❏ Create a PDF document
- ❏ Place objects on a page
- ❏ Define and use colors
- ❏ Lay out text and use fonts
- ❏ Handle graphics and pictures

Finally, we will see an example of how to create PDF documents using an object-oriented approach.

PDF

Portable Document Format (PDF) started off on the dream of a paperless office. Initially, it was an internal project at Adobe – about creating a file format such that the documents spread throughout the company could be displayed on any computer, using any operating system. Version 1.0 of PDF was announced at the Comdex Fall in 1992 where the technology won a 'Best of Comdex' award. Gradually, it evolved into a very powerful file format that is worthy in a Web environment as well as in prepress.

PDF is a format that has all the elements of a document as an image, which one can view, modify, print, or send across the Web. PDF documents are useful in cases where we need to preserve the graphic appearance of the file. PDF documents can include compressed (JPEG, ZIP, or LZW) images, text, and graphics. They can either include (embed) the complete type fonts or the definitions of the characters used in a particular document (subsetting). The resultant file usually is very small as compared to a PostScript file or a JPEG picture with the same graphic information. This is essential on the Web, as the majority of the Internet population does not have access to a broadband Internet connection. Thus if we want to deliver a high quality output that uses custom fonts, colors, and images, together with a more or less complex layout, which can be viewed and printed using almost any operating system, then PDF is the ideal solution.

The PDFlib Library

PDFlib is a library that allows a user to create files in Adobe's PDF. PDFlib runs on a wide variety of platforms such as Windows (9x, 2000, and NT), Macintosh, and several UNIX platforms. Moreover, EBCDIC-based platforms, such as IBM eServer iSeries (AS/400) and zSeries (S/390 with MVS, USS, or Linux) are also supported.

PDFlib GmbH (http://www.pdflib.com) produces the PDFlib library.

PDFlib is available under two separate licensing terms:

- ❑   The Aladdin Free Public license
- ❑   The Commercial PDFlib license

PDFlib can be used without any registration only for non-commercial purposes. For all commercial purposes the commercial PDFlib License has to be purchased. The cost, as announced on the PDFlib web site, is $500 for one server CPU (for PDFlib only) and $1000 for one server CPU (for PDFlib+PDI).

What PDFlib Can Do

The PDFlib library can be used to create simple or complex PDF documents.

We can use PDFlib with PHP to generate invoices, address labels, product catalogs, reports, and so on. They can include various PDF features, like:

- ❑   **Different colorspaces** (as in PDF created by the Adobe Distiller)
  These colorspaces can be gray, RGB, or CMYK. RGB colors are used mainly for on-screen viewing while CMYK colors are used mainly in prepress processing. We will discuss these colorspaces in the *Colors* section later in the chapter.

- ❑   **Process and spot colors**
  These are two ways of representing color, designed for prepress processing.

- ❑   **Hyperlinks**
  These help to link to other pages in a document, other PDF documents, or to a URL.

- ❑   **Bookmarks**
  Allows for better orientation in a PDF file.

❑ **Paths and clipping**
These are used for drawing all kinds of objects.

❑ **Patterns**
This is used for custom-made fills and strokes.

❑ **Fully formatted text with PostScript and TrueType font**

Thus, PDFlib is quick, portable, and fully suitable for the Web environment and online PDF creation.

What PDFlib Cannot Do

Though the library is quite powerful there are some limitations:

❑ The library on its own has very limited text layout ability. It allows no hyphenation (breaking of a word at the end of the line), no automatic letter-space (space added or subtracted from basic distance between characters) adjustments, limited automatic word-space (space added or subtracted from basic distance between words) adjustments, and no function to flow text over several pages. We would need user-defined functions/classes that accomplish these text layout features.

❑ It does not have any encryption support.

❑ The commercial PDF import library (PDI) can be used to import a PDF file, but we cannot subsequently modify it.

❑ It cannot import files in formats that may include vector graphics, like Encapsulated PostScript (EPS) or Windows Metafile Format (WMF).

Now that we have got an idea about PDF and PDFlib, their features and limitations, let us take a look at the various PDFlib packages and how to enable PDF support in our PHP distribution.

Getting Started

There are two PDFlib packages produced by PDFlib GmbH (http://www.pdflib.com):

❑ **Source distribution**
The source distribution contains the sourcecode, the PDFlib reference manual, and other documentation but it does not include the PDI library. Also, it does not have the watermark and we have to compile it with PHP on our own. The instructions can be found at http://www.pdflib.com/pdflib/faq/readme_php.txt.

❑ **Binary distribution**
The binary distribution contains both PDFlib and PDI. However, it will display a 'www.pdflib.com' demo stamp across all pages, which can be disabled with a license key.

Here is the screenshot of the demo stamp:

Now let's look at the easiest way to include PDF support in our PHP distribution.

Enabling PDF on UNIX

If PDF is installed as a dynamic module we will need to enable it by adding this line to the top of our PHP scripts:

```
dl(' libpdf_php.so');
```

Enabling PDF on Windows

PHP extensions exist as separate DLL files in the standard Windows distribution of PHP. This means that we need to manually load the PDF DLL for each script we want to use it in, using PHP's dl() function. The Windows distribution of PHP comes with php_pdf.dll, which can be enabled by adding this line to the top of our PHP scripts:

```
dl(' php_pdf.dll');
```

> For all other systems we need to compile PHP with the libpdf_php.* extension for
> the system. Here, * stands for the appropriate suffix for the operating system.

Cross-Platform Scripts

One of the nice features about PHP is that scripts written on a UNIX system will often run on Windows systems and vice versa. In this case, however, we can't always be sure whether PDF will be compiled statically into PHP, or whether it needs to be loaded as a .so file or a .dll file. If we want to ensure that our scripts will run on both UNIX and Windows systems, we need to check two things at the top of each script – which operating system (OS) the script is running on and, if that OS is Linux, whether or not PDF needs to be loaded using the dl() function.

To determine which operating system the script is running on, we can check the first few letters of the constant variable PHP_OS. If they are 'WIN', we know we're running on Windows. Otherwise, it's pretty safe to assume we are on a Unix-based platform.

To determine whether or not the PDF extension is already loaded (in the case of a UNIX server where it has been compiled into PHP), we can use the extension_loaded() function. When we put it all together, we get a snippet of code that will check to see if PDF is already loaded and, if it is not, load the correct version for the current operating system:

```php
<?php

if(!extension_loaded('pdf')) {
    if(strtoupper(substr(PHP_OS,0,3)) == 'WIN') {
        dl('php_pdf.dll');
    } else {
        dl('libpdf_php.so');
    }
}
?>
```

Testing the Installation

To ensure that PDF support is enabled with the PHP installation, use the phpinfo() script, including our new PDF detection script, first:

```php
<?php

if(!extension_loaded('pdf')) {
    if(strtoupper(substr(PHP_OS,0,3)) == 'WIN') {
        dl('php_pdf.dll');
    } else {
        dl('libpdf_php.so');
    }
}

phpinfo();
?>
```

When viewed in a web browser, phpinfo.php will get a detailed list of all the features that have been compiled into PHP on the server. Look for a section labelled pdf, as shown:

pdf	
PDF Support	enabled
PDFlib GmbH Version	4.0.2
Revision	$Revision: 1.106 $

Refer to Chapter 1 for detailed installation instructions.

Programming Concepts

In this section we will discuss the basic rules and techniques of PDF creation. We will look at:

❑   The scoping system

❑   The basic code flow of PDF creation

❑   The coordinate system transformation

❑   How to draw paths and use fills and strokes

❑   How to define templates and patterns

❑   Text handling including deploying fonts and text formatting

❑   Image handling

❑   PDF import with PDI

Scoping System

Scripts using PDFlib must obey certain structural rules. These rules are very straightforward, for example, we do not think about closing the page before we open it. In the same way, PDFlib enforces a correct ordering of functions with a strict scoping system. It means that functions can be used only within a certain scope. For example, we can only construct the path when we are within the path scope, we cannot change the color or the linewidth. We can change the color and linewidth either before we start the path construction or after we explicitly finish it.

The following picture illustrates the relation between the scopes as defined in the table below:

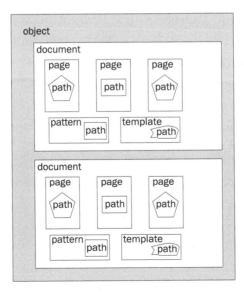

As we can see, pages cannot be nested and the patterns and templates must be defined outside pages. Also paths can be constructed only within a page, pattern, or template.

The following table lists the scopes and their definitions:

Scope	Definition
path	Started either by PDF_moveto(), PDF_circle(), PDF_arc(), PDF_arcn(), PDF_curveto() or PDF_rect() function, and terminated either by PDF_stroke( ), PDF_fill(), PDF_fill_stroke(), PDF_closepath_stroke(), PDF_closepath_fill_stroke(), PDF_clip(), or PDF_endpath() function.
page	Between PDF_begin_page() and PDF_end_page(), but outside the scope of path.
template	Between PDF_begin_template() and PDF_end_template(), but outside the scope of path.
pattern	Between PDF_begin_pattern( ) and PDF_end_pattern( ), but outside the scope of path.
document	Between PDF_open_( ) and PDF_close( ), but outside the scope of page, template, and pattern.
object	Between PDF_new( ) and PDF_delete( ), but outside the scope of document.
Null	Outside the scope of the object.

For example, here is a listing of the scopes of some functions:

Function	Scope
PDF_setcolor()	page, pattern, template
PDF_rect()	page, pattern, template, path; this function starts path scope
PDF_show()	page, pattern, template
PDF_setfont()	page, pattern, template

If we do not follow the scope of the functions, a PHP warning is thrown and no document is generated.

General Code Flow

When we construct the PDF object, the object's resource is returned. This resource is then used with all subsequent calls to the PDFlib functions. Therefore, while creating a PDF document we must follow a certain order for including the functions.

This is the general code flow when creating a PDF document:

1. Define a PDF object with `PDF_new()`

2. Start a PDF document with `PDF_open_file()`

3. Set the PDF information fields and parameters with `PDF_set_info()` and `PDF_set_parameter()`

4. Begin the new page with `PDF_begin_page()`

5. Draw objects and text on the page

6. Finish the page with `PDF_end_page()`

7. Close the document with `PDF_close()`

8. Use `PDF_get_buffer()` to get the buffer that contains the generated PDF document

9. Destroy the PDF object using `PDF_delete()`

The following 'Hello World' example complies with the general code flow, which we have to maintain while creating a PDF document:

```php
<?php

// helloworld.php

if(!extension_loaded('pdf')) {
    if(strtoupper(substr(PHP_OS,0,3)) == 'WIN') {
        dl('php_pdf.dll');
    } else {
        dl('libpdf_php.so');
    }
}

$pdf =PDF_new();                                    //define PDF object
PDF_open_file($pdf,"");                             //start PDF document

PDF_set_info($pdf,"Title","Hello world");           //set info fields
PDF_set_info($pdf,"Creator","helloworld.php");
PDF_set_info($pdf,"Author","wrox");
PDF_set_parameter($pdf,'openaction',"fitwidth");    //set parameters

PDF_begin_page($pdf,500,800);                       //begin new page

//draw objects on page
$font =PDF_findfont($pdf,"Helvetica-Bold","host",0);
PDF_setfont($pdf,$font,18.0);
PDF_set_text_pos($pdf,50,700);
PDF_show($pdf,"Hello world");
PDF_end_page($pdf);                                 //finish the page

PDF_close($pdf);                                    //close document

$buffer =PDF_get_buffer($pdf);                      //get the generated PDF document
$len =strlen($buffer);
```

```
header("Content-type:application/pdf");
header("Content-Length:$len");
header("Content-Disposition:inline;filename=hello_php.pdf");
print ($buffer);

PDF_delete($pdf);                                    //destroy PDF object
?>
```

This is the output:

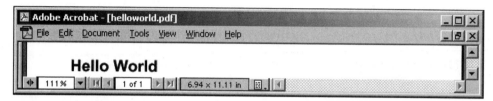

Code Fragment Wrapper Lines

To avoid repeating the same lines of code in all examples, we will place every fragment of code within the following wrapper lines:

```
<?php

if(!extension_loaded('pdf')) {
    if(strtoupper(substr(PHP_OS,0,3)) == 'WIN') {
        dl('php_pdf.dll');
    } else {
        dl('libpdf_php.so');
    }
}

$pdf =PDF_new();

PDF_open_file($pdf);

PDF_set_info($pdf,"Creator","pdflib");
PDF_set_info($pdf,"Author","wrox");
PDF_set_info($pdf,"Title","Example");

PDF_set_parameter($pdf,'openaction',"fitwidth");

PDF_begin_page($pdf,500,800);

//start of actual code fragment

  ...

//end of actual code fragment

PDF_end_page($pdf);
PDF_close($pdf);

$buffer =PDF_get_buffer($pdf);

$len =strlen($buffer);
```

```
header("Content-type: application/pdf");
header("Content-Length: $len");
header("Content-Disposition: inline;filename=example_php.pdf");

print $buffer;

PDF_delete($pdf);
?>
```

In most of the following examples only the actual code fragment is included unless otherwise specified.

Coordinate Systems

It is important to know the page layout before going into detailed discussions about the PDF document. To get a better idea we will take a look at:

❑   Default coordinates

❑   Metric coordinates

❑   Top-down coordinates

Default Coordinates

PDFlib uses PDF's default coordinate system (**default user space**). It originates from the lower-left corner of the page and uses DTP points.

> **72 DTP points = 1 inch**

The first coordinate increases to the right (x axis) while the second coordinate increases upward (y axis). Our script can change the default user space by rotating, scaling, translating, or skewing which results in a new user space. This way, we can draw rotated or skewed objects like rectangles and text.

The following code fragment generates a square and then another square rotated over it:

```
//start of fragment: rotate.php

PDF_setcolor($pdf,"stroke","gray",0,1,1,1);    //Set color to black
PDF_rect($pdf,100,500,100,100);                //Draw square
PDF_stroke($pdf);                              //Stroke it close path scope

PDF_save($pdf);                                //Save user space
PDF_translate($pdf,200,500);                   //Translate user space

PDF_rotate($pdf,30);                           //Rotate user space
                                               //Counterclockwise
PDF_rect($pdf,0,0,100,100);                     //Draw another square
PDF_stroke($pdf);                              //Stroke it close path scope
PDF_restore($pdf);                             //Restore user space
                                               //Next object won't rotate

//end of fragment
```

We get the following output, on executing the code:

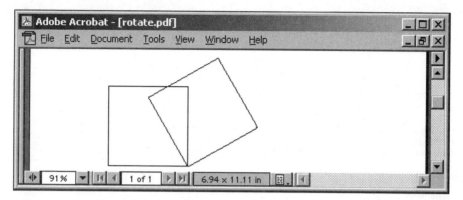

Once the object is drawn on a page it cannot be modified. The user space transformation does not affect existing objects; it only affects the future ones.

Hypertext functions – text annotations, links, and file annotations – are not affected by user space transformations and always use the default coordinate system. This means we cannot create rotated or skewed text annotation.

Metric Coordinates

The metric coordinates can be achieved by scaling the user space. The scaling factor is derived from the definition of the DTP point: 1 pt = (1 inch / 72) = (25.4 mm / 72) = 0.3528 mm. Thus, we have found the ratio by which we can scale the user space.

Once the following command has been executed within the page scope:

```
PDF_scale($pdf, 1/0.3528, 1/0.3528);
```

PDFlib will understand that all coordinates are in millimeters until the PDF_end_page () command.

Top-Down Coordinates

Some designers prefer top-down coordinates. We can achieve this with an appropriate user space transformation.

Placing Text with Top-Down Coordinates

Let us take a look at this transformation:

```
//start of the fragment: top-down_1.php

PDF_translate($pdf,0,800);                    // move the coordinate origin
PDF_scale($pdf,1,-1);                         // reflect at the horizontal axis

$font =PDF_findfont($pdf,"Helvetica-Bold","host",0);    // sample text

PDF_setfont($pdf,$font,18.0);
```

```
PDF_set_text_pos($pdf,200,100);

PDF_show($pdf,"Top-down coordinates!");

//end of fragment
```

which produces the output:

As we can see, the text is also 'top-down'. This is because the user space transformation affects everything including font size (except annotations). If we use the negative font size, with this command:

```
PDF_setfont($pdf,$font,-18.0);
```

the result is better but the text is mirrored.

Here then is the new code:

```
//start of the fragment: top-down_2.php

PDF_translate($pdf,0,800);                    // move the coordinate origin
PDF_scale($pdf,1,-1);                         // reflect at the horizontal axis

$font =PDF_findfont($pdf,"Helvetica-Bold","host",0);        // sample text

PDF_setfont($pdf,$font,-18.0);

PDF_set_text_pos($pdf,200,100);

PDF_show($pdf,"Top-down coordinates!");

//end of fragment
```

and this is the output:

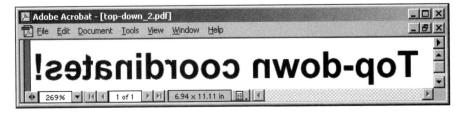

The following line of code can be used to compensate for the mirroring:

```
PDF_set_value($pdf,"horizscaling",-100);
```

Here is a better piece of code:

```
//start of fragment: top-down_3.php

PDF_translate($pdf,0,800);                    //move the coordinate origin
PDF_scale($pdf,1,-1);                         //reflect at the horizontal axis

$font =PDF_findfont($pdf,"Helvetica-Bold","host",0);            //sample text

PDF_setfont($pdf,$font,-18.0);                //make the text point upwards

PDF_set_value($pdf,"horizscaling",-100);      //compensate for the mirroring

PDF_set_text_pos($pdf,200,100);               //now use top-down coordinates

PDF_show($pdf,"Top-down coordinates!");

//end of fragment
```

and the output is:

Placing Images with Top-Down Coordinates

The scenario repeats when we try to place an image with top-down coordinates:

```
//start of fragment: top-down_image_mirrored.php

//set top-down coordinates

PDF_translate($pdf,0,800);                    //move the coordinate origin
PDF_scale($pdf,1,-1);                         //reflect at the horizontal axis

PDF_save($pdf);
PDF_translate($pdf,100,200);                  //Temporarily translate origin
                                              // to the desired coordinates

$img = PDF_open_image_file($pdf,"gif","php4.gif","",0);

if ($img) {
    PDF_place_image($pdf,$img,0,0,1);
}

PDF_restore($pdf);

//end of fragment
```

Make sure that the image file provided is in the same directory as the PHP script.

We end up with the mirrored image:

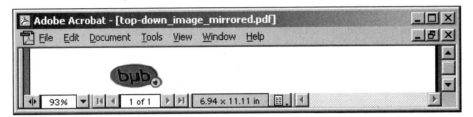

To compensate this we add `PDF_scale($pdf,1,-1)` in the code:

```
//start of fragment: top-down_image_ok.php

//set top-down coordinates

PDF_translate($pdf,0,800);              //move the coordinate origin
PDF_scale($pdf,1,-1);                   //reflect at the horizontal axis

PDF_save($pdf);

//Place the image's lower left corner to the desired coordinates - 100,200

PDF_translate($pdf,100,200);            //Temporarily translate origin
                                        // to the desired coordinates

PDF_scale($pdf,1,-1);

$img = PDF_open_image_file($pdf,"gif","php4.gif","",0);

if ($img) {
    PDF_place_image($pdf,$img,0,0,1);
}

PDF_restore($pdf);

//end of fragment
```

This is the result of the code:

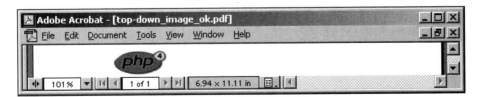

> Another viable alternative is to leave the bottom-up coordinates, but subtract every top-down y coordinate from the actual page height, like this: `$bottom_up_y = $page_height - $top_down_y;` which will give us the bottom-up y coordinate.

Page and Coordinate Limits

Let us get acquainted with the permissible page size and number of pages of a document.

Page Size

Although PDF and PDFlib do not restrict the usable page size, the Adobe Acrobat implementation does. The following table shows these limits:

Acrobat Version	Minimum Page Size	Maximum Page Size
Acrobat 3	1" = 72 pt = 2.54 cm	45" = 3240 pt = 114.3 cm
Acrobat 4 and 5	1/24" = 3 pt = 0.106 cm	200" = 14400 pt = 508 cm

Number of Pages in the Document

There is no limit to the number of generated pages in a document. If we avoid using the deprecated functions in PHP, the generated PDF document will be slim and fast regardless of its number of pages.

A comprehensive listing of deprecated functions is available at http://www.php.net/manual/en/ref.pdf.php.

Paths – Circles, Rectangles, Lines, and Curves

Paths are shapes made of an arbitrary number of curves, straight lines, circles, or rectangles. There are several operations that can be performed on a path:

❑ **Fill**
It paints the region enclosed by the path using the supplied parameter

❑ **Stroke**
It draws a line along the path using the supplied parameter

❑ **Clipping**
It reduces the image area for all subsequent operations by replacing the current clipping area with the intersection of the current clipping area and the path

The disconnected sections of a path are called subpaths.

Just drawing the path doesn't show anything – we have to stroke it or fill it. Most of the functions use the concept of a current point. We can imagine it as a location of the pen used for drawing. The general flow of code is:

1. Set color for fill and/or stroke using `PDF_setcolor()`

2. Set line parameters using PDF_linewidth(), PDF_setdash(), PDF_setpolydash(), PDF_setflat, PDF_setlinejoin(), PDF_setlinecap(), PDF_setmiterlimit()

3. Construct the path using PDF_moveto(), PDF_circle(), PDF_arc(), PDF_arcn(), PDF_curveto() or PDF_rect()

4. Finish the path using PDF_stroke( ), PDF_fill(), PDF_fill_stroke(), PDF_closepath_stroke(), PDF_closepath_fill_stroke(), PDF_clip(), or PDF_endpath()

We must not draw the path unless we finish it properly. The general rule is: 'Do not change the appearance within the path construction'. If we do not follow this rule, an error occurs and the PDF document is not generated. To get rid of such errors, we can do one of the following:

❑ Move the command PDF_setcolor() before the path construction.

❑ Add one of the path finishing commands before PDF_setcolor().

Before we go any further, it is best to explain the PDF_setcolor() function.

PDF_setcolor()

We can specify the color for stroking and filling the regions enclosed by the path and the interiors of the text characters using:

```
void PDF_setcolor(int pdf object, string type, string colorspace, float c1 [,
float c2 [, float c3 [, float c4]]]);
```

Let us take a look at the parameters:

❑ **pdf** – the resource handle.

❑ **type** – the type is fill for filling color, stroke for stroking color, and both for filling and stroking color.

❑ **colorspace** – colorspace is used to specify colors in the following manner:

   ❑ **gray**
      If the colorspace is gray, then the value of c1 should be between 0 (white) and 1 (black); the values of c2, c3, c4 are not specified in this case.

      For instance, a black fill is defined by:

      ```
      PDF_setcolor($pdf, "fill", "gray", 1, 0, 0, 0);
      ```

   ❑ **RGB**
      If the colorspace is RGB, then c1, c2, and c3 represent the percentages of red, green, and blue respectively. The value of c4 is not specified in this case. If the values of c1, c2, c3 are (0, 0, 0) then it corresponds to black and if the values are (1, 1, 1) then it corresponds to white.

      For instance, a green RGB stroke is defined by:

      ```
      PDF_setcolor($pdf, "stroke", "rgb", 0, 1, 0, 0);
      ```

      The default color value for stroke and fill is black (0 0 0) in the RGB colorspace.

❏ **CMYK**
This color space is defined by all the four parameters – c_1, c_2, c_3, and c_4. If the parameter value is 0, it means 'no color' (0%) and if the value=1, it means 'full color' (100%).

Also $(0, 0, 0, 0)$ = white, $(1, 0, 0, 0)$ = cyan, $(0, 1, 0, 0)$ = magenta, $(0, 0, 1, 0)$ = yellow, $(0, 0, 0, 1)$ = black.

For example, a magenta fill and stroke is defined by:

```
PDF_setcolor($pdf, "both", "cmyk", 0, 1, 0, 0);
```

❏ **spot color**
In this `colorspace`, c_1 is defined as the color handle and c_2 as the tint. However, before using a spot color we have to create it and obtain the spot color handle. We also specify the tint value, where 0=no color (0%) and 1=full color (100%).

For example, a spot color fill defined as 50% gray is given by:

```
PDF_setcolor($pdf, "fill", "gray", 0.5, 0, 0, 0);
$myGreySpot = PDF_makespotcolor($pdf,"myGrey");
PDF_setcolor($pdf, "fill", "spot", $myGreySpot, 1,0,0);
```

❏ **pattern**
This involves filling an object composed of text, paths, and/or images (not supported in Acrobat 3 PDF version 1.2).

In this case, c_1 is defined as the pattern handle. Here is how we set fill with pattern:

```
PDF_setcolor($pdf, "fill", "pattern", $patternHandle,0,0,0);
```

We will see how to define pattern and obtain its handle under *Patterns* in the *Templates* section.

Now that we have detailed the most important command, we can use the path commands. In the following example we will include three features.

Firstly, we will draw a simple dashed black line:

```
//start of fragment: fill_stroke_clipping.php

//a simple dashed black line
PDF_setdash($pdf,2,2);
PDF_setcolor($pdf,'stroke','rgb',0,0,0,0);
PDF_moveto($pdf,400,50);
PDF_lineto($pdf,450,150);
PDF_stroke($pdf);
```

then a rectangle (not dashed) and a blue circle:

```
//a rectangle and a blue circle
PDF_setdash($pdf,0,0);
PDF_setcolor($pdf,'stroke','rgb',0,0,0,0);
```

```
PDF_setcolor($pdf,'fill','rgb',0,0,1,0);
PDF_rect($pdf,50,100,100,50);
PDF_stroke($pdf);
PDF_circle($pdf,100,100,40);
PDF_fill_stroke($pdf);
```

and use the rectangle as a clipping path for the blue circle:

```
//the rectangle as a clipping path for the circle
PDF_rect($pdf,200,100,100,50);
PDF_clip($pdf);
PDF_setcolor($pdf,'stroke','rgb',0,0,0,0);
PDF_setcolor($pdf,'fill','rgb',0,0,1,0);
PDF_circle($pdf,250,100,40);
PDF_fill_stroke($pdf);

//end of fragment
```

To see the resulting image refer to *Fig 7.1* – `fill_stroke_clipping` in *Appendix G*.

Templates (XObjects)

PDFlib supports a PDF feature with the technical name XObjects, which is more commonly referred to as templates. A PDFlib template can be thought of as an off-page buffer where we can create objects like paths, text, images, and so on.

After finishing the template we can use it in the same way as a raster image (bitmap image) and place it any number of times in our document. We can also subject it to geometrical transformation like scaling, rotation, or skewing.

Even if the template is placed multiple times on one or more pages it is included only once in a PDF file, thus saving on the PDF output file size. Hence templates are used for elements that appear repeatedly on several pages such as a company logo, crop and registration marks, or a constant background.

Using Templates

Templates are defined only outside a page description (that is, within the document scope) and used only within the page description (that is, within the page scope). However templates may also contain other templates.

We define templates using `PDF_begin_template()` which returns a template handle that can be used later by the `PDF_place_image()` to refer to that template.

The following example shows a simple template definition. In this case the template has been placed 3 times on the page:

```php
<?php

//script templates.php

if(!extension_loaded('pdf')) {
    if(strtoupper(substr(PHP_OS,0,3)) == 'WIN') {
        dl('php_pdf.dll');
    } else {
        dl('libpdf_php.so');
    }
}

$pdf =PDF_new();
PDF_open_file($pdf);

PDF_set_parameter($pdf,'openaction',"fitwidth");

$template = PDF_begin_template($pdf,50,50);          //define the template

//create a path composed of 10 rectangles
PDF_setcolor($pdf,'stroke','rgb',0,0,0,0);

for ($i=0;$i<10;$i++) {
    PDF_rect($pdf,$i*3,$i*3,10+$i,10+$i);
}

PDF_stroke($pdf);

PDF_end_template($pdf);

//begin page
PDF_begin_page($pdf,500,800);

//place the template 3 times
PDF_place_image($pdf,$template,50,700,1.0);
PDF_place_image($pdf,$template,150,650,2.0);
PDF_place_image($pdf,$template,300,600,3.0);

PDF_end_page($pdf);
PDF_close($pdf);

$buf =PDF_get_buffer($pdf);
$len =strlen($buf);

header("Content-type: application/pdf");
header("Content-Length: $len");
header("Content-Disposition: inline;filename=hello_php.pdf");

ECHO $buf;

PDF_delete($pdf);
?>
```

This is the resultant PDF document:

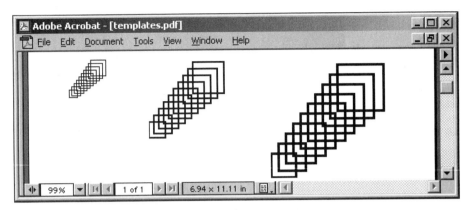

Patterns

A pattern can be thought of as an off-page buffer where we create objects – paths, text, images, and so on.

Besides colors, PDFlib also supports custom patterns, for fills and strokes. After finishing a pattern we can use it in PDF_setcolor() for fill, stroke, or both.

We define a pattern by:

```
int pdf_begin_pattern(int pdf, float width, float height, float xstep, float
ystep, int painttype);
```

Let us look at the parameters:

❑ width and height define the bounding box for the pattern.

❑ xstep and ystep give the repeated pattern offsets.

❑ painttype defines two types of parameters:

  ❑ If painttype = 1, it must define its own color specification which will be applied when the pattern is used.

  ❑ If painttype = 2, it must not contain any color specification but instead the current fill and stroke is used when the pattern is used. This means we can change the color of a particular pattern based on the fill and stroke color we define.

Using Patterns

Patterns are defined only outside a page description (that is, within the document scope) and can be used only within the page description (that is, within the page scope).

We use PDF_begin_pattern() that returns a pattern handle which can later be used by the PDF_setcolor() to set the pattern fill or stroke.

236

This example shows a simple pattern definition that is used to fill a rectangle:

```php
<?php

//script patterns.php

if(!extension_loaded('pdf')) {
    if(strtoupper(substr(PHP_OS,0,3)) == 'WIN') {
        dl('php_pdf.dll');
    } else {
        dl('libpdf_php.so');
    }
}

$pdf =PDF_new();
PDF_open_file($pdf);

PDF_set_parameter($pdf,'openaction',"fitwidth");

//define the pattern paint type = 2
$pattern = PDF_begin_pattern($pdf,20,20,20,20,2);

//create a path composed of 10 rectangles
for ($i=0;$i<4;$i++) {
    PDF_rect($pdf,$i*3,$i*3,10+$i,10+$i);
}

PDF_stroke($pdf);

PDF_end_pattern($pdf);

//begin page
PDF_begin_page($pdf,500,800);

//create rectangle with pattern fill
PDF_setcolor($pdf,'stroke','rgb',0,0,0,0);
PDF_setcolor($pdf,'fill','pattern',$pattern,0,0,0);
PDF_rect($pdf,50,550,300,200);
PDF_fill($pdf);

PDF_end_page($pdf);
PDF_close($pdf);

$buf =PDF_get_buffer($pdf);
$len =strlen($buf);

header("Content-type: application/pdf");
header("Content-Length: $len");
header("Content-Disposition: inline;filename=hello_php.pdf");

print ($buf);

PDF_delete($pdf);
?>
```

This is the result of the script:

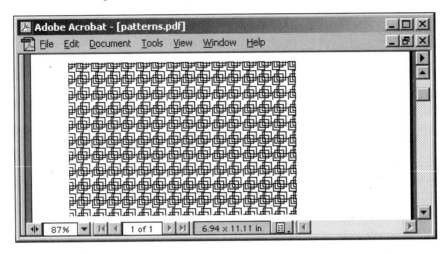

Now that we have looked at the coordinate systems, paths, and templates, let us focus on text handling in PDFlib.

Text Handling

In this section we will see how to:

❑   Use different fonts with PDFlib

❑   Use different encoding with PDFlib

❑   Lay out text in a block

❑   Lay out formatted text

Font

PDF supports a basic set of 14 core fonts, and PostScript and TrueType fonts.

Core Fonts

The core fonts need not be embedded in any PDF file. Here is a listing:

Core Font
Courier
Courier-Bold
Courier-Oblique
Courier-BoldOblique
Helvetica

Core Font
Helvetica-Bold
Helvetica-Oblique
Helvetica-BoldOblique
Times-Roman
Times-Bold
Times-Italic
Times-BoldItalic
Symbol
ZapfDingbats

Though the font is not embedded in the file, PDFlib needs to know about the width of the individual characters. This information, called the **metrics information**, is built into the PDFlib binary.

The metrics information of the core fonts built into the PDFlib binary can be used only with 'host' encoding (see the table in the *Encodings* section). Using an encoding other than the host encoding (for instance, macroman on a Windows system) requires metrics information files, which are included in the PDFlib distribution for just this purpose. The core fonts include only characters from the Windows ANSI set.

PDFlib supports both PostScript and TrueType fonts provided we supply the necessary information to PDFlib functions. In case of PostScript Type 1 fonts, the metrics information is stored in files with the extension *.pfm (PostScript Font Metrics) or *.afm (Adobe Font Metrics). Font outlines (actual shapes of characters) are stored in files with extension *.pfb (PostScript Font Binary) or *.pfa (PostScript Font ASCII). On the other hand, TrueType fonts store both types of information in one file with the extension *.ttf (TrueType Font).

PostScript Font

PDFlib supports the following formats for PostScript outline data and metrics on all platforms:

❑ Platform-independent AFM and Windows-specific PFM formats for metrics information. AFM has more information and can be used for any encoding supported by the font; PFM can only be used for a subset of encoding.

❑ Platform-independent PFA and Windows-specific PFB formats for font outline information in the PostScript Type 1 fonts (PostScript Type 3 fonts are not supported).

We must use the exact PostScript font name. We can find the PostScript font name in:

❑ The corresponding PFA or PFB file at the /FontName entry.

❑ The corresponding AFM file at the FontName entry.

❑ The font sample displayed by Adobe Type Manager (ATM). The font sample is displayed upon double-clicking the corresponding font (PFB) or metrics (PFM) file.

239

Note that these names can differ substantially from the ones in the Windows font menu.

Before embedding the font we must match its name with the font metric and outline files:

❑   By using the PDF_set_parameter()

❑   In the FontPFM and FontOutline section of the Resource Configuration file (see the *Resource Configuration File* section)

TrueType Font

PDFlib supports TrueType fonts on all platforms. The TrueType must be supplied in the Windows TTF format. Unlike with PostScript fonts there is no separate metric file for TrueType fonts. The following TrueType fonts are supported:

❑   Standard Latin text fonts with Windows character set (they must be used with winAnsi encoding)

❑   Unicode-compatible TrueType fonts (any encoding can be used provided it contains the required characters)

❑   Symbol fonts with custom character set (these must be used with built-in encoding)

On Windows platforms we can use the host font support of PDFlib. This means that PDFlib recognizes TrueType fonts available on the system without any additional configuration files. The exact TrueType name must be specified as it appears at the font menu at the user interface. For example, if we have font LIDSTFCE.ttf installed in the font folder, it shows up as 'Lido STF CE' in font menus and we have to reference it as 'Lido STF CE'.

On other platforms the font file must be configured by the PDF_set_parameter() function, or in the FontOutline section of the Resource Configuration file.

Encoding

Encoding is the vector mapping of the numerical code values to the character glyphs.

A glyph file is a file that defines the shapes of the characters in a font. The shapes can be defined either by outlines or by bitmaps.

PDFlib supports diverse encoding vectors for text handling. There are built-in encodings and custom encodings:

❑   The built-in encodings can be used in PDF_findfont() and need not be defined anywhere else.

❑   Custom encodings must be defined by an external code page file and this code page file must be referenced either by PDF_set_parameter() or in the Encoding section of the Resource Configuration File (see section to follow) before we use it with PDF_findfont().

The following table shows the built-in character encodings supported by PDFlib.

Built-In Encoding	Description
winansi	Windows code page 1252, a superset of ISO8859-1
macroman	Mac Roman encoding (the default Macintosh character set)
ebcdic	EBCDIC code page 1047 as used on IBM AS/400 and S/390 systems
builtin	Original encoding used mostly by non-text (symbol) or non-Latin text fonts
host	macroman on Macintosh, ebcdic on EBCDIC-based systems, and winansi on all others

The external character encodings distributed with the PDFlib source are:

External Encoding
ISO8859-2
ISO8859-3
ISO8859-4
ISO8859-5
ISO8859-6
ISO8859-7
ISO8859-8
ISO8859-9
ISO8859-10
ISO8859-15
CP1250
CP1251
CP1253
CP1254
CP1255
CP1256
CP1257
CP1258

We can also define our own code page. We can specify the external code page file that corresponds to a particular encoding, like this:

```
PDF_set_parameter($pdf,"Encoding","cp1250=cp1250.enc");
```

We can also specify the encoding that we wish to use with a particular font, like this:

```
$font = PDF_findfont($pdf,"Lido STF CE","cp1250", 1);
```

This command uses a font with Central Europe encoding.

Of course the font must be available for PDFlib through any one of the following:

❑   PDF_set_parameter()

❑   Resource Configuration File (for more details refer to the *Resource Configuration File* section)

❑   host font support on the Windows platform in which case the font must be installed in the host system

Most fonts do not include all encodings. Hence it is the user's responsibility that the given font includes all characters required by the given encoding. Otherwise we may end up with a document where we have missing characters on the lines.

Let us look at an example of bad encoding:

```php
<?php

//bad_font.php

////define the full path of the resource file
define("RESOURCE_FILE",'./pdflib1.upr');

$pdf =PDF_new();
PDF_open_file($pdf,"");

PDF_set_info($pdf,"Creator","hello.php");
PDF_set_info($pdf,"Author","wrox");
PDF_set_info($pdf,"Title","Hello world");

PDF_set_parameter($pdf,'openaction',"fitwidth");
PDF_set_parameter($pdf,'resourcefile',RESOURCE_FILE);

PDF_begin_page($pdf,500,800);

$font =PDF_findfont($pdf,"Helvetica-Bold","cp1250",0);

PDF_setfont($pdf,$font,18.0);

PDF_set_text_pos($pdf,50,700);

PDF_show($pdf,"Ceský text");
```

```
$font =PDF_findfont($pdf,"Helvetica-Bold","builtin",0);

PDF_setfont($pdf,$font,18.0);

PDF_set_text_pos($pdf,50,600);

PDF_show($pdf,"Ceský text");

PDF_end_page($pdf);

PDF_close($pdf);

$buffer =PDF_get_buffer($pdf);
$len =strlen($buffer);

header("Content-type:application/pdf");
header("Content-Length:$len");
header("Content-Disposition:inline;filename=hello_php.pdf");

print ($buffer);

PDF_delete($pdf);
?>
```

and here is the screenshot where we have a missing character on the second line:

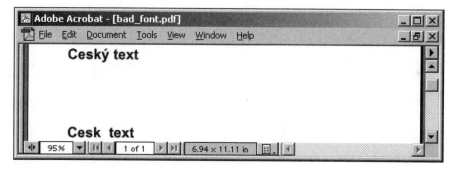

This problem exists with Acrobat core fonts too and it is significant for non-Latin character sets (for example, Central Europe, Baltic, or Greek). Therefore if we need to use these character sets, the best way to avoid problems is to use fonts including them, by setting the required encoding (for instance, CP1250) or built-in encoding if possible, or embedding the fonts (if the font license allows it).

Font Embedding

PDFlib is capable of embedding fonts into the generated PDF document. Alternatively, we can embed the font metrics (excluding the character outline data) into the document along with some general information. If the font is not embedded, the Acrobat reader will take it from the target system. If not available, it will replace it with a substitute font.

We must place the font files in a subfolder (FontFolder in our example). Also, we cannot use relative paths under Windows so we must define a constant (for instance, FONT_FOLDER in our example) and place the files in it.

Let us look at an example of font embedding in PDF:

```php
//start of code fragment: font_resource.php

//define path according to OS you are running under
if(strtoupper(substr(PHP_OS,0,3)) == 'WIN'){
    define("FONT_FOLDER","..\FontFolder");        //specify the full path
} else {                                          //of the sub folder
    define("FONT_FOLDER",'FontFolder');           // on OS other than Windows
}

//define external code page file
PDF_set_parameter($pdf,"Encoding","cp1250=".FONT_FOLDER."/cp1250.enc");

//first PostScript font example / embedded
PDF_set_parameter($pdf,'FontPFM',"DYLAN=".FONT_FOLDER."/DYLAN.PFM");
PDF_set_parameter($pdf,'FontOutline',"DYLAN=".FONT_FOLDER."/DYLAN.PFB");

$font = PDF_findfont($pdf,"DYLAN","host",1);
PDF_setfont($pdf,$font,18.0);
PDF_set_text_pos($pdf,20,750);
PDF_show($pdf,"Embedded Dylan PS Type 1 Font");

//second PostScript font example / not embedded
PDF_set_parameter($pdf,'FontPFM',"Euclair=".FONT_FOLDER."/Euclair.PFM");
PDF_set_parameter($pdf,'FontOutline',"Euclair=".FONT_FOLDER."/Euclair.PFB");

$font = PDF_findfont($pdf,"Euclair","host",0);
PDF_setfont($pdf,$font,18.0);
PDF_set_text_pos($pdf,20,700);
PDF_show($pdf,"Not embedded Euclair PS Type 1 Font");

//TrueType font example / embedded
PDF_set_parameter($pdf,'FontOutline',"Miltown=".FONT_FOLDER."/Miltown_.ttf");

$font = PDF_findfont($pdf,"Miltown","host",1);
PDF_setfont($pdf,$font,15.0);
PDF_set_text_pos($pdf,20,650);
PDF_show($pdf,"EMBEDDED MILTOWN TRUETYPE FONT");

//TrueType font example with different encoding / embedded
PDF_set_parameter($pdf,'FontOutline',"Lido STF CE=".FONT_FOLDER."/LIDSTFCE.TTF");

$font = PDF_findfont($pdf,"Lido STF CE","cp1250",1);
PDF_setfont($pdf,$font,18.0);
PDF_set_text_pos($pdf,20,600);
PDF_show($pdf,"Embedded Lido STF CE TrueType Font encoded cp1250 ešcržýáé");

//end of code fragment
```

When we execute this code, the result will look like this:

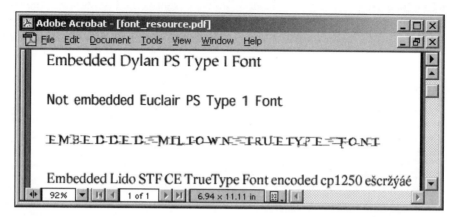

Make sure to specify the paths of the font files and the encoding file in the `PDF_set_parameter()`.

If we examine the fonts (listed in the `File/Document Properties/Fonts` of the Acrobat file) used in the PDF document created, we will see that four fonts are being used:

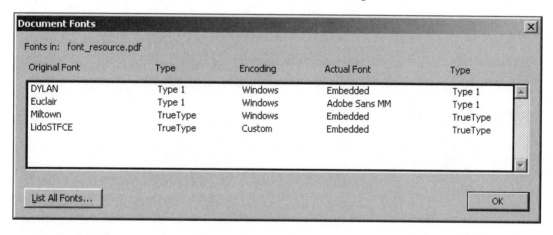

Font Subsetting in PDF

Only character glyphs actually used in the PDF document can be embedded. This technique significantly reduces the final file size.

Unfortunately, PDFlib cannot subset fonts. The workaround is to pass the created PDF to the Ghostscript, which will subset the fonts for us.

> **Ghostscript is a set of software that can read a PostScript or PDF file and display the results on the screen or convert them into a form you can print on a non-PostScript printer. Further information can be obtained at http://www.ghostscript.com.**

245

Of course the process takes a bit longer than normal, but provides a great effect on the size of a document. The time penalty is relatively small. If we have Ghostscript installed and we have the access rights to run its **ps2pdf** utility, then we can try the following example:

```
exec("ps2pdf $input_pdf $output_pdf");
```

Resource Configuration File

Font files and code page files are resources to PDFlib. Whenever we use a font other than the 14 core fonts or use a code page other than the ones built in the PDFlib binary, we have to define that resource, that is, match the name of the resource with the actual filename on the disk. There are 2 ways to define resources:

❑   Use PDF_set_parameter() for each resource

❑   Use the Resource Configuration file where we list all our available resources

We can combine both of them, but the definition of the particular resource shouldn't be duplicated.

Resource Categories

PDFlib uses four categories to define resources:

Resource Category Name	Description
FontAFM	PostScript font metrics file in AFM format
FontPFM	PostScript font metrics file in PFM format
FontOutline	PostScript, TrueType, or OpenType font outline file
Encoding	Text file containing an 8-bit encoding or the code page table

The same category names are used in PDF_set_parameter() as well as in the Resource Configuration File.

Defining the Resource Configuration File

In order to manage the PDFlib resources in a centralized fashion, PDFlib uses the Resource Configuration File. This is the place where the names of the available fonts are listed along with the paths to their metric and outline files. When porting our scripts to different hosts we just change the paths of the font files and not the scripts, thus making the scripts platform-independent. We can edit the configuration file in a text editor (like vi or Notepad) or it can be generated automatically by the **makepsres** utility available often as a part of X Window System.

The format of the Resource Configuration File is derived from a simple text format called Resource Configuration File (Unix PostScript Resource) that came to life in the era of Display PostScript and is still in use on several systems.

Here is an example of the Resource Configuration file `pdflib.upr`:

```
PS-Resources-1.0
FontAFM
FontPFM
FontOutline
Encoding
.

%Directory prefix example for Windows:
%/C:/apache/htdocs/wrox/fonts
%Directory prefix example for Linux:
%/home/httpd/html/wrox/fonts

FontAFM
%Example for an absolute path name
% with the prefix not applied (two equal signs)
Foo==Foo.afm
.

FontPFM
DYLAN=DYLAN.PFM
Euclair=Euclair.PFM
.

FontOutline
DYLAN=DYLAN.PFB
Euclair=Euclair.PFB
Lido STF CE=LIDSTFCE.TTF
Miltown=Miltown_.ttf
.

Encoding
cp1250=cp1250.enc
.
```

> **To use the Resource Configuration File successfully on Windows, we must have all the fonts we want to use, installed either directly or through Adobe Type Manager.**

If we place the above file in the same directory as the following script, it is not necessary to set the resources with `PDF_set_parameter()`.

Here is the code:

```php
//start of code fragment: font_resource_w_upr.php

//on Windows - uncomment and set appropriate directory
PDF_set_parameter($pdf,'resourcefile',"..\pdflib.upr"); //set the full path
//first PostScript font example / embedded
$font = PDF_findfont($pdf,"DYLAN","host",1);
PDF_setfont($pdf,$font,18.0);
PDF_set_text_pos($pdf,20,750);
PDF_show($pdf,"Embedded Dylan PS Type 1 Font");
```

```
//second PostScript font example / not embedded
$font = PDF_findfont($pdf,"Euclair","host",0);
PDF_setfont($pdf,$font,18.0);
PDF_set_text_pos($pdf,20,700);
PDF_show($pdf,"Not embedded Euclair PS Type 1 Font");

//TrueType font example / embedded
$font = PDF_findfont($pdf,"Miltown","host",1);
PDF_setfont($pdf,$font,15.0);
PDF_set_text_pos($pdf,20,650);
PDF_show($pdf,"EMBEDDED MILTOWN TRUETYPE FONT");

//TrueType font example with different encoding / embedded
$font = PDF_findfont($pdf,"Lido STF CE","cp1250",1);
PDF_setfont($pdf,$font,18.0);
PDF_set_text_pos($pdf,20,600);
PDF_show($pdf,"Embedded Lido STF CE TrueType Font encoded cp1250  š  žýáé");

//end of code fragment
```

The output will be the same as in the previous case.

Setting Resources without Resource Configuration File

The configuration can be also accomplished by PDF_set_parameter(). Here is the piece of code:

```
//specify the full path
PDF_set_parameter($pdf,"FontPFM","DYLAN=../DYLAN.PFM")

//specify the full path
PDF_set_parameter($pdf,"FontOutline","DYLAN=../ DYLAN.PFB")
```

How PDFlib Looks for Resources

When PDFlib wants to use a font (a resource) outside the 14 core fonts and not previously defined by PDF_set_parameter(), it needs to define the resource. In such a situation PDFlib searches for the Resource Configuration File in the following steps:

❑ On UNIX and Windows, the environment variable PDFLIBRESOURCE is examined and the filename is used.

❑ If no filename is found the resourcefile parameter is used, like this:

```
// give the full path
PDF_set_parameter($pdf,"resourcefile","../pdflib.upr");
```

❑ Else, the pdflib.upr in the current directory is used (this does not work on Windows). If the file cannot be opened or found, we will see a fatal error like this:

Fatal error: PDFlib error: Resource configuration file 'pdflib.upr' not found in ../font_resource.php

If the file is found, but the specified font is not found in the file, the fatal error will look like this:

Fatal error: PDFlib error: Metrics data for font 'DYLAN' not found in ../font_resource.php

Text Formatting

No graphic design can ignore text. We want a nice page layout for our e-invoice, report, or even address labels. Hence we want to work with the text in such a way that attributes like 'bold' and 'italic' get applied to the text as though we've done it in a word processor like Word or StarOffice.

Font Names – Bold and Italic Magic

In a text editor, if we want to change a part of the text to 'bold', we simply click the desired button. It appears as if 'bold' is the attribute of the font, but it is not.

For example, Helvetica and Helvetica-Bold are two different fonts. Together they form the Helvetica 'font family'. So, when we want to change a part of the text to 'bold', we also have to change the font of this text (for example, from Helvetica to Helvetica-Bold). The same applies to 'italic' – when we want to make the text italic, we have to use Helvetica-Oblique. Furthermore 'bolditalic' is also a separate font – Helvetica-BoldOblique in our case.

To use the selected font we have to create a font handle with `PDF_findfont()`, and then use it with `PDF_setfont()`. `PDF_findfont()` should be used only once in a document for a given font.

The following code fragment shows how to prepare a font, then set it active at size 12 and lay down the text at the desired position:

```
//start of code fragment: textformatting.php

$font = PDF_findfont($pdf,"Helvetica-Bold","host",0);
PDF_setfont($pdf,$font,12);
PDF_set_text_pos($pdf,20,700);
PDF_show($pdf,"Sample text");

//end of code fragment
```

This is the resulting PDF document:

Underline

Underline is a real attribute of the text. We can set PDFlib to draw a line at the appropriate position by:

```
PDF_set_parameter($pdf,"underline","true");
```

Text size is also an attribute of the text and is defined when we use `PDF_setfont()`. When using the metric system we must be careful that the size is understood in millimetres. Since the font size is usually given in points, we can simply use:

```
PDF_setfont($pdf,$font,$size_in_points*0.3528);
```

Text Layout of a Block of Text

The PDF_show_boxed() function is used to lay out a block of text (that is, several lines of text within the given boundaries). The PDF_show_boxed() function does the following:

❑ Lays the text within the given boundaries defined by the lower-left corner as in x, y, and width and height. It also honors line breaks.

❑ Aligns the text as defined by alignment: left, center, right, or justify

❑ Returns the number of characters that have not fitted within the given boundaries

❑ If feature is set to 'blind' no text is laid out. Only the number of characters which has not fitted within the given boundaries, is returned.

The following example demonstrates the use of the function:

```
//start of code fragment: show_boxed.php

//Here we define text
$text = "PDF_show_boxed() can lay out block of text of one-size, one-font. It can
align text left, center, right, or justify it. It cannot hyphenate words.";

$font = PDF_findfont($pdf,"Helvetica","host",0);      //prepare font
PDF_setfont($pdf,$font,11);                           //set font and size

//Layout text in boxes of width 150 and height 100
PDF_show_boxed($pdf,$text,50,650,150,100,'center');   //centered
PDF_show_boxed($pdf,$text,50,550,150,100,'justify');  //justified
PDF_show_boxed($pdf,$text,250,650,150,100,'right');   //right-aligned
PDF_show_boxed($pdf,$text,250,550,150,100,'left');    //left-aligned

//end of code fragment
```

When we execute the script the result looks like this:

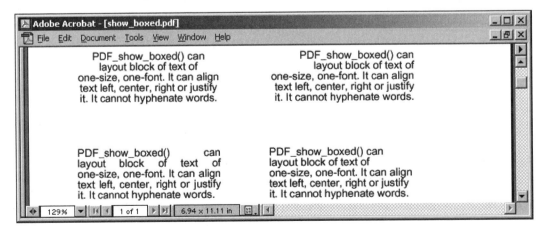

Text Layout of Bold, Italic and Different Font Sizes

In the previous section we have seen how to lay out a block of text. However, if we want to lay out text in bold or italic, or in different font sizes, we will have to create a simple layout engine function – a simple XML-to-PDF translator – as shown in the following example:

```
//start of code fragment: text_layout.php

//Here we define text with attributes with simple tags
$text = "Our text will be <b size=18>bold</b> and <i size=18>italic</i> and <n
size=36>huge</n>.";

//Define font for normal, bold, and italic text
$fontbold =PDF_findfont($pdf,"Helvetica-Bold","host",0);
$fontitalic =PDF_findfont($pdf,"Helvetica-Oblique","host",0);
$font = PDF_findfont($pdf,"Helvetica","host",0);

$base_size = 12;
$size = $base_size;
$font_face = $font;

//Set up basic font and starting point
PDF_setfont($pdf,$font,$base_size);
PDF_set_text_pos($pdf,50,600);

//Split the text
$r = preg_split("/(<[nib](?: size=[0-9]{1,2})?>)(.*?)(?:<\/[nib]>)/is", $text, -1,
PREG_SPLIT_NO_EMPTY|PREG_SPLIT_DELIM_CAPTURE);

//We walk through chunks of text
foreach($r as $chunk) {

  //In case of control tag we set the font and size appropriately
    if (preg_match("/<([nib])(?: size=([0-9]{1,2}))?>/is",$chunk,$m)) {
        $face = $m[1];
        $size = (!$m[2])?$base_size:$m[2];
        if ($face == 'b') {
            $font_face = $fontbold;
        } elseif ($face == 'i') {
            $font_face = $fontitalic;
        } else {
            $font_face = $font;
        }
    PDF_setfont($pdf,$font_face,$size);

    //Otherwise we lay out the given chunk of text
    } else {
        PDF_show($pdf,$chunk);                         //Layout text
        $textx = PDF_get_value($pdf,"textx",0);        //Retrieve the point
        $texty = PDF_get_value($pdf,"texty",0);        //Where text ended up
        PDF_set_text_pos($pdf,$textx,$texty);          //Prepare text position
        PDF_setfont($pdf,$font,$base_size);            //Return to base normal
    }                                                  //Font and base size
}

//end of code fragment
```

This is the resulting PDF document:

Image Handling

Images are an inherent part of graphic design. PDFlib is capable of sophisticated image placement and also supports many image file formats.

PDFlib supports the following formats:

- PNG images
- JPEG images
- GIF images
- TIFF images
- CCITT images – Group 3 and Group 4 faxes
- Raw data for images created directly in memory

Common Image Tasks

In this section we will look at the following image tasks:

- Embedding bitmap images
- Scaling and DPI calculations
- Forcing printed image size
- Non-proportional scaling
- Image masks and transparency

Embedding Bitmap Images

Embedding raster images (bitmap images) is easy. First we have to open the image with `PDF_open_image_file()` that returns an image handle. This handle is then used to call `PDF_place_image()` with positioning and scaling parameters.

Here is the demonstration code:

```
//start of code fragment: open_image.php

$image = PDF_open_image_file($pdf,"gif","php4.gif","",0);
if ($image) {
    PDF_place_image($pdf,$image,50,700,1.0);     //place once in 100% scale
    PDF_place_image($pdf,$image,200,650,2.0);    //place in 200% scale
```

```
      PDF_close_image($pdf,$image);
  } else {
      die("Cannot load the image.");
  }
  //end of code fragment
```

The resulting output of the script is:

> We must not call `PDF_close_image()` if we plan to use the image again in the same
> document. But we must call it before we close the PDF document with `PDF_close()`.

Scaling and dpi Calculations

The default resolution of PDF is 72dpi, and images are imported in this resolution (1 pixel is 1 unit in
user space). PDFlib does not change the number of pixels in an imported image – it does not do any
re-sampling.

The resolution contained in the original image (not all image formats contain resolution information) is
ignored. It may be queried by `resx` and `resy` parameters. Positive values mean resolution in pixels per
inch; negative values may be used to get the aspect ratio but do not have any absolute meaning. Zero
value means there is no information about the resolution.

The following example may be used to import `$image` with the resolution given in the image:

```php
  <?php

//script image_res.php

$pdf =PDF_new();
PDF_open_file($pdf);

$image = PDF_open_image_file($pdf,"gif","php4.gif","",0);

//Query the dpi values which may be present in the image file
$xDpi =PDF_get_value($pdf,"resx",$image);
$yDpi =PDF_get_value($pdf,"resy",$image);
```

```
//calculate scaling factors from the dpi values
if ($xDpi > 0 && $yDpi > 0) {          //Resolution is specified in the file
    $xScale = 72.0/$xDpi;
    $yScale = 72.0/$yDpi;
}elseif ($xDpi < 0 && $yDpi < 0){       //Only the aspect ratio is known
    $xScale = 1.0;
    $yScale = $yDpi / $xDpi;
}else {                               //There is no information about resolution
    $xScale = 1.0;
    $yScale = 1.0;
}

//We calculated scaling values from queried dpi_x and dpi_y. Now we
//create a new page sized exactly as the image size in the given resolution.

//Create a new page such that the scaled image exactly fits,
//and place the image
$width = PDF_get_value($pdf,"imagewidth",$image) * $xScale;
$height = PDF_get_value($pdf,"imageheight",$image) * $yScale;
PDF_begin_page($pdf,$width,$height);
PDF_scale($pdf,$xScale,$yScale);
PDF_place_image($pdf,$image,0,0,1);
PDF_close_image($pdf,$image);
PDF_end_page($pdf);
PDF_close($pdf);

$buf =PDF_get_buffer($pdf);
$len =strlen($buf);

header("Content-type: application/pdf");
header("Content-Length: $len");
header("Content-Disposition: inline;filename=hello_php.pdf");
ECHO $buf;
PDF_delete($pdf);

?>
```

The resulting PDF will look like this:

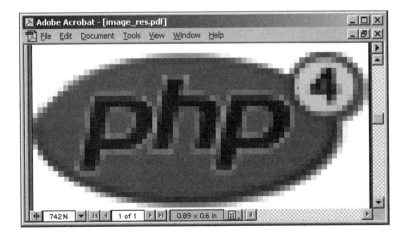

> We don't have to use **PDF_save()** and **PDF_restore()** here because we end the
> page immediately. Opening a new page restores the user space to default.

Forcing Printed Image Size

Often we may need to place an image into a given area on the page. In this case we have to calculate the necessary scaling. Of course we also have to avoid scaling the lower-left corner coordinates by translating user space before scaling.

Let us look at the following example:

```
//start of code fragment: image_size.php

$image = PDF_open_image_file($pdf,"gif","php4.gif","",0);
if (!$image) {
    die("Cannot load the image.");
}

//left corner coordinates
$x = 50;
$y = 600;

//forced height and width
$height = 150;
$width = 100;

//Calculate scaling necessary to force the width and height
$yScale = $height / PDF_get_value($pdf,"imageheight",$image);
$xScale = $width / PDF_get_value($pdf,"imagewidth",$image);

PDF_save($pdf);

PDF_translate($pdf,$x,$y);
PDF_scale($pdf,$xScale,$yScale);
PDF_place_image($pdf,$image,0,0,1);
PDF_close_image($pdf,$image);

PDF_restore($pdf);

//end of code fragment
```

The resulting PDF will look like this:

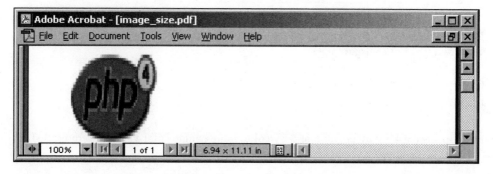

Non-Proportional Scaling

At times when we have an unproportionally scaled image, we simply scale the user space. Again we have to avoid scaling the lower-left corner coordinates by translating user space before scaling.

Let us look at the code:

```
//start of code fragment: image_unproportional.php

$image = PDF_open_image_file($pdf,"gif","php4.gif","",0);
if (!$image) {
    die("Cannot load the image.");
}

//left corner coordinates
$x = 50;
$y = 600;

PDF_save($pdf);

PDF_translate($pdf,$x,$y);   //Translate user space to the coordinate of the
                             //lower-left corner

PDF_scale($pdf,5,2);         //Scale to 500% horizontaly and 200% vertically
PDF_place_image($pdf,$image,0,0,1);
PDF_close_image($pdf,$image);

PDF_restore($pdf);

//end of code fragment
```

The resulting PDF will look like this:

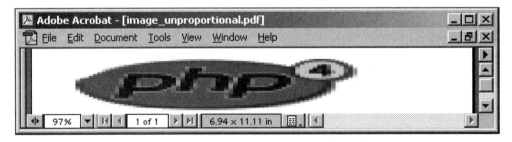

Image Masks and Transparency

There are two types of transparencies:

- ❑ Masking by position
- ❑ Masking by color

PDFlib supports masking by position and by color value (single color values, no ranges). Transparency information can be applied implicitly or explicitly.

In the implicit case the transparency information from the external image is honored in the following image file formats:

- ❑ GIF image files with a single transparent color value
- ❑ PNG image files may contain several flavors of transparency information (single transparency colors are retained)

Let us look at the code:

```
//start of code fragment: mask-implicit.php

PDF_setcolor($pdf,'fill','gray',0.8,0,0,0);
PDF_rect($pdf,0,0,500,800);
PDF_fill($pdf);

$image = PDF_open_image_file($pdf,"png","php4transparent.png");
if ($image) {
    PDF_place_image($pdf,$image,50,700,1.0);
    PDF_place_image($pdf,$image,200,650,2.0);
    PDF_close_image($pdf,$image);
} else {
    die("Cannot load the image.");
}

//end of code fragment
```

The masked PHP4 logo will look like this in the result of this script:

The explicit case requires two steps:

1. *First we load the image to be used as a transparency mask*
Only plain bitmaps are suitable for this task and they must be PNG or in-memory images. In order to be usable, the image must contain only a single color component and a bit depth of 1,that is, only plain bitmaps are suitable as a mask. Pixel values 0 are opaque, and pixel values 1 are transparent.

2. *Then we open the image with additional parameters*

Let us look at the code:

```
//start of code fragment: mask-explicit.php

PDF_setcolor($pdf,'fill','gray',0.8,0,0,0);
PDF_rect($pdf,0,0,500,800);
PDF_fill($pdf);

$mask = PDF_open_image_file($pdf,"png","mask.png","mask",0);
$image = PDF_open_image_file($pdf,"gif","php4.gif","masked",$mask);
if ($image) {
    PDF_place_image($pdf,$image,50,700,1.0);
    PDF_place_image($pdf,$image,200,650,2.0);
    PDF_close_image($pdf,$image);
} else {
    die("Cannot load the image.");
}

//end of code fragment
```

The output is the same as in the previous case.

> **Since PDF 1.3 (Acrobat 4) there is limited support for transparency.**

PDF Import with PDI

The PDF Import Library (PDI) contains a parser for the PDF file format, and prepares pages from the existing PDF documents for easy use with PDFlib. Imported PDF pages are treated just like imported raster images such as TIFF or PNG. We open a PDF document, choose a page to import and place it on an output page, applying any of PDFlib's transformation functions for translating, scaling, rotating, or skewing the imported page. Imported pages can easily be combined with new content by using any of PDFlib's text or graphics functions after placing the imported PDF page on the output page.

We have to understand that PDI will only import the actual page contents, not any hypertext features that may be present in the imported PDF document. Similarly, we cannot reuse individual elements of imported pages with other PDFlib functions. For instance, reusing fonts from imported documents for some other content is not possible. Instead, all required fonts must be configured in PDFlib. PDI will not remove any duplicate font data that may result from importing multiple pages. If an imported PDF document misses some fonts, the fonts will also be missing from the generated PDF output file.

Including the PDF Import Library with PDFlib

The PDF import library (PDI) is a part of the PDFlib binary code distribution. To include this feature, we must download the PDFlib binary package from http://www.pdflib.com. The bind directory of this package includes a PHP folder (along with other language-specific folders), in which there are various subfolders that contain DLL files for various PHP versions. We must use the DLL file that corresponds to the PHP version installed on our machine, copy it (or replace it with the source distribution DLL file, since it does not include this feature) in the extensions folder of our PHP installation directory and restart the web server.

Importing PDF Pages

Dealing with pages from imported PDF document is as easy as:

- ❏ Opening a PDF document with PDF_open_pdi().
- ❏ Checking the handle to see whether it has opened. The reasons for the check being incompatible PDF versions, corrupted, encrypted, or missing imported files.
- ❏ Opening the page with PDF_open_pdi_page().
- ❏ Again, checking the page handle to see if the page has opened. The reason we should do this is because at times a page may not be in imported PDF, as certain PDF pages use the LZW compression algorithm.
- ❏ Querying the width and height with PDF_get_pdi_value().
- ❏ Applying transformation, clipping, and so on.
- ❏ Placing the imported page with PDF_place_pdi_page().
- ❏ Closing the imported page with PDF_close_pdi_page().
- ❏ Closing the imported PDF document with PDF_place_pdi().

Let's now look at an example of placing a clipped PDF page. We will see how to import a page from a previously created document (the one that demonstrates font usage) and clip it with a rectangle from all four sides.

The PDF document that we want to import using PDF_open_pdi () must be in the same directory as our script. We must take care to see that we place the PDF document and not its PHP script along with the code. In our case, we will place the PDF document that is created when we run the font_resource.php script, in the same directory as this pdf_import.php code:

```php
<?php

if(!extension_loaded('pdf')){
    if(strtoupper(substr(PHP_OS,0,3)) == 'WIN') {
        dl('php_pdf.dll');
    } else {
        dl('libpdf_php.so');
    }
}

$pdf =PDF_new();
PDF_open_file($pdf);

PDF_set_info($pdf,"Creator","helloworld.php");
PDF_set_info($pdf,"Author","wrox");
PDF_set_info($pdf,"Title","Example");

PDF_set_parameter($pdf,'openaction',"fitwidth");

PDF_begin_page($pdf,500,800);
```

```php
//start of code fragment: pdf_import.php
$doc = PDF_open_pdi($pdf,"font_resource.pdf","",0);
if (!$doc) {
    return;
}

$page =  PDF_open_pdi_page($pdf,$doc,1,'');
if (!$page) {
    return;
}

$width =PDF_get_pdi_value($pdf,"width",$doc,$page,0);
$height =PDF_get_pdi_value($pdf,"height",$doc,$page,0);

PDF_rect($pdf,100,50,$width-200,$height-100);
PDF_clip($pdf);

PDF_rect($pdf,100,50,300,700);
PDF_stroke($pdf);

PDF_place_pdi_page($pdf,$page,0,0,1,1.0);

PDF_close_pdi_page($pdf,$page);
PDF_close_pdi($pdf,$doc);

//end of code fragment

//hide watermark
PDF_rect($pdf,0,0,1,1);
PDF_clip($pdf);

PDF_end_page($pdf);
PDF_close($pdf);

$buf =PDF_get_buffer($pdf);
$len =strlen($buf);

header("Pragma: no-cache");
header("Cache-Control: no-cache");
header("Content-type: application/pdf");
header("Content-Length: $len");
header("Content-Disposition: inline;filename=example_php.pdf");

print ($buf);

PDF_delete($pdf);

?>
```

This is the resulting PDF document:

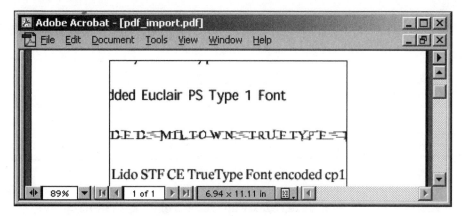

Implementing the PDFlib Functions

To explain the PDFlib functions better we will build a simple PDF layout class. We will create a one-page document which can be easily extended. We will use a collection of classes to define the layout of a page in an object-oriented manner. All we have to define are objects and their properties.

Let's see how the classes are organized:

❑ The PdfDoc class is the container class that represents the PDF document with one page

❑ The PdfObj class is an abstract class that represents an object on the page

❑ PdfObjRect, PdfObjLine, PdfObjCircle, PdfObjPict, PdfObjText, PdfObjPDF, and PdfObjNote, that extend PdfObj and represent appropriate kinds of objects on the document page

PdfDoc

We start with the definition of class PdfDoc. First we define some attributes with their default values:

```php
<?php

//script class.PdfDoc.php

class PdfDoc
{
    var $width = 500;                  // Default paper width
    var $height = 600;                 // Default paper height
    var $units =  2.834645669291;      // Millimeters in one DTP point
    var $debug = false;
    var $num_pages = 0;                // Page count
    var $curr_page = 0;                // Current page pointer
    var $pdf = 0;                      // Resource ID
    var $encoding = 'builtin';         // Encoding used by PDFLib
    var $objects = array();            // Objects' storage
    var $defaultFont = 'Helvetica';
    var $defaultFontBold = 'Helvetica-Bold';
    var $defaultFontItalic = 'Helvetica-Oblique';
```

Now let us focus on the constituents of the class. First, the PDFlib object is started with:

```
int PDF_new();
```

where `PDF_new()` returns the resource ID that can be used in the following function calls.

Next, we decide whether we want to create a PDF file using `filename`:

```
PDF_open_file(int pdf, string filename);
```

or generate the PDF file in memory:

```
PDF_open_file(int pdf);
```

Thus, `PDF_new()` and `PDF_open_file()` make up the basis of the class's constructor:

```
function PdfDoc($filename=false)
{
    //Init PDF document with defined filename or in-memory
    $this->pdf = PDF_new();
    $this->filename = $filename;

    PDF_open_file($this->pdf,$this->filename);
    PDF_set_parameter($this->pdf,'resourcefile',PATH_TO_RESOURCE_FILE);

    //Set some basic parameters
    PDF_set_parameter($this->pdf,'warning',"false");
    PDF_set_value($this->pdf,'compress',9);
    PDF_set_parameter($this->pdf,'openaction',"fitwidth");

    //Set info fields
    pdf_set_info($this->pdf, "creator", "pdfDoc 0.1.0");
    pdf_set_info($this->pdf, "author", "Wrox");
    pdf_set_info($this->pdf, "title", $this->filename);

    //init default fonts
    $this->fonts['defaultBold'] =
        PDF_findfont($this->pdf, "Helvetica-Bold","host",0);

    $this->fonts['defaultItalic'] =
        PDF_findfont($this->pdf,"Helvetica-Oblique","host",0);

    $this->fonts['default'] =
        PDF_findfont($this->pdf, "Helvetica","host",0);

}//PdfDoc()
```

Delete()

Once we finish with the PDF creation we have to destroy the object with:

```
PDF_delete(int pdf);
```

In the `Delete()` method we also include the possibility of not deleting the created file:

```
function Delete($unlink_file=true)
{
    if ($this->Filename && $unlink_file) {
        if (!unlink($this->Filename)) {
            print("Error deleting file");
        }
    }
    PDF_delete($this->pdf);

}//Delete()
```

Draw()

We have defined a new PDF document but there are no pages in it yet.

The page is defined by:

```
PDF_begin_page (int pdf, float width, float height);
```

Once we finish drawing objects we close it with:

```
PDF_end_page(int pdf);
```

If we do not want to add any more pages we will close the PDF document:

```
PDF_close(int pdf);
```

Now let's define the method for drawing the page and future objects on it:

```
function Draw()
{
    global $all_colors,$all_fonts;

    //Create page
    PDF_begin_page($this->pdf,$this->width,$this->height);

    //Go through all objects on the page and draw them with their own methods
    foreach ($this->objects as $key=>$rec) {
        $this->objects[$key]->draw();
    }

    //Close the page and close the document
    PDF_end_page($this->pdf);
    PDF_close($this->pdf);

} //Draw()
```

Output()

Once we have finished with the document drawing, we need to send the data to the browser. To do this, we collect the newly created PDF document with:

```
PDF_get_buffer(int pdf);
```

and then set headers so that the browser recognizes the incoming data as PDF.

Here is the method:

```
function Output($d=false)
{
    $buffer = PDF_get_buffer($this->pdf);

    header("Content-type: application/pdf");
    header("Content-Length: ".strlen($buffer));
    header("Content-Disposition:inline;filename=test.pdf");

    print ($buffer);

} // output

} //end of the PdfDoc class
```

This is all we need to do with the `PdfDoc` class.

PdfObj

In the previous section we created the `PdfDoc` class that represented the whole document with one page as a 'container' for the objects. Now we will create the `PdfObj` class and its descendants that will represent the different types of objects on the page.

Setting Stroke and Fill, Rotating, and Skewing

To create a PDF document with something on the page, we need to handle objects. First let us define a prototype class that will provide methods for object transformation (more precisely, user space transformation as discussed earlier) and setting fill and stroke.

These objects will be defined by an array of parameters. The most important are:

Parameters	Definition
xLB	X coordinate of left-bottom corner of the object (before transformation)
yLB	Y coordinate of left-bottom corner of the object (before transformation)
xRT	X coordinate of top-right corner of the object (before transformation)
yRT	Y coordinate of top-right corner of the object (before transformation)
fill	Fill color – array of RGB color components array (0,0,0) is black, array (1,1,1) is white
stroke	Stroke color – array of RGB color components (as fill)
linewidth	Linewidth of stroke
rotation	Rotation of the object
skew	Skew of the object
text	Text for layout
size	Size of text

The position of the object is defined by the bounding box with the coordinates (xLB, yLB) and (xRT, yRT):

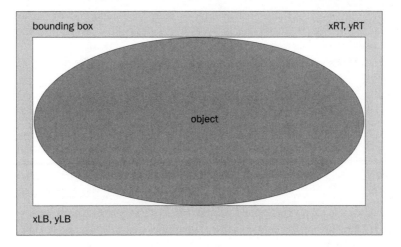

A bounding box is the smallest rectangle that encloses a geometric shape.

Let us initialize the class:

```
class PdfObj
{
    var $PdfDoc = false;                    //Link to parent pdfDoc object
    var $pdf = false;                       //Where to draw the PDF document
    var $pars = array();                    //Array of parameters
    var $saved = array();                   //Array of saved parameters

    //prototype constructor
    function PdfObj(&$PdfDoc, $pars=array())
    {
        $this->PdfDoc = &$PdfDoc;           //Store the reference to parent doc
        $this->PdfDoc->objects[] = &$this;  //Store itself to parent doc
        $this->pars = $pars;                //Store the parameters
        $this->pdf = &$this->pdfDoc->pdf;
    } // PdfObj()
```

SaveSpace()

Before we perform any user space transformations, we need methods to save the user space and also the parameters of the object. The parameters need to be saved because they may change, for instance, when the object is rotating.

Let us look at the method:

```
function SaveSpace()
{
    array_push($this->pars, $this->saved);      //Stack the parameters
    PDF_save($this->pdf);                        //Save the user space

} //SaveSpace()

function RestoreSpace()
{
    PDF_restore($this->pdf);                     //Restore user space
    $this->pars = array_pop($this->saved);       //Pop the parameters from
                                                 //stack
} //RestoreSpace()
```

Trasform()

The `Transform()` function will rotate and skew the object by transforming the user space. We want the objects to be rotated and skewed with the center of rotation (skewing) at the left-bottom corner; therefore we use the PDFlib function:

```
PDF_translate(int pdf, float x, float y)
```

to translate the origin of the user space (coordinate system) to the left-bottom corner and then change the object's coordinates.

Then we use the PDFlib functions to accomplish the rotation and skewing:

❑   `PDF_rotate()` to rotate the coordinate system by `rotation` degrees

```
PDF_rotate (int pdf, float rotation)
```

❑   `PDF_skew()` to skew the coordinate system

```
PDF_skew (int pdf, float skew)
```

Here is the complete method:

```
//Rotates and skews user space (de facto applies rotation and skew on
//object)

function Transform()
{
    if ($this->pars['rotation'] || $this->pars['skew']) {

        //Translate origin to left-bottom corner of the object
        PDF_translate($this->pdf, $this->pars['xLB'],
                    $this ->pars['yLB']);

        //Change appropriately the coordinates of the object
        $this->pars['xRT'] = abs($this->pars['xLB'] -
```

```
                                      $this->pars['xRT']);

        $this->pars['yRT'] = abs($this->pars['yLB']-
                                  $this->pars['yRT']);

        $this->pars['xLB'] = 0;

        $this->pars['yLB'] = 0;
        if ($this->pars['rotation'])
            PDF_rotate($this->pdf, $this->pars['rotation']);

        if ($this->pars['skew'])
            PDF_skew($this->pdf,0, $this->pars['skew']);
    }
} //Transform()
```

SetFillStroke()

Next we will create the `SetFillStroke()` function to define the fill, stroke, and linewidth that will be used on the object. We will use two functions:

❑   `PDF_setcolor()` to define the color

   `PDF_setcolor(int pdf, string type, string colorspace, float c1, float c2, float c3, float c4)`

❑   `PDF_setlinewidth()` to set the linewidth

   `PDF_setlinewidth(int pdf, float linewidth)`

To keep the example simple we use the RGB colorspace. In this case the values $c1$, $c2$, $c3$ are the respective RGB components of the desired color in an interval from 0 to 1, and $c4$ always stays 1. We also use simple lines; we don't use any dashed lines.

Let us look at the function:

```
//Set the fill, stroke, and linewidth

function SetFillStroke()
{
    if (is_array($this->pars['stroke'])) {
        list($c1,$c2,$c3) = $this->pars['stroke'];
        PDF_setcolor($this->pdf,'stroke','rgb',$c1,$c2,$c3,1);
    }

    if ($this->pars['linewidth']) {
        PDF_setlinewidth($this->pdf, $this->pars['linewidth']);
    }

    if (is_array($this->pars['fill'])) {
        list($c1,$c2,$c3) = $this->pars['fill'];
        PDF_setcolor($this->pdf,'fill','rgb',$c1,$c2,$c3,1);
    }
} //SetFillStroke()
```

FillStroke()

The `FillStroke()` function is used, after drawing the object, to fill and stroke the object with colors and linewidth defined in `SetFillStroke()`. It also finishes the **path scope**.

We will use three functions:

- ❑ `PDF_fill_stroke()` to fill and stroke the current path

  `PDF_fill_stroke(int pdf)`

- ❑ `PDF_fill()` to fill the interior of the path with the current fill color

  `PDF_fill(int pdf)`

- ❑ `PDF_stroke()` to stroke the path with the current color and linewidth and clear it

  `PDF_stroke(int pdf)`

If no fill or stroke is defined, `PDF_endpath(int pdf)` is used to finish the path scope.

Here is the function:

```
//Fills and strokes the object

function FillStroke()
{
    if (is_array($this->pars['stroke']) && is_array
                ($this->pars['fill'])) {
        PDF_fill_stroke($this->pdf);

    } elseif (is_array($this->pars['stroke'])) {
        PDF_stroke($this->pdf);

    } elseif (is_array($this->pars['fill'])) {
        PDF_fill($this->pdf);

    } else {
        PDF_endpath($this->pdf);
    }
} //FillStroke()

} // end of the PdfObj class
```

This is the `PdfObj` abstract class that represents the objects on the PDF page. In the following sections we will get down to defining the basic types of objects within the class.

PdfObjRect

We will start with a rectangle, using the function:

- ❑ `PDF_rect()` to draw a rectangle at lower left (x,y) with width and height:

  `PDF_rect(int pdf, float x, float y, float width, float height)`

Here is the class:

```
// Class PdfObjRect extends PdfObj class only in the Draw() function.

class PdfObjRect extends PdfObj
{
    function Draw()
    {
        $this->SaveSpace();

        //Prepare stroke and fill, transforms
        $this->SetFillStroke();
        $this->Transform();

        //Draw rectangle
        PDF_rect($this->pdf,$this->pars['xLB'],$this->pars['yLB'],
                            $this->pars['xRT']-$this->pars['xLB'],
                            $this->pars['yRT']-$this->pars['yLB']);

        $this->FillStroke();
        $this->RestoreSpace();

    }//Draw()

} //end of the PdfObjRect class
```

PdfObjLine

A line is drawn in the same way as by a plotter – move to certain coordinates, then draw a line from that point. For this we use two PDFlib functions:

❑   PDF_moveto() to set the current point.

    PDF_moveto(int pdf, float x, float y)

❑   PDF_lineto() to draw a line from the current point to (x,y):

    PDF_lineto(int pdf, float x, float y)

Here is the PDFObjLine class that is used to draw a line:

```
//Class PdfObjLine extends PdfObj class only in method Draw().

class PdfObjLine extends PdfObj
{
    function Draw()
    {
        $this->SaveSpace();

        //prepare stroke and fill, transforms
        $this->SetFillStroke();
        $this->Transform();

        PDF_moveto($this->pdf,$this->pars['xLB'],$this->pars['yLB']);
        PDF_lineto($this->pdf,$this->pars['xRT'],$this->pars['yRT']);
```

```
        $this->FillStroke();
        $this->RestoreSpace();

    } //Draw()

} // end of the PdfObjLine class
```

PdfObjCircle

This class defines a circle or ellipse by a bounding box (a rectangle), in which the circle or ellipse fits exactly.

First we have to make some calculations to find out the proper scaling, radius, and coordinates of the centre. Then we will use:

❑   PDF_circle() to draw the circle with centre (x, y) and radius r:

    PDF_circle(int pdf, float x, float y, float r).

Here is the object to draw an ellipse or a circle:

```
// Class PdfObjCircle extends the PdfObj class only in method Draw().

class PdfObjCircle extends PdfObj
{
    function Draw()
    {
        $this->SaveSpace();

        //Prepare stroke and fill, transforms
        $this->SetFillStroke();
        $this->Transform();

        //Calculate scaling if to be eliptical
        $xscale = abs($this->pars['xRT']-$this->pars['xLB'])/
        abs($this->pars['yRT']-$this->pars['yLB']);
        if ($f != 1) {
            PDF_scale($this->pdf,$xscale,1);
        }

        //Calculate centre coordinates and radius
        $x = ($this->pars['xLB']+($this->pars['xRT']-
            $this->pars['xLB'])/2)/$xscale;
        $y = $this->pars['yLB']+($this->pars['yRT']-$this->pars['yLB'])/2;
        $r = abs($this->pars['yRT']-$this->pars['yLB'])/2;

        PDF_circle($this->pdf,$x,$y,$r);

        $this->FillStroke();
        $this->RestoreSpace();

    } //Draw()

} // end of the PdfObjCircle class
```

PdfObjPict

As with the circle and rectangle, the position and scaling of a bitmap on the page is defined by the bounding box where it exactly fits. Therefore we have to query the width and height of the image by opening the image, placing it, and then closing it. The appropriate PDFlib functions used here are:

❑   PDF_open_image_file() to open the image file:

    PDF_open_image_file(int pdf, string type, string filename, string stringpar, int intpar)

❑   PDF_place_image() to place an image with the lower-left corner at (x, y) and scale it:

    PDF_place_image(int pdf, int image, float x, float y, float scale)

❑   PDF_close_image() to close the image retrieved with the PDF_open_image() function:

    PDF_close_image(int pdf, int image);

For the sake of simplicity this object does not use any masking and cannot utilize images from sources other than files.

Here is the PDFObjPict class:

```
//Object to draw bitmap (picture). Only GIF, TIFF, JPG, and PNG pictures

class PdfObjPict extends PdfObj
{
    function Draw()
    {
        //Open image, determine the format by picture extension
        switch (strtolower(preg_replace
                ('/^.*\.(.*)$/','\\1',$this->pars['filename']))) {

        case 'gif': $img = PDF_open_image_file
            ($this->pdf,'gif',$this->pars['filename']);
            break;

        case 'tif': $img = PDF_open_image_file
            ($this->pdf,'tiff',$this->pars['filename']);
             break;

        case 'jpg': $img = PDF_open_image_file
            ($this->pdf,'jpeg',$this->pars['filename']);
            break;

        case 'png': $img = PDF_open_image_file
            ($this->pdf,'png',$this->pars['filename']);
            break;

        default: return;
        }
```

```
        $this->SaveSpace();

        //Prepare rotation
        $this->Transform();

        //Calculate scaling of the image to fit in bounding box
        $height = abs($this->pars['yLB']-$this->pars['yRT']);
        $width = abs($this->pars['xLB']-$this->pars['xRT']);

        //Calculate scaling necessary to fit image in bounding box
        $yScale = $height / PDF_get_value($this->pdf,"imageheight",$img);
        $xScale = $width / PDF_get_value($this->pdf,"imagewidth",$img);

        PDF_scale($this->pdf,$xScale,$yScale);

        //Compensate for the lower-bottom coordinate
        $x = $this->pars['xLB']/$xScale;
        $y = $this->pars['yLB']/$yScale;

        PDF_place_image($this->pdf,$img,$x,$y,1);
        PDF_close_image($this->pdf,$img);

        $this->RestoreSpace();

    } //Draw()

} // end of the PdfObjPict class
```

PdfObjText

We will use `PdfObjText` to design a very basic line breaking and formatting mechanism. Our class will recognize the following formatting tags (based on HTML tags):

Tag	Description
<b></b>	For bold
<i></i>	For italic
<n></n>	For normal

Also, every tag can have an attribute size by which the text size can be set. For instance, `<i size=18></i>` would include an italicized 18pt-sized text.

Tags can neither overlap nor can they be nested.

The PDFlib functions used are:

1.   PDF_setfont() to set the current font in the given size

   PDF_setfont(int pdf, int font, float size):

2.   PDF_set_text_pos() to set the text output position

   PDF_set_text_pos(int pdf, float x, float y):

3.   PDF_show() to print the text in the current font and size at the current position

   PDF_show(int pdf, string text):

4.   PDF_stringwidth() to return the width of the text

   PDF_stringwidth(int pdf, string text, int font, float size):

As always we will define only the Draw() method, which will take care of actually drawing the text block on the page.

```
//Object to draw text block

class PdfObjText extends PdfObj
{
    function Draw()
    {
        $this->SaveSpace();

        //Prepare stroke and fill, transforms
        $this->SetFillStroke();
        $this->Transform();

        //Define local variables
        $text = $this->pars['text'];

        $leftEdge = $this->pars['xLB'];
        $rightEdge = $this->pars['xRT'];
        $bottomEdge = $this->pars['yLB'];
        $leading = $this->pars['leading'];

        $baseSize = $this->pars['size'];
        $size = $baseSize;
```

Now that we have defined the helper variables, let's set the font and base size. We will also set the values for leading and textrendering types.

Let's take a look:

```
//Set base font and size
$fontFace = $this->pdfDoc->fonts['default'];
PDF_setfont($this->pdf,$fontFace,$baseSize);

//Set leading and text rendering
PDF_set_value($this->pdf,"leading",$leading);
PDF_set_value($this->pdf,"textrendering",0);
```

We will read the ascender height so that we can adjust the starting point adequately; the text will fit in the defined bounding box:

```
//Read ascender height
$ascender = PDF_get_value($this->pdf,"ascender",
                    $this->pdfDoc->fonts['defaultItalic'])*$size;

//set where to start with text
PDF_set_text_pos($this->pdf,$leftEdge,$this->pars['yRT']-$ascender);
$textx = PDF_get_value($this->pdf,"textx",0);
$texty = PDF_get_value($this->pdf,"texty",0);
```

Now comes the finest part – we will split the text into an array. Whenever a control tag is encountered in the array, the appropriate font and text size will be set:

```
//Split text with tags
$r = preg_split("/(<[nib](?:size=[0-9]{1,2})?>)(.*?)(?:<\/[nib]>)/is",
            $text, -1,PREG_SPLIT_NO_EMPTY|PREG_SPLIT_DELIM_CAPTURE);

foreach($r as $v) {

    //if a tag is encountered then set appropriate fontface and size
    if (preg_match("/<([nib])(?:size=([0-9]{1,2})){0,1}>/is",$v,$m)) {
        $face = $m[1];
        $size = (!$m[2])?$baseSize:$m[2];

        if ($face == 'b') {
            $fontFace = $this->pdfDoc->fonts['defaultBold'];
        } elseif ($face == 'i') {
            $fontFace = $this->pdfDoc->fonts['defaultItalic'];
        } else {
            $fontFace = $this->pdfDoc->fonts['default'];
        }
```

We also check if the **chunk** is the line break \n. If yes, we adjust the text position to the beginning of the next line, and go directly to the next word. If the position reaches $bottomEdge we stop laying the text:

```
    } elseif ($v == "\n") {
        $textx = $leftEdge;         //Carridge return
        $texty -= $leading;         //New line

        if ($texty < $bottomEdge) {
            break;
        } else {                    //Otherwise lay down next chunk of text,
                                    // and take care of the line breaking
```

If the chunk is not a control tag, then it is the text to be laid out on the page. Since we want to 'line break' the text to fit into the bounding box ($leftEdge, $rightEdge, and $bottomEdge), we have to split the chunk again with spaces; this is simplified because comma, dot, and hyphen should also be a place for possible line break.

We use the explode() function to return an array of unbreakable words as we walk through it.

```
$w = explode(' ',$v);          //Split chunk with spaces
$i = 1;
foreach ($w as $word) {
```

First we calculate the string width of the current word with the PDF_stringwidth() and then check whether it fits between the edges. If $word alone does not fit into the bounding box, we exit immediately:

```
//Calculate string width of the word
$stringWidth = PDF_stringwidth
        ($this->pdf,rtrim($word),$fontFace,$size);

//If the word does not fit within margins, exit
if ($stringWidth > abs($rightEdge-$leftEdge)) {
    $this->RestoreSpace();
    return;
}
```

If the $stringwidth overlaps $rightEdge, we adjust the current text position at the beginning of the new line, like this:

```
//If the word does not fit, lay it on the next line
if ($textx + $stringWidth > $rightEdge) {
    $textx = $leftEdge;       //Carridge return
    $texty -= $leading;       //New line
    if ($texty < $bottomEdge) {
        break;
    }
}
```

Now we add space that was cut by explode() and we set the new PDF_set_text_pos() and PDF_show(). Finally we get the new current text position:

```
//Insert space if not at end of chunk
$space = ($i<count($w))?' ':'';

//Set the start point
PDF_set_text_pos($this->pdf,$textx,$texty);

//Lay the word
PDF_show($this->pdf,$word.$space);

//Read the new position
$textx = PDF_get_value($this->pdf,"textx",0);
$texty = PDF_get_value($this->pdf,"texty",0);
$i++;
}
```

After the layout of every chunk we return font and size to default:

```
            $fontFace = $this->pdfDoc->fonts['default'];
            $size = $baseSize;
        }
```

At the end of the cycle we use `PDF_setfont()` again to control the text position if it is not below `$bottomEdge`:

```
            PDF_setfont($this->pdf,$fontFace,$size);
            // Do not lay anything below the bottom edge
            if ($texty < $bottomEdge) {
                break;
            }
        }
        $this->RestoreSpace();

    } //Draw()

}// end of the PdfObjText class
```

PdfObjPDF

If we have the PDI library installed, we can use the function for placing existing PDF pages inside our new PDF file (as seen in the *PDF Import with PDI* section).

The usage of functions is similar to placing images:

```
//Object for PDF import
class PdfObjPDF extends PdfObj
{
    function
    {
```

First we have to open the PDF document and obtain the handle. If the handle is not valid, we exit. This may be the case when the placed file is not found or the file is not a valid PDF document. Here is the code:

```
        //open PDF
        $doc = PDF_open_pdi($this->pdf,$this->pars['filename'],"",0);
        if (!$doc) {
            return;
        }

        //open the page
        $pageno = (!$this->pars['page']) ? 1 : $this->pars['page'];
        $page =  PDF_open_pdi($this->pdf,$doc,$pageno,"");
        if (!$page) {
```

```
            return;
        }

    $this->SaveSpace();

    //Prepare rotation
    $this->Transform();

    //width and height of the bounding box
    $height = abs($this->pars['yLB']-$this->pars['yRT']);
    $width = abs($this->pars['xLB']-$this->pars['xRT']);

    //Calculate scaling necessary to fit PDF page in bounding box
    $yScale = $height / PDF_get_pdi_value($this->pdf,"height", $doc, $page);
    $xScale = $width / PDF_get_pdi_value($this->pdf, "width", $doc, $page);

    //Compensate for the lower-bottom coordinate
    $x = $this->pars['xLB']/$xScale;
    $y = $this->pars['yLB']/$yScale;

    //Place the page and close all resources
    PDF_place_pdi_page($this->pdf,$page,$x,$y,1);
    PDF_close_pdi_page($this->pdf,$page);
    PDF_close_pdi($this->pdf,$doc);

    $this->RestoreSpace();

    } //Draw()

} // end of the PdfObjPdf class
```

PdfObjNote

Hypertext functions allow us to insert annotations, file attachments, and links onto pages.

Here, we will look at the annotation note. It can be defined using:

❑   PDF_set_border_color() to set the border color for all kinds of annotations:

PDF_set_border_color(int pdf,float red, float green, float blue)

❑   PDF_add_note() to add an annotation for the current page:

PDF_add_note(int pdf, float xLB, float yLB, float xRT, float yRT, string contents, string title, string icon, int open)

Here is a listing of the icons that are visible when the corresponding icon name is passed through $icon in the PDF_add_note() function:

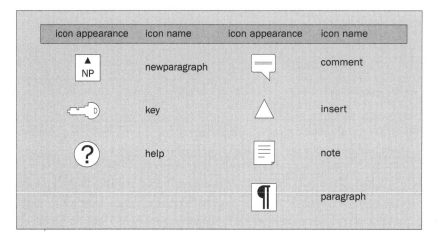

icon appearance	icon name	icon appearance	icon name
NP	newparagraph		comment
key	key		insert
?	help		note
		¶	paragraph

Further, the text in the annotation has to be in the PdfDoc encoding or Unicode.

Here is the code:

```
// Object to draw annotation

class PdfObjNote extends PdfObj
{
    function Draw()
    {
        extract($this->pars);

        //if the 'border color' is defined set it
        if (is_array($border_color)) {
            PDF_set_border_color($this->pdf,$r,$g,$b);
        }

        //create the annotation note
        PDF_add_note($this->pdf,$xLB,$yLB,$xRT,$yRT,
                     $text,$title,$icon,$note_open );

    }//Draw()

}// end of the PdfObjNote class
```

Putting It All Together

We have created a PdfDoc class that provides basic PDF document-handling capabilities and classes inherited from the PdfObj class, that represent the possible PDF objects usable on a page. To use it, we simply need to create a new instance of PdfDoc(), then add the objects on the page as we need, output it to the browser, and destroy it:

```
//Create a new PDF document
$p = new PdfDoc();

//Prepare some text
$text = "<b>PDFlib</b> \nsupports masking by <i size=12>position</i> and by <i
size=12>color</i> value (single color values, no ranges). Transparency information
can be applied implicitly or explicitly. In the implicit case the transparency
information from the external image is honored in the following image file formats:";

//Add a rectangle to the page
new PdfObjRect(&$p,array('fill'=>array(0,0,0),
                         'xLB'=>10,'yLB'=>10,'xRT'=>100,'yRT'=>100,
                         'linewidth'=>1,
                         'rotation'=>30));

//Add a picture on to the page
new PdfObjPict(&$p,array('xLB'=>200,'yLB'=>100,'xRT'=>300,'yRT'=>200,
                         'filename'=>'php4.gif', 'rotation'=>-30));

//Add a blue circle on to the page
new PdfObjCircle(&$p,array('fill'=>array(0,0,1),'xLB'=>100,
                           'yLB'=>50,'xRT'=>190,'yRT'=>140));

//Add some red text to the page
new PdfObjText(&$p,array('fill'=>array(1,0,0),
                         'xLB'=>300,'yLB'=>100,'xRT'=>400,'yRT'=>390,
                         'size'=>9,'leading'=>11,'text'=>$text,
                         'rotation'=>0));

//And finally some annotation
new PdfObjNote(&$p,array('border_color'=>array(0,0,1),
                         'xLB'=>300,'yLB'=>100,'xRT'=>350,'yRT'=>150,
                         'text'=>'annotation', 'title'=>'Title',
                         'icon'=>'help'));

$p->Draw();            //Draw the page
$p->Output();          //Send it to browser
$p->Delete();          //Destroy the object

?>
```

To see the resulting image refer to *Fig 7.2 – class.PdfDoc* in *Appendix G*.

Including PDF in HTML

There may be times when we need to display web elements, like search forms, banner updates, dynamically generated information such as stock quotes, news updates, and so on, on our PDF page. In this case, we will need to include our newly generated PDF document on the HTML pages.

There are four possibilities:

1. **Use PDF instead of the whole page**
    This is a standard solution. However, there is one disadvantage – we cannot include any form control element and the user has to go back or close the window to continue

2. **Use PDF in one of the frames in the frameset**

```
<frameset rows="2" cols="1">
  <frame src="navigation.php">
  <frame src"="http://server.maxdorf.cz/VIS/
                show_pdfdoc.php3?docID=0051&empty=-&sname=pdfdoc">
</frameset>
```

This does not create a problem with control elements but unfortunately IE may call the same document 3 times from within a frame, which is obviously not very good. The Netscape browser works fine.

3. **Use a floating frame (<iframe>)**

```
<iframe src="class.pdfdoc.php" width="100%" height="100%"></iframe>
```

4. **Use <OBJECT> and <EMBED> tags**

```
<OBJECT CLASSID="clsid:CA8A9780-280D-11CF-A24D-444553540000"
        WIDTH=100% HEIGHT=100% ID=Pdf1>
  <PARAM NAME="SRC" VALUE="class.pdfdoc.php">
</OBJECT>

<EMBED width=100% height=100% fullscreen=yes
       src="class.pdfdoc.php">
</EMBED>
```

These are a good alternative to using frames.

Removing or Hiding Acrobat Toolbars from the External Acrobat Window

Sometimes we need to hide Acrobat toolbar controls within the browser. We can do so, like this:

```
<a href="class.pdfdoc.php#toolbar=false">Link without toolbar</a>
```

The syntax #toolbar=false works in IE 5.5 SP2 on Windows 2000. In other cases, for instance in Netscape 4.7, the syntax ought to be #toolbar=0.

Summary

In this chapter, we looked at the basics of creating PDF documents using PDFlib.

We got acquainted with the various distribution packages of PDFlib and also discussed their possibilities and limitations.

We then detailed the basic programming concepts of PDFlib including the general rules for code flow and the scoping concept for PDFlib functions. We also discussed user space transformations in a PDF document, usage of colors and images, text handling, and font encodings with examples for each concept.

Finally we designed a PDF document using an object-oriented programming approach, where we created a basic container class (PdfDoc) for PDF document creation and a prototype class (Pdfobj) for defining the PDF objects.

We will use these foundation classes to build a PDF Template System in Chapter 12.

FDF – Sending Data To and From PDF Forms

The Internet has graduated from passive 'text' sites to dynamic 'form' sites. This dynamicity and interaction is possible as one can fill in online forms and submit the data thus posting the desired information on the server and getting the desired results.

HTML and HTTP provide a mechanism to perform this interaction quite easily through forms. A similar mechanism has been developed by Adobe for PDF documents. It is referred to as PDF Forms (Acrobat forms). The PDF form provides many advantages including cross-platform support, advanced layout and design features, document scaling and viewing, sophisticated printing setup, and field validation.

PDF Forms use the **Form Data Format** (FDF) which presents us with the possibility to populate a PDF document with data and dynamically customize it.

From the user's perspective, the only difference between HTML forms and PDF forms lies in the appearance. While HTML forms use the HTML format (they are rendered inside a HTML document by the browser), FDF documents use the Adobe Acrobat Reader to display their contents.

In the course of this chapter, we will cover the following aspects of PDF forms:

- ❑ PDF forms
- ❑ FDF
- ❑ Enabling FDF support with PHP

❏   Using FDF with PHP

❏   Creating a basic PDF form

❏   PDF form creation strategies

❏   FDF document structure

❏   Using JavaScript in PDF forms for validating PDF Forms

❏   FDF Functional Overview

Finally, we will discuss a detailed example where we will use most of the FDF functions we detail in the chapter.

PDF Forms

PDF forms are a special type of PDF document. We can use a PDF form to create interactive documents that contain form fields for an end user to complete. These form fields can be simple text fields, buttons, or something more complex. They can be designed to perform different types of functions, such as submitting or resetting a form, connecting to a hyperlink, or executing a script.

An FDF file is a specially formatted text file and is the by-product of a PDF form. This data can in turn be combined with a PDF form to make a completed (filled out) form or PDF file.

The FDF file or set of files may be generated from information contained in a database or gathered from data submitted on a web page. To do this kind of conversion requires the user to write scripts (such as PHP, JavaScript, and so on) to transform the raw data into the format required by FDF.

PDF Forms vs. HTML Forms

This is a good place to consider the criteria for going in for a PDF form rather than an HTML one. A graphical interface does not necessarily need a PDF form; we can do that easily with HTML. FDF forms are necessary if the form is really big or if we want to allow our users to complete the form offline.

Most forms that we see on the web are HTML-based. Users typically navigate to these pages and fill in the forms online. If the form is a single page HTML form, then we can go offline once the page loads, fill it in at our convenience and then connect to the Web to submit it. If it were a multi-page form then we would need a connection between the user and the server hosting the form, for each page load. Of course one may argue that we don't need an uninterrupted connection for multi-page HTML forms, just one for each page download, but this is quite a cumbersome way of filling in a form.

PDF forms are more flexible when used for online transactions. The PDF document itself can be downloaded by the user and completed offline, so a seamless Internet connection is not required for completing PDF forms.

Most web sites hosting forms provide users with various application documents available for downloading. These forms may be Microsoft Word documents, PDF, or other application software compatible file formats. These forms are usually downloaded from a server, printed using a laser printer by the end user, completed through hand-written methods, and faxed or mailed to the host. Two plausible applications of such forms that immediately come to mind are filing income tax returns and applying for a passport or visa.

Even when forms are necessary for analog signatures and hard-copy documents are required by licensing agencies, the use of PDF forms makes them easier to handle than their paper counterparts and offers the end user the ability to keep backup copies electronically stored. For electronic submission of forms, the benefits are obvious. Paper copies needn't be produced and the form author can collect data that can be submitted to a database and electronically stored. Also, the need for a technician to enter the data fields is eliminated. Of course, personnel will still be necessary when reviewing forms for authenticity and correctness although the frequency of errors would be dramatically reduced.

Besides, the final form data of a PDF form can be parsed and processed in two ways, either by submitting the data in **FDF** or **HTML format**. These two methods by which data from a PDF form can be handled, provide the development team the flexibility to use either of the options depending upon their suitability and relevance in a given situation.

What is FDF?

In Chapter 7 we saw that PDF is a file format which captures formatting information from disparate data sources like HTML pages and office documents and renders them uniformly in a device/system-independent manner.

FDF is used for submitting PDF form data to a server, receiving a response, and incorporating it into the form. It can also be used to generate (that is, 'export') standalone files containing form data that can be stored, transmitted electronically (for example, via e-mail), and imported back into the corresponding form. FDF can also be used to control the document structure. In other words, constructs within FDF allow it to control which PDF forms can be used in the creation of a new PDF document. This functionality can be used to create complex documents dynamically. FDF can also be used to define a container for annotations that are separate from the PDF document to which the annotations apply.

Thus FDF is a very powerful format featuring the following capabilities:

- ❑ Processing FDF data
- ❑ Generating personalized PDF documents
- ❑ Pre-populating existing PDF forms without modifying the source

We will look at all these features in our examples.

The general idea of FDF is very similar to HTML forms. A major difference, other than the appearance, is in the format in which the data is transmitted to the server on being posted. Let's consider two things – the form that users fill out and post using a submit button, and the server-side processing that handles the data and performs the necessary actions. Here the form is in the PDF format and when the submit button is pressed the data transmission and processing happens in FDF.

It is interesting to note that PDF forms can also be handled like HTML forms, with only the PDF user interface. When a PDF form used in this way is submitted to the server, the form data is available in the $_GET or $_POST request in exactly the same way an HTML form would make it available.

However, FDF supports capabilities that are not possible with HTML. We will discuss this in the next section.

FDF vs. HTML

FDF supports capabilities that are not possible with HTML, like:

❏ When sending the data back from the server, it is not necessary to re-send the form itself; the data can populate the same form that originated the data. For example, consider an HTML form – when the form is submitted, whatever the response, a new form is presented to the user. In case of PDF forms, the response can be used to populate the same form which posted it.

❏ FDF allows us to change the look of the buttons. Additionally, we can take advantage of this capability to send graphical information in either direction between the client and the server. In HTML, this involves working with stylesheets and developers often end up writing browser-specific code. In contrast PDF allows developers to come up with just one version of the form that can be used across all platforms.

❏ The form can be altered using FDF and sent back from the server. The various actions attached to the buttons can be modified, field properties can be changed, and list boxes and combo boxes can be populated with different choices.

❏ FDF can be used to dynamically synthesize PDF documents composed of a variable number of pages from templates found in PDF documents (specified by FDF) and to populate any fields in the spawned pages with data. A template is simply a page with a name attached that can be hidden. HTML forms do not have such a feature.

Thus, depending on the need, the PDF form can request either FDF-or URL-encoded format for server-side processing:

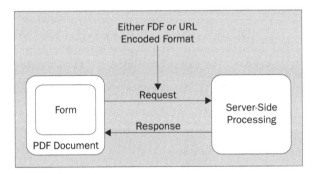

Getting Started

To work with PDF forms we need:

1. FDF Support

2. The `$HTTP_RAW_POST_DATA` variable

3. Adobe Acrobat

Enabling FDF Support

Adobe provides an API to use FDF functions on a variety of platforms and programming languages. The API is available for UNIX and Windows platforms. PHP has an inherent support for FDF. The FDF API is integrated into PHP as an extension. It comes with the PHP binary/sourcecode and can be readily used.

Refer to Chapter 1 for detailed installation instructions.

Enabling FDF Support on UNIX

Before enabling FDF support, we must ensure that the header file FDFTk.h and the library libFdfTk.so are present at fdftk-dir/include and fdftk-dir/lib, respectively. Then we can compile PHP with the --with-fdftk[=DIR] extension to include FDF support with PHP.

Enabling FDF Support on Windows

Before enabling FDF support with PHP we must ensure that two DLLs – php_fdf.dll and fdftk.dll are present in the WINNT/System32 directory on our system or any other place from where they can be loaded by the PHP engine.

To enable FDF support, we need to uncomment the line in the php.ini file that loads the php_fdf.dll associated with the FDF API, like this:

Note that on a Windows 98 machine, a reboot of the machine is required before we can start scripting away.

Cross-Platform Scripts

One of the nice features about PHP is that scripts written on a UNIX system will often run on Windows systems and vice versa. In this case, however, we can't always be sure whether FDF will be compiled statically into PHP or whether it needs to be loaded as a .so file or a .dll file. If we want to ensure that our scripts will run on both UNIX and Windows systems, we need to check two things at the top of each script – which operating system (OS) the script is running on and, if that OS is UNIX, whether or not FDF needs to be loaded using the dl() function.

To determine which operating system the script is running on, we can check the first few letters of the constant variable PHP_OS. If they are 'WIN', we know we're running on Windows. Otherwise, it's pretty safe to assume we are on a Unix-based platform.

To determine whether or not the FDF extension is already loaded (in the case of a UNIX server where it has been compiled into PHP), we can use the `extension_loaded()` function. When we put it all together, we get a snippet of code that will check if FDF is already loaded; otherwise load the correct version for the current operating system:

```php
<?php

if(!extension_loaded('fdf')) {
    if(strtoupper(substr(PHP_OS,0,3)) == 'WIN') {
        dl('php_fdf.dll');
    } else {
        dl('fdf.so');
    }
}
?>
```

Testing the Installation

To ensure that FDF support is enabled with the PHP installation, use the `phpinfo()` script, including our new FDF detection script first:

```php
<?php

if(!extension_loaded('gd')) {
    if(strtoupper(substr(PHP_OS,0,3)) == 'WIN') {
        dl('php_fdf.dll');
    } else {
        dl('fdf.so');
    }
}

phpinfo();
?>
```

When viewed in a web browser, `phpinfo.php` will get a detailed list of all the features that have been compiled into PHP on the server. Look for a section labeled fdf, as shown:

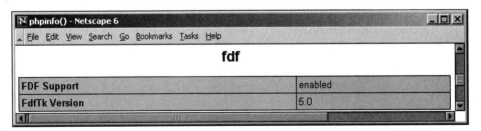

Even if we are running on a different platform, operating system, or web server the steps to be followed remain the same, and as long as we follow them, there should not be any problems in getting FDF running.

Enabling the $HTTP_RAW_POST_DATA Variable

As mentioned earlier, the difference between FDF and HTML format is the way in which the data is transmitted to the server.

The data posted to the server by the PDF forms is stored by PHP in the HTTP_RAW_POST_DATA environment variable, as opposed to the HTML data, which is stored in the HTTP_POST_DATA environment variable. The actual evaluation of the data has to be done in the PHP script, as opposed to the HTML POST data, which is evaluated by the PHP engine. What this means is that variables that are submitted as a part of the $_POST or $_GET requests are evaluated implicitly by the PHP engine. FDF variables however are different; they cannot be implicitly evaluated by the PHP engine and require a PHP script using the FDF API for this purpose.

We therefore need to explicitly enable the HTTP_RAW_POST _DATA variable in the php.ini file. To this effect, we must uncomment the always_populate_raw_post_data = On line in the php.ini file, like this:

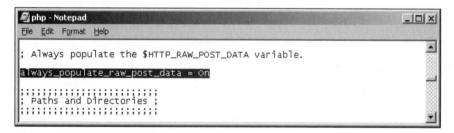

Now if we run the phpinfo() function in a script we will see this:

In the third row of the **PHP Core** table we see that both the **Local Value** and the **Master Value** for always_populate_raw_post_data are 1; 1 signifies that it is enabled and 0 otherwise.

Adobe Acrobat

We require the Acrobat Reader Plug-in for reading PDF documents and Acrobat 4.0 to develop our own PDF forms. This not a limitation to the end users of our developed forms, they would only need to have the Acrobat Reader Plug-in.

With the basics in place, we are now set to explore the FDF features in detail.

Using FDF with PHP

PHP can be used for:

1. Parsing the FDF data posted from a PDF form

2. Parsing the FDF data posted from a PDF form and using this data for server-side processing and populating another PDF form using this data

Creating a Basic PDF Form

For starters let's look at a basic PDF form. This will give us an idea of how PDF forms are created and will also lay the framework for the examples that we would see later on in the chapter.

For this purpose, let's assume that we have a specialized birthday tracking and reminder application where users can enter the birthdays of their friends and dear ones.

Our application will do two things:

❑ It sends automatic birthday wishes, on behalf of the user, to those who have been added to the list.

❑ The user has the option of being reminded about the birthday a day in advance. This one day prior alert and automatic wishes could take any form, from a simple e-mail message to an automated phone call.

We will not delve into the back-end logic, and only look at the frontend of the application here, since that is the area that makes use of PDF forms.

party.html

We begin by creating an HTML document (`party.html`), which creates the basic framework of the form:

```
<html>
  <body>
    <p><font face=Verdana size=2>Name</font></p>
    <p><font face=Verdana size=2>Date of Birth</font></p>
    <p><font face=Verdana size=2>Sex</font></p>
    <p><font face=Verdana size=2>Remind me one day in advance
                              of the Birthday</font></p>
  </body>
</html>
```

This document, when opened in Acrobat 4.0, looks like this:

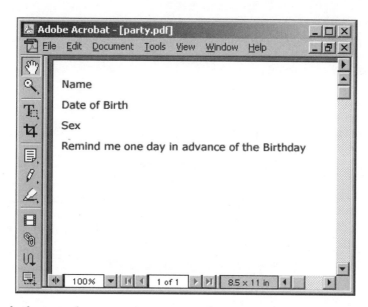

The form has only the textual matter written, we now have to go about adding textboxes, the checkbox, and the submit button to get the user input.

Adding Textboxes

We will start with selecting the **forms tool**, which is the last tool of the Tool Bar present on the left hand-side of the PDF document and drag a rectangle of suitable length in front of the Name label. This will pop up the Field Properties window where we fill in the properties of the form control we have just created:

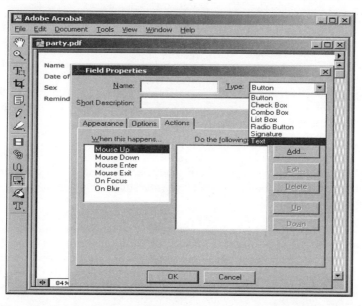

In the Name field, we will enter the name. This is the reference by which we can refer to the contents of the textbox once the form has been submitted. Next we change the Type to Text.

Similarly, we add a textbox named 'dob' in front of the Date of Birth label. For the Sex label, we create another textbox named 'gender' in which users can enter either M or F.

Adding a Checkbox

We add a checkbox, next to the Remind me one day in advance of the Birthday label, named 'remind' in case the user wants to be reminded about the birthday a day ahead of schedule, like this:

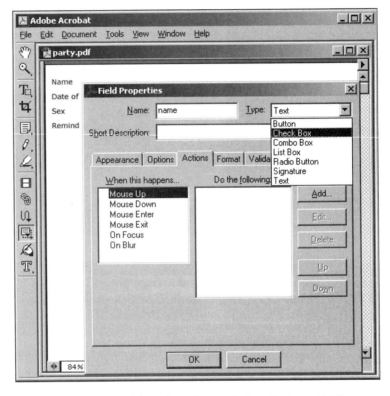

The form is now almost complete, all we have to do is add a submit button below the input fields.

Adding a Submit Button

Before we venture further, let's look at the theory behind the submit button in PDF forms.

PDF Forms are a group of extensions to PDF used by Adobe Acrobat. These extensions allow PDF files to contain fields and buttons and can be considered to be a new layer on top of a PDF file. The underlying PDF file may be created by any PDF producer including, but not limited to, PDF Writer, Acrobat Distiller, or Acrobat Capture. The fields are subsequently added manually using Acrobat, just as we have done in our sample PDF form.

After filling in a PDF form, the user will click on a button, which will submit the data to the server. For the form to be submitted, we must use a file format to transmit the form data stored in the PDF document to the server and back. As we have already seen, PDF forms support both the HTML form format (MIME type `application/x-www-form-URL encoded`) as well as FDF (MIME type `application/vnd.fdf`).

If HTML is selected, the format submitted is identical to HTML form submissions. Existing CGI scripts or any other server-side dynamic page technology (ASP, JSP, PHP, Servlets, and so on) for HTML forms may be used to parse data in this format. If FDF is selected, then there is a server library to parse and generate FDF files for this format. The URL to submit to is not restricted to the HTTP protocol; it can also be the mail to a scheme, for example, `mailto:someuser@somecompany.com`.

Using the 'form tool' we will drag a small rectangle in the shape of a button after the last textual field. As soon as we finish drawing the button a **Fields Properties** window pops up:

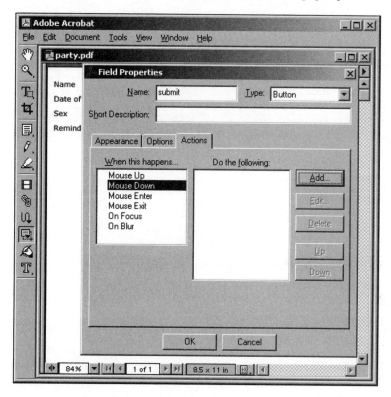

Here we enter **submit** in the **Name** box and set the **Type** to **Button**. Also in the **Actions** tab we select **Mouse Down**.

Now we set the action for the submit button, by clicking the **Add** button. This opens another window where we add the Action Type as **Submit Form** and click the **Select URL** button to enter the URL to the PHP script. We will also select the **Export Format** as **Forms Data Format (FDF)**. Here is how it looks:

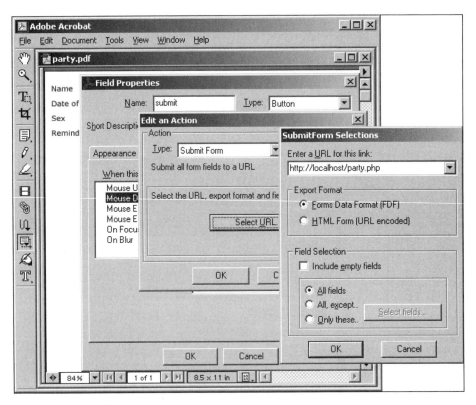

Next we will write the PHP script.

party.php

If PHP has FDF support compiled, it can parse FDF data and access any field by its name. FDF data is currently stored by PHP in the variable HTTP_RAW_POST_DATA (just as HTML data is stored in HTTP_POST_DATA). The actual evaluation of the data has to be done in the PHP script, as opposed to the HTML POST data which is evaluated by the PHP engine.

We will create a reference to a temporary file party.fdf, retrieve the data from the $HTTP_RAW_POST_DATA variable, save it to the FDF file, then close the file:

```php
<?php

if(!extension_loaded('fdf')) {
    if(strtoupper(substr(PHP_OS,0,3)) == 'WIN') {
        dl('php_fdf.dll');
    } else {
        dl('fdf.so');
    }
}

while (list($key, $val) = @each($HTTP_POST_VARS)) {
                        $GLOBALS[$key] = $val;

//Open a FDF document to get the data, which has been posted by the form
```

```
$fdffp=fopen("C:/party.fdf","w");
fwrite($fdffp, $HTTP_RAW_POST_DATA, strlen($HTTP_RAW_POST_DATA));
fclose($fdffp);
```

The `fdf_open()` function is used to open the file with form data, which is returned from the PDF form:

```
$fdf=fdf_open("C:/party.fdf");
```

We access the input fields by the names we used in the form and display the data entered in the HTML form to the client:

```
//Get the name
$name=fdf_get_value($fdf, "name");
print ("the name is '<B>$name</B>'<BR>");

//Get the date of birth
$date=fdf_get_value($fdf, "dob");
print ("the date of birth is '<B>$date</B>'<BR>");

//Get the gender
$gender=fdf_get_value($fdf, "sex");
print ("the gender is '<B>$gender</B>'<BR>");

//Get whether the checkbox was checked or not
if (fdf_get_value($fdf, "remind")=="Yes"){
    print ("You requested to be reminded one day ahead of schedule");
} else {
    print (" you will not be reminded ahead of schedule"{);
}

fdf_close($fdf);
?>
```

When we run this script from a browser, Acrobat Reader will open the PDF form where all the fields can be edited. Here is a sample form that has been filled in by the user:

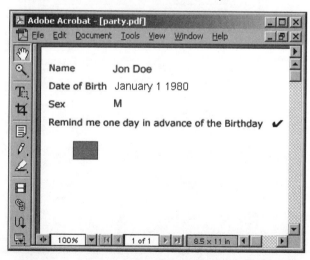

Now if we press the submit button, we will get the following response:

295

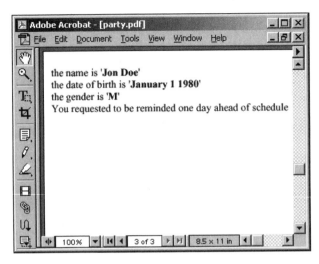

We have thus created our first PDF form having set the action of the form to the `party.php` script using FDF.

FDF Format vs. URL-Encoded Format

Let us now see how to change the format of our previous example from FDF to URL-encoded.

To edit the submit button action we have to open the `party.pdf` form, select the 'hand tool' and double click on the submit button. This would open the Fields Properties window. Here we would edit the action of the submit button by changing the Export Format to HTML Form (URL encoded). Here is how it all looks:

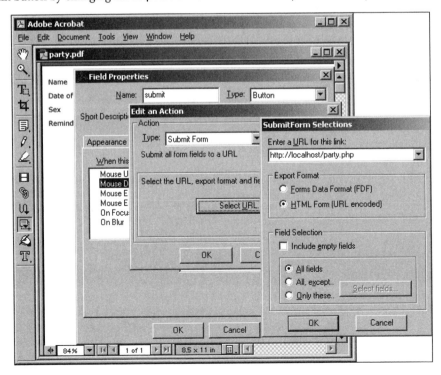

This is the resulting page that appears when we submit the form:

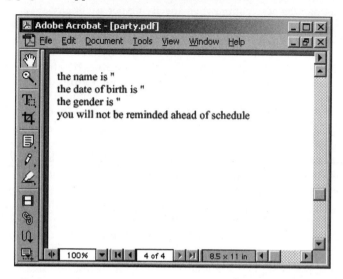

This is because the PHP script that we have written can only handle FDF format. In this case, we would need to modify the server-side script so that it can handle the traditional URL-encoded strings.

Also, since our PHP script is for FDF and we are processing HTML format in the above example, we will have to modify the error settings in our php.ini file such that the script continues even if it does not find a variable value. In case we do not modify the error settings, a host of error messages will be thrown instead of the above output.

PDF Form Creation Strategies

We have now learned how to create a PDF form. With this knowledge as a background, we will take a quick look at the various strategies that can be employed while creating FDF forms. There are a couple of points to remember when we create PDF forms. Since forms are the point of contact from where users are going to interact with our application, it often pays to be finicky with the appearance, layout, and formatting of the form.

Further, while working with PDF Forms, we need to constantly toggle between two modes:

❑ **Design mode**
To enter the design mode, we must select the 'form tool' from the Tool Bar. We will have to work in the design mode, to design the form and set programmatic actions.

❑ **Runtime mode**
To enter the run-time mode, we must select the 'hand tool' from the toolbox. The way our form looks in the run-time mode is the way it will finally appear to the end users. We can submit the form only in the run-time mode and not in the design mode.

Here are a few points to remember about naming conventions, character limits, web optimization, and form submission strategies:

❑ It is recommended that JavaScript developers building scripts for PDF forms should utilize some type of naming convention when specifying persistent global variables. One suggestion is to start all variables with the company name. For example, if the company name is Xyz, then start all variables with 'xyz_'. This will prevent collisions with other persistent global variable names throughout the documents. Another useful hint could be to precede each data type or field name with what it represents: str for String, bln for Boolean, txt for textbox, cmb for a combo box, sel for a select list, and frm for a form; this is the most popular Hungarian notation. Most importantly, the naming conventions should be consistent across the entire development team and sustained over a period of time.

❑ Careful selection of field names when creating forms is an important factor in data collection. If two fields share the same name, they also share the same value (we will discuss the value property in the next section). We can use this capability to create fields that have different appearances (that is, they appear on different pages and have different background colors) but have the same value. This means we can modify one field and the other field is updated automatically.

❑ If we are creating a text field, we must select a specific font size rather than setting it to automatic in the Field Properties dialog box. Doing so may require that we adjust the field's height to display the font and the blinking cursor during run-time mode.

❑ We can use the field's resize handles to adjust the height and width. It is often useful to view the form in run-time mode to see how it will look and work for users.

❑ We can create additional fields by using 'Ctrl + Click & Drag' to duplicate an existing field. We may also use one field's position to help line up other fields around it. Once we have copied a field, we can double-click on the new copy to modify its properties.

❑ While creating radio buttons we must ensure that all the buttons in the set share the same field name. We can differentiate each field by customizing the 'Export Value' (a feature of the radio buttons). For example, all radio buttons may have the same name ('Status'), but one radio button's 'Export Value' might be 'Classified' and another might be 'Student'. The 'Export Value' is the information used by a CGI application on a web server to identify the selected field.

❑ Every other save should be a Save As, saving over the existing file. The Save As option recompiles the PDF file keeping the file size small. Repeated Save commands will cause the file to bloat unnecessarily.

FDF Document Structure

Let's take a look at the FDF file that was created in the previous example, to learn its structure.

We'll navigate to the directory where we had created the file (C:/party.fdf) and open it using a text editor:

If we look at an FDF document we will find a catalog object named FDF. Such an object may contain a number of entries like Fields, F, Status, and so on. The most commonly used entries are Fields which point to a list of input fields and F which contains the filename of the PDF document this data belongs to. These entries are referred to in the FDF documentation as /F-Key or /Status-Key. To modify these entries, we use the PHP functions provided by the FDF API like `fdf_set_file()` and `fdf_set_status()`. Fields are modified with functions like `fdf_set_value()` and `fdf_set_opt()`.

The following diagram depicts the structure of an FDF document:

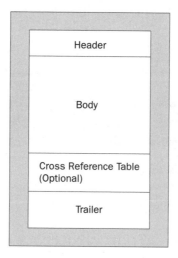

FDF is structured in the same way as PDF, but need only contain those elements that are required for PDF forms data export and import, like:

❑ **Header**
The first line of an FDF file specifies the version number of the PDF specification that FDF is a part of. This takes the format `%FDF-x.x`, where x.x is the version of PDF used.

❑ **Body**
The body consists of one `Catalog` object and additional indirect objects that it may reference. The `Catalog` object is a dictionary with only one (required) key in it, FDF. Its value is a dictionary, whose entries are described in the `FDF Catalog Object`. It is legal for the body to contain additional objects and for the `Catalog Object` to contain additional key-value pairs. Comments can appear anywhere in the body section of an FDF file. Just as in PDF, objects in FDF can be direct or indirect.

❑ **Cross Reference Table** (optional)

❑ **Trailer**
The trailer consists of a trailer dictionary, followed by the last line of the FDF file, containing the end of file marker, `%%EOF`. The trailer dictionary consists of the keyword trailer, followed by at least one key-value pair enclosed in double angle brackets. The only required key is `Root`, and its value is an indirect reference to the `Catalog` object in the FDF body. It is legal for the trailer dictionary to contain the additional key-value pairs described in the PDF specification.

This was a glimpse of the server-side scripting. Now let us get acquainted with the client-side scripting.

Validating the User Input in a PDF Form

On the client-side, JavaScript is employed for validation of the user inputs and also to populate a pre-created PDF document.

What is JavaScript?

JavaScript started out as a weakly typed language for client-side validations and has now grown into an indispensable element in any developer's arsenal. It is an interpreted programming/scripting language from Netscape and quite similar in capability to VB Script, Tcl, Perl, and REX.

JavaScript has come to play a very important role in the forms that are currently used over the Web and is useful for a host of functionalities, such as:

❑ **Client-side validation**
   It is good to validate the user input in our PDF forms to avoid user frustration by submitting wrong data to the server and getting an invalid response

❑ **Dynamic generation of presentation**
   Depending on the user input, we could decide what to show to the user on the fly; this enables us to provide personalized content to the users

❑ **Cookies**
   JavaScript can also be used to set and retrieve cookies

❑ **Client-side data processing**
   It can also be used to pre-populate the form fields based on the user input in another field

JavaScript has support for user-defined objects, as also intrinsic objects – Boolean, Number, Date, Math, String, and Array. Also, it has been specialized for Acrobat use with the help of predefined classes and objects. These objects – app, console, doc, event, field, global, util, and of course this – are available to us while working with JavaScript in PDF forms.

The use of JavaScript in PDF Forms can be separated into the following phases:

❑ Basics

❑ Validate, Calculate, and Actions

❑ Submit and Receive over the net

❑ Scripting simple things

❑ Scripting programs

> *For more information on using JavaScript with PDF Forms refer to JSSpec.pdf (www.planetpdf.com/codecuts/pdfs/tutorial/JSSpec.pdf) and AcroJS.pdf (www.planetpdf.com/codecuts/pdfs/tutorial/AcroJS.pdf).*

JavaScript for PDF is not the same as JavaScript for browsers and HTML pages. This is because JavaScript is, first and foremost, an interpreted language. The interpreter that runs JavaScript is inside the browser for browser-targeted JavaScript and inside Acrobat or Acrobat Reader for PDF-based JavaScript. This is important because Acrobat Reader does not have access to or exert control over web pages. It knows nothing about the Document Object Model (DOM) or the widgets attached to the HTML page running inside the browser at any given moment.

Acrobat Reader only knows about the Reader and the PDF environment. Accordingly, one cannot reach the browser's Document object (representing the open HTML page), the browser's Event object, the Window object, the Frame or Form objects, or any of the other canonical DOM objects that one is accustomed to manipulating if one is an experienced JavaScript programmer.

The PDF document does not adhere to a conventional DOM. In order to make JavaScript usable inside the Acrobat runtime environment, Adobe has to build its own unique object layer above the existing core JavaScript while removing browser-specific DOM classes. These objects along with their associated properties and methods are fully documented in the AcroJS.pdf file.

It is possible to have three levels of JavaScript while working with PDF forms:

1. Field level – This is used in field actions like validate, calculate, and so on.

2. Document level – This applies to the entire document per se and can be manipulated through Tools/Forms/Document JavaScripts.

3. Plug-In level – This concerns itself with the various plug-ins that are installed on the system. For instance, on a Windows platform this can be found at Program Files/Adobe/Acrobat 4.0/Acrobat/plug_ins/Acroform/Javascripts.

We will concentrate on the Field-level and Document-level scripts in the current discussion.

Modifying the Basic PDF Form

Let's open the party.pdf form which we created and enter the design mode. Add JavaScript to the Mouse Down action for the submit button, like this:

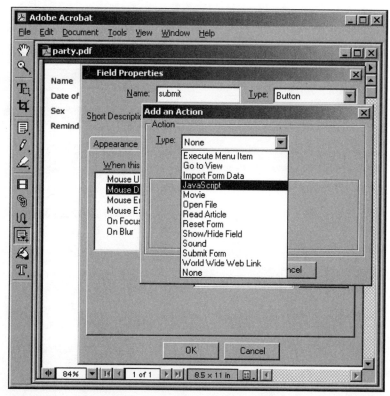

Now click on the **Edit** button. We get the following dialog box to create and edit our JavaScript:

In JavaScript for PDF Forms, the `app` object refers to the object at hand, that is, the current form. This object provides one method, `alert()`, which is used to inform the user of any necessary information.

Let's type the following code in this box:

```
var name = this.getField("name").value;

app.alert(name,1);
```

We now have two actions defined for the **Mouse Down** action of the submit button – **Submit Form** and **JavaScript**. The application looks like this:

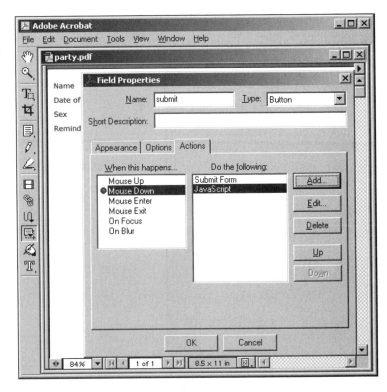

If we press the submit button in the run mode, we get a JavaScript message and then the form will be submitted.

How It Works

In this function, when we use `this.getField("name")` we get a reference to the textbox named **Name** on the form. The `value` property of the object returns the current contents of the textbox, which we alert using the next line `app.alert(name,1)`.

The `app.alert()` method takes some arguments to determine the kind of the alert message we want to show. In this case, we pass two arguments – `name` and `1`, so we get this message:

If we drop the second argument, we would get the following error dialog box:

If we passed 1, 3, and `name`, we would get the following dialog box:

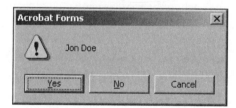

And if we passed 2, 3 as the arguments, we would get this alert:

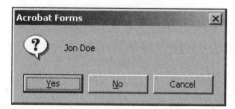

These dialog boxes are useful to determine what the user pressed and do further processing based on that.

In this section we discussed the basics of JavaScript support in PDF forms. Now that we have detailed the FDF form structure and created a basic PDF form, let's discuss the various FDF functions.

The PHP FDF API

The PHP API for FDF provides a host of useful functions. However documentation about them is very scanty. Hence in this section we will elaborate and explain the meaning, significance, and utility of each function in the following pages. This will serve as a ready reference for our PHP FDF development.

fdf_add_template()

Version

Support: PHP 3 >= 3.0.13, PHP 4 >= 4.0.0

Description

This function is used for the creation of dynamic PDF Forms using the templates feature; a template is a named page, which may be visible or invisible. FDF can act as the recipe to assemble a dynamic document composed of a variable number of pages and then populate those pages with data. Templates can also spawn pages using JavaScript.

This function adds a template to the FDF. There are two types of FDF:

❑ **Classic**
This was first introduced with Acrobat 3.0. We cannot add templates to a classic FDF, they are mutually exclusive.

❑ **Template-Based**
This constitutes the 'recipe' for, upon import into Acrobat, directing the construction of a brand new PDF document from templates found inside specified PDF documents. Many of the calls in the FDF Library are incompatible with a template-based FDF and will as well return if called with such an FDF. Other calls are valid with either kind of FDF. If called with a template-based FDF, they act on the most recently added template.

Function Prototype

```
bool fdf_add_template(int fdfdoc, int newpage, string filename, string template,
int rename)
```

Here:

❑ **fdfdoc** – is the reference of the FDF document to be used, obtained by making a call to `fdf_open()` function or by the `fdf_create()` function.

❑ **newpage** – if newpage is 1, the template starts a new page; if 0, a template is appended to the last page. If this is the first template added to the FDF, this parameter is ignored. When a template-based FDF is used to construct a new PDF document, each page can be the result of overlaying multiple templates one after another.

❑ **filename** – is a string containing the pathname of the PDF file to be used as the value for the /F key within the /TRef key. The Tref is the file specification for the PDF where the template is. It may be an empty string. In this case when the FDF gets imported into Acrobat, the template is expected to reside inside the PDF file currently being viewed. As a result the template will get replaced, as the topmost document, with the new PDF constructed because of importing the FDF.

❑ **rename** – if 0, it will add a /Rename key whose value is FALSE; otherwise it won't since TRUE is the default value for the /Rename key. When renaming is indicated, all fields in the template modified by the FDF (for example, because new values for them are included) get renamed. The purpose of the /Rename key is to provide flexibility concerning whether fields get renamed, as templates get spawned. The default is to do the renaming to prevent potential conflicts between field names originating in different templates. The renaming scheme consists of prepending "P" & page # & ".template name_." & template # before the field name. For example, if a template called 'flower' gets spawned into page 3 and this is the second template for that page in the FDF, then the field 'color' on that template gets renamed to 'P3.flower_1.color'.

❑ **template** – is the name of the template within the PDF file specified by the filename. Template functionality is not supported in Acrobat Reader. Therefore, if we create an Acrobat application that uses the template functionality, a user who only has access to Acrobat Reader would not be able to use the application.

Here is an example:

```php
<?php

$fdf = fdf_create();

fdf_add_template($fdf, 0, "c:/watermark.pdf", "watermark" ,0);

fdf_save($fdf, "c:/fdf_add_template.fdf");

fdf_close($fdf);
?>
```

Here we added a template to the FDF document that we created. In the arguments passed, c:/watermark.pdf is the PDF file, which contains a template named 'watermark' that we wish to associate with the document.

This is how the resultant document appears in a text editor:

```
%FDF-1.20%åáÍÓ

1 0 obj<< /FDF << /Pages 2 0 R >> >> endobj

2 0 obj[ << /Templates 3 0 R >> ]endobj

3 0 obj[ << /TRef << /F (c:/watermark.pdf)/Name (watermark)>>
            /Rename false >> ]]endobj

trailer<</Root 1 0 R >>

%%EOF
```

Practical Usage

Using Page Templates in Acrobat is a feature we'll want to use many times over. Any page in a PDF file can be used as a template and the template can be either visible or invisible. Templates can be used to spawn new pages much like how we would add a page in a layout application or as containers of information that we can add to existing documents like icons, images, graphics, and text blocks. Acrobat Reader does not support templates; we must consider this factor when developing or using template functionality in our code.

fdf_close()

Version

Support: PHP 3>= 3.0.6, PHP 4 >= 4.0.0

Description

The `fdf_close()` function closes the FDF document and frees the resources used by the FDF. Before exiting the application, we should call `fdf_close()` for each open FDF document. Once the FDF document has been closed, the reference is no longer available and the data within the document cannot be accessed.

Function Prototype

```
bool fdf_close (int fdf_document)
```

Here:

❑ **fdf_document** – is the reference of the FDF document to be used, obtained by making a call to the `fdf_open()` function or by the `fdf_create()` function

Here is an example:

```
<?php

$fdf = fdf_open("c:/test.fdf");

//The processing stuff goes here

//Close the FDF document we had opened earlier
fdf_close($fdf);
?>
```

Practical Usage

It is always good to explicitly close the reference to the document we are working with; this keeps the code easy to understand and to debug.

fdf_create()

Version Support

PHP 3>= 3.0.6, PHP 4 >= 4.0.0

Description

`fdf_create()` creates a new FDF document. This function is used to populate input fields in a PDF form with data. Once we have finished using the file created with this method, we close it by using the `fdf_close()` function.

Function Prototype

```
int fdf_create (void)
```

This function does not have any parameters.

Let's look at an example:

```php
<?php

$fdf = fdf_create();

// The rest of the processing information goes here

fdf_save($fdf, "c:/fdf_create.fdf");

fdf_close($fdf);
?>
```

Practical Usage

In many situations, we would like the fields of a PDF form to be populated using stored information about a person. This will be true of, say, a customer who logs in to his shopping cart and would like the order form to be filled up using the items he had saved or purchased during the last visit. This function can come in very handy to personalize user experience and reduce the time spent in filling up a cumbersome form.

fdf_get_file()

Version Support

PHP 3 >= 3.0.6, PHP 4 >= 4.0.0

Description

fdf_get_file() returns the value of the /F key. The return value is a string containing the value of FDF's /F key. This is assumed to be a PDF string since that is what Acrobat produces when exporting FDF. The /F key of the FDF document contains the path information of where the file is stored.

Function Prototype

```
string fdf_get_file (int fdf_document)
```

Here:

❑ **fdf_document** – is the reference of the FDF document to be used; it is obtained by making a call to fdf_open() or fdf_create()

Here is an example:

```php
<?php

//Open a pre-created FDF file.
//This is the same file from our earlier example

$fdf = fdf_open("c:/party.fdf");
```

```
//Make a call to the fdf_get_file() function to print the /F key

print (fdf_get_file($fdf));

fdf_close($fdf);

?>
```

This is a simple example that illustrates how this function can be used. We open an existing FDF document. In this case, it is the same document that we had created in our earlier example. Calling the fdf_get_file() function sends the path information stored in the /F key back to the user.

Practical Usage

Since the /F key of the FDF document contains the path information of where the file is stored, setting this key for every document we create is paramount. If this key is not set, a malformed document results. Getting the path information can help further processing of our application. We will see the format in which this key is stored when we detail the fdf_set_file() function.

fdf_get_status()

Version Support

PHP 3>= 3.0.6, PHP 4 >= 4.0.0

Description

fdf_get_status() returns the value of the /Status key in the FDF document. FDF exported from a PDF Form does not contain a /Status key. However, fdf_get_status() can still be useful when parsing an FDF produced some other way. For example, the FDF may have previously been produced along with a call to the fdf_set_status() function and then saved as a file.

Function Prototype

```
string fdf_get_status (int fdf_document)
```

Here:

❑ **fdf_document** – is the reference of the FDF document to be used, obtained by making a call to fdf_open() or fdf_create().

Here is an example:

```
<?php

//Open a pre-created FDF file.
$fdf = fdf_open("c:/party.fdf");

//Make a call to the fdf_get_status() function and print the ./F key
print (fdf_get_status($fdf));

fdf_close($fdf);

?>
```

This example is exactly similar to the previous example, except that the FDF file that we are referring to has been created using a PDF form and hence does not have a /Status flag. The example therefore will not produce any output. We will revisit this example when we detail the `fdf_set_status()` function.

Practical Usage

In many scenarios, we would like to set a custom status key for the forms that we are creating; this key can then be retrieved later on for any application-specific logic.

fdf_get_value()

Version Support

PHP 3>= 3.0.6, PHP 4 >= 4.0.0

Description

`fdf_get_value()` returns the value of a field from the FDF document. This is a string containing the value of the field. If we open the FDF document (`party.fdf`) and analyze the markup, we will see the following generic format:

```
/FDF << /Fields [ << /V (January 1 1980)/T (dob)>>...
```

The function thus returns the value of /V for a given field. In this case, it would return January 1 1980 if the `fieldname` parameter passed to it is `dob`.

Function Prototype

```
string fdf_get_value (int fdf_document, string fieldname)
```

Here:

❑ **fdf_document** – is the reference of the FDF document to be used, obtained by making a call to `fdf_open()` or `fdf_create()`.

❑ **fieldname** – is a string representing the fully qualified name of the field the value of which has to be retrieved from the FDF document.

Let us look at the `party.php` script:

```php
<? php

$fdf = fdf_open("c:/party.fdf");

//Get the name
$name = fdf_get_value($fdf, "name");
print ("The name is  '<B>$name</B>'<BR>");

//Get the date of birth
$date = fdf_get_value($fdf, "dob");
print ("The date of birth is  '<B>$date</B>'<BR>");

//Get the gender
```

```
$gender = fdf_get_value($fdf, "sex");
print ("The gender is  '<B>$gender</B>'<BR>");

//Get whether the checkbox was checked or not
if(fdf_get_value($fdf, "remind") == "Yes") {
    print ("You requested to be reminded one day ahead of schedule");
} else {
    print ("You will not be reminded ahead of schedule");
}
```

```
fdf_close($fdf);
?>
```

The first part of the original script (party.php), which retrieves the data from the $HTTP_RAW_POST_DATA variable and saves it to an FDF file, has been removed because the file has already been created.

In each call to the fdf_get_value() function, we pass the name of the field as created in the PDF form and hence stored in the FDF document as the fieldname parameter and get the /V value of that field as the return.

Practical Usage

This is one the most useful functions in the FDF set and one that we will be using more often than most of the other functions. It enables us to retrieve user inputs and do further processing on the server-side of the data.

fdf_next_field_name()

Version Support

PHP 3>= 3.0.6, PHP 4 >= 4.0.0

Description:

fdf_next_field_name() returns the name of the field after the field in the fieldname parameter or the field name in the first field (if the second parameter is NULL).

Function Prototype

```
string fdf_next_field_name (int fdf_document, string fieldname)
```

Here:

❏ **fdf_document** – is the reference of the FDF document to be used, obtained by making a call to fdf_open() or fdf_create().

❏ **fieldname** – is the string representing the fully qualified name of the previous field, such that fdf_next_field_name() will return the one that comes after it in the FDF. If fieldname is an empty string, the first field name in the FDF is returned.

Let's consider the FDF file that we have already created:

We'll use the above file in the following PHP script:

```php
<?php

//Open a pre-created FDF file.
$fdf = fdf_open("c:/party.fdf");

//Make a call to the fdf_next_field_name() function,
//and print the filed after the 'dob' field

print (fdf_next_field_name($fdf, "dob"));

fdf_close($fdf);
?>
```

This is the result on a browser:

We pass the string 'dob' as the field name and get the name of the next field ('gender' in this case) as the output. Note that the fields are stored in alphabetical order, no matter what their position on the actual form. Hence in this case, we get 'gender' as the field that comes after 'dob'.

Practical Usage

This function is used to enumerate the field names in FDF, it returns a string containing the fully qualified name of the field that comes after the one passed as parameter (if none are passed, it returns the first field name). Then the application can use the returned field name as a parameter for another method.

fdf_open()

Version Support

PHP 3>= 3.0.6, PHP 4 >= 4.0.0

Description

fdf_open() opens a file with form data and returns a reference to this file. This reference is used by all other methods in their operation. This file must contain the data as returned from a PDF form. Currently, the file has to be created 'manually' by using fopen() and fwrite() writes the content of $HTTP_RAW_POST_DATA into it. We must not forget to release the memory by calling the fdf_close() method for each open FDF document when we're done with it.

Function Prototype

```
int fdf_open (string filename)
```

Here:

❑   **filename** – is the pathname for the FDF file to be opened

Here is an example:

```php
<?php

while (list($key, $val) = @each($HTTP_POST_VARS)) {
                                $GLOBALS[$key] = $val;

// Save the FDF data into a temp file
$fdffp = fopen("test.fdf", "w");

fwrite($fdffp, $HTTP_FDF_DATA, strlen($HTTP_FDF_DATA));

fclose($fdffp);

// Open temp file and evaluate data
$fdf = fdf_open("test.fdf");

fdf_close($fdf);
?>
```

Practical Usage

This is the first method that we need to call when working with the functions in the FDF set. Needless to say, nothing will work without this function.

fdf_save()

Version Support

PHP 3>= 3.0.6, PHP 4 >= 4.0.0

Description

The `fdf_save()` function saves an FDF document. The FDF Toolkit provides a way to output the document to STDOUT if the parameter filename is '.'. This does not work if PHP is used as an Apache module. In this case we will have to write to a file and use `fpassthru()` to output it. The path name where the FDF file should be saved should be a local file path and not a network URL. The FDF document cannot be saved to a file that was opened with `fdf_open()` and hasn't yet been closed with `fdf_close()`.

Function Prototype

```
int fdf_save (string filename)
```

Here:

❑ **filename** – is the path to which the FDF document has to be saved and the filename to be associated with it

Here is an example:

```php
<?php

$outfdf = fdf_create();

//Do the processing

fdf_save($outfdf, "c:/fdf_save.fdf");

//Further processing, if at all
?>
```

We create an FDF document and then save it to the local drive using the `fdf_save()` function. This is the resultant FDF document in a text editor:

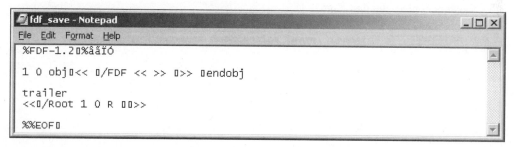

Practical Usage

This function can be used to save FDF documents on the fly using server-side processing. It can take the place of the Export Format tab we saw earlier in the chapter.

fdf_set_ap()

Version Support

PHP 3 >= 3.0.6, PHP 4 >= 4.0.0

Description

`fdf_set_ap()` sets the appearance of a field (that is, the value of the /AP key) in a PDF document. If the field does not exist in the FDF, it is created. If it does, the requested appearance in the /AP key is replaced. If the reference passed by the `fdf_document` parameter is a template-based FDF (that is, the FDF for which `fdf_add_template()` has been called), `fdf_set_ap()` acts on the most recently added template.

Function Prototype

```
bool fdf_set_ap (int fdf_document, string field_name, int face, string filename,
int page_number)
```

Here:

- **fdf_document** – is the reference of the FDF document to be used, obtained by making a call to the `fdf_open()` function or the `fdf_create()` function.

- **field_name** – is a string representing the fully qualified field name.

- **face** – specifies which face is to be set. It can be one of the following values:

    - 0 – /N key: Sets the normal appearance.

    - 1 – /R key: Sets the appearance associated with the rollover behavior.

    - 2 – /D key: Set the appearance on down behavior.

    The rollover and down behaviors are similar to their HTML counterparts. Rollover defines how the appearance of a field should respond to mouse rollovers. The down behavior captures how a field should look on the mouse down events.

- **filename** – is a string for the pathname of the PDF file, which represents the button's appearance.

- **page_number** – is an integer containing the page number within the PDF file to be used for the appearance (the first page is 1).

Here is an example:

```php
<?php

$outfdf = fdf_create();

fdf_set_ap ($outfdf, "Wrox", 0, "c:/watermark.pdf", 1);

fdf_save($outfdf, "c:/fdf_set_ap.fdf");
?>
```

In this example, we are telling the application to use whatever is contained in the `watermark.pdf` file as the appearance of the field entitled `Wrox`.

This produces a file containing the following data:

```
fdf_set_ap - Notepad                                              _ □ x
File  Edit  Format  Help
%FDF-1.2□%âåÏÓ

1 0 obj□<< □/FDF << /Fields 6 0 R >> □>> □endobj

2 0 obj□<< /Filter [ /FlateDecode ] /Length 109 /Type /XObject /Subtype
         /Form □/BBox [ 0 0 100 100 ] /FormType 1 /Matrix [ 1 0 0 1 -50 -50 ]
         /Name /FRM □/Resources 4 0 R >> □streamH%s□á2P□I□□å\®@Žž'□'¡□"ÒEå□
         ar.P□¡B9—S□—¾>□,¡%ž'©%%BH□—¡BH□□D•!HÜÐÄ□h„±ž™.....™BH.□\®□—Fyy'
         ^AJZNf'^r~®fH□Èr□ò□□Æ□endstream□endobj

3 0 obj□109 □endobj

4 0 obj□<< □/ProcSet [ /PDF /Text ] □/Font << /F0 5 0 R >> □>> □endobj

5 0 obj□<< □/Type /Font □/Subtype /Type1 □/Encoding /WinAnsiEncoding
         /BaseFont /Helvetica-Bold □>> □endobj

6 0 obj□[ << /T (wrox)/AP << /N 2 0 R >> >> ]□endobj
trailer
<<□/Root 1 0 R □□>>

%%EOF□
```

Practical Usage

When calling fdf_set_ap() in a web application, we pass the pathname as a parameter for the PDF file that contains the AP we want. Acrobat will only import a /AP key from FDF into fields of type 'Button'. In addition, only the FDFNormalAP will be imported (FDFDownAP and FDFRolloverAP will be ignored) unless the button that the /AP is being imported into has a 'Highlight' of type 'Push'. Also, the new imported /AP will not show if the 'Layout' for the button is of type 'Text only'.

Once the FDF containing the new /AP is imported into the PDF form, if the picture looks too small inside the button field (that is, with too much white space around it), we can use Acrobat to crop the PDF page used as the source of the /AP (that is, the one identified by parameters filename and page_number).

fdf_set_encoding()

Version Support

PHP 4 >= 4.1.0

Description

fdf_set_encoding() sets the character encoding in the FDF document (fdf_document). The parameter encoding should be the valid encoding name. The valid encoding names in Acrobat 5.0 are 'Shift-JIS', 'UHC', 'GBK', and 'BigFive'.

> 'Shift-JIS' was designed for Japanese support on Windows by Microsoft and is also referred to as MS Kanji. More information available at http://web.lfw.org/text/jp.html. UHC stands for Unified Hangul Code or Extended Wansung. GBK is a Simplfied Chinese encoding scheme, and BigFive is a Traditional Chinese Encoding Scheme.

Function Prototype

```
bool fdf_set_encoding (int fdf_document, string encoding)
```

Here:

- ❑ **fdf_document** – is the reference of the FDF document to be used, obtained by making a call to `fdf_open()` or `fdf_create()`.

- ❑ **encoding** – is a string containing the encoding name. It can take only one of these values: `'Shift-JIS'`, `'UHC'`, `'GBK'`, or `'BigFive'`.

Here is an example:

```
<?php

$outfdf = fdf_create();

fdf_set_encoding($outfdf,"UHC");

fdf_save($outfdf, "c:/fdf_set_encoding.fdf");
?>
```

In this example, we have set the encoding to UHC, which results in the following FDF markup:

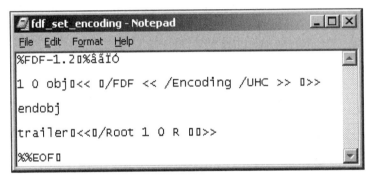

Practical Usage

Encoding is an important factor that determines whether or not the end users can view the applications in a format supported by their machines. In applications that address the locale-specific and internationalized applications, it can actually make or mar the fate of the application. Hence it is important to set an appropriate encoding for the FDF forms.

fdf_set_file()

Version Support

PHP 3>= 3.0.6, PHP 4 >= 4.0.0

Description

`fdf_set_file()` sets the value of the /F key in the FDF document. The /F key is just a reference to a PDF form which is to be populated with data. In a web environment it is a URL, for example, http:/testfdf/resultlabel.pdf.

The /F key is used to point the FDF data to the specific PDF form on a web server. When specifying the /F key, we must give the full URL of the PDF that the FDF data is meant for (for example, http://www.site.com/form.pdf). If the FDF already has a /F key, its old value is replaced.

Function Prototype

```
bool fdf_set_file (int fdf_document, string filename)
```

Here:

- **fdf_document** – is the reference of the FDF document to be used, obtained by making a call to fdf_open() function or by the fdf_create() function.

- **filename** – is a string which is the new value of the /F key. The value of /F can be a URL, a relative path, or a URL to the path of the FDF file. During import Acrobat uses the WebLink plug-in to retrieve it.

Here is an example:

```php
<?php

$outfdf = fdf_create();

fdf_set_file($outfdf,"C:/outtest.fdf");

fdf_save($outfdf, "c:/fdf_set_file.fdf");
?>
```

The resultant FDF document appears like this in a text editor:

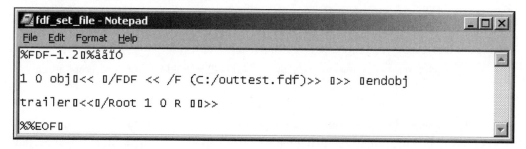

Practical Usage

When we create an FDF document using the API provided by the PHP functions, the document does not have the /F key value. Without the /F key, the document is invalid. This function sets the /F key and makes it a valid FDF document.

fdf_set_flags()

Version Support

PHP 4 >= 4.0.2

Description

`fdf_set_flags()` sets certain flags of the given field name. It sets the value of one of the /Ff, /F, SetFf, /ClrFf, /SetF, /ClrF flags of a field. If the field does not exist in the FDF, it is created. If it does, and already has flags, the old value is replaced.

If the document is a template-based FDF (that is, an FDF for which `fdf_add_template()` has been called), `fdf_set_flags()` acts on the most recently added template.

For more information about these flags refer the PDF Reference Manual.

Function Prototype

```
bool fdf_set_flags (int fdf_document, string fieldname, int whichFlags, int
newFlags)
```

Here:

- ❑ **fdf_document** – is the reference of the FDF document to be used, obtained by making a call to `fdf_open()` or `fdf_create()`.
- ❑ **fieldname** – is a string representing the fully qualified name of the field.
- ❑ **whichFlags** – must be one of the following flags:
    - ❑ 5 – FDFFf sets the /Ff key.
    - ❑ 6 – FDFSetFf sets the /SetFf key.
    - ❑ 7 – FDFClearFf sets the /ClearFf key.
    - ❑ 8 – FDFFlags sets the /F key.
    - ❑ 9 – FDFSetF sets the /SetF key.
    - ❑ 10 – FDFClrF sets the /ClrF key.
- ❑ **newFlags** – is the new value for flags. It must have one of the following values:
    - ❑ Invisible flag – specifies how an annotation is displayed when the corresponding annotation handler is not available.
    - ❑ Hidden flag – determines whether the annotation is to be shown.
    - ❑ Print flag – Indicates whether the annotation should be printed.
    - ❑ NoZoom flag – indicates that if the annotation has an appearance then the appearance should not zoom as the page is magnified by the viewer.
    - ❑ NoRotate flag – indicates that if the annotation has an appearance then the appearance should not be rotated with respect to the page before displaying the appearance.
    - ❑ NoView flag – indicates that if the annotation has an appearance, then that appearance should only be used for printing.
    - ❑ Read-only flag – indicates that the annotation should display but not interact with the user.

Here is an example:

```php
<?php

$outfdf = fdf_create();

fdf_set_flags ($outfdf, "test1", 5, 2);

fdf_save($outfdf, "c:/fdf_set_flags.fdf");
?>
```

The resultant FDF document appears like this in a text editor:

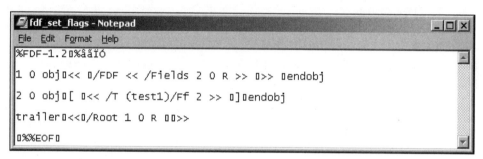

Practical Usage

PDF makes extensive use of the flags for various behaviors that are exhibited to the users. This function helps do that and makes the resultant documents more usable and functional.

fdf_set_javascript_action()

Version Support

PHP 4 >= 4.0.2

Description

fdf_set_javascript_action() sets a JavaScript action for the given field (fieldname).
It sets the value of either the /A or /AA keys, which is the action or additional actions performed in a field to an action of type JavaScript. If the field does not exist in the FDF, it is created. If it does, and already has a /A or /AA key, its old value is replaced. If the document is a template-based FDF, fdf_set_javascript_action() acts on the most recently added template.

Function Prototype

```
bool fdf_set_javascript_action (int fdf_document, string fieldname, int trigger,
string script)
```

Here:

❑ **fdf_document** – is the reference of the FDF document to be used, obtained by making a call to fdf_open() or fdf_create()

- ❑ **fieldname** – is a string representing the fully qualified name of the field
- ❑ **trigger** – is the event trigger for the action; it can be one of the following values:
  - ❑ 0 - FDFEnter
  - ❑ 1 - FDFExit
  - ❑ 2 - FDFDown
  - ❑ 3 – FDFUp (if the value is 3 , an /A entry is used, otherwise an /AA entry is created)
  - ❑ 4 - FDFFormat
  - ❑ 5 - FDFValidate
  - ❑ 6 - FDFKeystroke
  - ❑ 7 - FDFCalculate
- ❑ **script** – is a string containing the text of the script; we use Chr(13) to add a CR and Chr(9) for tabs

Here is an example:

```php
<?php

$outfdf = fdf_create();

fdf_set_javascript_action ($outfdf, "test1", 1, "c:/script.js");

fdf_save($outfdf, "c:/fdf_set_javascript_action.fdf");
?>
```

The resulting FDF document appears like this in a text editor:

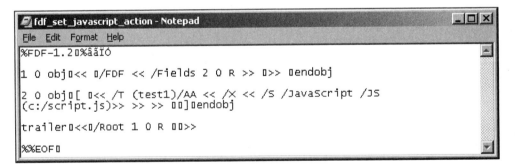

Practical Usage

This function helps to associate a JavaScript file with the actions that we perform on form fields.

fdf_set_opt()

Version Support

PHP 4 >= 4.0.2

Description

`fdf_set_opt()` sets options of the given field fieldname. It sets the value of one element in a field's /Opt key. Each element is either text representing one of the n potential values of the field or an array containing a text and a string – the text indicates a potential value and the string is used to produce the appearance. For example, in a list box, the potential value could be 'A' with the string value of 'Apples' to produce the appearance shown in the list box. If the field does not exist in the FDF, it is created. If it does exist and already has a /Opt array, the requested element in the array is replaced.

For template-based documents, `fdf_set_opt()` acts on the most recently added template. An FDF file used to dynamically change the /Opt of a field in a PDF form may also need to change the /V of that same field (that is, use `fdf_set_value()` when creating the FDF), particularly if the old /V of the field is not a member of the new /Opt being imported into the Form. We must remember that if the /Opt includes item names and export values, /V should use one of the export values, and not one of the item names.

Function Prototype

```
bool fdf_set_opt (int fdf_document, string fieldname, int element, string str1,
string str2)
```

Here:

- ❑ **fdf_document** – is the reference of the FDF document to be used, obtained by making a call to `fdf_open()` or `fdf_create()`.

- ❑ **fieldname** – is a string representing the fully qualified name of the field.

- ❑ **element** – is the index of the element to set in the field's /Opt array. The first element in the /Opt array has an index of 0 (zero).

- ❑ **str1** – if the /Opt array element to be set is composed of an array containing two strings, then `str1` contains the first string (the export value) and if the /Opt array element is a single string, `str1` contains that string (the item name).

- ❑ **str2** – if the /Opt array element to be set is composed of an array containing two strings, then `str2` contains the second string (the item name); otherwise `str2` is NULL.

Here is an example:

```php
<?php

$outfdf = fdf_create();

fdf_set_opt($outfdf, "test1", 1, "aaa", "Bbb");

fdf_save($outfdf, "c:/fdf_set_opt.fdf");
?>
```

The resulting FDF document appears like this in a text editor:

Practical Usage

This function is used to set the value of a select box or a drop-down list box dynamically.

fdf_set_status()

Version Support

PHP 3>= 3.0.6, PHP 4 >= 4.0.0

Description

The fdf_set_status() sets the value of the /Status key. If the FDF already has a /Status key, its old value is replaced. When an FDF document containing a /Status key is returned from a server after a submission, the value of this key is displayed in an alert box to the user.

Function Prototype

```
bool fdf_set_status (int fdf_document, string status)
```

Here:

❑   **fdf_document** – is the reference of the FDF document to be used, obtained by making a call to fdf_open() or fdf_create()

❑   **status** – is a string to use as new status

Here is an example:

```
<?php

$outfdf = fdf_create();

fdf_set_status($outfdf,"Wrox");

fdf_save($outfdf, "c:/fdf_set_status.fdf");
?>
```

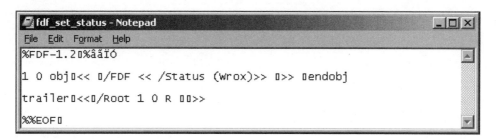

The resultant FDF document appears like this in a text browser:

Practical Usage

This function comes in handy when we want to dynamically change or set the /Status flag in our FDF document.

fdf_set_submit_form_action()

Version Support

PHP 4 >= 4.0.2

Description

fdf_set_submit_form_action() sets a submit form action for the given field fieldname.
It sets the value of either the /A or /AA keys that are the actions or additional actions performed in a field to the action of type 'Submit Form', using the passed URL. The created action will not include a /Fields key.

If the field does not exist in the FDF, it is created. If it does, and already has a /A or /AA key, its old value is replaced. For template-based documents, fdf_set_submit_form_action() acts on the most recently added template.

Function Prototype

```
bool fdf_set_submit_form_action (int fdf_document, string fieldname, int trigger,
string script, int flags)
```

Here:

- ❑ **fdf_document** – is the reference of the FDF document to be used, obtained by making a call to fdf_open() or fdf_create().

- ❑ **fieldname** – is a string representing the fully qualified name of the field.

- ❑ **trigger** – is the event trigger for the action. These are the integers that can be passed:

  - ❑ 0 - FDFEnter
  - ❑ 1 - FDFExit
  - ❑ 2 - FDFDown
  - ❑ 3 - FDFUp

323

If FDFUp is passed as a parameter, a /A entry used, otherwise a /AA entry is created. In the current version of Acrobat, only the FDFEnter, FDFExit, FDFDown, and FDFUp triggers can be used with a Submit Form action.

❑ **script** – specifies the name of an external JavaScript file that is to be executed when the form is submitted. This is used for client-side validation before posting the form to the server.

❑ **flags** – is the value for the /Flags key in the Submit Form action. By default it is 0. Other values that can be used for /Flags key are:

   ❑ bit1 (Include/Exclude flag) – this determines how the /Fields key is interpreted. If this bit is 0, then /Fields represents the individual fields to send. If the bit is 1, then all the name-value pairs in the AcroForm are sent, except for those in the /Fields array (and those that are flagged as 'no-export').

   ❑ bit2 (Include no-value fields flag) – it is used to further restrict which name-value pairs get sent.

   ❑ bit3 (Export format flag) – if 0, then the data is sent using the Forms Data Format (FDF). Otherwise it is sent using the HTML Form format.

   ❑ bit4 (Get Method flag) – if 0, the data is submitted using a POST action; if 1, a GET action is used for the submission. This bit has an effect only when bit3 is 1. If bit3 is 0, this bit must also be 0.

   ❑ bit5 (Submit Coordinates flag) – If this bit is 1, the x and y coordinates of the mouseclick that caused this action are sent as part of the AcroForm data. The x and y values are relative to the upper left-hand corner of the widget that contains the submit action.

Here is an example:

```php
<?php

$outfdf = fdf_create();

fdf_set_submit_form_action($outfdf,"test1",1,"c:/script.js",0);

fdf_save($outfdf, "c:/fdf_set_submit_form_action.fdf");
?>
```

The resultant FDF document appears like this in a text editor:

```
fdf_set_submit_form_action - Notepad
File  Edit  Format  Help
%FDF-1.2 0%âåîÓ

1 0 obj <</FDF << /Fields 2 0 R >> >> endobj

2 0 obj [ << /T (test1)/AA << /X << /S /SubmitForm /F
   (c:/script.js)>> >> >> ]] endobj

trailer <<0/Root 1 0 R >>

%%EOF
```

Practical Usage

Deciding what to do when a user submits a form is one the most important aspects of dynamic page generation and this function helps us to achieve just that.

fdf_set_value()

Version Support

PHP 3>= 3.0.6, PHP 4 >= 4.0.0

Description

`fdf_set_value()` sets the value of a field. The last parameter determines if the field value is to be converted to a PDF Name (isName = 1) or set to a PDF String (isName = 0). It sets the value of a field (that is, the value of the /V key). If the field does not exist, it is created. If it does and already has a value, the old value is replaced. For template-based FDF documents, `fdf_set_value()` acts on the most recently added template.

Function Prototype

```
bool fdf_set_value (int fdf_document, string fieldname, string value, int isName)
```

Here:

❑   **fdf_document** – is the reference of the FDF document to be used, obtained by making a call to `fdf_open()` or `fdf_create()`

❑   **fieldname** – is a string representing the fully qualified name of the field

❑   **value** – is a string to use as new value

❑   **isName** – determines if the field value is to be converted to a PDF Name (isName = 1) or set to a PDF String (isName = 0)

Here is an example:

```php
<?php

$fdf = fdf_create();

fdf_set_value($fdf, "ABCD", "XX", 0);

fdf_save($fdf, "c:/fdf_set_value.fdf");

fdf_close($fdf);
?>
```

In this example, we have created a document and set the value of the ABCD field to XX. The resultant file looks like this in a text editor:

```
fdf_set_value - Notepad
File  Edit  Format  Help

%FDF-1.2 %âãÏÓ

1 0 obj<< /FDF << /Fields 2 0 R >> >> endobj

2 0 obj[ << /T (ABCD)/V (XX)>> ]endobj

trailer<</Root 1 0 R >>

%%EOF
```

Practical Usage

This method is used to set the values of the fields when we create FDF documents programmatically.

Note that for all these functions, if we happen to refer to a non-existent field, the function will return without any further processing.

Now that we have covered the functional overview of FDF, let's discuss an example that makes use of most of these functions.

Creating a Complementary Application To the Basic PDF Form

Let's create a complementary application to the party form that we have been working with so far.

In that `party.pdf` form, the user could enter the name and date of birth of a person. This data would get saved on a remote database and an alert would be sent to the person one day in advance of the event. Also the other person would get automatic birthday wishes from the application.

What if the user wanted to check whose birthday falls on a given day? Let us create such an application. The form should allow users to enter a date, a month, and the names of all their friends who were born on that day.

> **The PDF forms used in this example are available with the code bundle from the Wrox web site.**

First we will create a `birthday.pdf` form that looks like this:

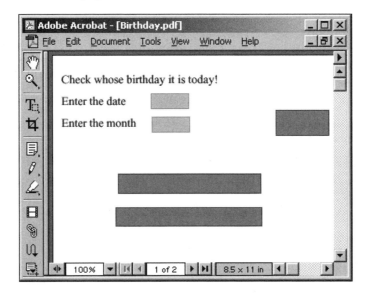

We will set `ProcessBirthday.php` as the action for the submit button:

```php
<?php

if(!extension_loaded('fdf')) {
    if(strtoupper(substr(PHP_OS,0,3)) == 'WIN') {
        dl('php_fdf.dll');
    } else {
        dl('fdf.so');
    }
}

while (list($key, $val) = @each($HTTP_POST_VARS)) {
                            $GLOBALS[$key] = $val;

//Open a FDF document to get the data that has been posted by the form
$fdffp = fopen("c:/bday.fdf", "w");

fwrite($fdffp, $HTTP_RAW_POST_DATA, strlen($HTTP_RAW_POST_DATA));

fclose($fdffp);

$fdf = fdf_open("c:/bday.fdf");

//Get the name
$day = fdf_get_value($fdf, "day");

//Get the month
$month = fdf_get_value($fdf, "month");

//This data can be stored in a database
$name[1] = "John Watson";
$name[2] = "Sherlock Holmes";

fdf_close($fdf);
?>
```

The server-side script retrieves the values the user has entered and sends back a list of those whose birthday falls on that day.

So far we have only used FDF functions to parse the FDF data posted from a PDF form. What if we wanted to populate another PDF document from this posted data? Let's modify our example to do just that.

Populating a PDF document with data is quite simple with FDF. We must:

❑   Create a PDF document.

❑   Add input fields to it with a tool like Acrobat.

❑   Put the document on the web server.

❑   Create the FDF document with PHP, which contains a reference to the PDF document which we want to populate. This will be done on the fly with PHP. The reference is a URL pointing to the PDF document.

Let us change the action of the submit button on the `birthday.pdf` document to point to a different script – `ProcessBirthdayAdvanced.php`:

```php
<?php

if(!extension_loaded('fdf')) {
    if(strtoupper(substr(PHP_OS,0,3)) == 'WIN') {
        dl('php_fdf.dll');
    } else {
        dl('fdf.so');
    }
}

while (list($key, $val) = @each($HTTP_POST_VARS)) {
                        $GLOBALS[$key] = $val;

//Open a FDF document to get the data which has been posted by the form
$fdffp = fopen("c:/bday1.fdf", "w");

fwrite($fdffp, $HTTP_RAW_POST_DATA, strlen($HTTP_RAW_POST_DATA));

fclose($fdffp);

$fdf = fdf_open("c:/bday1.fdf");

//Get the name
$day = fdf_get_value($fdf, "day");

//Get the date of birth
$month = fdf_get_value($fdf, "month");

fdf_close($fdf);

// This data can be stored in a database
$name[1] = "John Watson";
$name[2] = "Sherlock Holmes";

//This is the place where we include advanced functionalities

$outfdf = fdf_create();

fdf_set_value($outfdf ,"Name1",$name[1],0);

fdf_set_value($outfdf ,"Name2",$name[2],0);

fdf_set_file($outfdf,"http://localhost/Results.pdf");

fdf_save($outfdf,"c:/outtest.fdf");

fdf_close($outfdf);

header("Content-type: application/vnd.fdf");

$fp = fopen("c:/outtest.fdf", "r");
```

```
fpassthru($fp);
unlink("c:/outtest.fdf");

fdf_close($fdf);
?>
```

We will also need to create a PDF document (`Results.pdf`) to show the results. Here is a simple document with two textboxes to show the results:

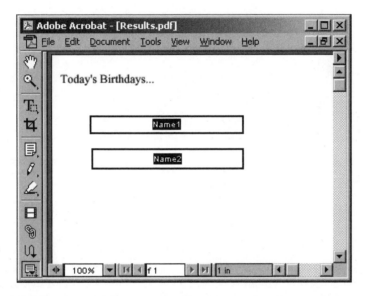

`Name1` and `Name2` are the two text fields. We will save it on the server so that it can be accessed using the HTTP protocol.

In this example we are performing the following steps:

❑   The user fills in the PDF form `Bday.pdf` and clicks on the submit button.

❑   Then the URL associated with the submit button is called; in this case, it is the `ProcessBirthdayAdvanced.php` script.

❑   The PHP script retrieves the data from the FDF data stream and creates a new FDF document, which contains the data for the resulting PDF document.

❑   The FDF document is sent back with the MIME Type `application/vnd.fdf`.

❑   The Acrobat Plug-In reads the data and displays the referred PDF document; in this case it is the `Results.pdf` page.

Now if we open the `Birthday.pdf` page, enter some data, and press the submit button, we will see the magic of populating a PDF document on the fly. The values we hard coded in the PHP script are seen in the `Results.pdf` document:

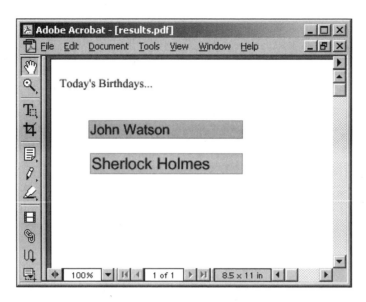

In this last example, we saw how to parse FDF data and populate a PDF document with it.

Summary

In this chapter we got acquainted with the advantages of PDF Forms and why it is good to use the FDF format for PDF Forms. Our next step was to get FDF running on Windows and UNIX machines.

Then we discussed how PHP can be used with FDF. We then went on to create a basic PDF form. This helped us in analyzing the advantages of the FDF format, the FDF document structure, and various FDF form creation strategies. We then looked at the role of JavaScript in validating and populating a pre-created PDF document.

Having done that, we saw a list of the functions available to us in PHP. We also saw how to use those functions. Finally we wrapped up with an example that made use of these functions and we saw how to process FDF data and populate PDF documents.

Regardless of whether forms are created for transactions or information archiving, they all need to be designed with the following aims:

❑   Ease of completion – The forms should be easy to fill in and complete

❑   Precision – In the form architecture, the smart forms need to be designed to prevent as much user error as possible

❑   Retrieval capability – Since the data on most analog forms eventually needs to be electronically cataloged, it would be good to have as many original forms submitted electronically as possible

Armed with this knowledge, we should now be ready to take any real-world FDF development using PHP.

Case Study – Ming Headline Grabber

9

In Chapter 3 and Chapter 4, we looked in detail at PHP/Ming and how we could use this module to create Flash SWF movies on the fly. Chapter 3 introduced us to the different classes that we use to create the graphical side of an SWF movie, and Chapter 4 demonstrated how we could add interactivity to the movie with **ActionScript**.

We shall now use this knowledge of the PHP/Ming module to create a useful application – a **Headline Grabber**. We will not only hone these skills, but also examine the process and thinking behind creating the application. Understanding the structure of a Flash movie is as important as knowing the tools used to create the movie.

Headline Grabber – Application Spec

In its most basic form, a headline grabber is an application, or a script that collects headlines from different news sites and displays them at one central point. The application, once developed, should allow the user to:

- ❑ Connect to different news web sites
- ❑ Retrieve data from these web sites
- ❑ Display data from these web sites
- ❑ Hyperlink to the news story

Now, before we think of writing a PHP script, we have to first identify the processes that we need to follow to develop our application. Once we do this, it will be easier for us to develop our application.

General Requirements

The Headline Grabber application should allow us to select a web site, retrieve headlines from it, store them at a proper location, and finally display the headlines. Alternatively, it should also provide us with the necessary links to the news articles on the selected web site. To do this, we can break the application into two distinct areas:

❑ **Interface**
Firstly, for selecting the web site, displaying headlines, and providing link to the news articles we have to rely on an interface. We have to provide some way for the user to select a news source and trigger the retrieval of the headlines. Secondly, once we have the headlines, we need to display them in a neat and easy-to-read manner; perhaps by providing a method of navigating through a longer list if necessary. Lastly, we need to provide a way for the user to link through to the news article itself.

❑ **Data retrieval and manipulation**
To start with, our data will not be stored on our local server, so we need to have some way in which we can retrieve the data from the news server that the user has selected. This data will not necessarily be in a format that we can readily use in our Flash movie, so we will have to do some sort of work on it to get it into a Flash-ready format. We will then need to get the data into the Flash movie so that our interface can display it to the user.

Later on in the chapter we will look at implementing some sort of local storage of headlines. This will save us the trouble of retrieving the headlines from the news server every time a user requests them. Also, this way we will provide a speedier response and, more importantly, not overburden the news site by visiting them every time for the headline data.

Now that we have looked in general terms at what is involved with the Headline Grabber, let's take a look at some of the specifics involved. This is where we think about how we intend to implement each of the steps in our application. It will also give us a clear picture of what we are creating, and what we are up against.

Usability

Our interface will be an SWF movie in the shape of a horizontal banner. That way, we will be using up minimal page real estate without sacrificing the usability of our application. We will need a button for each of the news services that we intend providing headlines for, an area to display the headlines themselves, and a method of scrolling through the headlines (if necessary).

Let's look at the layout:

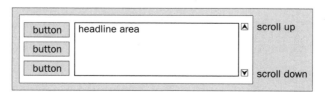

Here, we have three buttons on the left-hand side of the image and scrolling buttons on the far right. We will create these as Flash buttons using the SWFButton class in PHP/Ming. Chapter 4 detailed that we can load variables into a movie with ActionScript's loadVariables() function. Since we will be loading data into our movie, it makes most sense that we make use of this feature.

The contents in the headline area should be able to scroll and, as we saw in Chapter 4, the only object in Flash that we can move programmatically on the stage with ActionScript is a movie clip. Therefore, the headline area needs to be a movie clip created with the SWFSprite class. The buttons we use to scroll the headline area will therefore also be buttons with ActionScript attached to them that moves the headlines movie clip.

Within the movie clip itself we will need to show a list of headlines, each of which should be linked to a news item on a remote web site. Therefore, we need to have a number of buttons embedded within our headlines movie clip.

ActionScript has a function called loadMovie() that allows us to dynamically load another Flash movie into the current movie. It would be far easier for us to write the headlines portion of the application as separate movie clips that we dynamically load as and when we need them (that is, when the user clicks on one of the buttons).

Once the user has made the request for the headlines to be displayed, we will need to retrieve them from either the news server itself, or our local copy. The decision on whether to use the local copy or go directly to the source will be influenced by the amount of time that has elapsed since we last retrieved the headlines.

Retrieving the headlines from the source will require us to connect to the remote site and download the headlines. Some news sites provide their headlines as an RSS (RDF Site Summary) file – an XML document – and we will be using these files to populate our application with headline data.

RSS

According to the RSS-DEV working group (http://groups.yahoo.com/group/rss-dev/files/specification.html):

> "RDF Site Summary (RSS) is a lightweight multipurpose extensible metadata description and syndication format. RSS is an XML application, conforms to the W3C's RDF Specification, and is extensible via XML-namespace and/or RDF-based modularization."

This means that sites that use RSS files for providing headline data will all conform to the Rich Document Format (RDF).

Before we start looking at how RSS files are made up, here is a portion of the RSS file from Slashdot. All RSS files start with the following header, identifying them as being in RDF format:

```
<?xml version="1.0" ?>
  <rdf:RDF xmlns:rdf="http://www.w3.org/1999/02/22-rdf-syntax-ns#"
                  xmlns="http://my.netscape.com/rdf/simple/0.9/">


  <channel>
    <title>Slashdot: News for nerds, stuff that matters</title>
      <link>http://slashdot.org/</link>
```

```
          <description>News for nerds, stuff that matters</description>
      </channel>

      <image>
        <title>Slashdot: News for nerds, stuff that matters</title>
        <url>http://images.slashdot.org/topics/topicslashdot.gif</url>
        <link>http://slashdot.org/</link>
      </image>

      <item>
        <title>Cyber-Attacks?</title>
        <link>http://slashdot.org/article.pl?sid=02/06/27/0449259</link>
      </item>

      <item>
        <title>H2K2 Conference</title>
        <link>http://slashdot.org/article.pl?sid=02/06/27/0239212</link>
      </item>
  </rdf:RDF>
```

The important part for us within the RDF file is the part marked as:

```
<item>
  <title>Headline Title</title>
    <link>http://thenewssite.com/link/to/item</link>
</item>
```

These identify individual news items within the file, and it is these `<item>` tags that we will be using to build our headlines from.

PHP XML Functions

While ActionScript has XML-and socket-handling functions, PHP itself has a robust set of XML functions. Since we will be loading the headline data as a movie, we can use native PHP functions to fetch and parse the XML file before using PHP/Ming to build the SWF movie that will be loaded as the headline data.

PHP parses XML using an event-driven technique. As the parser arrives at tags signifying the beginning or end of an XML element, it fires off the relevant event. These events are handled by event handler functions called **callback functions** that we write in PHP. When we create the XML parser in PHP, we also tell it which PHP function to call when it reaches a start tag, and which function to call when it reaches an end tag. The parser will then call these functions, and pass it any relevant information for that tag.

> **For more information on using PHP with XML refer to** *Professional PHP4 XML* **from** *Wrox Press (ISBN 1-8610-072-1-3).*

The tags that we are interested in are the `<title>` and `<link>` tags that occur within the `<item>` tag. Therefore, our callback function needs to know whether we are inside an `<item>` tag or not and only needs to store information that is contained within `<title>` and `<link>` tags.

Local Storage

To alleviate load on the main news server, we will store the headline data on a local server, in a Microsoft Excel Comma Separated Values (CSV) format. Our interface will therefore have to be aware of the time elapsed between requests. The PHP script that retrieves the data and builds the headline movie will have to take this into account when deciding from where to retrieve the data. We will see how it is done once we finish developing our application.

Tools

Besides a web server, and PHP with Ming support, we will need the following:

- **An editor capable of saving files in UNIX format**
  Later in the chapter we will be using a here document. The terminating line of the here document cannot contain a carriage return character ($\backslash$r), but only a new line character ($\backslash$n). Windows editors insert $\backslash$r$\backslash$n at the end of a line. Fortunately, Windows editors, like Macromedia HomeSite, EditPlus, and ConTEXT, allow us to save a document in UNIX format, which will have the correct line termination character.

- **XML support for PHP**
  To process the RDF files we need to use the PHP XML functions. On UNIX, compile PHP with the -with-xml option to get XML support enabled with PHP. The Windows distribution will have this support by default.

Components

Our application will be made up of the following scripts:

- `newsgrabber.html` – This is the HTML script that we embed in our Flash application

- `mkbutton.php` – This include script allows us to build a button on the interface

- `grabber.php` – This script contains the PHP script that builds the Flash interface to our Headline Grabber application

- `parserdf.php` – This script builds the dynamic headline movie clip

- `class.parserdf.php` – This is a class script that we use to parse the headline RDF file

Application Development

Now that we have an idea of what we want to do, and how we intend to go about it, we can start coding the application. We will do this in a step-by-step fashion. The first part that we will create is the basic interface.

Creating the Basic Interface

In this first step we will only create the container portion of our application. The files we will be working on for this are the `newsgrabber.html` file, the `mkbutton.php` include file for creating the buttons, and the `grabber.php` skeleton code for the SWF movie itself.

newsgrabber.html

We will create an HTML file within which we will embed our SWF movie:

```html
<html>
  <head>
    <title>
      http://localhost/ProPHPMultimedia/Chapter09/newsgrabber.html
    </title>
  </head>

  <body>
    <object classid="clsid:D27CDB6E-AE6D-11cf-96B8-444553540000"
                    codebase="http://download.macromedia.com/pub/shockwave
                    /cabs/flash/swflash.c ab#version=5,0,0,0" width="500"
                    height="100" id="grabber">
      <param name="movie" value="grabber.php">
      <param name="quality" value="high">
      <param name="bgcolor" value="#FFFFFF">
      <embed src="grabber.php" quality="high" bgcolor="#FFFFFF"
             width="500" height="100" id="grabber"
             type="application/x-shockwave-flash" pluginspage=
             "http://www.macromedia.com/go/getflashplayer">
      </embed>
    </object>
  </body>
</html>
```

Don't test this file yet – we still have to create `mkbutton.php` and `grabber.php` files.

mkbutton.php

When we were planning what the interface was going to look like, we decided that we would be adding a number of buttons to the interface to allow the user to select the news-feed that they wished to view. Since this will be a repetitive process, it would be in our best interest to take the code for creating the button and create a function of it.

Let's create the function that will create a button for us. The following code should be saved in a file called `mkbutton.php`, in the same directory as `newsgrabber.html`:

```php
<?php
function MkButton($label,$width,$height,$linestyle)
{
```

We will be passing four arguments to the `MkButton()` function – the label that we want to appear on the button, the width of the button, the height of the button, and whether or not we want a line around the button.

In Chapter 3 we saw that the process of creating a button involves adding shapes to `SWFButton` for each of the states of the button. In our example we will only be using two shapes, one for the normal state of the button, and the other to highlight the button whenever the mouse is over it or clicking on it.

The SWFButton class in PHP/Ming does not have a way for us to add a label to the button, so we will have to work around this limitation. We will create a movie clip (SWFSprite), and add our text label to it. We will create a button with our two states, and add the button to the movie clip by positioning it on top of the text label. We can then add the movie clip to our main movie. To the user of the application, it will appear as a button.

However, if we position our button on top of the text we have already added, it will obscure the text below it. We get around this by setting the alpha value of the shape which we will be using for the normal state of the button, to 0, thus allowing the text to show through the button. For the over or clicked state of the button we set the alpha value of the fill to around 50%, which will give a highlighting effect to the text without obscuring it from the user.

Let's create our two shapes first:

```
$button_normal = new SWFShape();
if ($linestyle!=0){
    $button_normal->setLine(1,0,0,0);
}
```

If we set $linestyle to 0, there won't be a border around the button:

```
$bn_fill = $button_normal->addFill(255,255,255,0);
$button_normal->setRightFill($bn_fill);
```

The fill that we are using for the normal state of the button is white, with an alpha value of 0:

```
$button_normal->movePenTo(0,0);
$button_normal->drawLineTo($width,0);
$button_normal->drawLineTo($width,$height);
$button_normal->drawLineTo(0,$height);
$button_normal->drawLineTo(0,0);

$button_over = new SWFShape();
if ($linestyle!=0){
    $button_over->setLine(1,0,0,0);
}
```

For the over or clicked state of the button we are again using a white fill, but this time we set the alpha value to 150. Remember that an alpha value of 255 is opaque:

```
$bo_fill = $button_over->addFill(255,255,255,150);
$button_over->setRightFill($bo_fill);
$button_over->movePenTo(0,0);
$button_over->drawLineTo($width,0);
$button_over->drawLineTo($width,$height);
$button_over->drawLineTo(0,$height);
$button_over->drawLineTo(0,0);
```

We then create the button, and add our two previously created shapes to the button:

```
$button = new SWFButton();
$button->addShape($button_normal, SWFBUTTON_UP);
$button->addShape($button_over, SWFBUTTON_HIT | SWFBUTTON_OVER |
                                                SWFBUTTON_DOWN);
```

To put our button together, all we need now is to create the text label. We use the `SWFTextField` class rather than the `SWFText` class to maintain cross-platform compatibility with Windows machines. The `setBounds()` function sets the physical width and height of the textbox. We set this to the same as the width (`$width`) and height (`$height`) passed through to the `MkButton()` function so that no part of the font is cropped off:

```
$font = new SWFFont("_sans");
$textLabel = new SWFTextField();
$textLabel->setFont($font);
$textLabel->setBounds($width, $height);
$textLabel->setColor(0, 0, 0);
$textLabel->addString($label);
```

Now that we have all the pieces we need, we can create the movie clip:

```
$button_holder = new SWFSprite();
$hndLabel = $button_holder->add($textLabel);
$hndLabel->move(3,0);
$button_holder->add($button);
$button_holder->nextFrame();
```

We then return the newly created `SWFSprite` object to the script that called this function:

```
    return $button_holder;
}
?>
```

grabber.php

Our next step is to create the main PHP script that will output the SWF file that we embed into the page. Save this script as `grabber.php` in the same directory as the `newsgrabber.html` and `mkbutton.php`:

```
<?php

//Load the Ming module if necessary
if(!extension_loaded('ming')) {
    if(strtoupper(substr(PHP_OS,0,3)) == 'WIN') {
        dl('php_ming.dll');
    } else {
        dl('php_ming.so');
    }
}

require('mkbutton.php');
```

Since we will be calling the MkButton() function we need to include the code for the MkButton() function in our main script:

```
$movie = new SWFMovie();
$movie->setrate(25);
$movie->setbackground(255,255,255);
$movie->setdimension(500,100);
```

We will now add the three buttons to the interface using our MkButton() function. The four arguments we need to pass through to the function are the label for the button, the width, the height, and the parameter that decides whether we want a line or not. We will be providing news headlines from the following:

❑   http://www.slashdot.org

❑   http://www.freshmeat.net

❑   http://www.mozilla.org

Let's continue with the script:

```
$hndFreshmeat = $movie->add(MkButton("Freshmeat",70,15,1));
$hndFreshmeat->move(5,10);
$hndSlashdot = $movie->add(MkButton("Slashdot",70,15,1));
$hndSlashdot->move(5,30);
$hndMozilla = $movie->add(MkButton("Mozilla",70,15,1));
$hndMozilla->move(5,50);
```

While we are adding buttons, we can also add buttons to scroll the headlines:

```
$hndUpArrow = $movie->add(MkButton("^",10,10,1));
$hndUpArrow->move(489,0);
$hndDownArrow = $movie->add(MkButton("v",10,10,1));
$hndDownArrow->move(489,89);

header('Content-type: application/x-shockwave-flash');
$movie->output();
?>
```

If we now open up a web browser and take a look at newsgrabber.html we see:

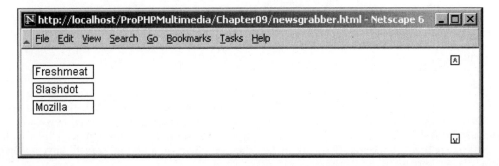

Taking the mouse over one of the buttons will highlight the text of that button:

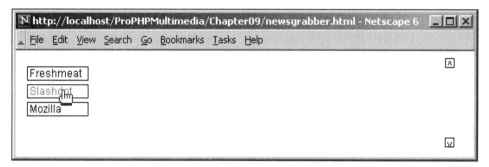

Completing the Interface

The next step in the development process for us is to add ActionScript to the buttons, so that when the user clicks on them it will actually do something. We will also add functionality to the scroll buttons.

The first thing that we will have deal with is adding the actions to the button. We will use the `setAction()` method from the `SWFButton` class that allows us to set the action for that button. Our button is being created inside the `MkButton()` function in `mkbutton.php`, so our first step is to go and alter the function to take this into account.

mkbutton.php

In `mkbutton.php`, we change the function signature of the `MkButton()` function:

```
function MkButton($label,$width,$height,linestyle)
{
```

to the following, by adding the `$action` parameter:

```
function MkButton($label,$width,$height,$linestyle,$action)
{
```

Within the `MkButton()` function we create an `SWFAction` object and associate it with the button with the `addAction()` method of the `SWFButton` class:

```
$button = new SWFButton();
$buttonAction = new SWFAction($action);
$button->addAction($buttonAction, SWFBUTTON_MOUSEUP);
```

When the user releases the mouse button, the ActionScript contained within the variable `$action` will be executed.

grabber.php

Now let's modify our `grabber.php` to pass the action that we want to associate with the button through to the `MkButton()` function. To make changing our code easier, the ActionScript that we add to the buttons will call the ActionScript functions that will be defined on the main timeline. This way, if we want to change the ActionScript that is run when the user clicks on a button, we will have a single central place where all of our ActionScript code is written.

Since we will be keeping all of our ActionScript at one single place, we will use the here document syntax to define the variable that stores the ActionScript functions. The here document syntax allows us to break the string that we want to store in a variable across multiple lines. This is especially useful for us when we want to add ActionScript to a button or frame that contains a complex block of code. Here is an example:

```
$actionstring = <<<EOD
   Example of string
   spanning multiple lines
   using heredoc syntax.
EOD;
```

We define the string with a <<< followed by an identifier, then the string we wish to store, and finally the identifier again, with a semicolon. The identifier has to appear by itself on its own line and must start at the beginning of the line. Thus, the $actionstring variable contains the entire block of ActionScript code.

Since the contents of grabber.php are quite different from the original one, we will include all the code for the script again. The first thing we will do is declare a variable called $root_actions, and using the here document syntax we will create ActionScript functions for each of the buttons in our interface. For the time being we will leave these functions empty as placeholder fields for the code (which we will write later). Here is the complete grabber.php script:

```php
<?php

//Load the Ming module if necessary
if(!extension_loaded('ming')) {
    if(strtoupper(substr(PHP_OS,0,3)) == 'WIN') {
        dl('php_ming.dll');
    } else {
        dl('php_ming.so');
    }
}

$root_actions = <<<EOD

function ClickFreshmeat()
{
}
function ClickSlashdot()
{
}

function ClickMozilla()
{
}
function ClickUp()
{
}
function ClickDown()
{
}
EOD;

require('mkbutton.php');
$movie = new SWFMovie();
```

```
$movie->setrate(25);
$movie->setbackground(255,255,255);
$movie->setdimension(500,100);
```

We then create our five buttons, but this time we add the fourth argument to the MkButton() function, passing through the action to perform:

```
$hndFreshmeat = $movie->add
              (MkButton("Freshmeat",70,15,1,"_root.ClickFreshmeat();"));

$hndFreshmeat->move(5,10);
$hndSlashdot = $movie->add
              (MkButton("Slashdot",70,15,1,"_root.ClickSlashdot();"));

$hndSlashdot->move(5,30);
$hndMozilla = $movie->add
              (MkButton("Mozilla",70,15,1,"_root.ClickMozilla();"));

$hndMozilla->move(5,50);
$hndUpArrow = $movie->add
              (MkButton("^",10,10,1,"_root.ClickUp();"));

$hndUpArrow->move(489,0);
$hndDownArrow = $movie->add
              (MkButton("v",10,10,1,"_root.ClickDown();"));

$hndDownArrow->move(489,89);
```

Then we add the contents of $root_actions as SWFAction to the root timeline of our movie, and output the SWF file:

```
$movie->add(new SWFAction($root_actions));

header('Content-type: application/x-shockwave-flash');
$movie->output();
?>
```

If we test this movie the buttons will still have no visible effect as they are calling empty ActionScript functions. Let's now write some code for each of the functions so that we can see it working.

Currently, we don't have any headline data to scroll through, so let's quickly create something that we can use in its place to scroll:

```
//Begin filler block
$movTest = new SWFSprite();
$font = new SWFFont("_sans");

$textTest = new SWFTextField(SWFTEXTFIELD_MULTILINE);
$textTest->setFont($font);
$textTest->setBounds(380,300);
$textTest->setColor(0, 0, 0);
$textTest->addString($root_actions);
```

```
$movTest->add($textTest);
$movTest->nextFrame();

$datablock = $movie->add($movTest);
$datablock->moveTo(100,0);
$datablock->setName("data");
//End filler block
```

```
$movie->add(new SWFAction($root_actions));
```

that adds the actions to the main timeline.

All that we are doing here is creating a movie clip that contains a multi-line textbox. The textbox has a height (300) that is larger than the height of our SWF movie, so, to see the entire contents, we will have to scroll it. We have filled the textbox with the text of the $root_actions variable and given the movie clip the name of the data, so that we can reference it from ActionScript.

If we run the movie now, we will get the following output:

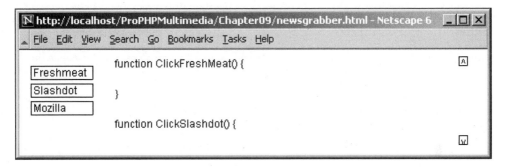

We cannot at the moment see the functions that allow us to scroll the data area, so let's go and add the ActionScript to do the scrolling.

We scroll the data by changing the _y value of the data movie clip. Since we don't want the data in the movie clip to scroll forever, we have to limit the distance that it can move up and down. We will do this by using the height of the movie clip in our ClickDown() function, to determine whether we have reached the lower extent of the movie clip or not.

When the page loads our movie will be laid out as follows:

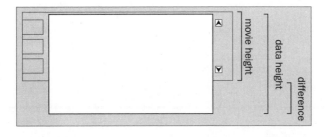

Depending on whether we have scrolled the data movie clip up or down, the value of _root.data._y can be positive or negative. If we click the down button, we want the movie clip to move up on our screen; in Flash terminology that means decreasing the _y value of the movie clip. Since we need to limit the extent of the scrolling, we need to know the height of the movie clip. We could hard code this value into our script, but at a later stage we will be loading this movie clip dynamically with the news headlines. Therefore, we will use the _height property (the height of the movie clip in pixels) in our calculations. The height of the movie clip less the height of our SWF movie is the section of the movie clip that is not visible.

When we have scrolled the data movie clip up as far as we wish to allow, the layout would be:

The _y value of the data movie clip is the negative of the data movie clip height less the SWF movie height. Our function needs to test whether we have exceeded this limit before moving the movie clip up any further.

Thus, the ClickDown() function, which we need to add to our heredoc section, looks like this:

```
function ClickDown()
{
    if (Math.abs(_root.data._y) <= (_root.data._height - 100)) {
        root.data._y -= 10;
    }
}
```

If the absolute value of _root.data._y is less than or equal to the height of the data movie clip less the height of the SWF movie (labeled **difference** in the figure above), then we have not yet reached the extent of the movie clip, and we can continue scrolling it up.

Once we have added this code to the ClickDown() function, we can test it by reloading the newsgrabber.html page and scrolling down, to see the new function we have added:

```
N http://localhost/ProPHPMultimedia/Chapter09/newsgrabber.html - Netscape 6    _ |□| X|

  File  Edit  View  Search  Go  Bookmarks  Tasks  Help

  Freshmeat        }
                   function ClickUp() {
  Slashdot             if (_root.data._y < 0) {
  Mozilla                  _root.data._y += 10;
                       }
                   }
```

The ClickUp() function will move the data movie clip down on the screen achieved in ActionScript by increasing the _y value. The function then only has to test whether the _y value has reached a positive value:

```
function ClickUp()
{
    if (_root.data._y < 0) {
        _root.data._y += 10;
    }
}
```

We will use ActionScript's loadMovie() function to load the headlines. loadMovie() loads an SWF movie into the current SWF movie, in place of an existing movie clip. This is the syntax:

```
loadMovie("url",level/target[, variables])
```

where url specifies the URL of the SWF movie that we want to load, level/target tells the function either at what level to load the new movie clip, or the name of the movie clip that this new movie is to replace, and variables is an optional argument that specifies the method to pass any variables through to the specified URL

In this case, the URL will be a PHP script that will retrieve the headlines and build them into an SWF movie. We will replace the data movie clip with this new movie clip.

Within the here document section of our grabber.php script, we can now update the code for our three button functions:

```
function ClickFreshmeat()
{
    loadMovie('parserdf.php?site=freshmeat',_root.data,"POST");
}

function ClickSlashdot()
{
    loadMovie('parserdf.php?site=slashdot',_root.data,"POST");
}

function ClickMozilla()
{
    loadMovie('parserdf.php?site=mozilla',_root.data,"POST");
}
```

parserdf.php

We will now write a script to create the headline data. Before we get into the details of how we are going to do that, we can test if loadMovie() is working by writing a test parserdf.php script to output just the name of the site that we have requested:

```php
<?php

//Load the Ming module if necessary
if(!extension_loaded('ming')) {
    if(strtoupper(substr(PHP_OS,0,3)) == 'WIN') {
        dl('php_ming.dll');
    } else {
        dl('php_ming.so');
    }
}

$movie = new SWFMovie();
$movie->setrate(25);
$movie->setbackground(255,255,255);

$font = new SWFFont("_sans");

$textSite = new SWFTextField();
$textSite->setFont($font);
$textSite->setColor(0, 0, 0);
$textSite->addString($_REQUEST["site"]);
$movie->add($textSite);

header('Content-type: application/x-shockwave-flash');
$movie->output();
?>
```

This is the output:

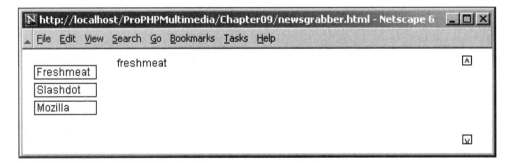

Grabbing and Using the Data

Now that we have created the interface we have to spend some time with the back-end `parserdf.php` script. Headline data is available on most sites as an RSS file.

class.parserdf.php

We will write a small class to process the RDF file.

> The latest version of PEAR (http://pear.php.net) has a class to do just this, but at the time of writing this class was not included with the PHP distribution.

Let's begin the class:

```php
<?php
class RDFParse
{
    var $headline_counter = 0;
    var $in_headline = FALSE;
    var $current_tag_state = '';
    var $headline_data = array();
```

Here we declare four variables:

- ❑ $headline_counter maintains a count of the number of headlines we have
- ❑ $in_headline tells us whether we are inside a headline (<item>) tag or not
- ❑ $current_tag_state tells us whether we have entered a <title> or a <link> tag
- ❑ $headline_data is an array of the headlines

The SetFile() function lets us set the URL of the RDF file that we want to open:

```php
function SetFile($file)
{
    $this->file = $file;
}
```

The Parse() function is the function that we will call to work through the RDF file:

```php
function Parse()
{
    $this->xml_parser = xml_parser_create();

    xml_set_object($this->xml_parser, $this);
    xml_set_element_handler
        ($this->xml_parser, "StartElementHandler","EndElementHandler");
    xml_set_character_data_handler
        ($this->xml_parser, "CharacterDataHandler");
    xml_parser_set_option
        ($this->xml_parser,XML_OPTION_CASE_FOLDING, FALSE);

    $fp = fopen($this->file,"r");

    while ($data = fread($fp, 4096)) {
        xml_parse($this->xml_parser, $data, feof($fp));
    }

    fclose($fp);
}
```

To begin with, we create an XML parser and then, because the callback functions exist within an object, we call the xml_set_object() function. We then tell the XML parser that, when it encounters a start tag the StartElementHandler() function should be called, and when it encounters an end tag the EndElementHandler() function should be called. Finally, when we encounter a character data we should call the CharacterDataHandler() function.

This is the `StartElementHandler()` function:

```
function StartElementHandler($xml_parser,
    $element_name,$element_attribs)
{
```

Here:

- ❑ `$xml_parser` is the XML parser
- ❑ `$element_name` is the name of the element for which this event was triggered
- ❑ `$element_attribs` is an associative array of the attributes for the element

Let's continue with the script:

```
if ($element_name == "item") {
    $this->in_headline = TRUE;
}
```

Remember the structure inside the RDF file that we are concerned with is:

```
<item>
  <title>Headline Title</title>
  <link>http://thenewssite.com/link/to/item</link>
</item>
```

Once we find an `<item>` tag we know that we are now inside a headline, and we incorporate it in our PHP script like this:

```
if ($this->in_headline == TRUE) {
    $this->current_tag_state = $element_name;
} else {
    $this->current_tag_state = '';
}
}
```

If we get a tag and are inside the headline, we set the `$current_tag_state` to the name of the tag that we are dealing with. Why we do this will become apparent when we look at the `CharacterDataHandler()` function that handles character data.

Here is the `EndElementHandler()` function:

```
function EndElementHandler( $xml_parser, $element_name)
{
    $this->current_tag_state = '';
```

If we have reached an end tag then we can safely set the $current_tag_state to an empty string:

```
        if ($element_name == "item") {
            $this->headline_counter++;
            $this->in_headline = FALSE;
        }
    }
```

If the tag that we just ended was an <item> tag then we know we have finished with a headline block and we can increment the headline counter and set our $in_headline variable to 0.

The CharacterDataHandler() function is passed two arguments – a reference to the parser and the data that fired off this callback function:

```
    function CharacterDataHandler($xml_parser, $data)
    {
```

If we are not inside a headline tag, then exit the function:

```
        if ($this->current_tag_state == '' || $this->in_headline == FALSE){
            return;
        }
```

If the $current_tag_state is a <title> tag, we store the title in our $headline_data array:

```
        if ($this->current_tag_state == "title" ) {
            $this->headline_data[$this->headline_counter]["title"] = $data;
        }
```

If the current tag is a <link> tag then we store the link in the array (any other tag is ignored):

```
        if ($this->current_tag_state == "link" ) {
            $this->headline_data[$this->headline_counter]["link"] = $data;
        }
    }
```

Here is the GetHeadlines() function:

```
    function GetHeadlines()
    {
        return $this->headline_data;
    }

} // End of class parsedf.php
?>
```

Our last function simply returns the headline data to the calling script.

parserdf.php

Before we start writing the code to grab the RDF file and parse the XML, we should store a local copy of the RDF files to work with. Using a web browser, we can grab and save the following three files into the same folder as the application files:

❑ http://slashdot.org/slashdot.rdf

❑ http://freshmeat.net/backend/fm.rdf

❑ http://mozilla.org/news.rdf

We wrote a very basic `parserdf.php` in the previous section so that we could make sure that our interface was working. Here's the `parserdf.php` script that works its way through the RDF file:

```php
<?php

//Load the Ming module if necessary
if(!extension_loaded('ming')) {
    if(strtoupper(substr(PHP_OS,0,3)) == 'WIN') {
        dl('php_ming.dll');
    } else {
        dl('php_ming.so');
    }
}

require('class.parserdf.php');

$xml = new RDFParse();

switch ($_REQUEST["site"]) {
case "slashdot":
    $xml->setFile("slashdot.rdf");
    break;

case "freshmeat":
    $xml->setFile("fm.rdf");
    break;

case "mozilla":
    $xml->setFile("news.rdf");
    break;
}
```

Now that we have set the filename for our XML parser, we can go ahead and parse it, and return the headline data:

```php
$xml->Parse();
$headline_data = $xml->GetHeadlines();
```

At this point we will have an array that contains the titles and headlines of all the headlines that are in the RDF file. We can now go ahead and use PHP/Ming to build the SWF movie:

```
$movie = new SWFMovie();
$movie->setrate(25);
$movie->setbackground(255,255,255);
require('mkbutton.php');
```

We already have a function (MkButton()) to make a button, so let's reuse the code:

```
for ($i=0;$i<count($headline_data);$i++) {
    $hndLabel = $movie->add
                (MkButton($headline_data[$i]["title"],380,15,0,
                "getURL('".$headline_data[$i]["link"]."','_blank');"));
    $hndLabel->moveTo(0,($i*20));
}
```

Now we loop around through each of the items in the $headline_data array, adding the title as the label of our button and using the link in a getURL() ActionScript function to open the link in a new browser window:

```
$movie->add(new SWFAction("stop();"));

$movie->nextFrame();

header('Content-type: application/x-shockwave-flash');
$movie->output();
?>
```

If we run the application now and click on one of the buttons we will get:

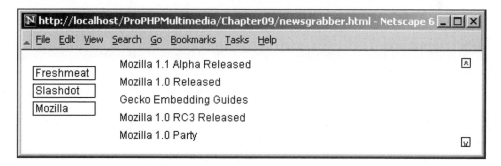

Enhancements

There is a glitch in this application – if we scroll down a set of headlines and then switch to another set of headlines, the new set will already be scrolled down. This is because when we load a movie with the loadMovie() function in ActionScript, it inherits the position, rotation, and scale of the targeted movie clip.

We can resolve this by altering the functions that call the loadMovie() function to also move the movie clip back to its initial position.

In `grabber.php`, change the three button functions to the following:

```
function ClickFreshmeat()
{
    loadMovie('parse_xml.php?site=freshmeat',_root.data,"POST");
    _root.data._y = 0;
}

function ClickSlashdot()
{
    loadMovie('parse_xml.php?site=slashdot',_root.data,"POST");
    _root.data._y = 0;
}

function ClickMozilla()
{
    loadMovie('parse_xml.php?site=mozilla',_root.data,"POST");
    _root.data._y = 0;
}
```

While we are working in the `grabber.php`, we should also alter the line that displays the root actions as the movie loads. Let's replace it with a message for the user, from:

```
$textTest->setBounds(380,300);
$textTest->setColor(0, 0, 0);
$textTest->addString($root_actions);
```

to:

```
$textTest->setBounds(380,50);
$textTest->setColor(0, 0, 0);
$textTest->addString("Welcome to the PHP/Ming Headline Grabber");
```

The output on the browser looks like this:

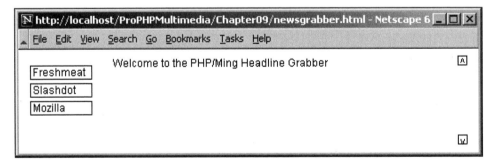

Adding Local Storage

As mentioned in the *Data Retrieval and Manipulation* section of this chapter, to avoid hammering the news server with requests for the RDF file we should implement some sort of local storage. We will use a flat text file to store our data. Since we have to make some changes to the `parserdf.php` file, we will write the entire script again.

Here is the `parserdf.php` script in its entirety:

```php
<?php

//Load the Ming module if necessary
if(!extension_loaded('ming')) {
    if(strtoupper(substr(PHP_OS,0,3)) == 'WIN') {
        dl('php_ming.dll');
    } else {
        dl('php_ming.so');
    }
}

require('class.parserdf.php');
require('mkbutton.php');
$site = $_REQUEST["site"];
$timenow = time();
```

Grab the current time as we have to compare it to the time when the headlines were retrieved from the source:

```php
if (file_exists($site.".csv")) {
    clearstatcache();
    $timelast = filemtime($site.".csv");
} else {
    $timelast = 0;
}
```

We will store the headline data in a CSV file named after the site where the headlines are from. We'll use the last modified time of the file to check the time that the headlines were last grabbed from the source at the main site.

If the difference between the timestamp now and the timestamp of the headline file is greater than ten seconds, we should retrieve the headlines from the RDF file again. We will use ten seconds so that we can test that the script is working correctly. We'll also use our local RDF file until we're sure that we've got it right:

```php
if (($timenow - $timelast) > 10) {
    $xml = new RDFParse();
    switch ($site) {
    case "slashdot":
        $xml->setFile("slashdot.rdf");
        break;
    case "freshmeat":
        $xml->setFile("fm.rdf");
        break;
    case "mozilla":
        $xml->setFile("news.rdf");
        break;
    }
    $xml->Parse();
    $headline_data = $xml->GetHeadlines();
```

Once we've retrieved the headlines, we can update the CSV file of headlines:

```
$fp = fopen($site.".csv","w");
for($i=0;$i<count($headline_data);$i++) {
    fwrite($fp,"\"".$headline_data[$i]["title"]."\",\"".
    $headline_data[$i]["link"]."\"\n");
}
fclose($fp);
```

If our interval was less than ten seconds then we can just grab the headlines from the local copy:

```
} else {
    $fp = fopen($site.".csv","r");
    $headline_data = array();
    $count = 0;
    while ($data = fgetcsv ($fp, 1000, ",")) {
        $headline_data[$count]["title"] = $data[0];
        $headline_data[$count]["link"] = $data[1];
        $count++;
    }
    fclose($fp);
}
```

The rest of the `parserdf.php` script remains unchanged:

```
$movie = new SWFMovie();
$movie->setrate(25);
$movie->setbackground(255,255,255);

for ($i=0;$i<count($headline_data);$i++) {
    $hndLabel =
    $movie->add(MkButton($headline_data[$i]["title"],380,15,0,
            "getURL('".$headline_data[$i]["link"]."','_blank');"));
    $hndLabel->moveTo(0,($i*20));
}

$movie->add(new SWFAction("stop();"));

$movie->nextFrame();

header('Content-type: application/x-shockwave-flash');
$movie->output();
?>
```

To test the script on Windows machines, we can open the command prompt in the directory where our script files are, then clicked on the Freshmeat button in the application:

```
07/03/2002  05:09p            641 freshmeat.csv
```

After about 20 seconds when we click on the Freshmeat button again, the listing shows that the file modification time has been updated:

```
/03/2002  05:11p            641 freshmeat.csv
```

We then clicked a few more times in succession, and we can see that the modification time remains the same until 10 seconds have elapsed:

```
07/03/2002  05:13p                641 freshmeat.csv
07/03/2002  05:13p                641 freshmeat.csv
07/03/2002  05:13p                641 freshmeat.csv
```

> **To get the output on the UNIX system, open the shell prompt and use the command:**
> `ls -l --full-time *.csv`

Our code works as we expected it to, so we can go and change the ten second value in the `parserdf.php` script to a value that is considerate to the news site. For instance, Slashdot asks that one shouldn't request the file more than once every 30 minutes, so let's go for 45 minutes by changing the value from 10 to 2700.

We can also change the URLs that `fopen()` is calling, to the actual URLs of the RDF files that live on the Web, from:

```
if (($timenow - $timelast) > 10) {
```

to:

```
if (($timenow - $timelast) > 2700) {
```

and the lines:

```
$xml->setFile("slashdot.rdf");
$xml->setFile("fm.rdf");
$xml->setFile("news.rdf");
```

to:

```
$xml->setFile("http://slashdot.org/slashdot.rdf");
$xml->setFile("http://freshmeat.net/backend/fm.rdf");
$xml->setFile("http://mozilla.org/news.rdf");
```

We have thus completed a fully tested and working Headline Grabber application.

Summary

Over the course of this chapter we have built a working PHP/Ming Headline Grabber application. We have looked at how to begin tackling a project like this, and how by using a combination of ActionScript, PHP/Ming, and other PHP functions, we could bring it to completion.

We covered some new areas by finding out how the `loadMovie()` function works in ActionScript and delved into the world of RDF files and XML processing.

This chapter has given us some insight into the processes and methodologies of building a Flash application. We can build on this application by adding error checking, more sophisticated database integration, and better visual effects to the interface.

10

Case Study – Using GD on WAP Sites and PDA

One of the obvious uses of PHP's image manipulation capabilities is to automate the preparation of a single-source image for deployment on more than one platform. In this case study we'll use the GD image functions to automatically generate images optimized for a mobile web application.

Here's our hypothetical situation. Our client has a web site featuring a searchable database of coffee shops. The MySQL database includes information such as the address, telephone number, and even URLs and photographs when available. The client wants to make the database available to mobile users and to reach out to the widest possible audience; it should be accessible from both PDAs and web-enabled cell phones.

We'll come up with a detailed specification later, but first let us take a look at the platforms we're going to design for – WAP and PDA.

WAP

Wireless Application Protocol (WAP) was developed by a forum of companies from the mobile communications industry as a standard protocol for Internet applications on mobile phones and other handheld devices. Before WAP was developed, many of the large mobile phone companies had developed their own protocols for sending messages and other data from mobile devices, and although each one worked, the market became fragmented. With so many different platforms, there was little incentive for companies to develop services for each one.

Since it was introduced, WAP has been widely deployed and it has become the de facto standard for creating mobile-phone-friendly pages. In August 2001 the WAP Forum announced the WAP 2.0 specification, which uses Extensible Hypertext Markup Language (XHTML) and Cascading Style Sheets (CSS) to deliver applications to mobile browsers. Although WAP 2.0 is not yet widely supported, this convergence of the WAP protocol with the XHTML standards promises to make developing applications that work on both traditional PCs and mobile devices a much smoother process than it is now.

WAP consists of several layers of protocols (Application Environment Layer, Session Layer, Transport Layer, and so on), which in combination allow WAP clients to access information from the Internet wirelessly. The only component we're concerned with for our application is the **Wireless Markup Language** (WML).

WML vs. HTML

WML documents live on web servers just like HTML documents and can be accessed by URLs using HTTP. Both use a hierarchical tag structure to mark up content, for example, <p>, <img>, <br>, and <a> tags.

There are numerous differences between WML and HTML and we must familiarize ourselves with them if we plan to start building WML pages on our site. Here are some of the most important ones:

- **Decks and Cards vs. Sites and Pages**
  A collection of HTML resources is called a **site** and is made up of any number of linked individual **pages**. Pages are stored as separate files on the web server. On the other hand, a collection of WML resources is called a **deck**, and consists of any number of linked individual **cards**. Unlike HTML Pages, WML cards are all part of the same deck, which form a single WML file.

- **WML is XML**
  Although the web is moving slowly towards the W3C's XML-compliant version of HTML known as XHTML, the vast majority of sites still deploy pages using HTML 4 or even HTML 3.2. A lot of that HTML isn't 100% valid when checked against the W3C specification. Most of the major desktop web browsers are still very forgiving when it comes to rendering HTML with improperly nested or missing tags, but the WML specification is more demanding (though a filter program can be written or the ones available with the vendor may be used to translate HTML pages into WML pages).

  Hence, we will need to pay special attention and keep all of our tags in lowercase, making sure to close empty tags with a closing slash, like <br/> and <img/>. Most importantly, our WML decks must be 'well-formed', meaning that they follow the WML Document Type Definition (DTD) to the last detail.

- **The <head> tag and the <body> tag**
  We don't use the <head> tag in WML, instead the HTTP header information is sent using a scripting language. The page title is written inside the <card> tag instead of the <head> tag. Also, there is no <body> tag in WML.

A Basic WML Deck

Providing details about WML is beyond the scope of this case study, but let's take a quick look at a simple WML deck with a couple of cards:

```
<?xml version="1.0"?>

<!DOCTYPE wml PUBLIC "-//WAPFORUM//DTD WML 1.1//EN"
"http://www.wapforum.org/DTD/wml_1.1.xml">

<!-- This is a comment. -->

<wml>
  <card title="Card One" id="card1">
    <p>This is the first card in the deck.</p>
    <p>Here's a link to another card: <a href="#card2">Card 2</a></p>
  </card>

  <card title="Card Two" id="card2">
    <p>This is the second card in the deck.</p>
    <p><a href="#card1">Go Back</a></p>
  </card>
</wml>
```

The first three lines are the XML and DTD declarations. The deck itself is contained between the `<wml>` and `</wml>` tags, which are analogous to the `<html>` and `</html>` tags of an HTML document. Within the `<wml>` tags are the `<card>` tags, which in turn contain the actual content of the deck.

WAP on the Desktop

If we want to develop WAP pages but don't have a WAP-enabled cell phone, or other mobile device, there are a couple of options that we can use on the desktop:

❑ **DeckIt**
DeckIt is a free WAP emulator from PyWeb.com (http://www.PyWeb.com/tools/). It is available for Windows and UNIX systems.

❑ **Openwave SDK**
The Openwave SDK from Openwave Systems (http://www.openwave.com/) includes a WAP emulator and tools for developing WAP applications. It is available for Windows 95/98/ME and Windows NT/2000.

PDA Web Content – AvantGo

AvantGo is one of the most popular web browsers available for handheld devices. AvantGo's service allows users to add **channels** of content, which are updated whenever the PDA is synced to the desktop computer. On devices with Internet connectivity (through wireless communication or an external modem, for instance) AvantGo acts as a regular web browser, making it an ideal platform for handheld web-based applications.

We'll use AvantGo as our target PDA platform since it can be installed on most PDAs.

AvantGo Considerations

In the World Wide Web's infancy, browsers were much simpler as compared to today's multimedia powerhouses – no Flash animation, no MIDI or WAV sound files, no streaming video plug-ins, not even images. Not surprisingly, the HTML that made up the earliest web pages was similarly minimalist. As browsers evolved, and companies like Microsoft and Netscape added proprietary extensions to HTML, designers began using HTML for graphical page layout rather than providing the user agent (browser) with contextual information about the text on the page.

We can get away with as many `<font>` tags and spacer GIFs as we want in a desktop web browser, but creating web pages for handheld devices requires a little more restraint. Since AvantGo is one of the most widely used handheld browsers, we must familiarize ourselves with some of its requirements and limitations:

❑ **Image sizes**
AvantGo runs on many different devices with varying screen resolutions. If an image is larger than a particular device's resolution, AvantGo automatically scales it to fit. However, if we want to make sure our image looks consistent on all platforms we must limit our images to 150x150 pixels, which is the maximum image resolution for standard PalmOS displays. Making our images less than 150x150 pixels will keep bandwidth and memory usage down, and if we avoid scaling of images by AvantGo we can be assured that they'll look consistent across all platforms.

❑ **Image formats**
AvantGo displays JPEG and GIF images, but not PNG. If we plan to use GD to manipulate images for use in AvantGo, we're limited to one format – JPEG.

❑ **Page size**
AvantGo will not display pages with images and text totaling more than 32K. This probably won't be an issue, especially when the application will also be deployed on WAP devices, but it's something to keep in mind.

There are many other ways to optimize our HTML for AvantGo. For further information, see AvantGo's HTML style guide at http://avantgo.com/doc/developer/styleguide/styleguide.html.

AvantGo with a PDA

To download AvantGo, create a user account at http://www.AvantGo.com/ and follow the instructions for downloading and installing AvantGo on the PDA platform.

AvantGo without a PDA

If we want to try AvantGo but don't have a PDA, Palm Computing offers a free desktop Palm emulator called Palm Operating System Emulator (POSE), which is available for Windows, Macintosh, and UNIX. Precompiled binaries of POSE are available for Red Hat and Debian GNU/Linux, while other versions of UNIX are able to download and compile the POSE sourcecode.

To use POSE we will also need a ROM image from a PalmOS device. The ROM image is a read-only snapshot of the core operating system, which is stored on a chip in an actual PalmOS device. On our desktop the ROM image is stored as a file.

There are two ways to obtain ROM files for PalmOS devices:

❑   Download a ROM image from the Palm Resource Pavillion

❑   Upload a ROM image from a PalmOS device to our computer

Palm provides ROM images for free, but they do require us to sign up as a Palm Developer. They provide ROMs for many different types of PalmOS devices; even if we have an older, monochrome model we can still see what our HAWHAW pages will look like on a color device.

For more information about obtaining PalmOS ROMs or uploading them from our PDA, visit the Palm developers' web site at http://www.palm.com/developers/.

> **Refer Appendix H for detailed instructions to set up Palm Desktop, POSE, and AvantGo on a Windows desktop. UNIX users will have to go through the AvantGo sign-up and installation process to get the necessary .PRC files for the POSE.**

Delivering Custom Content with PHP

Now that we're familiar with the platforms we'll be developing for, we need to think about how we can best use PHP to create an application that will work with both WAP WML, and PDA-optimized HTML. We already know that we can use GD to resize images and save them in both WBMP and JPEG format (we need to do it for our coffee shop photos). The tricky part now is finding a way to tailor our scripts' output to two different platforms.

Determining the User Agent

The first thing we need to know is the browser that is requesting our script; this will tell us which type of markup – WML or HTML – our scripts need to return.

This is easy enough to determine by accessing PHP's built-in $_SERVER array. Specifically, we need to examine the contents of $_SERVER["HTTP_USER_AGENT"]. We'll also need a list of user agents and the HTTP_USER_AGENT header they send, so we know which user agents expect which kind of content.

WML/HTML on the Fly

The next step will be to figure out a way to take information from the database, and generate WML or HTML pages on the fly. We could come up with an elaborate system of headers and footers, or separate sets of templates for WML and HTML pages, but then we'll be locked into a fairly static format and we'll end up updating two different files any time we want to adjust the page layout.

On top of that, we've only just scratched the surface of WML; mixing PHP code and WML templates is a less than ideal situation when we're not very familiar with WML alone.

Does this sound like a headache yet? Fortunately there's another option that will make our lives a lot easier.

HAWHAW

HTML and WML Hybrid Adapted Webserver (HAWHAW) is a toolkit that makes developing cross-platform mobile applications a lot easier than developing a proprietary template system. Even better, it creates applications that are compatible with platforms other than WAP and PDA-friendly HTML. In addition to WAP and HTML, HAWHAW supports **HDML** (a WML predecessor), **i-Mode** (i-Mode is the packet-based service for mobile phones offered by NTT DoCoMo, Japan), and **MML** (Multimedia Markup Language).

> *i-Mode, since it was developed by a Japanese wireless communications company, is mostly used in Japan. MML is another wireless markup language widely used in Japan, and was developed by J-Phone Communications Co Ltd.*

The HAWHAW toolkit comes with several components:

❑ **HAWHAW XML**
HAWHAW XML is the markup language used by the HAWHAW toolkit. It is similar in appearance to WML but is somewhat simplified. We can think of HAWHAW XML as an abstraction layer between our content and the different platforms that HAWHAW supports.

❑ **HAWXY**
HAWXY is a proxy server in the form of a PHP script that translates HAWHAW XML into the appropriate markup for any user agent requesting that document, based on the `$_SERVER["HTTP_USER_AGENT"]` variable.

❑ **The HAWHAW PHP class library**
The HAWHAW PHP class provides a set of functions for building standalone mobile applications that don't need to use HAWHAW XML or HAWXY. It generates the appropriate markup on its own. We'll be using the HAWHAW PHP class extensively in our Coffee Shop Finder mobile application.

Object-Oriented Web Pages

The HAWHAW PHP class uses an object-oriented (OO) approach for building the pages of our application. At the beginning of each script, we create a `HAW_deck` object, which has several properties and methods associated with it. Page elements contained within the `HAW_deck` are also represented by objects, which in turn have their own properties and methods for setting attributes, and adding child objects.

Here's what a simple script using the HAWHAW class looks like:

```php
<?php

include_once("hawhaw.inc");

$haw = new HAW_deck("My HAWHAW Deck");

$hello = new HAW_text("Hello, World!");

$haw->add_text($hello);

$haw->create_page();
?>
```

That's all there is to it. The HAWHAW class takes care of figuring out what type of user agent is requesting the page, and transforms the HAW_deck object into the correct markup. Here's what our 'Hello, World!' script returns when called from a WAP device:

```
<?xml version="1.0"?>

<!DOCTYPE wml PUBLIC "-//WAPFORUM//DTD WML 1.1//EN"
"http://www.wapforum.org/DTD/wml_1.1.xml">

<!-- Generated by HAWHAW V4.06 (C) Norbert Huffschmid -->

<wml>
  <card title="My HAWHAW Deck">
    <do type="prev" label="Back">
      <prev/>
    </do>
    <p>
    Hello, World!
    <br/>
    </p>
  </card>
</wml>
```

And here's what the same script returns when called by AvantGo:

```
<!doctype html public "-//w3c//dtd html 4.0 transitional//en">

<html>

  <head>
    <meta http-equiv="Content-Type" content="text/html; charset=iso-8859-1">
    <meta name="GENERATOR" content="HAWHAW V4.06 (PHP) (C) Norbert
        Huffschmid">
    <meta name="HandheldFriendly" content="True">
    <title>My HAWHAW Deck</title>
  </head>

  <body>
    <div align="left">
    Hello, World!
    <br>
    </div>
  </body>

</html>
```

The HAWHAW class methods and properties are intuitive and consistent, as we'll see when we start building our application.

Coffee Shop Finder – Application Spec

We will use GD's image functions and the HAWHAW PHP class to automatically generate Coffee Shop Finder images for both WAP sites and PDA.

Now that we know what platforms we're developing for and what tools we'll be using, let's add some details to our specification.

General Requirements

Let's refresh ourselves on our client's basic requirements. The client has an existing web site, powered by a MySQL database, which allows users to search for local coffee shops and retrieve shop addresses and ratings. Phone numbers, URLs, and photographs are also provided, if they are available. The user can also add a rating for a particular coffee shop in the database, on a scale of 1 to 5. The client wants to make this database available to PDA and mobile phone users.

The Database

For our application we are going to use the MySQL database, and to define the structure of the database we need to create tables and populate them. Let's first look at the structure of these tables that we are going to use. We can then query the database with our application. We will need six tables for our sample Coffee Shop Finder application.

The general structure of these tables is as follows:

- **city table**
  This table holds records for each individual city in the database.

- **state table**
  This table contains the names and two-letter postal abbreviations for the states.

- **zip table**
  This table matches ZIP codes to cities; the city_id field in this table corresponds to the city_id field in the city table.

- **city_state table**
  This table is a joining table, matching the city_id field from the city table, and the st_abbrev field with the st_abbrev field from the state table.

- **coffee_shop table**
  The coffee_shop table contains records for each individual coffee shop in the database. The city_id field matches the city_id field from the city table.

- **rating table**
  The rating table contains user ratings. The shop_id field matches the shop_id field in the coffee_shop table. $score is a value from 1 to 5. There are no unique indexes on this table, since we want to be able to store more than one rating per coffee shop.

This is the physical design of the database, with the relationships added and primary keys underlined:

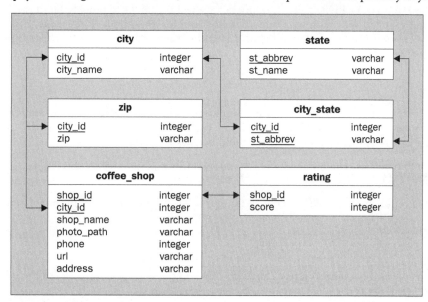

This may look like a lot of tables with relatively few distinct fields of data; putting the city, state, and zip code information into the `coffee_shop` table would knock the database down to just two tables – `coffee_shop` and `rating`. While having two tables would simplify our queries, it could cause us more trouble in the long run.

Suppose city names were stored in the `coffee_shop` table, and there were a dozen different coffee shops in the same city. What would happen if somebody added another coffee shop in that same city to the database, but accidentally misspelled the name of the city? The data would become inconsistent, and while one misspelled city name might be easy to catch and repair, maintenance of such a database would become a nightmare if it grew to contain hundreds, or even thousands of records.

By giving cities their own table and using the `city_id` field to link them to coffee shops and zip codes, our database will be much easier to maintain. The process of designing databases to reduce redundancy within tables is called normalization. Database normalization is beyond the scope of this case study, but it's good to be aware of it.

For more information about database normalization refer to Beginning Databases with PostgreSQL from Wrox Press (ISBN 1-861005-15-6).

Tools

We will use PHP to build this application as it easily accommodates the functionality we need for various components of the application:

❑ **Image Manipulation**
PHP's GD functions will be perfect for automatically converting the client's existing, full-size photos into smaller, AvantGo-friendly JPEGs and WAP WBMP graphics. We can also use GD to generate graphics indicating each coffee shop's rating, from 1-5 stars.

❑ **HAWHAW**
The HAWHAW PHP class – `hawhaw.inc` – will enable us to quickly build the mobile Coffee Shop Finder application by eliminating the need for an intimate knowledge of WML and the need to develop a complex template system for transforming the client's data into PDA and WAP-friendly content.

Usability

We must pay special attention to our mobile application's interface; screen real estate is at an absolute premium, especially on many mobile phones. The user should be able to get the desired information in as few screens as possible, and the process should be easy and intuitive.

Components

Based on the requirements we've laid out so far, our application will consist of the following files:

❑ **hawhaw.inc**
The HAWHAW PHP class library.

❑ **common.php**
This file will contain common functions that will be used by some or all of the other scripts in the application.

❑ **config.php**
This file will contain configuration information such as database connection parameters and image formatting instructions. Keeping configuration information in a separate file will make changes easy.

❑ **index.php**
The main page of the application, where the user can choose how to search: by Zip code, or by state and city.

❑ **form.php**
This script will create the search form based on the user's criteria from `index.php`. The Zip code option will have a single 5-digit field, and the state/city option will have two fields – a two-letter field for the state abbreviation, and a five-letter field for the city name. Entering text is a cumbersome process on many mobile devices, so we'll let the user enter just the first two or three letters of the city they wish to search in, and match cities against that substring.

❑ **search.php**
This script is called when the user submits `form.php`. It connects to the database and executes a query based on the user's search criteria. The script returns a list of matching coffee shops with the name of the city in which they're located and a graphics representing the restaurant's user rating from 1 to 5 stars. Results will be sorted by score from highest to lowest, with a link from each coffee shop listed, to a detailed page that will contain all the contact information and a photo (if available).

❑ **details.php**
This script queries the database for the address, phone, URL, and photo information available for the coffee shop specified by the link from `search.php`.

❑ **rate.php**
This script inserts the user's rating of a coffee shop into the database.

We will cover each script in detail as we get into the program listings.

Program Listings

Let's put our application together, starting with the common functions that will be used by the other scripts.

hawhaw.inc

hawhaw.inc contains the HAWHAW PHP class library, which we're using to build the application. This file can be downloaded from the HAWHAW web site at http://hawhaw.de/.

It also comes bundled with PHPLib, which can be downloaded from http://phplib.netuse.de/. To include this class, simply update the include_path statement in the php.ini file to point to the PHP distribution directory.

Basic HAWHAW objects and methods will be explained as we go on. A full documentation for the HAWHAW class is available at the HAWHAW web site.

common.php

common.php contains functions that will take care of repetitive tasks and can be used by all the scripts in our application. Let's view the synopsis for this file:

```php
<?php

/************************************************************************
This file contains functions that are used by all of the scripts in the
Coffee Shop Finder.
************************************************************************/

/* Load the GD module if necessary; since this file is common to all of
   the others in the application, this is the only place we need to load
   the module. */

if(!extension_loaded('gd')){
    if(strtoupper(substr(PHP_OS,0,3)) == 'WIN'){
        dl('php_gd2.dll');
    } else {
        dl('gd.so');
    }
}
```

We will now see each and every function in detail.

DbConnect

```
mysql_handle DbConnect (string db_host, string db_user, string db_pass,
                        string db_name);
```

At first glance, DbConnect() might look a little redundant; other than the fourth db_name parameter it looks identical to PHP's standard mysql_connect(). However, DbConnect() also provides error handling with ErrorPage() in the event of a failed connection.

Here's the `DbConnect()` function:

```
function DbConnect($db_host,$db_user,$db_pass,$db_name)
{
    /* Try to connect to the database, suppressing error messages: */

    $db = @mysql_connect($db_host, $db_user, $db_pass);
    if(!$db){
        /* If the connection fails, send the user an error page: */
        $message = "Can't connect to the database.";
        ErrorPage($message);
    }

    /* If the connection is successful, try to select the database
       named '$db_name': */
    $selected = @mysql_select_db($db_name,$db);

    if(!$selected){

        /* If the database can't be selected, send the user an error page:*/
        $message = "Can't use database '$db_name'";
        ErrorPage($message);
    }

    /* If we've connected and selected the database without any error,
       return the MySQL connection handle: */
    return $db;

} // DbConnect()
```

DbQuery

```
result DbQuery (string query, mysql_handle connection);
```

At a glance this function looks identical to its standard PHP equivalent – `mysql_query`, however, this function adds error handling with the `ErrorPage()` function. This means that if the query fails, the user will get a nicely formatted error page. Remember that WAP browsers expect 100% valid XML content, and if a page ends unexpectedly it's possible that they won't render it at all. By intercepting errors in this function we can avoid that problem altogether.

We write the `DbQuery()` function like this:

```
function DbQuery($query,$connection)
{
    /* Attempt to execute the query, suppressing error messages: */
    $result = @mysql_query($query,$connection);

    if(!$result){

        /* If the query fails, send the user an error page: */
```

```
        $message = "The database query failed.";
        ErrorPage($message);

    } else {

        /* If the query was successful, return the result pointer: */
        return $result;

    }
} // DbQuery()
```

InitDeck

```
HAW_deck InitDeck (string title, string html_bg="#FFFFFF",
                   int html_border=0);
```

This function is a wrapper for the HAWHAW HAW_deck constructor, which automatically sets the background color and table border width of the deck (the way it will appear in a standard HTML browser). Since we want all the pages in our application to look consistent, it's better to write a reusable function that handles all the initial formatting. In our case the background color defaults to white (#FFFFFF), and the border width defaults to 0.

Let's look at the function:

```
function InitDeck($title,$html_bg = "#FFFFFF", $html_border = 0)
{
    /* Create a new HAWHAW deck object: */
    $deck = new HAW_deck($title);

    /* Set the background colors of the deck and the HTML page: */
    $deck->set_bgcolor($html_bg);
    $deck->set_disp_bgcolor($html_bg);

    /* Set the border width of the table containing the deck: */
    $deck->set_border($html_border);

    /* Return the new deck object: */
    return $deck;

} // InitDeck()
```

ErrorPage

```
void ErrorPage (string message="An error occurred.");
```

ErrorPage () uses InitDeck() to create a new HAW_deck object, adds the contents of the message to it, and exits the script. By suppressing error messages with the @ operator in other parts of the application, and calling ErrorPage() in the event of an error, we can make sure the application exits gracefully. The error message defaults to 'An error occurred'.

371

Let's look at the function:

```php
function ErrorPage($message = "An error occurred.")
{
    /* Create a new HAWHAW deck titled "Error": */
    $error_page = InitDeck("Error");

    /* Create a text object containing the
       error message with two line breaks: */

    $text = new HAW_text($message);
    $text->set_br(2);

    /* Create a "Back" link object that points to the referring page: */
    $link = new HAW_link("Back", $_SERVER['HTTP_REFERER']);

    /* Add the text and link objects to the deck: */
    $error_page->add_text($text);
    $error_page->add_link($link);

    /* Send the page to the browser: */
    $error_page->create_page();

    /* Exit the script: */
    exit();

} // ErrorPage()
```

FormatPhone

```
string FormatPhone (string number);
```

Our client has phone numbers stored as strings of 10-digit numbers with no parenthesis or dashes to indicate area codes or prefixes. FormatPhone() takes an unformatted phone number '##########' and returns a nicely formatted string '(###)###-####'.

Here is the function:

```php
function FormatPhone($number)
{
    /* Split "$number" into its individual components: */
    $areacode = substr($number,0,3);
    $prefix   = substr($number,3,3);
    $number   = substr($number,6,4);

    /* Reassemble the components with formatting, and return the
       resulting string: */
    return "($areacode)$prefix-$number";

} // FormatPhone()
```

ImageForceTwoColor

image_resource ImageForceTwoColor (image_resource img,
int threshold=128);

If we use GD's `ImageWbmp()` function to convert a color image created from a JPEG into a 1-bit, black-and-white WBMP graphic, we'll know that the results can be frustratingly unpredictable.

Since we want to be sure our photos get consistently converted into WBMP images, we'll use our own algorithm to handle the conversion from 256 colors down to only 2, black and white. Here's how it works:

1. First, we create a new GD image resource with the same dimensions as the image resource that was passed to the function using `imagesx()` and `imagesy()`, to determine the correct dimensions.

2. Next, we define white and black color resources for our new image using `ImageColorAllocate()`. We define white first, so it will be the background color.

3. Now, using nested x and y `for` loops for the width and height of the images, we go through each individual pixel in the source image, one at a time.

4. Using `ImageColorAt()` and `ImageColorsForIndex()`, we can access the individual red, green, and blue values for that pixel.

5. By adding the RGB values together and dividing by three, we get the average brightness, from 0 to 255, for that pixel.

6. This is where the threshold parameter comes in. By comparing the average brightness of the source pixel to the value of threshold, we know whether to set the corresponding pixel in the new image to black or white. If the average brightness is less than the threshold, the pixel is set to black. If it's above the threshold, it's set to white.

7. Once the x and y loops are finished, so is our new 1-bit image that we return.

This is a relatively simple algorithm that doesn't do anything fancy like dithering. To get a sense of what the filter does, let's try it on a larger image first:

Now if we use `ImageForceTwoColor()` on this photo with a threshold of 100, here's what we see:

The resulting high contrast image will lend itself nicely to the small displays on WAP devices.

Here's the code for `ImageForceTwoColor()`:

```
function ImageForceTwoColor($img, $threshold = 128)
{
    /* Determine the width and height to make a new black-and-white image:*/
    $width = imagesx($img);
    $height =imagesy($img);

    /* Create a new image resource: */
    $newimg = ImageCreate($width, $height);

    /* Define black-and-white color resources: */
    $white = ImageColorAllocate($newimg, 255,255,255);
    $black = ImageColorAllocate($newimg, 0,0,0);

    /* Cycle through each pixel in the source image, and determine the
       average brightness. If the average brightness is less than
       the value of $threshold, set the corresponding pixel in the
       new image resource to black. If the average brightness is greater
       than $threshold, set the corresponding pixel to white. */

    for($y = 0; $y < $height; $y++){

        for($x = 0; $x < $width; $x++){
            $colorindex = ImageColorAt($img,$x,$y);
            $colorinfo = ImageColorsForIndex($img,$colorindex);
            $coloraverage = ($colorinfo["red"] +
            $colorinfo["green"] + $colorinfo["blue"]) / 3;

            if($coloraverage < $threshold){
                /* Force pixel to black: */
                ImageSetPixel($newimg,$x,$y,$black);
            } else {
```

```
                /* Force pixel to white: */
                ImageSetPixel($newimg,$x,$y,$white);
            }
        }
    }

    /* Return the 2-color image resource. */
    return $newimg;

} // ImageForceTwoColor()
```

ImageResize

```
image_resource ImageResize (image_resource img, int percent);
```

ImageResize() provides a simple way to resize the $img GD image resource to $percent percent of its original size using ImageCopyResampled():

```
function ImageResize($img, $percent)
{
    /* Determine the width and height of the source image "$img" : */
    $width = imagesx($img);
    $height =imagesy($img);

    /* Determine the multiplier we'll use to calculate the reduced
       width and height dimensions of the resized image: */
    $multiplier = $percent/100;

    /* Calculate the new width and height, using floor() to force the
       results to the next lowest integer - for example, floor(72.7) will
       return 72, floor(48.3) will return 48, etc: */
    $new_width = floor($width * $multiplier);
    $new_height = floor($height * $multiplier);

    /* Create a new image with our new reduced width and height dimensions*/
    $new_img = ImageCreate($new_width, $new_height);

    /* Copy the entire source image into the reduced image: */
    ImageCopyResampled($new_img,$img,0,0,0,0,$new_width, $new_height,
                       $width, $height);

    /* Return the reduced image: */
    return $new_img;

} // ImageResize()
```

MakeRatingGraphic

```
void MakeRatingGraphic (int score, string src_graphic, string
                        format["wbmp"|"jpeg"]);
```

MakeRatingGraphic() creates an image resource from the file at $src_graphic (in our case this will be star.png from the config.php file) and a new image with $score copies of that image. The new image is then written to the disk as a WBMP or JPEG graphic depending on the value of $format.

Here's how it works:

1. The function creates a GD image resource from the file $src_graphic, and gets its width and its height with imagesx() and imagesy().

2. Then, to determine how wide the rating graphic needs to be, the function multiplies the width of the source image by the value of $score. In other words, if $src_graphic is 15 pixels wide and $score is 3, our 3-star rating graphic needs to be 45 pixels wide to accommodate three copies of $src_graphic. The height of the rating graphic will be the same as the height of the source graphic.

3. Next, the function uses a for loop to copy the source image into the new image resource, repeating $score times. The loop uses a variable called $offset to tell ImageCopy() where to position the copied graphic in the new image. Every time the loop runs, $offset is increased by the width of the source graphic.

4. Finally, the function examines $format. If $format is JPEG, the new image is written to disk as a JPEG with 100% quality. If $format is WBMP, there are a couple of extra steps. Firstly, the new image is reduced by 50% using our ImageResize() function to make sure it doesn't take too much room on the small screen of a WAP device. Secondly, it is forced to black and white with our ImageForceTwoColor() function. Lastly, it is written to the disk. The filename of the new image is determined by the value of $score – 1.jpg, 2.jpg, 3.jpg, 1.wbmp, 2.wbmp, and 3.wbmp, for example.

Let's take a look at the code for MakeRatingGraphic():

```
function MakeRatingGraphic($score,$src_graphic,$format)
{
    /* Open the source rating graphic as a GD resource */
    $src = ImageCreateFromPng($src_graphic);
    $src_width  = imagesx($src);
    $src_height = imagesy($src);

    /* Calculate the size of our new rating graphic based on the value of
    '$score', and create a new image resource: */
    $new_width  = $score * $src_width;
    $new_height = $src_height;

    $rating = ImageCreate($new_width, $new_height);

    /* Copy the source graphic into the new graphic one time for each point,
    offsetting the x position by '$src_x' pixels each time: */
    for($x = 0; $x < $score; $x++) {
        $offset = $x * $src_x;
        ImageCopy($rating, $src, $offset, 0, 0, 0, $src_width, $src_height);
    }

    /* Now write the image to disk */
    switch($format){
    case "jpeg" :
        ImageJpeg($rating,"$score.jpg",100);
```

```
            break;

    case "wbmp" :
        $rating = ImageResize($rating,50);
        $rating = ImageForceTwoColor($rating);
        ImageWbmp($rating,"$score.wbmp");
        break;
    }

} // MakeRatingGraphic()

// common.php
?>
```

config.php

`config.php` contains variables that will be frequently used by other scripts in the application. These variables are pretty straightforward:

❑ **MySQL Configuration**
The variables in this section contain information that our application will use to connect to the MySQL server.

❑ **Ratings Configuration**
We're going to generate our ratings graphics (1-5 stars) on the fly by repeating a single source graphic. By setting the filename of that graphic as a variable, we'll be able to easily change the rating graphics' appearance.

❑ **Photo Configuration**
These variables specify the maximum width that should be used when creating the JPEG images for PDA browsers and the WBMP graphics for WAP devices.

Here is the code:

```
<?php

/***************************************************************************
Common variables used by the Coffee Shop Finder
***************************************************************************/

/* MySQL Configuration */
$db_host = "localhost";
$db_name = "coffee_shop";
$db_user = "php";
$db_pass = "mypassword";

/* Ratings configuration */
$rating_graphic = "star.png";

/* Photo configuration */
$wbmp_max_width = 75;
$jpeg_max_width  = 150;

// config.php
?>
```

index.php

This is the first deck of our application, the first resource the user will see on connecting to the Coffee Shop Finder with a WAP or PDA device. This script doesn't do anything fancy; it just displays a title and provides two links to form.php, one for searching by Zip code and the other for searching by state and city.

However, this is where we start to delve a little deeper into the various objects and functions HAWHAW provides for making decks, so we'll take a look at each new object as it comes up.

The script begins with files that contain the HAWHAW class, our common functions, and configuration information:

```php
<?php

/**********************************************************************
This is the script that generates the main menu screen of the application
**********************************************************************/

/* Include external files */
include_once("hawhaw.inc");
include_once("common.php");
include_once("config.php");
```

Now we'll create a new HAWHAW deck called $haw, using our own InitDeck() defined in common.php.

Once $haw is defined we want to add some text to it, to let the user know what they will be seeing. To add text to a HAWHAW deck, we have to create a new HAW_text object. The HAW_text constructor takes two arguments:

❑　A parameter text which the object will contain

❑　An optional parameter, which can contain a special constant telling HAWHAW how to format the text

In our case, we want our title to appear in boldface on devices that support it, so we'll use the HAW_TEXTFORMAT_BOLD constant.

Once our HAW_text object is created, we use the add_text method of our HAW_deck object to add it to the deck. This is how all HAWHAW decks are built: by creating different HAWHAW objects, setting their properties, and then adding them to the HAW_deck at the top of the hierarchy.

Here is the code:

```php
/* Create a new HAW deck and title: */

$haw     = InitDeck("Coffee Shop Finder");
$title   = new HAW_text("Coffee Shop Finder",HAW_TEXTFORMAT_BOLD);
$haw->add_text($title);
```

Some HAWHAW objects contain other HAWHAW objects, HAW_linkset is one of them. It contains HAW_link objects and is used to build numbered menus on WAP user agents that support them. The links will appear on the device screen with a number, and the user can press that number on their phone's keypad to follow that link. On other devices, HAW_linksets are rendered as a simple list of links.

Once our HAW_linkset object is created, we need to create some HAW_link objects to put into it. The HAW_link constructor takes two arguments – the link text and the URL it should point to.

The statement:

```
$link=new HAW_link ("My Link", "my_other_script.php")
```

is the HAWHAW equivalent of the HTML markup:

```
<a href="my_other_script">My Link</a>
```

We'll set up an array of menu items, and use a foreach loop to walk through the array and add HAW_link objects to our HAW_linkset object automatically. The loop creates a new object for each key/value pair in the array, and then uses HAW_linkset's add_link method to add it to $menu, and our HAW_linkset object.

Let's look at the code:

```
/* Create a menu of the ways the user can search: */
$menu = new HAW_linkset();

/* Set the URL of the script that will generate the search form: */
$form_url = "form.php";

/* Create an associative array of each menu item, with the link text as
   the array key and the URL as its value. For this menu, all items will
   point to the script at $form_url, and specify which type of form is
   being requested by setting the 'type' variable on the query string: */

$menuitems = array("By Zip Code"   => "$form_url?type=zip",
                   "By State/City" => "$form_url?type=st_city");

/* Now that the link information is stored in an array, we can use a loop to
   build the menu: */

foreach(array_keys($menuitems) as $linktext){
    $link = new HAW_link($linktext, $menuitems[$linktext]);
    $menu->add_link($link);
    }
```

Once our HAW_linkset object ($menu) is built we add it to the HAW_deck object with the add_linkset method. As we can see, building HAWHAW decks is a consistently structured, intuitive process that makes development a breeze, once we become familiar with the different HAWHAW objects.

Once our `HAW_deck` object (`$haw`) is complete we use the `create_page()` method to render the HAWHAW deck into markup, and send it to the user. This is where the real magic happens – `create_deck()` takes care of figuring out what type of device is requesting the page, and renders the appropriate markup automatically.

Here is the final piece of code:

```
/* Add the menu to the deck */
$haw->add_linkset($menu);

/* Render the deck */
$haw->create_page();

// index.php
?>
```

This is how `index.php` appears on the WAP device:

> Make sure to disable the **Enable Cache** option in the DeckIt browser. In the main browser window, click on **Options** and then unclick the checkbox.

And here's how it appears on the PDA screen:

form.php

`form.php` creates the form which allows the user to enter their search criteria for finding coffee shops. This script expects the variable `$type` to be set on the query string. `$type` indicates which type of form to send to the user. A value of `zip` will result in a form for searching by Zip code, and a value of `st_city` will result in a form for searching by state and city.

The script starts by including the HAWHAW class, our common functions, and the global configuration scripts:

```php
<?php

/*******************************************************************************
This script generates the search forms.
*******************************************************************************/

/* Include external files */
include_once("hawhaw.inc");
include_once("common.php");
include_once("config.php");

/*Next we need to get the value of $form from the query string by using the
  extract function to process the contents of the global $_GET array into
  local variables; calling extract ($_GET) converts the global $_GET
  ["type"] into the local $type. */

extract($_GET);

/*Then we create a new HAW_deck called $haw and add the text "Search:" in
  bold. */
$haw       = InitDeck("Search:");
$title     = new HAW_text("Search:",HAW_TEXTFORMAT_BOLD);
$haw->add_text($title);
```

Now we're ready to create a HAW_form object to hold the search form. The HAW_form constructor takes one argument, the URL, which the form should submit to. In our case it will submit to the search.php script:

```php
/* Create a new form that submits to "search.php" */
$form = new HAW_form("search.php");
```

The statement:

```php
$form = new HAW_form("search.php");
```

is the HAWHAW equivalent to the HTML markup:

```html
<form action="search.php">
```

There is no 'method' option for HAW_form objects; HAWHAW forms always use the GET method (AvantGo and WAP do support POST as well). However, since HAWHAW is intended for creating mobile applications, it's unlikely that the size of the form data being sent from a cell phone or a PDA will exceed the maximum length allowed by the browser and the server for the GET query string.

Now we'll create the HAW_form input objects based on the value of $type; a zip form will have one input named zip and a st_city form will have two inputs, st and city.

The `HAW_input` constructor takes three arguments:

❑ The name of the object

❑ The default value of the object

❑ A text label that will appear in front of the input

The following line of code:

```
$zip = new HAW_input("zip","","Zip Code:")
```

is the HAWHAW equivalent of the XHTML markup:

```
Zip Code: <input type="text" name="zip" value="" />
```

`HAW_input` objects also have methods for restricting the size and maximum length of the input:

❑ `set_size` specifies the number of characters the input should be displayed with

❑ `set_maxlength` specifies the maximum number of characters that can be entered

Let's put everything together, using `switch` to determine which `HAW_inputs` to add to `$form`:

```
/* Now examine $type and build the appropriate form elements: */

switch($type){
case "zip" :
    /* Make a text input for zip code: */
    $zip = new HAW_input("zip","","Zip:");

    /* Limit zip code field to 5 characters: */
    $zip->set_size(5);
    $zip->set_maxlength(5);

    /* Add the zip field to the form: */
    $form->add_input($zip);

    break;

case "st_city" :
    /* Make a text input for state abbreviation: */
    $state = new HAW_input("st","","State:");

    /* Limit state input to two characters (If we needed longer state
       or province abbreviations for a different country, we would
       need to make sure to use the size of our st_abbrev database
       field as the value for set_size and set_maxlength) */
    $state->set_size(2);
    $state->set_maxlength(2);

    /* Make a text input for first few letters of city: */
    $city = new HAW_input("city","","City (1st few letters):");

    /* Limit city name to 5 characters: */
```

```
        $city->set_size(5);
        $city->set_maxlength(5);

        /* Add the state and city inputs to the form: */
        $form->add_input($state);
        $form->add_input($city);

        break;

    default:
        /* If '$type' is not set or unknown, exit with an error page: */
        $message = "No search method was specified.";
        ErrorPage($message);
    }
```

We also need to pass $type to search.php as a hidden variable, to tell the script how to query the database. We'll use a HAW_hidden object to do this.

The HAW_hidden constructor takes two arguments, the name of the object and its value:

```
    /* Pass along the value of '$type' as a hidden variable */

    $searchtype = new Haw_hidden("type",$type);
    $form->add_hidden($searchtype);
```

The last component of our form will be a HAW_submit object. The HAW_submit constructor takes one argument, the text that should appear on the submit button:

```
    /* Create the submit button and close the form: */

    $submit   = new HAW_submit("Go");
    $form->add_submit($submit);
```

Now that our form is complete, we can add it to our deck and create the page:

```
    /* Add the form to the deck: */
    $haw->add_form($form);

    /* Render the deck: */
    $haw->create_page();

    // form.php
    ?>
```

Here's what form.php looks like, when $type is set to zip, on the WAP device:

And here's what `form.php` looks like, when `$type` is set to `st_city`, on the PDA screen:

search.php

`search.php` is called by `form.php` and it queries the database for coffee shops matching the user's search criteria. It looks up four pieces of information:

- ❑ The coffee shop's name
- ❑ The coffee shop's ID
- ❑ The name of the city the coffee shop is in
- ❑ The average rating of the coffee shop

If the query returns one or more rows from the database, the name, rating, and city of the matching coffee shops are listed in a results page. The shop name is linked to `details.php` with the shop's ID number on the query string.

Before we get to the database-related parts of the script, let's take care of the familiar initialization process:

```php
<?php
/*****************************************************************
This file takes the form inputs sent by form.php and searches the database for
matching coffee shops.
*****************************************************************/

/* Include external files */
include_once("hawhaw.inc");
include_once("common.php");
include_once("config.php");

/* Process form variables: */
extract($_GET);

/* Create a new HAW deck: */
$haw = InitDeck("Results:");
```

The next step is to establish a link to the database server using our database variables from
`config.php`, and `DbConnect()` from `common.php`:

```
/* Connect to the database and choose our database*/
$db = DbConnect($db_host, $db_user, $db_pass, $db_name);
```

Now it's time to build our database query. The `$type` variable, sent as a hidden variable from `form.php`
and extracted from the `$_GET query string` array, tells us what fields we need to match against:

❑ **zip**

If `$type` is `zip`, we'll need to write our query to select only coffee shops whose `city_id` field
matches the `city_id` field of the `zip` table, where `zip` matches the `$zip` variable sent by
`form.php`.

❑ **st_city**

If `$type` is `st_city`, we'll need to write our query to select only coffee shops whose
`city_name` field has the same first few letters as the `$city` variable sent by `form.php`. The
`city_id` can be found in the `city_state` table where `st_abbrev` matches the value of `$st`
sent by `form.php`.

To achieve this we'll use a few MySQL `LEFT JOIN` statements in our queries.

To get the average rating for matching coffee shops we can use some of MySQL's built-in math
functions. We'll use `SUM()` to add up all of the matching values in the score field of the rating table, and
then divide that sum by the `COUNT()` of matching `shop_id` fields to get the average rating. The
`ROUND()` function will round the result to the nearest integer. In order to use the `SUM()` and `GROUP()`
functions, we'll have to add a `GROUP BY rating.shop_id` clause to the query. Finally, we'll render the
results in the descending order of the average score of the coffee shops.

Here is the code:

```
switch($type){
case "zip" :
    if($zip == ''){
        /* We can't search without a zip code.Exit with error page. */
        $message = "You must enter a zip code.";
        ErrorPage($message);
    } else {
        $query = "SELECT shop_name, coffee_shop.shop_id, city_name,
        ROUND(SUM(score) / COUNT(rating.shop_id)) as score
        FROM coffee_shop
        LEFT JOIN rating ON rating.shop_id = coffee_shop.shop_id
        LEFT JOIN city ON city.city_id = coffee_shop.city_id
        LEFT JOIN zip ON city.city_id = zip.city_id
        WHERE zip.zip = $zip GROUP BY rating.shop_id
        ORDER BY score DESC, shop_name";
    }
    break;

case "st_city" :
    if($st == '' || $city == ''){
        /* If state or city have been omitted, exit with error page. */
        $message = "You must enter a State and the first few letters of a
                    city name.";
```

```
            ErrorPage($message);
        } else {
            /* Get the length of '$city' so we can match the substring from
               the database */
            $city_length = strlen($city);

            /* Force '$city' and '$st' to uppercase
               to make the match case-insensitive. */
            $city = strtoupper($city);
            $st = strtoupper($st);
            $query = "SELECT shop_name, coffee_shop.shop_id, city_name,
                        ROUND(SUM(score) / COUNT(rating.shop_id)) as score
                        FROM coffee_shop
                        LEFT JOIN rating ON rating.shop_id = coffee_shop.shop_id
                        LEFT JOIN city ON city.city_id = coffee_shop.city_id
                        LEFT JOIN city_state ON city_state.city_id = city.city_id
                        LEFT JOIN state ON city_state.st_abbrev = state.st_abbrev
                        WHERE state.st_abbrev = '$st'
                        AND upper(substring(city_name,1,$city_length)) = '$city'
                        GROUP BY rating.shop_id
                        ORDER BY score DESC, shop_name, city_name";
        }
        break;
    }
```

Now that we have the appropriate query string built, we'll query the database using our DbQuery() from, common.php. If no matches are found, we'll exit with an error page.

Let's look at the code:

```
/* Query the database */
$result = DbQuery($query, $db);

/* If there are no matches, exit with an error page: */

if(mysql_num_rows($result) == 0){
    $message = "No Coffee Shops were found matching your criteria.";
    ErrorPage($message);
}
```

Now we need to display our results. We'll use a while loop to retrieve each result row in object form, and then begin adding content to the deck:

1. First we'll create a HAW_link object whose text is the shop name. The URL of the link will be details.php, and we'll pass the shop_id to the query string as ID.

2. Next we'll add a HAW_image object containing the rating graphic. The HAW_image constructor takes three arguments:

❑ The WAP-friendly (WBMP) image source.

❑ The HTML-friendly (JPEG or PNG) image source.

❑ The alternative text, which should be displayed if the user agent can't display images. We'll use str_repeat to make our alternative text a string containing score of asterisks.

3. Our MakeRatingGraphic() saves the rating images to the hard drive, so that we don't need to generate them on the fly every time search.php is called; we can check to make sure the files exist using file_exists first, and call MakeratingGraphic() only when needed.

4. The last part of the listing will be the city name, which gets added as a plain HAW_text object.

Here is the final piece of code:

```
/* Use a loop to display all matching results, each with links to the
   'details.php' page */

while($row = mysql_fetch_array($result)){

    /* Extract the result object properties into their local equivalents: */
    extract($row);

    $link = new HAW_link("$shop_name","details.php?id=$shop_id");
    $link->set_br(0);

    /* Set up file names for rating graphics. We're using jpeg for PDA/Web
    browsers because AvantGo doesn't implement PNG */
    $wbmp = "$score.wbmp";
    $jpeg = "$score.jpg";
    $alt = str_repeat("*",$score);

    /* Only make the rating graphics if the files don't already exist: */
    if(!file_exists($wbmp)){
        MakeRatingGraphic($score,$rating_graphic,"wbmp");
    }

    if(!file_exists($jpeg)){
        MakeRatingGraphic($score,$rating_graphic,"jpeg");
    }

    /* Create an image object for the rating graphic and make sure there's a
    line break after it: */
    $score_img = new HAW_image($wbmp, $jpeg, $alt);
    $score_img->set_br(1);

    /* Create a text object containing the city name: */
    $city_name = new HAW_text($city_name);

    /* Add the link, rating graphic, and city name to the deck: */
    $haw->add_link($link);
    $haw->add_image($score_img);
    $haw->add_text($city_name);
}

/* Render the deck: */
$haw->create_page();

// search.php
?>
```

This is the display on the WAP device:

And this is how it appears on the PDA screen:

We can see our MakeRatingGraphic() at work. The WBMP displayed on the WAP page is solid black, and smaller.

details.php

details.php is called by links on the search.php results page, which sends the variable $id in the query string. $id indicates the ID of the coffee shop whose details are to be retrieved.

Let's include our external files, make sure $id is set and connect to the database:

```php
<?php

/*********************************************************************
This file displays details about an individual coffee shop, and provides links for
rating it.
*********************************************************************/

/* Include external files */
include_once("hawhaw.inc");
include_once("common.php");
include_once("config.php");

/* Process form variables: */
extract($_GET);
```

```
/* Make sure all necessary variables have been set *
if($id == ''){
    $message = "No coffee shop was selected.";
    ErrorPage($message);
}


/* Connect to the database server and choose our database*/
$db = DbConnect($db_host, $db_user, $db_pass, $db_name);
```

We want to display all available information about the coffee shop, so we'll be selecting the shop_name, shop_id, photo_path, phone, url, address, st_abbrev, city_name, zip, and score (average rating) fields from the database where the value of the coffee_shop.shop_id field matches the value of $id.

As with our queries in search.php, we'll need to do several LEFT JOINs to get the appropriate data across all the database tables, and group the results by the rating.shop_id field. If, for some reason, the query returns an empty result, we exit with an error page.

Here is the code:

```
/* Get the shop id, name, address, city, state, rating, and zip.
   get Phone #, url, and photo if available. */

$query = "SELECT shop_name, coffee_shop.shop_id, photo_path,
            phone, url, address,
            st_abbrev, city_name, zip,
            round(sum(score) / count(rating.shop_id)) as score
            FROM coffee_shop
            LEFT JOIN city ON city.city_id = coffee_shop.city_id
            LEFT JOIN zip ON zip.city_id = city.city_id
            LEFT JOIN city_state ON city_state.city_id = zip.city_id
            LEFT JOIN rating ON rating.shop_id = coffee_shop.shop_id
            WHERE coffee_shop.shop_id = $id
            GROUP BY rating.shop_id";


$result = DbQuery($query, $db);

/* If information for $id can't be retrieved, make an error page: */

if(mysql_num_rows($result) == 0){
    $message = "Could not retrieve information for coffee shop $id";
    ErrorPage($message);
}
```

Now we can begin building our deck. First, we'll fetch the matching result row as an associative array, which we can then extract into its local equivalents; $row["shop_name"] gets copied into $shop_name along with the rest of the fields from the query.

Once we have the coffee shop details, we can create a new HAW_deck and add a bold-formatted HAW_text object of the shop name at the top:

```
/* We only need to fetch the first row, since the query will
   only return one result: */
$row = mysql_fetch_assoc($result);

/* Extract the row variables into their local equivalents: */
extract($row);

/*  Create a new HAW deck: */
$haw = InitDeck($shop_name);

/* Make the Title - disable the line break and add it to the deck */
$name = new HAW_text($shop_name, HAW_TEXTFORMAT_BOLD);
$name->set_br(0);
$haw->add_text($name);
```

Next, we'll add a `HAW_image` object containing the rating graphic as we did in `search.php`. This time we'll assume that the graphics have already been created, since the user has to view a search results page before getting to this one.

Let's take a look:

```
/* Display the score graphic (It will already be created by the search
   results script. */
$wbmp  = "$score.wbmp";
$jpeg  = "$score.jpg";
$alt   = str_repeat("*", $score);

$rating = new HAW_image($wbmp, $jpeg, $alt);
$rating->set_br(1);

$haw->add_image($rating);
```

If the `photo_path` is set, we check to see if friendly copies of the source image already exist. If they do, we can add a `HAW_image` object to the deck containing the photo of the coffee shop.

Otherwise, we create them using the `$wbmp_max_width` and `$jpeg_max_width` variables defined in `config.php`, to calculate how much we need to reduce the original image. If the photo path is incorrect, or PHP does not have permission to write the new image files to the current directory, users will simply see the alternative text (Photo).

If we are using PHP on Windows, we must make sure to escape each backslash in our file path with another one, otherwise PHP may interpret the single slashes in our file path as the beginning of escape sequences. In other words, if the path to our photo file is `C:\apache\htdocs\photos\star.png`, we should save it in the database as `C:\\apache\\htdocs\\photos\\star.png`.

Here is the code that creates the new image files:

```
if($photo_path != ''){

    /* Determine the wbmp and jpeg filenames, and the alt text*/
    $wbmp_file = "shop_$shop_id.wbmp";
    $jpeg_file = "shop_$shop_id.jpg";
    $alt = "(Photo)";
```

```
    if(!file_exists($wbmp_file)){

        /* If the WBMP file does not exist, create it */
        $photo = ImageCreateFromJpeg($photo_path);
        $width = imagesx($photo);

        /* Calculate the amount to reduce the photo: */
        $wbmp_reduce = ($wbmp_max_width / $width) * 100;

        /* Create a new, resized image and force it to black and white: */
        $new_wbmp = ImageResize($photo,$wbmp_reduce);
        $new_wbmp = imageForceTwoColor($new_wbmp);

        /* Save the WAP-friendly WBMP to disk: */
        ImageWbmp($new_wbmp,$wbmp_file);

        /* Destroy the image resources: */
        ImageDestroy($photo);
        ImageDestroy($new_wbmp);
}

if(!file_exists($jpeg_file)){

    /* If the JPEG file does not exist, create it */
    $photo = ImageCreateFromJpeg($photo_path);
    $width = imagesx($photo);

    /* Calculate the amount to reduce the photo: */
    $jpeg_reduce = ($jpeg_max_width / $width) * 100;

    /* Create a new, resized image: */
    $new_jpeg = ImageResize($photo,$jpeg_reduce);

    /* Save the PDA-friendly JPEG to disk: */
    ImageJpeg($new_jpeg,$jpeg_file);

    /* Destroy the image resources: */
    ImageDestroy($photo);
    ImageDestroy($new_jpeg);
}

    /* Create the HAW photo object, make sure there's a line break
       after it and add it to the deck. */
    $shop_photo = new HAW_image($wbmp_file,$jpeg_file,$alt);
    $shop_photo->set_br(1);
    $haw->add_image($shop_photo);
}
```

Now we can display the rest of the contact information. If the phone number is available, we can add it to the deck as a HAW_phone object. On WAP browsers that support it, HAW_phone objects display the phone number as a link. When the user follows the link, their phone will automatically dial the number. On devices that don't support this feature, the phone number is rendered as plain text.

The `HAW_phone` constructor takes two arguments – the phone number and the text that will appear over the soft key that will follow the link (if supported by the user agent).

After the phone number, we will add a `HAW_rule` object, which is similar to an HTML horizontal rule (`<hr>`):

```
$address_info = new HAW_text($address);
$haw->add_text($address_info);

$city_state_zip = new HAW_text("$city_name, $st_abbrev, $zip");
$haw->add_text($city_state_zip);

if($phone != ''){

    /* If a phone number is available, add it as a phone object: */
    $phone = FormatPhone($phone);
    $phone_number = new HAW_phone($phone,"Call");
    $haw->add_phone($phone_number);
}

if($url != ''){

    /* If a URL is available, add it as a link object: */
    $homepage = new HAW_link("Homepage",$url);
    $haw->add_link($homepage);
}

/* Add a rule between info and rating menu: */
$rule = new HAW_rule();
$haw->add_rule($rule);
```

This is what the `HAW_phone` object looks like in WML:

```
<a title="Call" href="wtai://wp/mc;3105551212">310-555-1212</a>
```

> **Wireless Telephony Application Interface (WTAI) is the WAP component that allows us to dial the number by selecting the link. It has a wp library which includes the WTAI-compliant mc (make call) function.**

The last part of the details page is a menu that allows the user to add a rating for this coffee shop to the database.

Before building that menu, we need to check if the variable `$user_score` was passed to this script on the query string. If `$user_score` is set it means the user has already rated this coffee shop, so we don't need to display the rating menu. `$user_score` is set by the `rate.php` script, as we shall see shortly.

We'll define our five ratings as an array, and use a `foreach` loop to generate each `HAW_link` automatically.

Here is the code:

```
/* See if we should display the rating menu; if '$user_score' is already set,
display the user's rating instead: */

if(isset($user_score)){

    $score_text = new HAW_text("You gave this coffee shop $user_score
                            stars.");
    $haw->add_text($score_text);

} else {

    /* Build the link menu for rating this shop: */
    $rate_text = new HAW_text("Rate it!",HAW_TEXTFORMAT_BOLD);
    $haw->add_text($rate_text);

    /* Define the array of menu items, in order of best possible rating
        to worst; since many phone browsers only display a few lines we
        don't want "Terrible" to be the first link the user sees! */

    $menu_items = array("Excellent","Good","Fair","Poor","Terrible");
    $rating_menu = new HAW_linkset();
    $score_value = 5;

    /* Create a HAW_link that passes a score of '$score_value' for
        '$shop_id' on the command line to rate.php. Decrease '$score_value'
        by one at each iteration of the loop: */

    foreach($menu_items as $item){
        $link = new HAW_link($item,"rate.php?id=$shop_id&score
                            =$score_value");
        $rating_menu->add_link($link);
        $score_value--;
    }

$haw->add_linkset($rating_menu);
}
```

Now that all of the available content has been added to the page, all that remains is to send it to the user. Here is the final piece of the code:

```
/* Render the deck: */
$haw->create_page();

// details.php
?>
```

This is the result on the WAP device:

And this is how it appears on the PDA screen:

Depending on the size of the display area of a WAP device or PDA screen, the details page will probably scroll.

> **Some mobile browsers may have trouble understanding URLs with spaces in them, like 'http://localhost/Chapter 10/index.php' or ' http://localhost/Chapter20%10/index.php'.**
>
> **The mobile browser seems to understand URL-encoded spaces (%20), but it doesn't appear to use them internally when it's trying to access the images, which would throw up an HTTP 404 error. To avoid this problem use underscores (Chapter_10) or eliminate the spaces (Chapter10) altogether.**

rate.php

rate.php is called when the user follows one of the rating links from a page produced by details.php. It expects two variables to be passed to it on the query string – $id (the unique database ID of the coffee shop being rated) and $score (the user's rating).

This script is pretty straightforward:

1. First, the script includes the files containing the HAWHAW class, our common functions, and configuration information. It then uses extract() to parse the variables contained in the $_GET global array into their local equivalents; extract() copies ($_GET["id"] and $_GET["score"]) into $id and $score.

2. Then it checks to make sure both $id and $score are properly set. If either one is missing or empty, the application displays an error page.

3. If $id and $score are properly set, the script uses DbConnect() to connect to the database and DbQuery() to insert the coffee shop ID/score pair into the database rating table.

4. Once the database has been updated, the script disconnects from the database and uses the
`header()` function to send the user back to the details page for the coffee shop just rated. To
provide simple protection against people abusing the rating system, the variable `$user_score`
is sent back to `details.php` indicating that the user has already rated the shop.

Let's look at the code:

```php
<?php

/*******************************************************************************
This script inserts the user's rating of a coffee shop into the database.
*******************************************************************************/

/* Include external files */
include_once("hawhaw.inc");
include_once("common.php");
include_once("config.php");

/* Extract the 'type' variable from the query string: */
extract($_GET);

/* If this script somehow gets called with no coffee shop ID
   or score, display an error page: */

if(!isset($id) || !isset($score)) {
    $message = "No Coffee Shop or no score was specified.";
    ErrorPage($message);
}

/* Connect to the database and select our database: */
$db = DbConnect($db_host, $db_user, $db_pass, $db_name);

/* Build the query string */
$query = "INSERT INTO rating (shop_id,score) VALUES ($id,$score)";

/* Do the query */
DbQuery($query, $db);

/* Close the database connection: */
mysql_close($db);

/* Redirect back to the details page, with a flag indicating that
   the user has already rated this shop: */
header("Location: details.php?id=$id&user_score=$score");

// rate.php
?>
```

Possible Enhancements

Our Coffee Shop Finder uses a very simple protection against user abuse of the ratings system – by
sending `$user_score` back to `details.php` after `rate.php` is run, we make it hard for the user to
simply keep rating a restaurant 'Excellent' or 'Terrible'; when `details.php` sees that `$user_score` is
set, it simply won't display the rating menu. This simple protection won't prevent the user from
backtracking and re-rating, but it will prevent them from simply clicking 'Excellent' or 'Terrible' over
and over again from the result screen.

If someone was really determined to artificially inflate or deflate the ratings, they would be able to backtrack to the search results page, and reload a fresh copy of the details page that would once again display the ratings menu. Backtracking is quite easy in a web browser, but harder on a PDA and even more cumbersome on a cell phone – it would be tedious, but it would work. We can't rely on IP addresses to determine if a user has already entered a rating, since AvantGo and many mobile phone users' requests will be coming from proxy servers shared by other users.

Creating **sessions** would be a good option for abuse prevention. We can assign a session ID to each user when they first visit. Then, checking for a session ID at the start of each subsequent script will prevent the same session ID from rating a shop more than once. Further, by sending users without a session ID back to index.php, we would make it considerably more inconvenient to abuse the system. In order to get a new session ID and access to the rating menu, the user would have to completely close their mobile browser, reload index.php and start the whole search from scratch again. The only catch is that we can't rely on cookies either, since WAP browsers don't support them, and people accessing the application from the web could simply disable them.

Fortunately, PHP can also implement sessions by appending the session ID as a variable on the query string. If PHP is compiled with the option –enable-trans-sid, it will automatically add the session ID to link for us or we can add the session ID manually by using the constant SID. For more information about PHP's session handling functions refer to *Professional PHP 4* from *Wrox Press* (*ISBN 1-861006-91-8*) and http://www.php.net/session.

Summary

In this case study, we were faced with the task of making an existing web site available to mobile phone and PDA users. The web site, which allows users to search for local coffee shops by city and state/Zip code, also provides ratings, URLs, and photos of the restaurants when available. The final component that we added to the application was a feature that allows the user to contribute their rating of a shop to the average score.

After looking over the possibilities and limitations of our target WAP and PDA platforms, we began to realize how difficult it would be to develop a cross-platform mobile application that would generate both WML for WAP devices and HTML for the AvantGo browser. The solution to our dilemma was the HAWHAW toolkit and the HAWHAW PHP class in particular. The HAWHAW class provides a platform-neutral way to build mobile applications, and it automatically takes care of determining what type of user agent is requesting the page. Once it determines the user agent, HAWHAW generates the appropriate markup language, thus eliminating the need for us to create a complex template system for developing our application for two different platforms.

With our development tools selected, we began to organize our project. We determined that we would need common files containing configuration information and frequently used functions, as well as separate pages for the home, search, results, details, and rating. By using desktop emulators available for PalmOS and WAP devices, we could see the results on WAP and PDA devices. We were able to see the way HAWHAW creates markup for them. We also saw how quickly our mobile application came together thanks to the HAWHAW class.

After combining the image manipulation capabilities of PHP's GD functions, with the ease and flexibility of the HAWHAW class, we now have a clear idea about what is possible on these platforms with PHP and we'll be comfortable developing similar projects in the future.

11

Case Study – Image Gallery

In Chapters 3 and 4 we looked at how we could create dynamic Flash content using Ming. We also looked at some features that allowed us to incorporate an existing image within our Flash content. Then in Chapter 6 we discussed how to use ImageMagick's Convert, Mogrify, and Identify tools to modify an existing image. In this chapter we will put to use the skills that we have acquired to build a fully functional **Image Gallery** application.

When we think of an Image Gallery, we might think of a web page displaying a list of images and wonder how this relates to ImageMagick. As we shall see in this chapter, ImageMagick can provide some nifty functionality to our gallery and some cool features as well.

Image Gallery – Application Spec

Our Image Gallery application displays images to the user browsing the web site. Before we delve into actual coding, let's add some details to our specification.

Storage

Where and how do we store the images for the gallery? It would be nice if we let the user browse through the images by category or allowed them to search for images with specific keywords – the best way to do this would be to use a database.

Even though it is possible to store binary (image) data in a database, the purpose of this chapter is to look at how we can add functionality to an image gallery with the ImageMagick tools, so we'll keep the storage solution simple – the image files themselves will be saved in a folder on the web server and the details of the image will be stored in a database for quick and easy searching.

Now that we have an idea as to how we will be storing the images, we can think about how we will be getting them onto the server: that is, administration.

Administration

Our administration tools will have two main tasks. The first is to administer the categories that we can store our images under. Second, and more important, will be the tool we use to get our images into the gallery. This tool will not only have to handle the uploading of images and store them in the appropriate place, but will also have to make sure than any images that we upload are in a suitable format for the Web. This is a web application, so, for example, we will not be able to display a Tag Image File Format (TIFF) file – we will have to convert it to a format that is viewable by a web browser.

> **To view a TIFF file directly on the Web, we have to use a helper application (for example, Kodak Imaging for Windows) outside our web browser.**

Front End

The front end should provide the following functionality to the end user:

❑ **Browse images**
The user should be able to browse through the images by category. Rather than displaying the full image size, which might take a long time to download, we will display a thumbnail of the image.

❑ **Search images**
The user should also be able to search through the images using a specific keyword.

❑ **View images**
Once users find an image that they want to view then they should to be able to view its full size.

❑ **Features**
Since we are dealing with ImageMagick, we can add some features to our front end that will allow the user to do some interesting things to the image.

Features

While this is not something that we would typically see in an image gallery, it doesn't hurt to include some features that allow the user to add cool effects to the image. We will use this section of the application to provide some fun effects that the user can apply to the image.

Tools

In this chapter we shall use the ImageMagick class that we created in Chapter 6. Since the class uses the ImageMagick tools, we should have them installed on our machines. Refer to Chapter 6 to know more about how to install these tools on UNIX and Windows platforms.

Besides the ImageMagick tools, we will also need the following:

❑ **A database server**
In this application we will use the MySQL database, to store the image information. We will also need permissions to create tables in a new MySQL database.

❑   **A web server with writable folders**
In this application we will be uploading and creating images on the fly and for this we will
need to store our images somewhere. Since the end users will want to view these images, the
folder where these images will be stored has to be somewhere inside our web directory
structure. Further, the web server should be able to write to this directory.

Components

Before we delve into writing our PHP scripts, let's look at the components that we would be creating for
our Image Gallery application.

The Database

To enable quick and easy searching, we will store the details of the images in a `gallery` database with
two tables. The first table stores the categories that we will assign images to:

```
create table category (
            cat_id int(11) not null auto_increment,
            cat_name varchar(30),
            primary key(cat_id)
);
```

The `images` table will store information about each of the images that we upload. Besides the category,
we will also store the keywords associated with the image, the name that we have given the image as
stored in the `data` directory, and the original name of the file that we uploaded:

```
create table images (
            im_id int(11) not null auto_increment,
            im_category int(11),
            im_keywords varchar(100),
            im_filename varchar(33),
            im_original varchar(255),
            primary key(im_id)
);
```

Classes, Functions, and Configuration

As mentioned earlier we will be using the **class.imagemagick.php** file that we created in Chapter 6.
In the class we created a constructor function that retrieved all relevant information about the image.
We also created some functions that allowed us to interface into the ImageMagick tools to resize and
convert our image. Rather than reinvent the wheel, we will use as much functionality from this class as
possible. Also, some functionality that we require is not related to the ImageMagick class, so we will
create a few helper functions in **tools.php**. Further, our application will have certain settings, so we
will have to create a **config.php** file to store these settings.

Administration

The administration of the application includes three files. **admin.php** is the top-level script that allows
us to choose administration options. The administration options are to manage the categories and to
upload images. **catadmin.php** will allow us to add and delete categories from the MySQL database.
upload.php will let us upload new images; the images will be stored in a directory on the web server,
converted to an appropriate format and a thumbnail generated.

Front End

The front end, **index.php**, will allow the user to select a category to browse and optionally enter a keyword. If a keyword is entered, the results within that category will be filtered by the keyword specified. The images are displayed as thumbnails to reduce download time to the end user. We will also provide links to the various features that are available.

Features

Since ImageMagick is more than just retrieving image information, converting and resizing images, we will add some features to the image gallery that let the user experience some of these. In Chapter 6 we wrote a script that interfaced with the ImageMagick convert tool and allowed us to add effects like flipping the image, converting it to grayscale, and embossing it. Here we will once again provide similar functionality and also write an interface into the ImageMagick montage tool.

montage.php takes a number of images and creates a photo montage from them. The user of our image gallery will be able to select images that they want and then create a photo montage from these images.

Program Listings

Now that we have a clear idea about the different components that we need to build our Image Gallery, let's put them all together, starting with scripts that will be used by other scripts.

Configuration

The first section that we will deal with is the configuration section. In this section we will look at the code that makes up the configuration file and the code for the helper functions.

config.php

This file will contain the system settings:

```php
<?php

$default_thumbnail_resolution = 80;
```

This is the maximum height and width that we will allow for the thumbnails of the image. All images will be scaled proportionately to fit within the 80x80 area.

As mentioned earlier, ImageMagick can deal with a vast number of image formats while our web browsers cannot. This array lists the file formats that are accepted by a web browser to display images:

```php
$acceptable_image_formats = array('JPEG', 'JPG', 'GIF', 'PNG');
```

The upload.php script, which we will write later, will use this array to check whether the file needs to be displayed in a web browser or not.

Next we create two directories that will be used by the upload.php and effects.php scripts:

```php
$default_base_directory = 'data/';
$default_temp_directory = 'tmp/';
```

The base directory (data) is where the images will be stored within the directory structure of the web server, and the temporary (tmp) directory is the directory that the Convert and Montage tools will use to output the altered images.

The last set of variables defines our MySQL connection:

```
$database_host = '127.0.0.1';
$database_port = '3306';
$database_name = 'gallery';
$database_user = 'jon';
$database_pass = 'secret';
?>
```

Note that these settings will have to be changed to reflect the settings on the local machine.

tools.php

During the upload process, in a number of places, we will need to extract the extension and the name of the file we are uploading. We'll put these functions into a script called tools.php:

The first function returns the file extension. To do this, we split the string on the period and return the last element of the resultant array:

```
<?php

function ReturnExtension($filename)
{
    $r = explode(".", $filename);
    return ($r[sizeOf($r) - 1]);
}
```

The second function returns the file name. In this case we want the exact opposite – we want everything up to and including the last period. Again we split the string up by the period and then concatenate all except the last element of the array (the extension):

```
function ReturnName($filename)
{
    $r = explode(".", $filename);

    for ($i = 0; $i < sizeOf($r) - 1; $i++) {
        $n .= $r[$i];

        if ($i < (sizeOf($r) - 2)) {
            $n .= ".";
        }
    }

    return $n;
}
?>
```

Administration

The administration section of the application is where we can create and delete categories from our database and upload images to the database. Before we write scripts to allow these functionalities we need a script to link to each of them.

admin.php

This is the top-level script of the administrative tool:

```html
<html>
  <head>
    <title>Gallery Admin</title>
  </head>

  <body bgcolor="#FFFFFF">
```

In order to use the administration section we need to make sure that our configuration file exists, otherwise the script should generate an error message:

```php
<?php

if (file_exists("config.php")) {
    require_once "config.php";
```

We also need to make sure that the directories, specified to store the data and information about the generated images, also exist; otherwise the script should generate an error message:

```php
if(is_dir($default_base_directory)&&
    is_dir($default_temp_directory)){
    ?>
```

If everything is in order we can provide links to the scripts to administer the categories, and upload files:

```php
            <a href="upload.php">Upload Images</a><br />
            <a href="catadmin.php">Administer Categories</a>
            <?php
        } else {
            ?>
            The directories specified in the configuration script
              do not exist.
            <?php
        }
    } else {
        ?>
        Configuration file was not found.
        <?php
    }
    ?>
  </body>
</html>
```

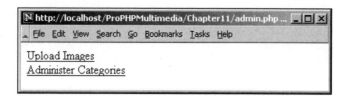

catadmin.php

This script allows the user to add categories to the `category` table. This is the second layer of our administration section:

```
<a href="admin.php">Admin</a><br />
<?php
```

First we make sure we've included our configuration script, as this script contains the settings for our database connection:

```
require_once "config.php";

mysql_connect($database_host, $database_user, $database_pass);
mysql_select_db($database_name);
```

We will create a form with a submit button that has a value, `Add`. We can then test to see if this value exists in the `$_POST` variables. If it does then we submit the form and insert the category:

```
if ($_POST['submit'] == 'Add') {

    $sql = "INSERT INTO category (cat_name)
            VALUES ('".htmlspecialchars($_POST['category'],ENT_QUOTES)."')";

    mysql_query($sql) or die(mysql_error().'<br>'.$sql);

    print ('Record Inserted: '.$_POST['category'].'<br />');
```

We should also be able to delete records, and we will do this through a link next to the relevant record. Since this will be coming through to our script in the form of a URL, we need to check for it in the `$_GET` variable:

```
} elseif ($_GET['action'] == 'Delete') {

    $sql = 'SELECT im_id FROM images WHERE im_category='.$_GET['item'];
    $dRes = mysql_query($sql) or die(mysql_error().'<br>'.$sql);
```

We must make sure that we do not remove a category for which images exist. To do this we will have to search the database, to check the database for images for that particular category. If there are none we can go ahead and delete the category from the database:

```
    if (mysql_num_rows($dRes) == 0) {
        $sql = 'DELETE FROM category WHERE cat_id='.$_GET['item'];
        mysql_query($sql) or die(mysql_error().'<br>'.$sql);
        print('Record deleted.<br />');
    } else {
        print('Record not deleted: Images exist for this category.<br />');
    }
}
?>
```

We display the current categories, on the page itself, with a link next to each one to delete the record:

```
<strong>Current Categories:</strong><br />

<?php

$sql = 'SELECT * FROM category ORDER BY cat_name';
$cRes = mysql_query($sql) or die('Database Connection Failed');

if (mysql_num_rows($cRes)==0) {
    print('No Current Categories');
} else {
    print('<table border=0>');
    while ($cRow = mysql_fetch_array($cRes)) {
        ?>

        <tr>

          <td><?php print $cRow['cat_name']; ?>
          <td><a href="<?php print $PHP_SELF; ?> ?action=Delete&item=
                    <?php print $cRow['cat_id']; ?>">Delete</a>
        </tr>

        <?php
    }
    print('</table>');
}
?>
<br />
<hr />
```

The last thing in this script is the form to insert a new category:

```
<br />
<form action="<?php print $PHP_SELF; ?>" method="POST">
  Category: <input type="text" name="category"> 
  <input type="submit" name="submit" value="Add">
</form>
```

Here is the output:

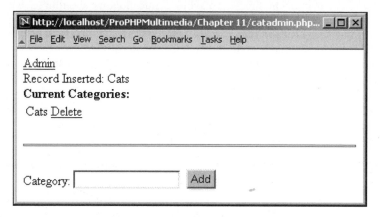

The category administration script is fairly straightforward. Up to this point we haven't used any of the ImageMagick tools. Our next script – `upload.php`, will do just that.

upload.php

This script is the final layer of our administration section:

```
<a href="admin.php">Admin</a><br />
<?php
```

Since this script will be making use of ImageMagick tools, we will need to include the ImageMagick class file along with the configuration file. We also need to include `tools.php`, as we will be using the functions from this file as well:

```
require_once "config.php";
require_once "tools.php";
require_once "class.imagemagick.php";
```

This script only has one function, and that is to upload files. As we did in the category administration page, we test for the value of the submit button to check if the form has been posted or not:

```
if ($_POST['submit'] == 'Upload') {
```

Our form will have a number of fields. The first and most important is the name of the file on the local disk that we are uploading. We will also need the category and optionally some keywords. If the category has not been selected or if we have not yet entered any categories into our database, then we need to exit the script and print a relevant error message:

```
if ($_POST['category']==0) {
    print('Please Use the admin tool to create categories');
} else {
```

When we upload the file, we will be storing it in a directory with all the other images, hence we need to generate a random file name for the image. To avoid duplication, we shouldn't use the filename of the image already present on the local disk. We will use the PHP's mt_rand() function to generate a random number from 97 to 122, and then use this with the chr() function to convert the returned number into a letter from the alphabets. In the earlier versions of PHP (prior to PHP version 4.2.0), we first had to seed the random number generator with the mt_srand() function.

> *By default, PHP uses the libc random number generator with the rand() function. mt_rand()*
> *function is a drop-in replacement for this. It uses a random number generator with known*
> *characteristics, the Mersenne Twister, which will produce random numbers that should be suitable*
> *for seeding some kinds of cryptography and is four times faster than what the average libc provides.*

We can test whether the version of PHP on our local system is older than 4.2.0 with the version_compare() function and if it is, seed the random number generator:

```
if (version_compare(PHP_VERSION, "4.2.0") < 0) {
    list($usec, $sec) = explode(' ', microtime());
    $seed = (float) $sec + ((float) $usec * 100000);
    mt_srand($seed);
}
```

$fname will store the randomly generated filename, and $oname will store the original file name from the local disk. We will only want the name part, not the extension, as we will be altering the type of our image file to a Web-suitable format:

```
$fname = '';
$oname = ReturnName($_FILES['upload']['name']);
for ($i=0;$i<25;$i++) {
    $fname .= chr(mt_rand(97,122));
}
```

Once the image is uploaded, we can create a new ImageMagick object from it. Remember, when we create the object, the constructor function sets a number of properties of that object, which we can use to determine whether the image is in a suitable format or not:

```
$image = new ImageMagick($_FILES['upload']['tmp_name']);
if (!in_array($image->imageType, $acceptable_image_formats)) {
```

If the image is not in a suitable format we need to convert it to one that is. We will take the first image type from the $acceptable_image_formats array and convert to that. We will use the MoveUploadedFile() function to move the uploaded file, from the temporary directory on the web server, to the data directory. Since we are using MoveUploadedFile() we can't convert to a different filename; we have to retain the same filename. To do this we call ImageMagick's Convert tool and use the following syntax to change the format without altering the filename:

```
convert imagename FORMAT:imagename
```

where FORMAT: is an image format that is known to ImageMagick. For example, if we had a Windows bitmap called mom.bmp that we wanted to convert to a JPEG format, but retain the original filename, we would issue the command in the following manner:

```
convert mom.bmp JPEG:mom.bmp
```

The resultant mom.bmp would actually be a JPEG file. This suits our purpose well because if we change the filename in any way, the MoveUploadedFile() function would fail:

```
$cmdString = 'convert '.$image->imageName.'
              '.$acceptable_image_formats[0].':'.$image->imageName;
`$cmdString`;
```

Once we have converted the file, we can build the new $fname and $oname variables by adding the new image format extension to the end of the filename:

```
$fname .= '.'.strtolower($acceptable_image_formats[0]);
$oname .= '.'.strtolower($acceptable_image_formats[0]);
} else {
```

If the file is in an acceptable format then we don't have to do any conversions, we can just update the $fname and $oname variables:

```
$fname .= '.'.ReturnExtension($_FILES['upload']['name']);
$oname .= '.'.ReturnExtension($_FILES['upload']['name']);
}
```

Now we can move the uploaded file to the $default_base_directory and as we move it we will rename it to our new randomly generated name:

```
move_uploaded_file($image->imageName,
                   $default_base_directory.$fname);
```

Once we have moved the file, we can generate a thumbnail for the image. The thumbnail must be proportionately sized, and must fit within the area specified by the $default_thumbnail_resolution variable. To do this we first create an ImageMagick object of the newly uploaded file. We then determine which of the dimensions, width or height, is larger. This is the dimension that we will scale down to $default_thumbnail_resolution and scale the other dimension proportionately.

```
$image = new ImageMagick($default_base_directory.$fname);
if ($image->imageHeight > $image->imageWidth) {
    $proportion = ($image->imageHeight /
                   $default_thumbnail_resolution);
} else {
    $proportion = ($image->imageWidth /
                   $default_thumbnail_resolution);
}
```

Once we have the proportion, we can determine the new height and width of the thumbnail, and then resize the file to this new size, saving the resultant image with the same name as of the original, but with thumb_ prefixed to it:

```
            $newWidth = ($image->imageWidth / $proportion);
            $newHeight =( $image->imageHeight / $proportion);

            $image->c_resize($default_base_directory.'thumb_'.$fname, $newWidth,
                            $newHeight);
```

Now that have uploaded and created the thumbnail, we can insert this information into the database:

```
        mysql_connect($database_host, $database_user, $database_pass);

        mysql_select_db($database_name);

        $sql = "INSERT INTO images (im_category, im_keywords, im_filename,
            im_original) VALUES (".$_POST['category'].",'".htmlspecialchars
            ($_POST['keywords'],ENT_QUOTES)."','".htmlspecialchars
            ($fname,ENT_QUOTES)."','".htmlspecialchars
            ($oname,ENT_QUOTES)."')";
        mysql_query($sql) or die(mysql_error().'<br>'.$sql);
    }
}
?>
```

Our form needs to have a field for the file, the category, and the keywords. We generate the category from the database. If there are no categories or if there was an error generating the list of categories, then we output a single <option> tag with a value of 0. Remember that we tested for this value earlier in the script to make sure that we had a category to insert into the database:

```
<form action="<?php print $PHP_SELF; ?>" method="POST"
        enctype="multipart/form-data">
  File: <input type="file" name="upload"><br />
  Category: <select name="category">

    <?php
    mysql_connect($database_host, $database_user, $database_pass);
    mysql_select_db($database_name);
    $sql = 'SELECT * FROM category ORDER BY cat_name';

    $cRes = mysql_query($sql) or die('<option value=0>Database Connection
        Failed</option>');

    if (mysql_num_rows($cRes)==0) {
        print('<option value=0>No Categories available</option>');
    } else {
        while ($cRow = mysql_fetch_array($cRes)) {
            print('<option value='.$cRow['cat_id'].'">'
                .$cRow['cat_name'].'</option>');
        }
    }
    ?>

  </select><br />
    Keywords: <input type="text" name="keywords" size="40"><br />
    <input type="submit" name="submit" value="Upload">
</form>
```

Here is the output:

Front End

Our front end is made up of a single script, `index.php`. The script will allow the user to select a category and optionally specify keywords to filter the images by.

index.php

The first thing we will do is include our `config.php` and `class.imagemagick.php` files, then connect to the database:

```php
<?php

include_once('config.php');
require_once "class.imagemagick.php";

mysql_connect($database_host, $database_user, $database_pass);
mysql_select_db($database_name);
?>
```

We will put the forms for selecting the category and keywords right at the top of the page. The categories are presented as a drop-down list of categories:

```php
<form action="<?php print $PHP_SELF; ?>" method="POST">
  <select name="category">
  <?php
      $sql = 'SELECT * FROM category ORDER BY cat_name';
      $cRes = mysql_query($sql) or die('<option value=0>Database Connection
                                  Failed</option>');
  if (mysql_num_rows($cRes)==0) {
      print('<option value=0>No Categories available</option>');
  } else {
      while ($cRow = mysql_fetch_array($cRes)) {
          print('<option value='.$cRow['cat_id']."">".
                              $cRow['cat_name'].'</option>');
      }
  }
  ?>

  </select> <input type="text" name="keyword">
           <input type="submit" name="submit" value="View">
</form>
```

Below the form we will display the images from the category that has been selected. The submit button of the form has a value, View, which we can use to test whether the form has been submitted or not:

```
<hr>
<?php
if ($_POST['submit'] == 'View') {
```

The first thing that we do is grab the current category name and output it as a heading to the page:

```
    $sql = 'SELECT cat_name FROM category
            WHERE cat_id='.$_POST['category'];

    $cRes = mysql_query($sql) or die($sql);

    $cRow = mysql_fetch_array($cRes);

    $currentCategory = $cRow['cat_name'];
?>

<strong><?php print $currentCategory; ?></strong><br />
```

We now test to see whether the user has entered a keyword or not. If they have, we must include the keyword in the SQL SELECT statement. If not, we select all the images in that category:

```
<?php
if (strlen($_POST['keyword'])==0) {
    $sql = 'SELECT * FROM images
            WHERE im_category='.$_POST['category'];
} else {
    $sql = 'SELECT * FROM images
            WHERE im_category='.$_POST['category'].'
            AND im_keywords LIKE %'.
            htmlspecialchars($_POST['keyword'],ENT_QUOTES).'%"';
}

$iRes = mysql_query($sql) or die($sql);
if (mysql_num_rows($iRes) == 0) {
    print('No images found.');
} else {
```

If we have some images in our result set then we can output them on the page. In this chapter we are trying to keep things as simple as possible – to highlight the way in which we can use ImageMagick, so in the output the images are simply presented one below the other:

```
    print('<table border=0>');
    while ($iRow = mysql_fetch_array($iRes)) {
```

Once this is done, we grab the file name of the current image, and create a new ImageMagick object with it. Once this object is created we will quickly be able to retrieve the width and height of the image, then use them to display the full size of the image:

```
$image = new ImageMagick($default_base_directory.
                         $iRow['im_filename']);
?>
<tr>
```

If the user clicks on the thumbnail, we will use JavaScript to open a new window containing the full-size image. The `window.open` method allows us to specify the width and height of the new window, and we will make the new window a little bit larger than the image we are displaying in it. By doing this we will be able to see the full size of the image:

```
<td><a href="javascript:;" onClick="window.open
       ('<?php print $image->imageName; ?>','theView',
       'width=<?php print ($image->imageWidth+20); ?>,
       height=<?php print ($image->imageHeight+20); ?>');">
       <img src="<?php print $default_base_directory.'thumb_'.
                         $iRow ['im_filename']; ?>" border="0">
       </a>
```

The second cell, next to the thumbnail of the image, contains a form that allows us to apply certain effects to the current image. Some of these effects have been detailed in Chapter 6, therefore we will not explain each one of them here. Notice though that some of the effects that we pass to the convert script require additional information to be passed with the `effect` switch, and this information is included in the `<option>` tag. The form calls the `effects.php` script, and shows the output in a new window. We will look at the contents of this script in a short while:

```
<td>
   <form action="effects.php" method="post" target="_blank">
     <input type="hidden" name="image"
            value="<?php print $iRow['im_filename']; ?>">
     <select name="effect">
       <option value="flip">Vertical Mirror</option>
       <option value="flop">Horizontal Mirror</option>
       <option value="monochrome">Black & White</option>
       <option value="charcoal 1">Charcoal</option>
       <option value="emboss">Emboss</option>
       <option value="implode 0.4">Implode</option>
       <option value="paint 1">Paint</option>
       <option value="swirl 180">Swirl</option>
     </select> <input type="submit" value="--&gt;">
   </form>
```

We have already mentioned that we would provide a way for the user to create a photo montage. We do this by providing a kind of 'shopping cart' page that lists the images that the user has selected. The script that handles this is called `list.php`. We will see this script once we are done with our `effects.php` script:

```
<a href="javascript:;" onClick="window.open
   ('list.php?image=<?phpprint $iRow['im_filename']; ?>',
   'theList','width= 400,height=500');">Add to List</a><br>
   <?php
 }
 print('</table>');
   }
 }
?>
```

This is the output of index.php:

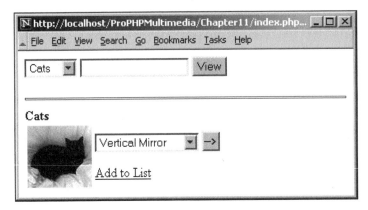

Features

The features that we will detail are the effects that we can apply to the image and the montage facility.

effects.php

Here, we will get the image name and effect from the $_POST array and pass these directly through to the ImageMagick class to do the conversion. The output is saved in the directory specified by $default_temp_directory and the image is outputted in an <img> tag. Note that ImageMagick's Convert tool updates the imageName property with the name of the new outputted image:

```php
<?php

require_once "config.php";
require_once "class.imagemagick.php";

$image = new ImageMagick($default_base_directory.$_POST['image']);

print;

$image->convert($default_temp_directory.
                $_POST['image'], '-'.$_POST['effect']);
?>

<img src="<?php print $image->imageName; ?>">
```

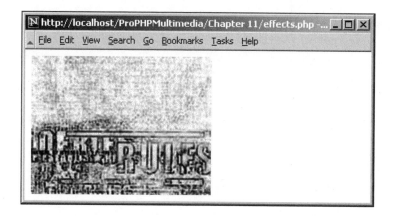

list.php

list.php has to work with sessions to store the list of images that we have chosen to add to our 'shopping cart'.

The first thing we do is start the session. Once we have done that we can include the config.php file.

```php
<?php

session_start();
require_once "config.php";
```

We check to see if the session variable $imageList is registered, and if not, we register it:

```php
if (!session_is_registered($imageList)) {
    session_register('imageList');
}
```

We will give the user the option of removing an image from the list by a link in the page. If the $_GET['action'] is set to Delete, then we need to remove the item from the $imageList array with the array_splice() function. We will pass the position in the array through in the URL as well as the offset, so we will retrieve that value through the $_GET['offset'] variable:

```php
if ($_GET['action']=='Delete') {
    array_splice ($_SESSION['imagelist'], $_GET['offset'], 1);
} else {
```

If we are not deleting an image from the list then we are adding one. We need to make sure that we have been passed an image name, and that it is not already present in the $imageList array.

```php
    if (strlen($_GET['image'])!=0 &&
        !in_array($_GET['image'],$_SESSION['imagelist'])) {
```

If we have an image name and it is not already in the array, then we can safely add it to the array:

```
            $_SESSION['imagelist']
                    [count($_SESSION['imagelist'])] = $_GET['image'];
    }
}
?>
```

We will display the images that are currently in the list on the page itself, along with the option to remove them from the list:

```
<strong>Current Images:</strong><br />

<table border="0">
    <?php
```

Loop through the imageList session variable:

```
        for ($i=0;$i<count($_SESSION['imagelist']);$i++) {
            ?>
```

As we did in the gallery, we will display the thumbnails of the images, rather than the images themselves:

```
            <tr><td><img src="<?php print $default_base_directory.
                            'thumb_'.$_SESSION ['imagelist'][$i]; ?>">
```

Next to each image we will provide a link to remove the image from the list. We pass $i as the offset, since this is the position where the image occurs in the array:

```
            <td><a href=<?php print $PHP_SELF; ?>
                ?action=Delete&offset=<?php print $i; ?>">Remove</a>
            <?php
        }
    ?>
    </table>
    <hr />
```

Beneath the list of images we provide a form for the user to create a photo montage of the current images. We will allow the user to provide the dimensions of the images as they will appear in the montage. Once again we set the target of the form as a new blank window:

```
<form action="montage.php" method="POST" target="_blank">
    Width:
    <select name="width">
        <option value="50">50</option>
        <option value="100">100</option>
        <option value="150">150</option>
    </select><br />

    Height:
    <select name="height">
```

```
            <option value="50">50</option>
            <option value="100">100</option>
            <option value="150">150</option>
        </select><br />
    <input type="submit" value="Montage">
    </form>
```

To see the resulting image refer to *Fig 11.1 – list.php* in *Appendix G*.

montage.php

The script to create the montage is also quite straightforward. The Montage tool has the following syntax:

```
montage image1 image2 image3 -geometry WxH outputfile
```

where WxH is the dimension of the image as it will appear in the montage and image1, image2, and image3 are the images the user wants to add to the montage. outputfile is the name of the file that Montage will pass the output to. We can also add borders, text, and effects to the image using the Montage tool.

Let's start the script:

```
<?php

session_start();
require_once "config.php";
```

We need to pass the Montage tool a space-separated list of images that we want to add to the montage. The list at the moment only has the image name and not the path to the image in the array, so we use the implode() function to join the image list together with a space and the $default_base_directory. The first image will not have the $default_base_directory prepended to it, so we will have to do this manually:

```
$strFiles = implode(' '.$default_base_directory, $_SESSION['imagelist']);
$strFiles = $default_base_directory.$strFiles;
```

Once we have the image list, we can build a command string for the montage command including the geometry we get from the values posted from the form, and the session ID as the filename – to maintain a unique filename for the new image in the $default_temp_directory. We can then execute the Montage tool by inserting the $cmdString variable inside the backtick operator:

```
$cmdString = 'montage -geometry '.$_POST['width'].'x'.$_POST['height'].'
            '.$strFiles.' '.$default_temp_directory.session_id().'.jpg';
`$cmdString`;
?>
```

Finally we display the image:

```
<img src='<?php print $default_temp_directory.session_id(); ?>.jpg'>
```

To see the resulting image refer to *Fig 11.2 – montage.php* in *Appendix G*.

Possible Enhancements

We have tried to keep the Image Gallery as simple as possible and concentrated on the aspects that use the ImageMagick tools. But there is definite scope for enhancement:

❑ **Administration**
In the current application anyone with the URL can alter categories and upload images. So it will be good to add some protection to the administration script.

❑ **Front End**
The images are displayed in a list. If we had a large number of images this would become unmanageable. A great enhancement would be to alter the layout of the page to display the images in a tabular format – across, as well as down the page. Also, our images are stored in a database, which would make it easy for us to select a specific number of images from the database at a time using the LIMIT keyword.

❑ **Features**
Not all of the features that we can achieve with the ImageMagick tools have been included in the application. We can add many extra effects to the images, and also give the user the facility to set the options that are passed through with these effects.

Summary

We've gone through the design and development of a fully functional Image Gallery that allows us to store images, browse and search them, and alter them using ImageMagick effects.

In this chapter, we used ImageMagick tools to:

❑ **Upload Images**
The script that we used to upload images made use of the ImageMagick class to first retrieve information about the uploaded image, and then used that image information and a class member function to convert the image to a suitable format for the Web. We also used the ImageMagick class to create a thumbnail of the newly uploaded file.

❑ **Display Images**
In the front end of the application we used the ImageMagick class to grab the image information. We then used the width and height to build a single line of JavaScript that opened the image in a new window of the correct size to display it.

❑ **Add Effects**
We built a script that allowed us to apply certain ImageMagick effects to the images in our gallery.

❑ **Create a Photo Montage**
We built a script that allowed us to add images to a list. Then we used ImageMagick's Montage tool to convert the images in that list into a photo montage.

12

Case Study: PDF Template System

Web applications often need some kind of facility for generating reports and subsequently printing them. HTML Template Systems are already a standard part of designing a web application. However, HTML output is not very suitable for this as there is neither an effective control over the page layout, nor the freedom to use custom fonts. One of the formats that can deliver these requirements is **PDF** (Portable Document Format).

In this case study we will create a general-purpose PDF **Template System** that can be used with almost any web application. With this system we will be able to produce PDF documents filled with dynamic content.

> **The Template System is built on the object-oriented classes that we have seen in Chapter 7, and also uses an object model from an example in that chapter, as a skeleton.**

HTML vs. PDF Template System

The HTML template system allows separating design from the application logic, so that web designers do not have to know much about programming. Essentially, the templates are HTML files with placeholder fields that are parsed through some engine, and those fields are filled with more or less dynamic content. Some examples of HTML templates are the FastTemplate, the PHPlib Template, and the Smarty.

A PDF Template System can also separate the design from the application logic. However, unlike in an HTML file, we cannot just find and replace text in a PDF file. First we have to create an object-oriented representation of this PDF in our application, find and change the placeholder fields with our content, and then send that PDF file (or data stream) to the browser.

The following table compares features of HTML and PDF Template Systems:

Feature	HTML Template System	PDF Template System
Placeholder fields are filled with data	Yes	Yes
Separates presentation and application logic	Yes	Yes
Page size	Depends on client's browser	Fixed
Available fonts	Limited set	Any font installed on the server host system
Template design	Same as the HTML page	Defining pages and objects with desired properties in PHP
Interactive features	Yes	No
Positioning of objects	Mostly relative	Mostly absolute
Type of layout	Floating (relative)	Fixed with a few floating layout features

Basic Layout Types

In the above table we saw one important difference between the HTML and PDF Template System – the type of layout. There are two basic types of layout:

❑ **Fixed layout**
Fixed layout has objects placed on the page with absolute coordinates, and fixed space for the text in text blocks. Pages follow the same pattern – fields are always at the same place. This type of layout is good for simple forms and reports, for example a phone directory, an invoice listing, and a to-do list.

❑ **Floating layout**
Floating layout has objects that are positioned relative to each other on a page, and the space for the text in the text block is not fixed (though some objects like headers and footers are placed on the page with absolute coordinates). Therefore, the objects 'float' over pages as the text is pushed into the fields. This type of layout is suitable for long texts, like books, articles, and lengthy and complex reports, but is much more difficult to accomplish with **PDFlib**. We have to, more or less, replicate what a browser does when parsing HTML.

In this case it is better to use some typographically well-equipped tool, for example, the pdfTex. This is because some kind of justification/line breaking/hyphenation mechanism is needed (we do have to create TeX sourcecode with PHP to obtain our layouts). pdfTex is a powerful and free publishing tool that is capable of producing professionally typeset documents. We can find more about it on http://wwww.pdftex.org.

PDF Template System – Application Spec

Before we start with our template system, let's first look at the requirements that we need to set up, and the tools that we are going to use while building our case study.

General Requirements

Let's set up the requirements for the Template System. Once we implement this system it should be:

- Easy to define fixed layouts for a new document, with some simple features of floating layout
- Easy to link and integrate with any PHP database application
- Extensible while using new types of objects on pages, and relations among objects
- Able to create multi-page documents
- Able to use arbitrary colors and fonts in documents
- Able to fill fields (placeholders) with data from a database
- Able to output the created PDF document to a browser, or to a file on a disk

We will also look at some features of floating layout like the ability to create relations among objects. Hence, the templates will be most suitable for forms and simple reports. However, we will not try to solve the following tasks:

- Complex text layouts with hyphenation and justification
- Long text floating layouts

Tools

We will use PDFlib extension to create PDF documents. As we learned in Chapter 7, PDFlib is a library that allows a user to create files in Adobe's Portable Document Format. It can be downloaded from http://www.pdflib.com.

Usability

We will use an object-oriented model of the PDF document that will allow us to achieve extensibility. The PDF Template System can be useful in a web environment for producing orders, or e-invoices, and in Intranet solutions for creating automated address labels, reports, invoices, price offers, and product catalogs.

Components

Based on the requirements we have discussed so far, the Templates System will create a new structure based on the object-oriented structure we created in Chapter 7.

Class Description

Let's detail the classes:

- **PdfDocument class**
  This class represents the whole PDF document that we create. It is a container for all page objects, font objects, and color objects. It can draw itself to PDF; it can fill all placeholders on all pages with data from a database. This class will include the following features:

❑ Fonts – ability to use arbitrary fonts (and of course those available on host system)

❑ Colors – ability to use arbitrary colors with different color models (RGB, CMYK, or Gray)

❑ Relations – ability to define relations among objects (for example, a box around text blocks, or clipping)

❑ Pages – ability to create documents with more than one page

❑ Page templates – ability to store the defined page layout, and use it later with merged data

❑ Data merging – ability to fill placeholders with data from a database

❑ **PdfFont class**
This class represents the font family used in PDF. It stores information about a particular font family (for example, which of the fonts is regular, bold, italic, or bold italic). It provides the appropriate font handle when requested by the PdfObjText class.

❑ **PdfColor class**
This class represents the color used in PDF. It stores information about a particular color. Almost all PdfObj descendants to set fill and/or stroke use it.

❑ **PdfRel class**
This class and its descendants (PdfRelBoxAround and PdfRelClip) represent relations between objects in PDF.

❑ **PdfPage class**
This class represents one page of the document that will be created when the final PDF is produced. It contains all objects on a particular page, and can draw itself to the PDF.

❑ **PdfPageTemplate class**
This class is a container for templates that can quickly form new pages.

❑ **PdfObj class**
This class and its descendants represent objects in PDF. Every single object has ability to draw itself to the PDF. Objects are defined by an array of parameters – params. This array may also contain relations for a particular object. For example, it may contain PdfRel objects. Descendants of this class defined in this chapter are: PdfObjRect, PdfObjLine, PdfObjCircle, PdfObjText, PdfObjPict, PdfObjBookmark, PdfObjNote, and PdfObjPDF.

Class Relationship

The relationship between classes reflects the relations of the objects in the PDF document. The PdfDocument contains pages, fonts, colors, and the PdfPage contains objects. Every object can have relations with other objects.

The following picture shows the relationship of classes in a UML diagram (the filled diamond shows aggregations while the white triangle shows inheritance).

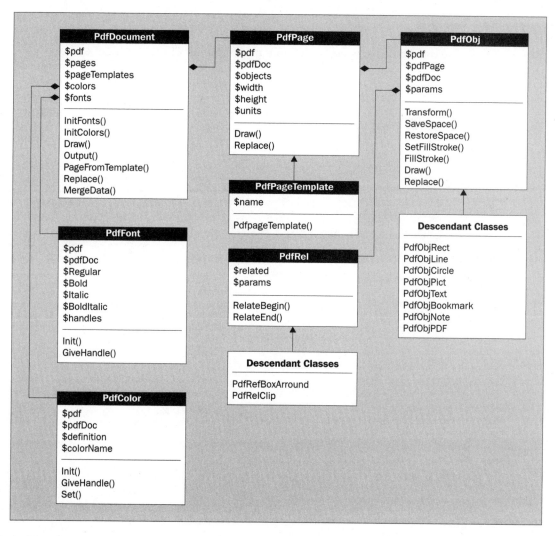

Data Merging

Data merging depends on the ability to find and replace placeholders in text objects throughout the document, or a particular page. Therefore, we define the `Replace()` function at all levels – `PdfDocument`, `PdfPage`, and `PdfObjText`. The placeholders are text fields delimited with brackets, for example, `{text}`. However, the delimiters could be changed to constants (`L_DELIM`) and (`R_DELIM`).

Now that we have discussed different classes, and their relations, let's see how we can build them. We will start with a discussion on constants, which we will be using in our Template System, and then go on to introduce the new class – `PdfDocument`. We will then use the most simple database access mechanism to fill documents with data from the MySQL database.

Program Listing

First we will define some basic constants to use in our application. The RESOURCE_FILE is dependent on installation, and is necessary only if we want to use custom fonts (other than one of the fourteen PDF core fonts). The default page size will be A4 with millimeters as units. The default encoding will be host.

Here is our class.PdfDocument.php file:

```php
<?php

//class.PdfDocument.php

//PDF detection script
if(!extension_loaded('pdf')) {
    if(strtoupper(substr(PHP_OS,0,3)) == 'WIN') {
        dl('php_pdf.dll');
    } else {
        dl('libpdf_php.so');
    }
}

//Path to the resource file - dependent on installation
define("RESOURCE_FILE", "/Resource/Font/pdflib.upr");

//Values for pdf info fields of
define("AUTHOR", "Jon Doe");
define("CREATOR", "PDF Template System 0.1");

//Default values for page sizes and units
define("DEFW", 210);                       //A4 page size
define("DEFH", 297);
define("DEFUN", 2.834645669291);           //Millimeters as units
define("DEFEN", "host");                    //Default encoding

//Delimiters for placeholders' fields
define("L_DELIM", "{");
define("R_DELIM", "}");

//Default values for pdf parameters
define("PDF_WARNING", "FALSE"); //Defines if PDFlib should generate warnings
define("PDF_COMPRESS", 9);      //Compression level (1 lowest, 9 highest)
define("PDF_OPENACTION", "fitpage"); //Defines what PDF will do when opened
```

Let's also define the constants for accessing our database:

```php
//Database constants
define("HOST", "localhost");
define("USER", "jon");
define("PASSWORD", "secret");
define("DATABASE", "mydtb");
```

> **Remember to change the host, user, password, and database to reflect local configuration.**

Let's now build the different classes used in the template system.

Class PdfDocument

First, we will define the container and the basic attributes for the whole PDF document:

```
class PdfDocument
{
    var $defaultWidth;                      //Default paper width
    var $defaultHeight;                     //Default paper height
    var $defaultUnits;                      //Millimeters in one DTP point
    var $defaultEncoding;                   //Encoding used by PDFLib

    var $pdf;                               //Resource ID

    //Storage
    var $pages = array();                   //Pages' storage
    var $pageTemplates = array();           //PageTemplates' storage
    var $fonts = array();                   //Fonts' storage
    var $colors = array();                  //Colors' storage
    var $xForms = array();                  // X-Forms' storage
    var $patterns = array();                // patterns' storage
```

The constructor of this class only stores the document's local default page size, units, and encoding values (users can always stay with default values). It is written as follows:

```
//Constructor
function PdfDocument($filename=FALSE, $defaultWidth=DEFW,
        $defaultHeight=DEFH,$defaultUnits=DEFUN, $defaultEncoding=DEFEN)
{
    $this->filename = $filename;
    $this->defaultWidth = $defaultWidth;
    $this->defaultHeight = $defaultHeight;
    $this->defaultUnits =  $defaultUnits;
    $this->defaultEncoding =  $defaultEncoding;
} // PdfDocument()
```

Next, we will detail the methods used in the PDFDocument class.

Draw()

This method starts the new PDF document with PDF_new() and PDF_open_file(). It will draw the defined document. Here are the steps:

- ❑ Start the new PDF document with PDF_new() and PDF_open_file()
- ❑ Set up parameters:

- ❑ Path to the resource file
- ❑ Decide whether to suppress warnings
- ❑ Decide the compression level
- ❑ Decide the action the document will take when it opens in a viewer
- ❑ Set info fields
- ❑ Initialize fonts (more precisely PdfFont objects)
- ❑ Initialize colors (more precisely PdfColor objects)
- ❑ Draw all the defined pages, page by page
- ❑ Close the PDF document

```
function Draw()
{
    //Start document
    $this->pdf = PDF_new();
    PDF_open_file($this->pdf,$this->filename);

    //Set some basic parameters
    PDF_set_parameter($this->pdf, "resourcefile",RESOURCE_FILE);
    PDF_set_parameter($this->pdf, "warning", PDF_WARNING);
    PDF_set_value($this->pdf, "compress", 9);
    PDF_set_parameter($this->pdf, "openaction", "fitpage");

    //Set info fields
    PDF_set_info($this->pdf, "creator", CREATOR);
    PDF_set_info($this->pdf, "author", AUTHOR);
    PDF_set_info($this->pdf, "title", $this->filename);
```

In order to have at least one instance of the PdfFont class available we will define the default font, which will be used if no font is defined for use with PdfObText. Then we initialize all fonts and all colors:

```
    //Define default font if not defined
    if (!$this->fonts['default']) {
        new PdfFont(&$this, 'default', 'Helvetica','Helvetica-Bold',
                    'Helvetica-Oblique');
    }

    //Initialize all fonts
    $this->InitFonts();

    //Initialize all spot colors
    $this->InitColors();
```

Finally we will cycle through all pages and draw them:

```
    //Go through all pages and draw them with their own methods
    foreach($this->fonts as $key=>$rec) {
        $this->pages[$key]->draw();
    }
    //Close the document
    PDF_close($this->pdf);

} // Draw()
```

InitFonts()

This function will cycle through all the defined fonts and initialize each of them with their `Init()` method:

```
//Initializes all defined fonts
function InitFonts()
{
    //Go through all fonts and initialize them with their own method
    foreach($this->fonts as $key=>$rec) {
        $this->fonts[$key]->init();
    }

} // InitFonts()
```

InitColors ()

Here is the procedure for initialization of colors:

❑ Create the appropriate scope for subsequent calls to the PDFlib functions – `PDF_fill()` and `PDF_makespotcolor()`, and `PDF_begin_template()`. (refer to Chapter 7 for details about PDFlib scope)

❑ Go through the array of all defined colors and call the `Init()` method of each of them

❑ Finish the scope with the PDFlib function `PDF_end_template()` and clean up $t with `PDF_close_image()`

Here is the function:

```
//Initializes all defined colors
function InitColors()
{
    //Create appropriate scope
    $t = PDF_begin_template($this->pdf,50,50);

    //Go through all colors and init each of them
    foreach($this->colors as $key => $rec) {
        $this->colors[$key]->init();
    }

    //Close the scope and clean up
    PDF_end_template($this->pdf);
    PDF_close_image($this->pdf,$t);

} // InitColors()
```

PageFromTemplate ()

This method creates a new page named $newPageName from pageTemplates[$name]. We cannot use simple assignment because we must update references of all objects in the given pageTemplates[] array, and we have to:

❑ Go through all objects in pageTemplates[]

❑ Update the reference in PdfPage

❑ Copy the object

Here is the function:

```
//Creates new page from template $name
function PageFromTemplate($name,$newPageName=FALSE)
{
    //Test if template exists
    if (is_object($this->pageTemplates[$name])) {

        //If $newPageName is set, create the new page under this name
        if ($newPageName) {
            $this->pages[$newPageName] = $this->pageTemplates[$name];
            $pc = $newPageName;

        //Else just add it to the array
        } else {
            $this->pages[] = $this->pageTemplates[$name];
            $pc = count($this->pages)-1;
        }

        //Now we can use the key to new page - $pc
        $this->pages[$pc]->objects = array();

        //Duplicate each object on page separately
        $this->pages[$pc]->objects = array();

        foreach($this->pageTemplates[$name]->objects as $k=>$obj) {
            $obj->PdfPage = &$this->pages[$pc]; //Update the reference
            $this->pages[$pc]->objects[$k] = $obj; //copy object
        }

        //Return the key
        return $pc;

    //If there is no pageTemplate[] with $name, return FALSE
    } else {
        return FALSE;
    }

} // PageFromTemplate()
```

Replace ()

This method goes through all pages and calls the Replace() function with argument $what and $count:

❑ $what is an array that defines what is to be replaced by $key=>$val pairs

❑ $count defines the maximum number of objects where the replacement can be made

For example, if $what = array ("black" => "white","long"=>"short"), and if $count = 2, then all occurrences of black, in a maximum of 2 objects, will be replaced with white, and all occurrences of long, in a maximum of 2 objects, will be replaced with short.

Further, if $count is −1 all occurrences are replaced, and if $lastpage is TRUE we will replace only on the last page.

Here is the function:

```
function Replace($what,$count=-1,$lastpage=FALSE)
{
    //Replace only at last defined page
    if ($lastpage) {
        $pc = count($this->pages)-1;
        $this->pages[$pc]->replace($what,$count);

    //Replace on all pages
    } else {
        foreach($this->pages as $key => $rec)) {
            $count = $this->pages[$key]->replace($what,$count);

            //If $count occurrences, allow replaced return
            if ($count == 0) { break; }
        }
    }
    return $count; //Return the occurrences left to fulfill $count

} //Replace ()
```

MergeData( )

This function uses a simple database connection to fill the placeholder $fields with data from $query:

```
function MergeData($fields,$query,$pageTemplateFirst,$pageTemplateNext)
{
    //Create the first page
    $this->PageFromTemplate($pageTemplateFirst);
    $left = FALSE;
    $noStop = TRUE;
    $i = 0;

    //MySQL queries can be done with some DB abstraction class

    $conn = mysql_pconnect(HOST, USER, PASSWORD) or die(mysql_error());
    $selected = mysql_select_db(DATABASE) or die(mysql_error());
    $result = mysql_query($query);

    while (($row = mysql_fetch_array($result)) && $noStop) {

        //Change fields, only one change per field
        $what = array();

        foreach($fields as $key) {
            if (isset($row[$key])) {
                $what[L_DELIM.$key.R_DELIM] = $row[$key];
            }
        }

        //Replace 1 occurrence of each field on the last page
        $left = $this->replace($what,1,TRUE);
```

```
            //If there are still some data to be filled, add a page to
            //prevent indefinite page inserting loops when no field matches
            if ($left && $i > 0) {
                $this->PageFromTemplate($pageTemplateNext);
                $noStop = $this->Replace($what,1,TRUE);
            }
            $i++; //Count number of times replace was called
        }

        //Cleanup
        mysql_free_result ($result);

    } // MergeData()
```

Output () and Delete()

The Output() function outputs the final document to the browser:

```
//Outputs document to browser
function Output()
{
    if ($this->filename) {
        $fp = fopen($this->Filename,"r");
        $buffer = fread($fp,filesize($this->Filename));
        fclose($fp);
    } else {
        $buffer = PDF_get_buffer($this->pdf);
    }
    header("Content-type: application/pdf");
    header("Content-Length: ".strlen($buffer));
    header("Content-Disposition:inline; filename=test.pdf");

    print $buffer;

} // Output()
```

In case of the Delete() method, we may decide not to delete (unlink) the PDF file, for example, if we have to send it by e-mail, or simply store it in some directory for future use. The PDFlib function, PDF_delete() deletes the PDF object, but not the created PDF file:

```
//Final cleanup - deletes PDF object, may delete PDF file
function Delete($unlink_file=TRUE)
{
    if ($this->Filename && $unlink_file) {
        if (!unlink($this->Filename)) {
            print("Error deleting file");
        }
    }
    PDF_delete($this->pdf);

} // Delete()

} // End of class PdfDocument
```

Next, we will include the ability to use fonts that are available on the host system in our template model, using the PdfFont class.

Class PdfFont

This class helps to abstract the relationship between individual fonts in font families; for example, the font family Helvetica includes Helvetica-Regular (regular), Helvetica-Bold (bold), Helvetica-Oblique (italic), and Helvetica-BoldOblique (bold italic). Therefore, we will have to define fonts for regular, bold, italic, and bold italic font faces.

PdfFont also stores information about whether to embed the font into a document, and what encoding is to be used. When the fonts are initialized, the resulting handles are stored for future use by PdfObjText. Here are the constituents of the class:

❑ The constructor stores the information, and the reference of the object itself in the fonts array, in PdfDocument

❑ The Init() function initializes the font using PDF_findfont() and stores the handles of each font face to the handles[] array

❑ The GiveHandle() function provides the font handle (used by PdfObjText)

Let's take a look at this class:

```
class PdfFont
{
    //Properties
    var $pdf;
    var $pdfDoc;
    var $handles = array();

    //Constructor

    function PdfFont(&$pdfDoc,$fontName, $Regular=FALSE,$Bold=FALSE,
            $Italic=FALSE,$BoldItalic=FALSE,$embed=FALSE,$encoding=FALSE)
    {
        $this->pdf = &$pdfDoc->pdf;
        $this->pdfDoc = &$pdfDoc;
        $pdfDoc->fonts[$fontName] = &$this;

        $this->regular = $Regular;
        $this->bold = $Bold;
        $this->italic = $Italic;
        $this->boldItalic = $BoldItalic;

        $this->embed = ($embed === FALSE)?$pdfDoc->defaultEmbed:$embed;
        $this->encoding = ($encoding === FALSE)? $pdfDoc->defaultEncoding:
                        $encoding;

    } // PdfFont()

    //Initialize font
    function Init()
    {
```

```
        if ($this->pdf) {
            if ($this->regular) {
                $this->handles['regular'] = PDF_findfont
                ($this->pdf, $this->regular,$this->encoding,$this->embed);
            }
            if ($this->bold) {
                $this->handles['bold'] = PDF_findfont
                ($this->pdf,$this->bold,$this->encoding,$this->embed);
            }
            if ($this->italic) {
                $this->handles['italic'] = PDF_findfont
                ($this->pdf,$this->italic,$this->encoding,$this->embed);
            }
            if ($this->boldItalic) {
                $this->handles['boldItalic'] = PDF_findfont
                ($this->pdf,$this->boldItalic,$this->encoding,$this->embed);
            }
        }
    } //Init ()
```

The `GiveHandle()` function is used by the `PdfObjText` object to obtain the appropriate handle for the appropriate font face (by default, `'regular'`):

```
    //Return handle of the font
    function GiveHandle($name='regular')
    {
        if ($this->handles[$name]) {
            return $this->handles[$name];
        } else {
            return $this->handles['regular'];
        }

    } // GiveHandle()

} // End of class PdfFont
```

We shall include the ability to use arbitrarily named colors with different color models in our PDF Template System, using the `PdfColor` class.

Class PdfColor

In order to use arbitrary colors in our application we will store each named color as an object in the `colors[]` array of the `PdfDocument` object. Each color is defined by a:

❑ Unique name

❑ Colorspace (RGB, CMYK, gray)

❑ Numeric definition

❑ Spot or process flag
  The spot colors must be initialized to obtain a handle that is later used as a reference to this spot color (spot colors have their name and definition stored within a PDF file, therefore, they need to be initialized or created first. Process colors do not need initialization.

Refer to Chapter 7 for details about color setting in PDF.

Here are the constituents of this class:

- ❑ The constructor stores the provided color definition, and the reference of itself in the colors[] array of the PdfDocument parent class
- ❑ The Init() function initializes the spot color (if present) and stores the handle
- ❑ The GiveHandle() function provides the color definition (or spot color handle) as the array
- ❑ The Set() function sets the fill or stroke by calling the PDFlib function PDF_setcolor(); it is used by the SetFillStroke() function of the PdfObj class.

Let's take a look at the class:

```
//This class handles color definitions
class PdfColor
{
    var $pdf;
    var $pdfDoc;
    var $definition = array();
    var $colorName;
    var $spot;
    var $handle;

    //Constructor
    function PdfColor(&$pdfDoc,$colorName,$colorSpace,
                    $c1=1,$c2=1,$c3=1,$c4=1,$spot=FALSE)
    {
        $this->pdf = &$pdfDoc->pdf;
        $this->pdfDoc = &$pdfDoc;
        $pdfDoc->colors[$colorName] = &$this;
        $this->colorName = $colorName;
        $this->spot = $spot;
        $this->definition = array($colorSpace,$c1,$c2,$c3,$c4);
    } //PdfColor()

    //Initialize spot color
    function Init()
    {
        if ($this->spot && !$this->handle) {
            PDF_save($this->pdf);
            list($colorSpace,$c1,$c2,$c3,$c4) = $this->definition;
            PDF_setcolor($this->pdf, "fill",$colorSpace,$c1,$c2,$c3,$c4);
            $this->handle = PDF_makespotcolor($this->pdf,$this->colorName);
            PDF_restore($this->pdf);
        }

    } // Init()

    //Returns definition of the color
    function GiveHandle()
    {
```

```
        if ($this->spot) {
            return array('spot',$this->handle,1,0,0);
        } else {
            return $this->definition;
        }
    } // GiveHandle()

    //Sets the fill or stroke color
    function Set($fillOrStroke)
    {
        list($colorSpace,$c1,$c2,$c3,$c4) = $this->giveHandle();
        PDF_setcolor($this->pdf,$fillOrStroke,$colorSpace,$c1,$c2,$c3,$c4);
    } // Set()

} // End of class PdfColor
```

Class PdfRel

In order to add some elements of the floating layout to our application we will design the `relations` element, which represents the relations between objects.

This diagram shows an example (`PdfRelBoxAround`) relation:

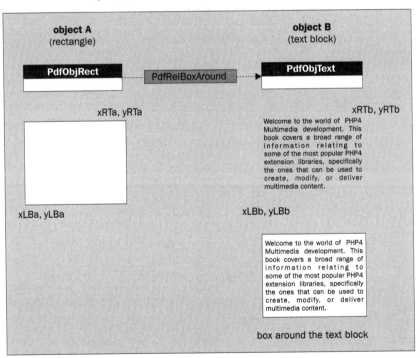

The diagram shows an example of a box positioning itself around the text block. It takes object A (a rectangle) and modifies its parameters to fit around the text in object B; that is, it modifies (xRTa, yRTa) and (xLBa, yLBa) to include the text in the coordinates (xRTb, yRTb) and (xLBb, yLBb)). We will look at the `PdfRelBoxAround` class later in the section.

`PdfRel` is the abstraction class that represents the objects on the page. Object A stores its relations in an array in `params[relations]`. Every relation defines object B by name. Here are the constituents:

- The constructor stores the parameters
- The `RelateBegin()` function is used before object A is drawn
- The `RelateEnd()` function is used after object A is drawn

Here is the class:

```php
//This object will produce a relation to the other object
class PdfRel
{
    var $related;
    var $params = array();

    function PdfRel($related,$params=array())
    {
        $this->related = $related;
        $this->params = $params;
    } // PdfRel()

    function RelateBegin(&$pdfObj)
    {
        return TRUE;
    } // RelateBegin()

    function RelateEnd(&$pdfObj)
    {
        return TRUE;
    } // RelateEnd()

}//End of class PdfRel
```

Next, we will look at a few example relations to get a better picture.

Class PdfRelBoxAround

This class takes object A (`$pdfObj`), and modifies its parameters in order to create a box around object B (`$relObj`):

```php
class PdfRelBoxAround extends PdfRel
{
    function RelateBegin(&$pdfObj)
    {
        if (isset($this->params['distance'])) {
            $relObj = &$pdfObj->pdfPage->objects[$this->related];
```

If the object is a text block (for instance, `PdfObjText` or its descendant), we first have to find its actual bottom edge by drawing it with the parameter `blind` (without actually drawing anything) or use its coordinates:

```
        if (get_class($relObj) == 'pdfobjtext' ||
            is_subclass_of($relObj,'pdfobjtext')) {
            $relObj->draw('blind');
            $yLB = $relObj->params['yBottomReal'];
        } else {
            $yLB = $relObj->params['yLB'];
        }
```

Next, we take the coordinates of object B and add or subtract the `distance` parameter appropriately. We finish with setting the same rotation and skew:

```
        $pdfObj->params['yRT'] = $relObj->params['yRT'] + $distance;
        $pdfObj->params['yLB'] = $yLB - $distance;
        $pdfObj->params['xRT'] = $relObj->params['xRT'] + $distance;
        $pdfObj->params['xLB'] = $relObj->params['xLB'] - $distance;
        $pdfObj->params['rotation'] = $relObj->params['rotation'];
        $pdfObj->params['skew'] = $relObj->params['skew'];
    }
    return TRUE;

    } // RelateBegin()
} // End of class PdfRelBoxAround
```

Class PdfRelClip

This class takes object A (`$pdfObj`), and uses it as a clipping path for object B (`$relObj`). First we set the value of `params[clip]` to `TRUE`, so that object A is drawn as a clipping path, like this:

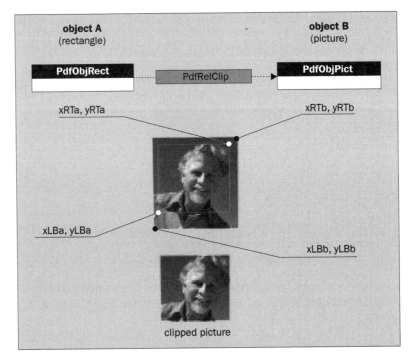

clipped picture

Here is the class:

```
class PdfRelClip extends PdfRel
{
    function RelateBegin(&$pdfObj)
    {
        $pdfObj->params['clip'] = TRUE;
    } // RelateBegin()
```

When the clipping path is created we have to:

❑ Draw object B (clip one) immediately, so that the clipping path is active – it will be reset before we move to the next object on the page (a call to PDF_restore() is always issued after the object is drawn)

❑ Issue PDF_save() so that we save the users space

❑ Draw() object B, and set its noDraw property to TRUE so that it will not be drawn again

❑ Use PDF_restore() to restore our user space (coordinate system) from object A.

Here is PdfRelClip's function:

```
    function RelateEnd(&$pdfObj)
    {
        $relObj = &$pdfObj->pdfPage->objects[$this->related];
        PDF_save($relObj->pdf);

        $relObj->draw();
        $relObj->noDraw = TRUE;

        PDF_restore($relObj->pdf);

        return TRUE;
    } // RelateEnd()

} // End of class PdfRelClip
```

In order to be able to use more than one page in our document, and also create templates that can be used to define new pages, we will define:

❑ PdfPage
This class will be a container for objects on one page. These objects are actually drawn when the whole document is drawn.

❑ PdfPageTemplate
This class will be a container for templates that can quickly form new pages (for example, as in the MergeData() function).

Class PdfPage

The PdfPage class is a container class that represents one page of the document. It stores all the objects in the $objects array. When instantiated, the PdfPage class writes a reference to itself in the $pages array of the PdfDocument class, and is then passed to the constructor of PdfPage. We can also set the page size and units used within the page. Here are the constituents of the class:

❑ The constructor writes a reference to itself in the $pages array of PdfDocument, and sets the default page size and units

❑ The Draw() function draws all objects on the page

❑ The Replace() function replaces $count occurrences of $key=>$val pairs in the $what argument in all the objects defined on the page

Here is the class:

```
//Page object
class PdfPage
{
    var $pdf;                        //Pdf handle
    var $pdfDoc;                     //Parent document
    var $objects = array();          //Objects' storage
```

The constructor stores information about one page of the document:

```
//Constructor
function PdfPage(&$pdfDoc, $width=FALSE, $height=FALSE, $units=FALSE)
{
    $this->pdfDoc = &$pdfDoc;
    $this->pdfDoc->pages[] = &$this;
    $this->pdf = &$pdfDoc->pdf;

    $this->width = ($width)?$width:$pdfDoc->defaultWidth;
    $this->height = ($height)?$height:$pdfDoc->defaultHeight;
    $this->units = ($units)?$units:$pdfDoc->defaultUnits;

} // PdfPage()
```

Let's now discuss the methods that we are going to use in the PdfPage class.

The Draw() function cycles through the $objects array, checks the noDraw property, and then calls the object's Draw() method within the PDF_save() – PDF_restore() pair. Thus, it draws all the objects on the page:

```
function Draw()
{
    if ($this->pdf) {

        //Start page and scale to units
        PDF_begin_page($this->pdf,$this->width*$this->units,
                       $this->height*$this->units);
        PDF_scale($this->pdf,$this->units,$this->units);

        //Go through all objects on the page and draw them with their own
        //methods
        reset($this->objects);

        while (list($key,) = each($this->objects)) {
            if (!$this->objects[$key]->noDraw) {
```

```
                    PDF_save($this->pdf);
                    $this->objects[$key]->draw();
                    PDF_restore($this->pdf);
                }
            }
            //Close the page
            PDF_end_page($this->pdf);
        }
    } // Draw()
```

The `Replace()` function is analogous to that of `PdfDocument`. It replaces `$key=>$val` pairs in the `$what` parameter in a maximum of `$count` objects. It cycles through all the objects in the `objects[]` array and calls their `Replace()` method. It also returns the number of replaces that are left to `$count`:

```
    function Replace($what, $count=-1)
    {
        reset($what);
        while (list($wh, $wi) = each($what)) {
            $all = $count;
            foreach($this->objects as $key=>$rec) {

                //After $all replacements quit; -1 for all replace
                if ($this->objects[$key]->replace($wh, $wi)) {
                    $all -= 1;
                }
                if ($all == 0) { break; }
            }
        }

        return $all;

    } // Replace()
} // End of class PdfPage
```

Class PdfPageTemplate

`PdfPageTemplate` differs from `PdfPage` in two ways:

- ❑ It stores itself in the `pageTemplates[]` array in `PdfDocument`
- ❑ For further retrieval, we have to assign a `$name` to `PdfPageTemplate`

Here is the class:

```
class PdfPageTemplate extends PdfPage
{
    var $name = '';

    function PdfPageTemplate(&$pdfDoc,$name)
    {
        $this->pdfDoc = &$pdfDoc;
        $this->pdfDoc->pageTemplates[$name] = &$this;
        $this->pdf = &$pdfDoc->pdf;
        $this->width = ($width)?$width:$pdfDoc->defaultWidth;
        $this->height = ($height)?$height:$pdfDoc->defaultHeight;
        $this->units = ($units)?$units:$pdfDoc->defaultUnits;
```

```
            $this->name = $name;

    } // PdfPageTemplate()

} // End of class PdfPageTemplate
```

This completes our objective of building upon the PdfDoc class from Chapter 7, to include additional features for our PDF Template System. However, we also need some modules which deal with the various shapes and text layouts. This can be obtained by building the PdfObj class.

Thus, our next task is to build the PdfObj class and its descendants.

Class PdfObj

This is an abstract class that defines the basic methods; we cannot draw anything using this class.

We will first look at the various objects that help us in drawing lines, circles, ellipses, bitmap pictures, and in the layout of text. These objects are just an extension of the class PdfObj. The objects are defined by an array of parameters, like the following:

Parameter	Description
name	The name of the object (not required)
xLB	X coordinate of left-bottom corner the object, before transformation
yLB	Y coordinate of left-bottom corner the object, before transformation
xRT	X coordinate of top-right corner the object, before transformation
yRT	Y coordinate of top-right corner the object, before transformation
fill	Fill color – array of RGB color components or named color
stroke	Stroke color – array of RGB color components or named color
clip	If TRUE the object will be drawn as a clipping path
linewidth	Line width of stroke
rotation	Rotation of the object
skew	Skew of the object
text	Text to be laid-out
size	Size of the text
leading	Text leading (the vertical distance between two lines)
font	Font name (as defined in the fonts[] array in PdfDocument)
relations	Array of 'relations' (includes the references to PdfRel objects)
filename	Filename of the picture or the PDF file

Here is the `PdfObj` class:

```
class PdfObj
{
    var $pdf;                     //Where to draw the PDF document
    var $pdfPage;                 //Link to parent pdfPage object
    var $pdfDoc;                  //Link to grandparent pdfDoc object
    var $params = array();
```

The constructor stores parameters and vital references. It also stores the reference of itself to array `objects` in the parent `PdfPage` (or `PdfPageTemplate`) object, so that it maintains a link with it.

Here is the `PdfObj()` function:

```
//Prototype constructor
function PdfObj(&$pdfPage,$params=array())
{
    $this->pdfPage = &$pdfPage;

    //If name is defined store reference of itself under this name
    if ($params['name']) {
        $this->pdfPage->objects[$params['name']] = &$this;

    //Else add to the objects[] array
    } else {
        $this->pdfPage->objects[] = &$this;
    }

    $this->pdf = &$pdfPage->pdf;
    $this->pdfDoc = &$pdfPage->pdfDoc;
    $this->params = $params;

} // PdfObj()
```

The `Transform()` function rotates and skews the objects (more exactly the user space). It uses the center of the object (as defined by the coordinates) as the center of rotation or skewing:

```
function Transform()
{
    if ($this->params['rotation'] || $this->params['skew']) {

        $width = abs($this->params['xLB']-$this->params['xRT']);
        $height = abs($this->params['yLB']-$this->params['yRT']);

        PDF_translate($this->pdf,$this->params['xLB']+$width/2,
                     $this->params['yLB']+$height/2);

        $this->params['xRT'] = $width/2;
        $this->params['yRT'] = $height/2;
        $this->params['xLB'] = -$width/2;
        $this->params['yLB'] = -$height/2;

        PDF_rotate($this->pdf,$this->params['rotation']);
        PDF_skew($this->pdf,0,$this->params['skew']);
        $this->transformed = TRUE;
    }

} // Transform()
```

The `SaveSpace()` function is always called at the beginning of the `Draw()` method of any particular object. It simply takes all the relations and calls their `RelateBegin()` method. Then it saves parameters in the `params[]` array. This way they can be restored after the object is drawn:

```
function SaveSpace()
{
    //Do relations
    if (is_array($this->params['relations'])) {
        foreach ($this->params['relations'] as $rel) {
            $rel->RelateBegin(&$this);
        }
    }

    //Save parameters
    $this->saved = $this->params;

} // SaveSpace()
```

The `RestoreSpace()` function reverses the basic transforms (if they were performed in `Transform()`). Once all relations are taken care of, the `RelateEnd()` function is called:

```
function RestoreSpace()
{
    //Restore transforms as they were before
    if ($this->transformed) {
        PDF_skew($this->pdf,0,-$this->params['skew']);
        PDF_rotate($this->pdf,-$this->params['rotation']);

        $this->params = $this->saved;

        $width = abs($this->params['xLB']-$this->params['xRT']);
        $height = abs($this->params['yLB']-$this->params['yRT']);
        PDF_translate($this->pdf, -$this->params['xLB']-$width/2,
                      -$this->params['yLB']-$height/2);

        $this->transformed = FALSE;

    } else {

        $this->params = $this->saved;

    }

    //Do relations
    if (is_array($this->params['relations'])) {
        foreach ($this->params['relations'] as $rel) {
            $rel->RelateEnd(&$this);
        }
    }
} // RestoreSpace()
```

The `SetFillStroke()` function sets the fill, stroke, and clipping based upon the `params['fill']`, `params['stroke']`, and `params['clip']` respectively. The color definition is taken directly from the `params[]` array, or as a named color from the color object (all color objects are stored in the `colors[]` array in the `PdfDocument` class):

```
function SetFillStroke()
{
    $fill = $this->params['fill'];
    $stroke = $this->params['stroke'];

    if ($stroke) {
        if (is_array($stroke)) {
            list($c1,$c2,$c3) = $stroke;
            PDF_setcolor($this->pdf,'stroke','rgb',$c1,$c2,$c3,1);
        } elseif (is_object($this->pdfDoc->colors[$stroke])) {
            $this->pdfDoc->colors[$stroke]->set('stroke');
        }
    }

    if (isset($this->params['linewidth'])) {
        PDF_setlinewidth($this->pdf, $this->params['linewidth']);
    }

    if ($fill) {
        if (is_array($fill)) {
            list($c1,$c2,$c3) = $fill;
            PDF_setcolor($this->pdf,'fill','rgb',$c1,$c2,$c3,1);
        } elseif (is_object($this->pdfDoc->colors[$fill])) {
            $this->pdfDoc->colors[$stroke]->set('stroke');
        }
    }

} // SetFillStroke()
```

The FillStroke() function finalizes the drawing (with the fill or stroke set earlier). It is used at the end of the Draw() function:

```
function FillStroke()
{
    if ($this->params['clip']) {
        PDF_clip($this->pdf);
    } elseif ($this->params['stroke'] && $this->params['fill']) {
        PDF_fillstroke($this->pdf);
    } elseif ($this->params['stroke']) {
        PDF_stroke($this->pdf);
    } elseif ($this->params['fill']) {
        PDF_fill($this->pdf);
    } else {
        PDF_endpath($this->pdf);
    }

} // FillStroke()
```

Here is the Replace() function:

```
function Replace($wh,$wh)
{
    return FALSE;
} // Replace()

} // End of class PdfObj
```

Now let's look at the various extensions of the `PdfObj` class – these functions are mainly used for drawing different objects, rectangles, lines, and circles, and so on.

Class *PdfObjRect*

This object draws a rectangle:

```
class PdfObjRect extends PdfObj
{
    function Draw()
    {
        $this->SaveSpace();

        //Prepare stroke and fill, transforms
        $this->SetFillStroke();
        $this->Transform();

        PDF_rect($this->pdf,$this->params['xLB'],$this->params['yLB'],
            $this->params['xRT']-$this->params['xLB'],$this->params['yRT']
            -$this->params['yLB']);

        $this->FillStroke();
        $this->RestoreSpace();

    }//Draw()

} // end of class PdfObjRect
```

This class is identical to the `PdfObjRect` *class detailed in Chapter 7.*

Class *PdfObjLine*

This object draws a line:

```
class PdfObjLine extends PdfObj
{
    function Draw()
    {
        $this->SaveSpace();

        //Prepare stroke and fill, does not need transforms
        $this->SetFillStroke();

        PDF_moveto($this->pdf,$this->params['xLB'],$this->params['yLB']);
        PDF_lineto($this->pdf,$this->params['xRT'],$this->params['yRT']);

        $this->FillStroke();
        $this->RestoreSpace();
    }//Draw()

} // End of class PdfObjLine
```

This class is identical to the `PdfObjLine` *class detailed in Chapter 7.*

Class *PdfObjCircle*

This object draws a circle or an ellipse:

```
class PdfObjCircle extends PdfObj
{
    function Draw()
    {
        $this->SaveSpace();

        //Prepare stroke and fill, transforms
        $this->SetFillStroke();
        $this->Transform();

        //Calculate scaling for it to be elliptical
        $width = abs($this->params['xRT']-$this->params['xLB']);
        $height = abs($this->params['yRT']-$this->params['yLB']);
        $xscale = $width/$height;

        if ($xscale != 1) {
            PDF_scale($this->pdf,$xscale,1);
        }

        PDF_circle($this->pdf,($this->params['xLB']+$width/2)/$xscale,
            $this->params['yLB']+ $height/2,$height/2);

        $this->FillStroke();
        $this->RestoreSpace();

    } // Draw()

} // End of class PdfObjCircle
```

This class is identical to the `PdfObjCircle` *class detailed in Chapter 7.*

Class *PdfObjPict*

This object draws a picture (bitmap):

```
//Currently this class accepts only GIF, TIFF, JPG, and PNG images
class PdfObjPict extends PdfObj
{
    function Draw()
    {
        //Open the image and recognize it by its extension
        $f = $this->params['filename'];

        switch (strtolower(preg_replace('/^.*\.(.*)$/','\\1',
                $this->params['filename']))) {
        case 'gif':
            $img = PDF_open_image_file($this->pdf,'gif',$f);
            break;
        case 'tif':
```

```
          $img = PDF_open_image_file($this->pdf,'tiff',$f);
          break;
    case 'jpg':
          $img = PDF_open_image_file($this->pdf,'jpeg',$f);
          break;
    case 'png':
          $img = PDF_open_image_file($this->pdf,'png',$f);
          break;
    default:
          return;
    }

    $this->SaveSpace();

    //Prepare rotation
    $this->Transform();

    //Calculate the scaling of the image to fit in bounding box
    $yScale = abs($this->params['yLB']-$this->params['yRT'])
                  /PDF_get_value($this->pdf,"imageheight",$img);
    $xScale = abs($this->params['xLB']-$this->params['xRT'])
                  /PDF_get_value($this->pdf,"imagewidth",$img);

    PDF_scale($this->pdf,$xScale,$yScale);

    PDF_place_image($this->pdf,$img,
          $this->params['xLB']/$xScale,$this->params['yLB']/$yScale,1);

    PDF_close_image($this->pdf,$img);

    $this->RestoreSpace();

    } // Draw()

} // End of class PdfObjPict
```

This class is identical to the PdfObjPict *class shown in Chapter 7.*

Class PdfObjText

The PdfObjText object is used to design a very basic line-breaking and formatting mechanism. Our class will know only the following formatting tags (based on HTML tags):

Tag	Description
<b></b>	For bold
<i></i>	For italic
<e></e>	For bold/italic
<n></n>	For normal

Every tag can have attribute size by which the text size can be set:

Tag	Description
`<i size=18></i>`	For italic, text size of 18pt

Tags can neither overlap nor can they be nested.

Though this class is almost identical to that shown in Chapter 7, there are a few differences:

❑ The `$blind` parameter that controls the text actually laid-out to PDF

❑ The `textrendering` parameter is handled by the `setFillStroke` method of `PdfObjText`

❑ The `<e></e>` tag is used for the boldItalic font face

❑ The font handle is provided by the `PdfFont` object

Here is the class:

```
class PdfObjText extends PdfObj
{
    function Draw($blind=FALSE)
    {
        if ($blind == 'blind') { $blind = TRUE; }

        $this->SaveSpace();

        //Prepare stroke and fill, transforms
        $this->SetFillStroke();
        $this->Transform();

        //Define the local variables
        $text = $this->params['text'];
        $leftEdge = $this->params['xLB'];
        $rightEdge = $this->params['xRT'];
        $leading = $this->params['leading']/$this->pdfPage->units;
        $baseSize = $this->params['size']/$this->pdfPage->units;
        $size = $baseSize;
```

Next, we will read the parameters concerning the font and font size. If the given font name is unknown we will use `default`.

The ascender height (the height of the tallest character in the font, for instance, 'f' in the diagram overleaf) is read, so we can adjust the starting point of the text layout adequately. The text will fit in the defined bounding box like this:

Let's continue with the class:

```
//Set the default font if it is not defined among font objects
if (!$this->pdfDoc->fonts[$this->params['font']]) {
    $this->params['font'] = 'default';
}

$this->font = &$this->pdfDoc->fonts[$this->params['font']];

$fontHandle = $this->font->GiveHandle();

$ascender = PDF_get_value($this->pdf,"ascender",
                          $this->font->GiveHandle())*$size;

//Set font, size and leading in PDF
PDF_setfont($this->pdf,$fontHandle,$baseSize);
PDF_set_value($this->pdf,"leading",$leading);

//Set where to start with text
PDF_set_text_pos($this->pdf,$leftEdge,$topEdge-$ascender);
$textx = PDF_get_value($this->pdf,"textx",0);
$texty = PDF_get_value($this->pdf,"texty",0);
```

Now we will split the text into an array with `preg_split()`, so that we recognize control tags in the text. Then, as we walk through this array, whenever the control tag is encountered, the appropriate font and text size is set. Note that we use the font handle provided by the font object (`$this->font->GiveHandle('bold')`):

```
//Split text with tags
$r = preg_split("/(<[nibe](?: size=[0-9]{1,2})?>)(.*?)(?:<\/[nibe]>)
                | (\\n)/is", $text, -1, PREG_SPLIT_NO_EMPTY |
                PREG_SPLIT_DELIM_CAPTURE);

foreach($r as $chunk) {

    //If tag is encountered, set appropriate font face and size
    if (preg_match("/<([nibe])(?: size=
                        ([0-9]{1,2})){0,1}>/is",$chunk,$m)) {

        $face = $m[1];
```

```
            if (!$m[2]) {
                $size = $baseSize;
            } else {
                $size = $m[2]/$this->pdfPage->units;
            }


            if ($face == 'b') {
                $fontHandle = $this->font->GiveHandle('bold');
            } elseif ($face == 'i') {
                $fontHandle = $this->font->GiveHandle('italic');
            } elseif ($face == 'e') {
                $fontHandle = $this->font->GiveHandle('boldItalic');
            } else {
                $fontHandle = $this->font->GiveHandle();
            }
```

We also check if $chunk is a line break (\n). If yes, we adjust the text position to the beginning of the next line, and directly go to the next word. If the position reaches $bottomEdge, we stop rendering the text so that it does not overflow. The rest of the text will not be written to the PDF dcoument:

```
            } elseif ($chunk == "\n") {
                $textx  = $leftEdge;                    //Carriage return
                $texty -= $leading;                     //New line
                if ($texty < $bottomEdge) break;
                    continue;
            //Otherwise lay down next chunk of text, and take care of the
            // line breaking
            } else {
```

If $chunk is not a control tag, then it is the text to be displayed on the page. Since we want to line break the text within the bounding box ($leftEdge, $rightEdge, and $bottomEdge), we have to split the chunk again with spaces (this is simplified because a comma, dot, or hyphen also point towards possible line breaks). We use the function explode() to create an array of words that cannot be broken further:

```
                $w = explode(' ',$chunk);               //Split chunk with spaces
```

Let us walk through the array:

```
                foreach ($w as $word) {
```

First, we calculate the string width of the current word with the PDF_stringwidth(), and ask whether it fits between the edges. If $word alone does not fit into the bounding box, exit immediately:

```
                    //Calculate the string width
                    $stringWidth = PDF_stringwidth($this->pdf,rtrim($word),
                                             $fontHandle,$size);
```

If $stringwidth overlaps $rightEdge, we adjust the current text position at the beginning of the new line:

```
//This word to next line
if ($stringWidth > abs($rightEdge-$leftEdge)) {
    $this->RestoreSpace();
    return;
}

//If the word does not fit
if ($textx + $stringWidth > $rightEdge) {
    $textx  = $leftEdge;                //Carriage return
    $texty -= $leading;                 //New line
    if ($texty < $bottomEdge) { break; }
}
```

Now we add space that was cut by explode(), and we set the new PDF_set_text_pos() and PDF_show(). Finally we get the new current text position. In case $blind is TRUE we do not use PDF_show() and only read the string width:

```
//Insert space if not at the end of chunk
$space = (count($w))?' ':'';
PDF_set_text_pos($this->pdf,$textx,$texty);
//Actually do not lay out any text (used the example in
// relations) ask only for the string width
if ($blind) {
    PDF_show($this->pdf,$word.$space);
} else {
    $stringWidth + PDF_stringwidth($this->pdf,$word.
                                $space,$fontHandle,$size);
    PDF_set_text_pos($this->pdf,$textx+$stringWidth,
                                $texty);
}
$textx = PDF_get_value($this->pdf,"textx",0);
$texty = PDF_get_value($this->pdf,"texty",0);
}
```

After the layout of every chunk, we return values of font and font size as defined in params array:

```
$fontHandle = $this->font->GiveHandle();
$size = $baseSize;
}
```

After the cycle we use PDF_setfont() to set font face and font size. We also check if the text position is not below $bottomEdge (so that we do not overflow it):

```
PDF_setfont($this->pdf,$fontHandle,$size);

//Do not lay anything below bottom edge
if ($texty < $this->params['yLB']) { break; }
}

$this->RestoreSpace();
```

Finally we set the `yBottomReal` parameter, which indicates where the actual bottom edge of the text block lies:

```
        $this->params['yBottomReal'] = $texty;
        if ($textx == $leftEdge) {
            $this->params['yBottomReal'] += $leading;
        }

    } // Draw()
```

For `PdfObjText`, the `SetFillStroke()` function must be extended from the `PdfObj` class. We also have to use the `textrendering` parameter to achieve the appropriate mode of rendering of text.

The following table shows the values of parameter `textrendering` used in `PDF_set_parameter()`:

Value	Description	Value	Description
0	Fill text	4	Fill text and add it to the clipping path
1	Stroke text (outline)	5	Stroke text and add it to the clipping path
2	Fill and stroke text	6	Fill and stroke text, and add it to the clipping path
3	Invisible text	7	Add text to the clipping path

Here is the extended `SetFillStroke()` function:

```
    function SetFillStroke()
    {
        //Call the inherited method
        PdfObj::SetFillStroke();

        //Text rendering based on fill and stroke
        if ($this->params['stroke'] && $this->params['fill']) {
            $textrendering = 2;
        } elseif ($this->params['stroke']) {
            $textrendering = 1;
        } elseif ($this->params['fill'])  {
            $textrendering = 0;
        } else {
            $textrendering = 3;
        }

        //Clip if defined
        if ($this->params['clip']) {
            $textrendering += 4;
        }

        PDF_set_value($this->pdf,"textrendering",$textrendering);

    } // SetFillStroke()
```

The `Replace()` function changes the text in a text object. This function is called by the `Replace()` function in the `PdfPage` parent object. The replacements are made with `str_replace()`. The method returns TRUE if any replacements were made, FALSE otherwise:

```
function Replace($wh,$wi)
{
    $s = $this->params['text'];
    $this->params['text'] = str_replace($wh,$wi,$s);

    if ($s != $this->params['text']) {
        return TRUE;
    } else {
        return FALSE;
    }

}//Replace()

} // End of class PdfObjText
```

Class PdfObjBookmark

This object creates a bookmark:

```
class PdfObjBookmark extends PdfObj
{
    function Draw()
    {
        //If the 'bookmarkdest' is defined set it
        if (is_array($this->params['bookmarkdest'])) {
            PDF_set_parameter($this->pdf,'bookmarkdest',
                                $this->params['bookmarkdest']);
        }

        //Create the bookmark to current page
        PDF_add_bookmark($this->pdf,$this->params['text'],0,
                            $this->params['child_open']);
    } // Draw()

} // End of class PdfObjBookmark
```

Class PdfObjNote

This object creates an annotation note:

```
class PdfObjNote extends PdfObj
{
    function Draw()
    {
        //If the 'border color' is defined set it
        if (is_array($this->params['border_color'])) {
            list($r,$g,$b) = $this->params['border_color'];
            PDF_set_border_color($this->pdf,$r,$g,$b);
        }
```

```
            //Create the annotation note
        PDF_add_note($this->pdf,$this->params['xLB'],$this->params['yLB'],
                    $this->params['xRT'],$this->params['yRT'],
                    $this->params['text'],$this->params['title'],
                    $this->params['icon'],$this->params['note_open']);
    } // Draw()

} // End of class PdfObjNote
```

Class PdfObjPDF

If we have the PDI library installed, we can use this function for placing the PDF pages.

The PDI library is available only with the binary distribution of PDFlib. For more information, refer the PDF Import with PDI *section in Chapter 7.*

The usage of functions is similar to that of placing images:

```
class PdfObjPDF extends PdfObj
{
    function Draw()
    {
        //Open PDF
        $doc = PDF_open_pdi($this->pdf,$this->params['filename'],"",0);
        if (!$doc)
        {
            return;
        }

        $pageno = (!$this->params['page']) ? 1 : $this->params['page'];
        $page =  PDF_open_pdi($this->pdf,$doc,$pageno,"");
        if (!$page)
        {
            return;
        }

        $this->SaveSpace();

        //Prepare rotation
        $this->Transform();

        //Calculate scaling of the image to fit in bounding box
        $height = abs($this->pars['yLB']-$this->pars['yRT']);
        $width = abs($this->pars['xLB']-$this->pars['xRT']);

        //Calculate scaling as it is necessary to fit image in bounding box
        $yScale = $height / PDF_get_pdi_value($this->pdf,"height",
                                              $doc,$page);
        $xScale = $width / PDF_get_pdi_value($this->pdf,"width",$doc,$page);

        PDF_place_image($this->pdf,$img,$this->params['xLB']/$xScale,
                        $this->params['yLB']/$yScale,1);
```

```
            PDF_close_image($this->pdf,$img);

            $this->RestoreSpace();

    }//Draw()

} // End of class PdfObjPdf

// End the class.PdfDocument.php script
?>
```

Testing the PDF Template System

In order to test the PDF Template System we will have to:

- ❑ Create a simple database table (storing only 3 addresses)
- ❑ Define a template layout (we choose to create a simple envelope merged with addresses in our database table)

We will use the Times font that is included in the basic 14 fonts available in PDF.

Database Table Definition

Here is the `person` table with 3 records, which will be called in the `MergeData()` function:

```
CREATE TABLE 'person' (
                    'name' varchar(100) NOT NULL default '',
                    'address' varchar(100) NOT NULL default '',
                    'title' varchar(50) NOT NULL default '',
                    'zip' varchar(10) NOT NULL default '',
                    'city' varchar(100) NOT NULL default ''
                    ) TYPE=MyISAM PACK_KEYS=1;

INSERT INTO person VALUES ('Wrox Press Ltd.',
                    'Arden House','To,','1102',
                    'Warwick Road, UK, Birmingham'
                    );
```

Layout Design

Let's start the layout by defining the document, and its default page size:

```
<?php

//envelope.php

include_once('class.PdfDocument.php');

$d = &new PdfDocument(FALSE,210,100);
```

Define the Times font family:

```
$f = &new PdfFont(&$d,"Times","Times-Roman","Times-Bold",
                  "Times-Italic","Times-BoldItalic");
```

Define the colors that we will use; blue will be the spot color:

```
$c = &new PdfColor(&$d,'blue','cmyk',0.83,0.7,0,0,TRUE);
$c = &new PdfColor(&$d,'black','cmyk',0,0,0,1);
$c = &new PdfColor(&$d,'grey','gray',0.8,0,0,0);
```

Define `pageTemplate[envelope]`:

```
$p = &new PdfPageTemplate(&$d,'envelope');
```

Define the relation between an object named `Address` and the clipping of an object named `picture`:

```
$boxArround = &new PdfRelBoxAround('address',array('distance'=>5));
$clip = &new PdfRelClip('picture');
```

We will create a rectangle that will be used as a box around the address using the relation we have created above:

```
new PdfObjRect(&$p,array('stroke'=>'blue','xLB'=>10,'yLB'=>10,
              'xRT'=>100,'yRT'=>100,'linewidth'=>0.175,'rotation'=>0,
              'relations'=>array(&$r)));
```

We continue with the address text block. Note the placeholder fields in `text`:

```
//Address
new PdfObjText(&$p,array('fill'=>'black','xLB'=>115,'yLB'=>10,
        'xRT'=>190,'yRT'=>50,'size'=>10,'leading'=>11,'text'=>"{title}\n<b>
        {name}</b>\n{address}\n{zip} - {city}",'rotation'=>0,'font'=>"Times",
        'name'=>'address'));
```

Then we create a postage stamp-sized rectangle:

```
//Postage rectangle
new PdfObjRect(&$p,array('stroke'=>'black','xLB'=>186,'yLB'=>74,
              'xRT'=>204,'yRT'=>94,'linewidth'=>0.1,'rotation'=>0));
```

Finally, we draw the circle that will clip the picture (using the relation created above):

```
//Clipping circle
new PdfObjCircle(&$p,array('stroke'=>array(0,0,1),'linewidth'=>0.5,
        'xLB'=>6,'yLB'=>74,'xRT'=>26,'yRT'=>94,'relations'=>array(&$clip)));

//Picture to be clipped
new PdfObjPict(&$p,array('xLB'=>0,'yLB'=>65,'xRT'=>30,'yRT'=>95,
              'filename'=>'php4.gif','rotation'=>10,'name'=>'picture'));

// End of the envelope.php script
?>
```

Looking at the Template

Let's take a look at the template that we have created. To do this, we create a regular page from the `pageTemplate[]` array named `envelope`, draw it, and output it to the browser:

```php
<?php

//envelope_template.php

include_once('envelope.php');

$d->pageFromTemplate('envelope');
$d->Draw();
$d->Output();
$d->Delete();

// End of the envelope_template.php script
?>
```

The result looks like this:

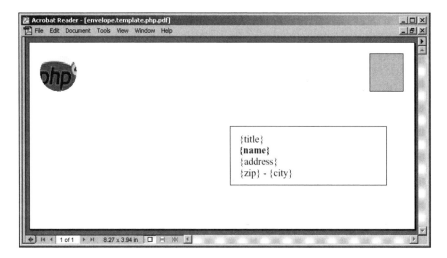

Note that the placeholder fields are enclosed in brackets.

Linking with the Database

Finally we will merge the `pageTemplate[]` array named `envelope` with data from the SQL query, draw it, and output it to the browser:

```php
<?php

//envelope_merged.php

include_once('envelope.php');
```

```
$d->mergeData(array('title','name','address','zip','city'),
             "SELECT * from person",'envelope','envelope');
$d->Draw();
$d->Output();
$d->Delete();

// End of the envelope_merged.php script
?>
```

This will create a 3-page PDF document. The first page looks like this:

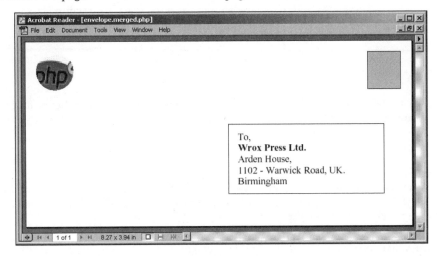

Possible Enhancements

Our case study is quite simple, but if we try to create precisely crafted complex layout, it takes a lot of time and accurate measurements. One way to avoid this is to use some visual tool to create the layout. Here are a few examples:

- ❑ Several graphic programs from Adobe that can produce the SVG format, which then can be parsed to objects in PHP.

- ❑ The OpenOffice suite (http://openoffice.org) that uses an XML-based format, which can again be parsed to objects in PHP.

- ❑ The PDFTemplates (http://sourceforge.net/projects/pdftemplates) class can import templates from Adobe PageMaker, convert the object properties to a MySQL table, and then to the objects in PHP. It uses PDFlib for PDF creation and PHPlib for database access.

We can enhance the text layout engine of the PdfObjText class that allows us to parse XML with more formatting options. We could include extending classes with new objects, like:

- ❑ Polygons
- ❑ Curves
- ❑ Text on path objects
- ❑ Tables

We can also extend relations by including:

- ❑ Snaps below, above, left, and right to create lines below, above, left, and right of the paragraphs, respectively
- ❑ Masks to use object A as a mask for object B
- ❑ Page breaks to flow the text over several pages
- ❑ Conditions to make object A visible or hidden, based on properties of object B

Further, instead of using the MySQL database, we can use a database abstraction class to make the application more portable.

Summary

In this chapter we learned how to build a PDF Template System that provides better functionality than HTML templates.

While developing the system we built a collection of classes:

- ❑ PdfDocument
  A basic class that takes care of PDF document creation, outputting, and filling placeholder fields with data from the database table. It serves as container for PdfFont, PdfColor, PdfPage, and PdfPageTemplate.
- ❑ PdfFont
  A class that takes care of font family management.
- ❑ PdfColor
  A class that takes care of color definitions and initialization.
- ❑ PdfRel
  A prototype class for defining relations between PDF objects. It had two descendent classes:
  - ❑ PdfRelBoxAround
    A class that modifies object A to create a box around object B.
  - ❑ PdfRelClip
    A class that modifies object A to serve as clipping path to object B.
- ❑ PdfPage
  A class that represents a page of the PDF document and serves as container for the descendants of the PdfObj class.
- ❑ PdfPageTemplate
  A class that represents a page of the PDF document. It is used as template for new pages in the document, for example, during data merging.
- ❑ PdfObj
  A prototype class for defining PDF objects. It had eight descendent classes:
  - ❑ PdfObjRect
    A class for drawing a rectangle object
  - ❑ PdfObjLine
    A class for drawing a line
  - ❑ PdfObjCircl
    A class for drawing a circle and ellipse object.

- ❑   `PdfObjPict`
  A class for drawing a bitmap (image) object

- ❑   `PdfObjText`
  A class for designing a text block object (able to parse simple HTML-like tagged file)

- ❑   `PdfObjBookmark`
  A class for creating a bookmark object

- ❑   `PdfObjNote`
  A class for creating an annotation note object

- ❑   `PdfObjPDF`
  A class for importing pages from the PDF file

Finally, we created a simple envelope, and filled the address fields with data from the MySQL database. Further, we discussed possible enhancements of the PDF Template System. Though it provides only the basic features of PDFlib and produces fixed layouts with some simple features of floating layout, it can serve as a basis for an extended system that is suited to individual PHP applications.

PHP Ming Language Reference

This is a listing of the methods available with the 13 classes in PHP/Ming.

SWFMovie

Function	Returns	Description
SWFMovie->add	Void	Adds any type of data (shape, text, fonts, and so on) to the movie
SWFMovie->init()	Class	Returns a new SWFMovie object
SWFMovie->labelFrame(string name)	Void	Appends the given label to the current frame of the movie
SWFMovie->nextFrame()	Void	Moves to the next frame of the movie
SWFMovie->output()	Void	Dumps the movie to the browser
SWFMovie->remove	Void	Removes something from the movie display list

Table continued on following page

Function	Returns	Description
SWFMovie->save(file)	Void	Saves the movie to the given file
SWFMovie->setBackground(r,g,b)	Void	Sets the color of the movie background to (r,g,b)
SWFMovie->setDimension(width, height)	Void	Sets the width and height of the movie accordingly
SWFMovie->setFrames(number)	Void	Sets the total number of frames in the movie to number
SWFMovie->setRate(rate)	Void	Sets the movie's display rate to frames per second
SWFMovie->streamMp3(mp3file)	Void	Streams an MP3 file over the movie

SWFShape

Function	Returns	Description
SWFShape->addFill(r,g,b[,a])	Integer	Defines a new solid color fill for the shape
SWFShape->addFill(fill[, flags])	Integer	Sets up either a bitmap or a gradient as the new fill for the shape
SWFShape->drawArc(radius, start, end)	Void	Draws an arc of given radius centred round the current pen position, anticlockwise from start degrees to end degrees, relative to the positive y axis
SWFShape->drawCircle(radius)	Void	Draws a circle of given radius centred round the current pen position anticlockwise
SWFShape->drawCubicTo(bx, by, cx, cy, dx, dy)	Void	Draws a cubic Bezier curve from the pen's current coordinates to (dx,dy) using (bx,by) and (cx,cy) as control points

Function	Returns	Description
SWFShape->drawCubic(bx, by, cx, cy, dx, dy)	Void	Same as SWFShape_drawcubicto() but the given coordinates are calculated relative to the pen's current coordinates
SWFShape->drawCurveTo(ax, ay, bx, by[, dx, dy])	Void	Draws either a curve from current coordinates to (bx,by) using (ax,ay) as a control point, or draws a Bezier curve to (dx,dy) using (ax,ay) coordinates as control points
SWFShape->drawCurve(adx, ady, bdx, bdy[, cdx, cdy])	Void	Same as SWFShape_drawcurveto(), but the points given are relative to the current coordinates of the pen
SWFShape->drawGlyph(font, string)	Void	Draws the first character of the given string using the given font into the shape
SWFShape->drawLine(x, y)	Void	Draws a line from the current pen coordinates (origx, origy) to (origx+x,origy+y)
SWFShape->drawLineTo(x, y)	Void	Draws a line from the current pen coordinates to (x,y)
SWFShape->init()	Class	Returns a new SWFShape object
SWFShape->movePen(x, y)	Void	Moves the pen in the shape by (x, y)
SWFShape->movePenTo(x, y)	Void	Moves the pen to shape coordinates (x,y)
SWFShape->setLeftFill(r,g,b[,a])	Void	Defines a solid color fill on the left side of the edge segment

Table continued on following page

Function	Returns	Description
SWFShape->setLeftFill(fill)	Void	Defines either a bitmap or a gradient as the fill on the left side of the edge segment
SWFShape->setRightFill(r,g,b[,a])	Void	Defines a solid color fill on the right side of the edge segment
SWFShape->setRightFill(fill)	Void	Defines either a bitmap or a gradient up as the fill on the right side of the edge segment

SWFFont

Function	Returns	Description
SWFFont->getAscent()	Integer	Returns the ascent of the font, 0 otherwise
SWFFont->getDescent()	Integer	Returns the descent of the font, 0 otherwise
SWFFont->getLeading()	Integer	Returns the leading of the font, 0 otherwise
SWFFont->getWidth(string)	Integer	Returns the width of the given string written in the current font at full height
SWFFont->init(file)	Void	Returns a new SWFFont object from the given file

SWFText

Function	Returns	Description
SWFText->addString(text)	Void	Adds the given text into the current text object at the current pen position
SWFText->getAscent()	Double	Returns the ascent of the current font at its current size, 0 otherwise
SWFText->getDescent()	Double	Returns the descent of the current font at its current size, 0 otherwise

Function	Returns	Description
SWFText->getLeading()	Double	Returns the leading of the current font at its current size, 0 otherwise
SWFText->getWidth(string)	Double	Returns the width of the given string in the text object's current font and size
SWFText->init()	Class	Returns a new SWFText object
SWFText->MoveTo(x,y)	Void	Moves the current pen to coordinates (x,y) within the text object
SWFText->setColor(r,g,b[,a])	Void	Sets the current text's color to the given (r, g, b) value
SWFText->setFont(font)	Void	Sets the text object's current font
SWFText->setHeight(height)	Void	Sets the current text object's height to the given height
SWFText->setSpacing(value)	Void	Sets the current text's character spacing to the given value

SWFButton

Function	Returns	Description
SWFButton->addShape(shape, state)	Void	Defines a shape for a particular state of the button – up, over, down, or hit
SWFButton->init()	Object	Returns a new SWFButton object
SWFButton->keyPress(char)	Integer	Returns the action flag corresponding to the key press
SWFButton->setDown(SWFchar)	Void	Sets the SWFChar for the button's down state
SWFButton->setHit(SWFchar)	Void	Sets the SWFChar for the button's hit state
SWFButton->setOver(SWFchar)	Void	Sets the SWFChar for the button's over state
SWFButton->setUp(SWFchar)	Void	Sets the SWFChar for the button's up state

We can add the following states to the button:

State	Description
SWFBUTTON_UP	This is the normal state of the button
SWFBUTTON_OVER	This is the state when the mouse is hovering over the button
SWFBUTTON_DOWN	This is the state when the user clicks the button
SWFBUTTON_HIT	This state is never displayed but describes the shape of the button that responds to the previous 3 events

SWFDisplayItem

Function	Returns	Description
SWFDisplayitem->addColor(r, g, b [, a])	Void	Adds the given (r,g,b) color to this display item's color transform
SWFDisplayitem->move(x,y)	Void	Moves the display item on the screen by (x,y)
SWFDisplayitem->moveTo(x,y)	Void	Moves the display item to new coordinates (x,y)
SWFDisplayitem->multColor(r, g, b [, a])	Void	Sets the multiply color to (r,g,b) in the display item's color transform
SWFDisplayitem->rotate(angle)	Void	Rotates the display item angle degrees clockwise
SWFDisplayitem->scale(x,y)	Void	Multiplies the display item's x and y scale factors by x and y respectively
SWFDisplayitem->scaleTo(x [, y])	Void	Scales the display item by x horizontally and y (x if y is not given) vertically
SWFDisplayitem->setDepth(depth)	Void	Sets the object's z-level for the display item to the given depth
SWFDisplayitem->setMatrix(a, b, c, d, x, y)	Void	Sets the display item's transformation matrix

Function	Returns	Description
SWFDisplayitem->setName(name)	Void	Sets the display item's name to the given name
SWFDisplayitem->setRatio(ratio)	Void	Sets the display item's ratio to the given ratio; only useful for morphs
SWFDisplayitem->skewX(xskew)	Void	Adds xskew to the display item's current horizontal skew setting
SWFDisplayitem->skewXTo(xskew)	Void	Sets the display item's horizontal skew setting to xskew
SWFDisplayitem->skewY(yskew)	Void	Adds yskew to the display item's current vertical skew setting
SWFDisplayitem->skewYTo(yskew)	Void	Sets the display item's vertical skew setting to yskew

SWFill

Function	Returns	Description
SWFFill->init()	Class	Returns a new SWFFill object
SWFFill->moveTo(x, y)	Void	Moves the fill to coordinates (x, y)
SWFFill->rotateTo(angle)	Void	Rotates the fill angle degrees clockwise
SWFFill->scaleTo(x [, y])	Void	Scales the fill by x horizontally and y (x if y is not given) vertically
SWFFill->skewXto(xskew)	Void	Sets the fill's horizontal skew setting to xskew
SWFFill->skewYto(yskew)	Void	Sets the fill's vertical skew setting to yskew

SWFGradient

Function	Returns	Description
SWFGradient->addEntry(ratio, r, g, b [, a])	Void	Adds a color to the gradient at a point specified by ratio
SWFGradient->init()	Class	Returns a new SWFGradient object

SWFMorph

Function	Returns	Description
SWFMorph->getShape1()	SWFShape	Returns this morph's starting shape
SWFMorph->getShape2()	SWFShape	Returns this morph's ending shape
SWFMorph->init()	Class	Returns a new SWFMorph object

SWFBitmap

Function	Returns	Description
SWFBitmap->init(file[, mask])	Class	Returns a new SWFBitmap object from the given JPEG (and mask) or DBL file
SWFBitmap->getHeight()	Void	Returns the height of the current bitmap
SWFBitmap->getWidth()	Void	Returns the width of the current bitmap

SWFTextField

Function	Returns	Description
SWFTextfield->addString(string)	Void	Adds the given string to the text field
SWFTextfield->align(align)	Void	Sets the text alignment within the text field to align

Function	Returns	Description
SWFTextfield->init()	Class	Returns a new SWFTextField object
SWFTextfield->setBounds(width, height)	Void	Sets the height and width of the text field
SWFTextfield->setColor(r, g, b [,a])	Void	Sets the color of the text field to the given (r, g, b) value
SWFTextfield->setFont(font)	Void	Sets the text field's current font
SWFTextfield->setHeight(height)	Void	Sets the new font height for the text field
SWFTextfield->setIndentation(value)	Void	Sets the indentation for the first line of text in this text field to value
SWFTextfield->setLeftMargin(value)	Void	Sets the left margin of the text field to the given value
SWFTextfield->setLinespacing(value)	Void	Sets the line spacing for this text field to the given value
SWFTextfield->setMargins(lvalue, rvalue)	Void	Sets the left and right margins for the text field to lvalue and rvalue respectively
SWFTextfield->setName(name)	Void	Sets the new name for the text field
SWFTextfield->setRightMargin(value)	Void	Sets the right margin of the text field to the given value

These are the optional arguments we can pass to the constructor:

Optional Parameter	Description
SWFTEXTFIELD_DRAWBOX	The text field will have an outline
SWFTEXTFIELD_HASLENGTH	The text field will restrict the number of characters
SWFTEXTFIELD_HTML	Allows HTML markup
SWFTEXTFIELD_MULTILINE	Creates a multi-line text field
SWFTEXTFIELD_NOEDIT	This text field is not editable

Table continued on following page

Optional Parameter	Description
SWFTEXTFIELD_NOSELECT	The user cannot select any text in the field
SWFTEXTFIELD_PASSWORD	The text is obscured by a password character (*)
SWFTEXTFIELD_WORDWRAP	The text will wrap inside the text field

SWFSprite

Function	Returns	Description
SWFSprite->add(object)	Void	Adds the named object to the current sprite
SWFSprite->init()	Class	Returns a new SWFSprite object
SWFSprite->labelFrame(label)	Void	Gives the current frame for the sprite a specified label
SWFSprite->nextFrame()	Void	Moves the sprite to its next frame
SWFSprite->remove(object)	Void	Removes the given object from the current sprite
SWFSprite->setFrames(number)	Void	Sets the number of frames in the sprite

SWFAction

Function	Returns	Description
SWFAction->init(script)	Object	Compiles the Flash script and returns an SWFAction object

Misc

Function	Returns	Description
ming_setcubicthreshold(value)	Void	Sets the global cubic threshold to value.
ming_setscale(value)	Void	Sets the global scale factor to value, by using the TWIP unit scale (1PIXEL = 20 TWIPS).
ming_useswfversion(int version)	Void	Makes Ming compile code in the Flash version 4 format, instead of 5.

Function	Returns	Description
`swf_placeobject ( int objid, int depth)`	Void	Places the object specified by `objid` in the current frame at a depth of `depth`. The `objid` parameter and the depth must be between 1 and 65535.

B

PHP GD Language Reference

Here is a listing of the PHP GD functions:

Function	Returns	Description
GetImageSize (filename [,image_info])	Array	Returns the size of the image with the specified filename
Image2wbmp (image[, filename [, threshold]])	Integer	Saves the image as a WBMP file with the given filename
ImageAlphaBlending (image, blendmode)	Integer	Switches the alpha blending mode ON or OFF for image by setting blendmode to TRUE or FALSE
ImageArc (image, cx, cy, width, height, start, end, col)	Integer	Draws a partial ellipse in an image centered at cx, cy with the specified width and height, from the start angle to the end angle, in the color
ImageChar (image, font, x, y, c, col)	Integer	Draws a character horizontally
ImageCharUp (image, font, x, y, c, col)	Integer	Draws a character vertically

Table continued on following page

Function	Returns	Description
ImageColorAllocate (image, red, green, blue)	Integer	Allocates a color for an image and returns a color identifier
ImageColorAt (image, x, y)	Integer	Returns the index of the color of the pixel at the specified point in an image
ImageColorClosest (image, red, green, blue)	Integer	Returns the index of the closest color to the specified color in the palette of the specified image
ImageColorClosestAlpha (image, red, green, blue, alpha)	Integer	Returns the index of the closest color to the specified color plus alpha in the palette of the specified image
ImageColorClosestHwb (image, red, green, blue)	Integer	Returns the index of the color with the hue, white, and blackness closest to the specified color in the palette of the specified image
ImageColorDeallocate (image, index)	Integer	De-allocates a color for an image
ImageColorExact (image, red, green, blue)	Integer	Returns the index of the specified color in the palette of the specified image
ImageColorExactAlpha (image, int red, int green, int blue, int alpha)	Integer	Returns the index of the specified color plus alpha in the palette of the specified image
ImageColorResolve (image, red, green, blue)	Integer	Returns the index of the specified color or its closest possible alternative
ImageColorResolveAlpha (image, int red, int green, int blue, int alpha)	Integer	Returns the index of the specified color plus alpha or its closest possible alternative
ImageColorSet (image, index, red, green, blue)	Boolean	Sets the color for the specified palette index
ImageColorsForIndex (image, index)	Array	Returns an associative array containing the red, green, and blue values for the specified color index
ImageColorsTotal (image)	Integer	Returns the total number of colors in the specified image's palette

Function	Returns	Description
ImageTrueColorToPalette (image, bool dither, int ncolors)	Void	Converts a true-color image to a palette image; if dither is TRUE then dithering will be used, which will result in a more speckled image but with better color approximation *Requires GD 2 and later.*
ImageColorTransparent (image [,color])	Integer	Sets color as the transparent color
ImageCopy (dst_image, src_image, dst_x, dst_y, src_x, src_y, src_w, src_h)	Integer	Copies part of an image src_im to dst_im, from the src_ coordinates to the dst_ coordinates
ImageCopyMerge (dst_image, src_image, dst_x, dst_y, src_x, src_y, src_w, src_h, pct)	Integer	Copies part of image src_im from the coordinates (src_x, src_y) of width src_w and height src_h onto image dst_im at coordinates (dst_x, dst_y); the extent of the merge is given by pct, a value between 0 (none) and 100
ImageCopyMergeGray (dst_image, src_image, dst_x, dst_y, src_x, src_y, src_w, src_h, pct)	Integer	Works as ImageCopyMerge(), except that the portion dst_im to be merged is converted to grayscale first, to preserve its hue value
ImageCopyResampled (dst_image, src_image, dstX, dstY, srcX, srcY, dstW, dstH, srcW, srcH)	Integer	Copies and resamples part of an image, using dstX and dstY as top-left coordinates
ImageCopyResized (dst_image, src_image, dstX, dstY, srcX, srcY, dstW, dstH, srcW, srcH)	Integer	Copies and resizes part of an image, using dstX and dstY as top left coordinates
ImageCreate (width, height)	Integer	Creates a new image with the specified height and width
ImageCreateFromGif (filename)	Integer	Creates a new image from the specified GIF file
ImageCreateFromJpeg (filename)	Integer	Creates a new image from the specified JPEG file
ImageCreateFromPng (filename)	Integer	Creates a new image from the specified PNG file

Table continued on following page

Function	Returns	Description
`ImageCreateFromString (string)`	Integer	Creates a new image from the data in the given string
`ImageCreateFromWbmp (filename)`	Integer	Creates a new image from the given WBMP file
`ImageCreateFromXbm (filename)`	Integer	Creates a new image from the given XBM file
`ImageCreateFromXpm (filename)`	Integer	Creates a new image from the given XPM file
`ImageCreateTrueColor (width, height)`	Integer	Create a new true color image with `width` and `height`
`ImageDashedLine (image, x1, y1, x2, y2, col)`	Integer	Draws a dashed line in the specified image
`ImageDestroy (image)`	Integer	Destroys the image specified by `image`
`ImageEllipse (image, x, y, width, height, color)`	Integer	Draws an ellipse centered at (x,y) of given width, height and line color
`ImageFill (image, x, y, color)`	Integer	Flood fills the image specified by `image` with `color`
`ImageFilledArc (image, x, y, width, height, start, end, color, style)`	Integer	Draws a partial ellipse centered at (x,y) of given width and height between the angles of start and end degrees in the given color, and style
`ImageFilledEllipse (image, x, y, width, height, color)`	Integer	Draws an ellipse centered at (x,y) of given width, height, filled with color
`ImageFilledPolygon (image, points, num_points, color)`	Integer	Draws a filled polygon in the image between the points in the `points` array
`ImageFilledRectangle (image, x1, y1, x2, y2 color)`	Integer	Draws a filled rectangle in the image
`ImageFillToBorder (image, x, y, border, col)`	Integer	Performs a flood fill in the image with a border color (`border`)
`ImageFontHeight (font)`	Integer	Returns the height of the specified font in pixels

Function	Returns	Description
`ImageFontWidth (font)`	Integer	Returns the width of the specified font in pixels
`ImageGammaCorrect (image, inputgamma, outputgamma)`	Integer	Applies a gamma correction to the GD image
`ImageGif (image [,filename])`	Integer	Sends the GIF image filename to a file or browser as image
`ImageInterlace (image [,interlace])`	Integer	Turns interlacing ON or OFF for the specified image
`ImageJpeg (image [,filename [,quality]])`	Integer	Sends the JPEG image to a file or browser; use an empty string (`' '`) to replace no filename when specifying quality
`ImageLine (image, int x1, int y1, int x2, int y2, int col)`	Integer	Draws a line from (x1, y1) to (x2, y2) (top-left is 0, 0) in the image of color (color)
`ImagePng (image [, string filename])`	Integer	Sends the GD image stream in PNG format to a browser or file
`ImageSetPixel (image, int x, int y, int color)`	Integer	Draws a pixel at x, y (top-left is 0, 0) in the image of color (color)
`ImagePolygon (image, array points, int num_points, int color)`		Takes an array of coordinates (points) and connects each point with lines; num_points is the total number of vertices contained in the polygon
`ImageRectangle (resource image, int x1, int y1, int x2, int y2, int col)`	Integer	Creates a rectangle of color in an image starting at upper-left coordinate x1, y1 and ending at bottom-right coordinate x2, y2; 0, 0 is the top-left corner of the image
`ImageString (image, int font, int x, int y, string s, int col)`	Void	Writes the text contained in string to image using color at the coordinate (x, y) where x is the beginning of the text and y is the top of the text (not the baseline)
`ImageTTFString (image, int size, int angle, int x, int y, int color, string fontfile, string text)`	Void	Draws the contents of text starting at the coordinate (x, y) at an angle (angle) in the color (color), using the TrueType font located at fontfile

Table continued on following page

Function	Returns	Description
ImageTTFText (resource image, int size, int angle, int x, int y, int color, string fontfile, string text)	Array	Draws the contents of text in the image identified by image, starting at coordinates x, y (top-left is 0, 0), at an angle in color, using the TrueType font file identified by fontfile
ImageWbmp (image [, string filename [, int foreground]])	Integer	Creates the WBMP file in filename from the image (image), the image argument is returned from the ImageCreate() function

HAWHAW Reference

HAWHAW (HTML And WML Hybrid Adapted Webserver) is a toolkit that helps web masters to make their web sites mobile, that is, it makes developing cross-platform (including WAP-and PDA-friendly HTML) mobile applications a lot easier than developing a proprietary template system. In addition to WAP and HTML, HAWHAW supports HDML (Handheld Device Markup Language – a WML predecessor), i-mode (Japan's wireless Internet system), and MML (Multimedia Markup Language).

The HAWHAW toolkit consists of three components:

❑   HAWHAW XML – The markup language

```
<?xml version="1.0"?>
  <hawhaw>
    <deck>
      <text>Hello World</text>
    </deck>
  </hawhaw>
```

❑   hawhaw.inc – The PHP class library

```
<?php
require("hawhaw.inc");
$myPage = new HAW_deck("Welcome");
$myText = new HAW_text("Hello World!");
$myPage->add_text($myText);
$myPage->create_page();
?>
```

❏   HAWXY – The HAWHAW proxy

HAWHAW users can select the components that fit their personal requirements. Web masters can use the HTML-like HAWHAW XML markup language, to provide wireless accessible content without requiring any programming skills or special web server support. PHP gurus can use the PHP class library to set up tailor-made standalone mobile applications on their PHP-enabled web server. They can also set up their own HAWHAW proxy, which can be used by the webmasters for the required markup conversion.

The whole HAWHAW code, both for the HAWHAW PHP class library and the HAWHAW proxy server is open source and available for free under GPL. Users of the HAWHAW XML markup language don't need any code at all, because they just have to edit HAWHAW XML files, which are accessed via other user's proxies.

> In some Windows installations HAWHAW's output is destroyed by some PHP warnings of notice level. In this case we can turn off the notices by editing the php.ini file, like this: error_reporting = E_ALL & ~E_NOTICE; to display all errors and warnings.

The HAWHAW PHP Class Library

To use the HAWHAW PHP class library all we need is a PHP-enabled web server and a little experience with server-side scripting.

Next we will detail the PHP HAWHAW classes.

Class HAW_banner

```
public class HAW_banner
```

This class provides a banner in a HAW_deck object (HTML only).

Here is an example:

```
$myPage = new HAW_deck(...);
...
$myBanner1 = new HAW_banner("http://wwww.adpartner1.org/images/adp1.gif",
                "http://www.adpartner1.org/", "Welcome at adpartner1!");
$myPage->add_banner($myBanner1);
...
$myBanner2 = new HAW_banner("http://wwww.adpartner2.org/images/adp2.gif",
                            HAW_NOLINK, "Buy products of adpartner2!");
$myBanner2->set_size(300,50);
$myBanner2->set_br(0);
$myPage->add_banner($myBanner2,HAW_TOP);
```

Constructor Summary

```
HAW_banner(var $image, var $url, var $alt)
```

Explanation:

- ❑ `$image` – Stands for the ad-partners banner in `.gif`, `.jpg`, or any other HTML compatible formats
- ❑ `$url` – Links to the ad-partner or `HAW_NOLINK` (if no is link available)
- ❑ `$alt` – Includes alternative text for the banner

Method Summary

Here are the methods of the class:

Method	Description
`public void set_size(var $width, var $height)`	Sets the number of line breaks (CRLF) after the banner, where `$width` and `$height` are the width and height of the banner in pixels. The default is 1.
`public void set_br(var $br)`	Sets the number of line breaks (CRLF) after the banner, where `$br` is the number of the line breaks.

> Though not mandatory, usage of the `set_size()` function will accelerate page setup.

Class HAW_checkbox

```
public class HAW_checkbox
```

This class provides a single checkbox element in a `HAW_form` object.

Here is an example:

```
$myCheckbox = new HAW_checkbox("agmt", "yes", "I agree");
```

which is equivalent to:

```
$myCheckbox = new HAW_checkbox("agmt", "yes", "I agree", HAW_NOTCHECKED);
```

Here's another instance:

```
$myCheckbox = new HAW_checkbox("agmt", "yes", "I agree", HAW_CHECKED);
```

Method Summary

This is the method of the class:

Method	Description
public HAW_checkbox(var $name, var $value, var $label, var $state)	Here $name is the variable in which $value is sent to the destination URL. If the box is checked then $label describes the checkbox on the user's screen, $state is optional. The allowed values are HAW_CHECKED and HAW_NOTCHECKED (default). The allowed values are HAW_CHECKED and HAW_NOTCHECKED (default).

Class HAW_deck

```
public class HAW_deck
```

This class is the top-level class of all HAWHAW classes. Our page should consist of exactly one HAW_deck object. For WML browsers one deck with one card will be generated. For HDML browsers one deck that includes as much cards as necessary will be generated. HTML browsers will receive a normal HTML page. For AvantGo and i-mode browsers the appropriate HTML code is created.

> Do not overload HAW_deck objects. A lot of WAP clients cannot handle more than about 1400 bytes of compiled data.

Here is an example:

```
$myPage = new HAW_deck();
$myPage = new HAW_deck("My WAP page");
$myPage = new HAW_deck("", HAW_ALIGN_CENTER);
...
$myPage->set_bgcolor("blue");
...
$myPage->add_text($myText);
...
$myPage->create_page();
```

Constructor Summary

```
public HAW_deck(var $title, var $alignment)
```

Explanation:

❑ $title – If a string is provided here, it will be displayed in the HTML title bar, respectively somewhere on the WAP display. WAP devices can display very few lines and if we use a title bar then we would be using at least one line from these already few available lines. If we consider that some WAP and PDA devices don't display the title at all then the default is HAW_NOTITLE.

❏ `$alignment` – We can enter `HAW_ALIGN_CENTER`, or `HAW_ALIGN_RIGHT` to modify the alignment of the whole page. The default is `HAW_ALIGN_LEFT`.

Method Summary

Here is a listing of the methods of the class:

Method	Description
`public void add_banner (var $banner, var $position)`	Adds a `HAW_banner` object. It has no effect on WML/handheld pages.
`public void add_form (var $form)`	Adds a `HAW_form` object.
`public void add_image (var $image)`	Adds a `HAW_image` object.
`public void add_link (var $link)`	Adds a `HAW_link` object.
`public void add_linkset (var $linkset)`	Adds a `HAW_linkset` object to `HAW_deck`.
`public void add_phone (var $phone)`	Adds a `HAW_phone` object to `HAW_deck`.
`public void add_rule (var $rule)`	Adds a `HAW_rule` object to `HAW_deck`.
`public void add_table (var $table)`	Adds a `HAW_table` object to `HAW_deck`.
`public void add_text (var $text)`	Adds a `HAW_text` object to `HAW_deck`.
`public void create_page ()`	Creates the page in the appropriate markup language. Depending on the clients' browser type HTML (pure HTML, handheld-friendly AvantGo HTML, i-mode cHTML, or MML), WML or HDML code is created.
`public void disable_cache ()`	Disables deck caching in the user's client. This object function allows changing content under the same URL.
`public_set_background(var $background)`	Sets wallpaper.
`public void set_bgcolor(var $bgcolor)`	Sets the background color.
`public void set_border (var $border)`	Sets the thickness of the HTML display frame.
`public void set_charset (var $charset, var $unicodemaptab)`	Sets a given character set. The default is ISO-8859-1.
`public void set_color (var $color)`	Sets the color for all characters.
`public void set_disp_background (var $background)`	Sets display wallpaper.

Table continued on following page

Method	Description
`public set_disp_bgcolor` `(var $disp_bgcolor)`	Sets the display background color.
`public void set_face (var $face)`	Sets the font for all characters.
`public void set_height (var $height)`	Sets the display height.
`public void set_link_color` `(var $link_color)`	Sets the color of links.
`public void set_redirection` `(var $timeout, var $red_url)`	Redirects automatically after timeout, to another URL (this feature is not supported in HDML browsers, due to the missing timer functionality).
`public void set_size (var $size)`	Sets the font size for all characters.
`public void set_vlink_color` `(var $vlink_color)`	Sets the color of visited links.
`public void set_waphome(var $waphome)`	Sets the URL of a WAP site, an HTML-browsing user is invited to enter via WAP. It has no effect on WML created pages.
`public void set_width (var $width)`	Sets the display width. It has no effect on WML/handheld pages.
`public void use_simulator ()`	Activates the built-in device simulator on big-screen browsers. Device simulator can be displayed only by IE and Netscape 6, as the layout requires a scrollable table element, which unfortunately is not supported by other browsers. With old browsers, the classic HAWHAW layout will be displayed.

Class HAW_form

```
public class HAW_form
```

This class defines a form with various possible input elements. These input elements have to be defined as separate objects and they are linked to the form with a special add function. One HAW_deck object can contain only one HAW_form object.

Here is an example:

```
$myPage = new HAW_deck(...);
...
$myForm = new HAW_form("/mynextpage.wml");
```

```
$myText = new HAW_text(...);
$myForm->add_text($myText);
$myInput = new HAW_input(...);
$myForm->add_input($myInput);
$mySubmit = new HAW_submit(...);
$myForm->add_submit($mySubmit);
...
$myPage->add_form($myForm);
...
$myPage->create_page();
```

Constructor Summary

```
HAW_form (var $url)
```

Explanation:

❑ $url – Holds the address where the user input is sent to.

Method Summary

Here is a listing of the methods of the class:

Method	Description
public void add_checkbox(var $checkbox)	Adds a HAW_checkbox object
public void add_hidden (var $hidden)	Adds a HAW_hidden object
public void add_image (var $image)	Adds a HAW_image object
public void add_input (var $input)	Adds a HAW_input object
public void add_radio (var $radio)	Adds a HAW_radio object
public void add_rule (var $radio)	Adds a HAW_rule object
public void add_select (var $select)	Adds a HAW_select object
public void add_submit (var $submit)	Adds a HAW_submit object
public void add_table (var $table)	Adds a HAW_table object
public void add_text (var $text)	Adds a HAW_text object

Class HAW_hidden

```
public class HAW_hidden
```

This class provides a hidden element in a HAW_form object.

489

Here is an example:

```
$myHiddenElement = new HAW_hidden("internal_reference", "08154711");
```

Constructor Summary

```
HAW_hidden(var $name, var $value)
```

Explanation:

- ❏ $name – This is the variable in which $value is sent to the destination URL
- ❏ $value – This is the value sent to the destination URL

Class HAW_image

```
public class HAW_image
```

This class allows inserting bitmap images into a HAW_deck, HAW_form, or HAW_table object.

Here is an example:

```
$myImage1 = new HAW_image("my_image.wbmp", "my_image.gif", ":-)");
$myImage2 = new HAW_image("my_image.wbmp", "my_image.gif", ":-)",
                          "my_image.bmp");
$myImage2->set_br(1);
```

Constructor Summary

```
HAW_image(var $src_wbmp, var $src_html, var $alt, var $src_bmp)
```

Explanation:

- ❏ $src_wbmp – Holds the bitmap in WAP-conformable .wbmp format.
- ❏ $src_html – Holds the bitmap in .gif, .jpg, or any other HTML-compatible format.
- ❏ $alt – Holds alternative text for the bitmap. This text will be displayed if the client cannot display any graphic formats.
- ❏ $src_bmp – Holds the bitmap in monochrome (.bmp) format. This image will be sent if the user signals in the HTTP request header that he's only able to display images in .bmp format and not in vnd.wap.wbmp (for instance, the UPSim 3.2 included this feature). It is optional.

Method Summary

Here is a listing of the methods of the class:

Method	Description
`public void setbr (var $br)`	Sets the number of line breaks (CRLF) after the image. The default is zero.
`public void use_chtml_icon(var $icon)`	Uses CHTML icon instead of HTML bitmap on i-mode devices. Using built-in icons, mobile devices don't have to download bitmap images. It has no effect on non-i-mode devices.
`public void use_localsrc(var $icon)`	Uses the `localsrc` attribute on WAP/HDML devices. Using built-in icons, mobile devices don't have to download bitmap images. If the device can not render the specified icon, it will download the appropriate bitmap as specified in the `HAW_image` constructor.
`public void use_mml_icon(var $icon)`	Uses the MML icon instead of HTML bitmap on MML devices. Using built-in icons, mobile devices don't have to download bitmap images. It has no effect on non-MML devices.

Class HAW_input

```
public class HAW_input
```

This class provides a text input area in a `HAW_form` object.

Here is an instance:

```
$myInput1 = new HAW_input("cid", "", "Customer ID");

$myInput2 = new HAW_input("cid", "", "Customer ID", "*N");
$myInput2->set_size(6);
$myInput2->set_maxlength(6);

$myInput3 = new HAW_input("pw", "", "Password", "*N");
$myInput3->set_size(8);
$myInput3->set_maxlength(8);
$myInput3->set_type(HAW_INPUT_PASSWORD);
```

Constructor Summary

```
public HAW_input(var $name, var $value,  var $label, var $format)
```

Explanation:

- ❏ $name – This is the variable in which the input is sent to the destination URL.

- ❏ $value – The initial value (string) that will be presented in the input area.

- ❏ $label – This describes our input area on the surfer's display.

- ❏ $format – Input format code according to the WAP standard. For example, allows the WAP user client to input only digits and not characters. On an HTML-generated page this format has no significance. It is optional and the default is *M.

Method Summary

Here is a listing of the methods of the class:

Method	Description
`public void set_br(var $br)`	Sets the number of line breaks (CRLF) after the input field, where $br denotes the number of line breaks. The default is 1 and has no effect in WML/HDML.
`public void set_maxlength(var $maxlength)`	Sets the maximum of allowed characters in the input area, where $maxlength is the maximum number of characters the user can enter. It will be ignored in case of HDML output.
`public void set_mode(var $mode)`	Sets the input mode/style for Japanese MML/i-mode devices, where $mode is the input mode. This mode can be HAW_INPUT_ALPHABET (default), HAW_INPUT_KATAKANA, HAW_INPUT_HIRAGANA, or HAW_INPUT_NUMERIC.
`public void set_size(var $size)`	Sets the size of the input area, where $size denotes the number of characters fitting into the input area. This will be ignored in case of HDML output.
`public void set_type(var $type)`	Sets the input type, where $type denotes the allowed values which can be HAW_INPUT_TEXT (default) or HAW_INPUT_PASSWORD.

Class HAW_link

```
public class HAW_link
```

This class provides a link in a HAW_deck, HAW_linkset, or in the HAW_table object.

Here's an example:

```
$myPage = new HAW_deck(...);
...
$myLink = new HAW_link("Continue","/mynextpage.wml");
$myPage->add_link($myLink);
```

Constructor Summary

```
public HAW_link(var $label, var $url, var $title)
```

Explanation:

- ❏ $label – Describes the link on the surfer's display.

- ❏ $url – Holds the next destination address.

- ❏ $title – If a string is provided here, it will be displayed in the HTML browser status bar during 'MouseOver' state, respectively somewhere on the WAP display. In order to work well with a broad range of user agents, keep the title under 6 characters. It is optional.

Method Summary

This is the method of the class:

Method	Description
public void set_br(var $br)	Sets the number of line breaks (CRLF) after link, where $br denotes the number of breaks. The default is 1.

Class HAW_linkset

This class is similar to HAW_link:

```
public class HAW_linkset
```

This class defines a set of links. The links have to be defined as separate HAW_link objects and are attached to the linkset with a special add_link() function. For WAP devices browser-dependent WML code will be created.

On UP-browser-based WAP devices linksets allow easier navigation through WML decks by using the 'onpick' WML option. This improves the usability of an application. Instead of painfully navigating through the links sports->football->results->today, the mobile user, for example, can press '2431' on the keypad to enter his favorite deck. For all other WAP devices normal <a> tags are created. One HAW_deck object can contain only one linkset object.

Here is an example:

```
$myPage = new HAW_deck(...);
...
$myLinkset = new HAW_linkset();
$myLink1 = new HAW_link("Phonebook", "/wap/phonebook.wml");
$myLinkset->add_link($myLink1);
$myLink2 = new HAW_link("DateBook", "/wap/datebook.wml");
$myLinkset->add_link($myLink2);
...
$myPage->add_linkset($myLinkset);
...
$myPage->create_page();
```

Constructor Summary

```
public HAW_linkset()
```

Method Summary

This is the method of the class:

Method	Description
public void add_link(var $link)	Adds a HAW_link object to HAW_linkset. Here $link is a HAW_link object.

Class HAW_phone

```
public class HAW_phone
```

This class provides a phone number in a HAW_deck object. If supported by their mobile device, users can establish a voice connection to the specified number.

Here is an instance:

```
$myPage = new HAW_deck(...);
...
$myPhone = new HAW_phone("123-45678", "CALL");
$myPage->add_phone($myPhone);
```

Constructor Summary

```
public HAW_phone(var $phone_number, var $title)
```

Explanation:

❏ $phone_number – Holds the phone number to dial.

❑ $title – If a string is provided here, the call button on a WAP/HDML device will be entitled. In order to work well with a broad range of user agents, keep the title under six characters. It is optional.

Class HAW_radio

```
public class HAW_radio
```

This class provides a radio button element in a HAW_form object.

Here is an example:

```
$myRadio = new HAW_radio("country");
$myRadio->add_button("Finland", "F");
$myRadio->add_button("Germany", "G", HAW_CHECKED);
$myRadio->add_button("Sweden", "S");
```

Constructor Summary

```
public HAW_radio(var $name)
```

Explanation:

❑ $name – Denotes the variable in which the information about the pressed button is sent to the destination URL

Method Summary

This is the method of the class:

Method	Description
public void add_button(var $label, var $value, var $is_checked)	Adds one radio button to a HAW_radio object, where $label describes the radio button on the surfer's display and $value is the value sent in the $name variable. If this button is selected, the values allowed for $is_checked (optional) are HAW_CHECKED, or HAW_NOTCHECKED (default).

> **Setting to 'checked' will overwrite previously checked radio buttons of this HAW_radio object.**

Class HAW_row

```
public class HAW_row
```

This class defines the rows that a HAW_table object consists of.

Here is an example:

```
...
$image1 = new HAW_image("my_image.wbmp", "my_image.gif", ":-)");
$text1 = new HAW_text("my text");
$row1 = new HAW_row();
$row1->add_column($image1);
$row1->add_column();
$row1->add_column($text1);
...
```

Constructor Summary

```
public HAW_row()
```

Method Summary

This is the method of the class:

Method	Description
public void add_column(var $cell_element)	Adds a cell element to a HAW_row object where $cell_element can be a HAW_text object, a HAW_image object, a HAW_link object, or the NULL pointer (default). The latter results in an empty cell element.

Class HAW_rule

```
public class HAW_rule
```

This class will cause a (horizontal) rule to be drawn across the screen. It can be used to separate text paragraphs in HAW_deck or HAW_form objects.

Here is an example:

```
$myDefaultRule = new HAW_rule();
$mySpecialRule = new HAW_rule("60%", 4);
...
$myPage->add_rule($myDefaultRule);
...
$myPage->add_rule($mySpecialRule);
```

Constructor Summary

```
public HAW_rule(var $width, var $size)
```

Explanation:

- ❏ $width – Sets the percentage of screen width or absolute value in number of pixels (for example, '50%' or 100). It is optional.

- ❏ $size – Sets the height of the line to be drawn in pixels. It is optional.

Class HAW_select

```
public class HAW_select
```

This class provides a `select` element in a `HAW_form` object. It allows creating optimized WML for WAP devices, which are capable of interpreting the Openwave GUI extensions for WML 1.3. All other WAP devices receive WML 1.1 compatible markup code, which is quite similar to the markup code created by the `HAW_radio` class.

Here is an example:

```
$mySelect = new HAW_select("color");
$mySelect->add_option("Blue", "b");
$mySelect->add_option("Red", "r", HAW_SELECTED);
$mySelect->add_option("Yellow", "y");
```

Constructor Summary

```
public HAW_select(var $name, var $type)
```

Explanation:

- ❏ $name – This is a variable in which the information about the selected option is sent to the destination URL.

- ❏ $type – Sets the type of `select` area with `HAW_SELECT_POPUP` that pops up the whole selection list (default) or `HAW_SELECT_SPIN` that rotates options on a WAP device screen. It is optional.

Method Summary

This is the method of the class:

Method	Description
public void add_option(var $label, var $value, var $is_selected)	Adds one option to a HAW_select object where $label describes the option on the surfer's display, and $value sets the value (string!) sent in the $name variable. If this option is selected then $is_selected (optional) holds HAW_SELECTED or HAW_NOTSELECTED (default).

> **Setting to 'selected' will overwrite the previous 'selected' options of this HAW_select object.**

Class HAW_submit

```
public class HAW_submit
```

This class provides a submit button in a HAW_form object. One HAW_form object can contain only one HAW_submit object.

Here is an example:

```
$mySubmit = new HAW_submit("Submit");
$mySubmit = new HAW_submit("Submit", "user_pressed");
```

Constructor Summary

```
public HAW_submit(var $label, var $name)
```

Explanation:

❑ $label – This is written on the button.

❑ $name – This is the variable in which $label is sent to the destination URL. It is optional.

Class HAW_table

```
public class HAW_table
```

This class allows inserting tables into a HAW_deck or HAW_form object. Not all WAP clients are able to display tables properly. HDML is not supporting tables at all. The contents of the table will be generated column-by-column for HDML users and row-by-row for WAP devices where each table cell will result in one separate line on the display.

Here is an example:

```
...
$myTable = new HAW_table();
$row1 = new HAW_row();
$row1->add_column($image1);
$row1->add_column($text1);
$myTable->add_row($row1);
$row2 = new HAW_row();
$row2->add_column($image2);
$row2->add_column($text2);
$myTable->add_row($row2);
$myDeck->add_table($myTable);
...
```

Method Summary

This is the method of the class:

Method	Description
public void add_row(var $row)	Adds a HAW_row object to HAW_table where $row is the HAW_row object.

Class HAW_text

```
public class HAW_text
```

This class allows inserting plain text into a HAW_deck, HAW_form, or HAW_table object.

Here is an example:

```
$myText1 = new HAW_text("Hello WAP!");
$myText2 = new HAW_text("Welcome to HAWHAW", HAW_TEXTFORMAT_BOLD);
$myText3 = new HAW_text("Good Morning", HAW_TEXTFORMAT_BOLD |
HAW_TEXTFORMAT_BIG);

$myText3->set_br(2);
```

Constructor Summary

```
public HAW_text(var $text, var $attrib)
```

Explanation:

❑ $text – This is the string we want to display.

❑ $attrib – This can hold HAW_TEXTFORMAT_NORMAL (default), HAW_TEXTFORMAT_BOLD, HAW_TEXTFORMAT_UNDERLINE, HAW_TEXTFORMAT_ITALIC, HAW_TEXTFORMAT_BIG, or HAW_TEXTFORMAT_SMALL. This is optional.

Method Summary

This is the method of the class:

Method	Description
public void set_br(var $br)	Sets the number of line breaks (CRLF) after text, where $br is some number of line breaks. The default is 1.

PHP PDF Language Reference

Here is a listing of the PHP PDF functions:

Function	Returns	Description
`PDF_add_annotation(pdfdoc, xll,` `yll, xur, yurtitle, text)`	Void	Adds an annotation for the defined box on the PDF. This function is deprecated. Use `PDF_add_note()` instead.
`PDF_add_bookmark(pdfdoc, text` `[,parent, open])`	Integer	Adds a bookmark called `text` for the current page.
`PDF_add_launchlink(pdfdoc, llx,` `lly, urx, ury, filename)`	Void	Adds a launch annotation (to a target of arbitrary file type) in a box described by lower-left and upper-right coordinates (`llx`, `lly`) and (`urx`, `ury`).
`PDF_add_locallink(pdfdoc, llx,` `lly, urx, ury, page, dest)`	Void	Adds a link annotation to a target within the current PDF file in a box described by lower-left and upper-right coordinates (`llx`, `lly`) and (`urx`, `ury`).

Table continued on following page

Function	Returns	Description
PDF_add_note(pdfdoc, llx, lly, urx, ury, contents, title, icon, open)	Void	Adds a note annotation in a box described by lower-left and upper-right coordinates (llx, lly) and (urx, ury).
PDF_add_outline		Alias for PDF_add_bookmark().
PDF_add_pdflink(pdfdoc, llx, lly, urx, ury, PDFfile, page, dest)	Void	Creates a link on the PDF to the given PDF file from the box defined with lower-left corner at (llx, lly) and upper-right corner at (urx, ury).
PDF_add_thumbnail(pdfDoc, image)	Void	Adds an existing image as thumbnail for the current page. It works only with PDFlib 4.0.
PDF_add_weblink(pdfDoc, llx, lly, urx, ury, url)	Void	Creates a link on the PDF to the given URL from the box defined with lower-left corner at (llx, lly) and upper-right corner at (urx, ury)
PDF_arc(pdf, x, y, r, start, end)	Void	Draws a circular arc anticlockwise with centre (x, y) between start and end degrees relative to the positive y axis.
PDF_arcn(pdf, x, y, r, start, end)	Void	Draws a circular arc clockwise with centre (x, y) between start and end degrees relative to the positive y axis. It works only with PDFlib 4.0.
PDF_attach_file(pdfDoc, lly, lly, urx, ury, filename, description, author, mimetype, icon)	Void	Adds a file attachment annotation in a box described by lower-left and upper-right coordinates (llx, lly) and (urx, ury).
PDF_begin_page(pdfDoc, width, height)	Void	Adds a new page of given width and height to the document.
PDF_begin_pattern(pdfDoc, width, height, xstep, ystep, painttype)	Integer	Starts a new pattern definition. It works only with PDFlib 4.0.

Function	Returns	Description
`PDF_begin_template(pdf, width, height)`	Integer	Starts a new template definition. It works only with PDFlib 4.0.
`PDF_circle(pdfDoc, x, y, radius)`	Void	Draws a circle with centre (x, y) and given radius.
`PDF_clip(pdfDoc)`	Void	Uses the current path as the clipping path.
`PDF_close(pdfDoc)`	Void	Closes the named PDF document.
`PDF_close_image(pdfDoc, pdfimage)`	Void	Closes an image retrieved with one of the `PDF_open_image()` functions.
`PDF_closepath(pdfDoc)`	Void	Closes the current path.
`PDF_closepath_fill_stroke(pdfDoc)`	Void	Closes, fills, and draws a line along the path with the current fill and line color.
`PDF_closepath_stroke(pdfDoc)`	Void	Closes the path and draws a visible line across it.
`PDF_close_pdi(pdfDoc, doc)`	Void	Closes the named input PDF document. It works only with PDFlib 4.0.
`PDF_close_pdi_page(pdfDoc, doc, page)`	Void	Closes the page handle on the named page. It works only with PDFlib 4.0.
`PDF_concat(pdfDoc, a, b, c, d, e, f)`	Void	Concatenate a matrix to the current transformation matrix for text and images.
`PDF_continue_text(pdfDoc, text)`	Void	Continues the text area with the given text from the next line down.
`PDF_curveto(pdfDoc, x1, y1, x2, y2, x3, y3)`	Void	Draw a Bezier curve from the current point, using 3 more control points.
`PDF_delete(pdfDoc)`	Void	Deletes the given PDF object.
`PDF_end_page(pdfDoc)`	Void	Finishes the page.

Table continued on following page

Function	Returns	Description
PDF_endpath(pdfDoc)	Void	Ends the current path.
		This function is deprecated. Use one of the strokes, fill, or clip functions instead.
PDF_end_pattern(pdfDoc)	Void	Finishes the pattern definition.
		It works only with PDFlib 4.0.
PDF_end_template(pdfDoc)	Void	Finishes the template definition.
		It works only with PDFlib 4.0.
PDF_fill(pdfDoc)	Boolean	Fills the interior of the path with the current fill color.
PDF_fill_stroke(pdfDoc)	Boolean	Fills and draws a line along the path with the current fill and line color.
PDF_findfont(pdfDoc, font, encoding[, embed])	Integer	Prepares a font for later use with PDF_setfont().
PDF_get_buffer(pdfDoc)	String	Gets the contents of the PDF output buffer. The result must be used by the client before calling any other PDFlib function.
PDF_get_font(pdfDoc)	Integer	PDF_get_font() returns the current font.
		This function is deprecated.
PDF_get_fontname(pdfDoc)	String	Returns the current font family name.
		This function is deprecated. Use PDF_get_value() instead.
PDF_get_fontsize(pdfDoc)	Double	Returns the current font size.
		This function is deprecated. Use PDF_get_value() instead.
PDF_get_image_height(pdfDoc, image)	Integer	Returns the height of the specified image.
		This function is deprecated. Use PDF_get_value() instead.

Function	Returns	Description
PDF_get_image_width(pdfDoc, image)	Integer	Returns the width of the specified image.
		This function is deprecated. Use PDF_get_value() instead.
PDF_get_parameter(pdfDoc, parameter, modifier)	String	Returns the value of the named PDFlib parameter.
PDF_get_pdi_parameter(pdf, parameter, doc, page, index)	String	Returns the contents of the named parameter for a PDI document that has a text-based value.
		It works only with PDFlib 4.0.
PDF_get_pdi_value(pdf, parameter, doc, page, index)	Double	Returns the contents of the named parameter for a PDI document that has a numerical value.
		It works only with PDFlib 4.0.
PDF_get_value(pdfDoc, parameter, modifier)	Double	Returns the value of the named PDFlib parameter.
PDF_initgraphics(pdfDoc)	Boolean	Resets all implicit color and graphics state parameters to their defaults.
		It works only with PDFlib 4.0.
PDF_lineto(pdfDoc, x, y)	Boolean	Draws a line from the current point to (x, y).
PDF_makespotcolor(pdfDoc, spotname)	Integer	Makes a named spot color from the current color.
		It works only with PDFlib 4.0.
PDF_moveto(pdfDoc, x, y)	Boolean	Sets the current cursor point to (x, y).
PDF_new()	Integer	Creates a new PDF object.
PDF_open([file])	Integer	Opens the named PDF file.
		This function is deprecated. Use PDF_new() or PDF_open_file() instead.

Table continued on following page

Function	Returns	Description
`PDF_open_ccitt(pdfDoc, filename, width, height, bitreverse, k, blackls1)`	Integer	Opens a file containing raw CCITT compressed bitmap data and returns an image for placement.
`PDF_open_file(pdfDoc[, file])`	Integer	Opens a new PDF document file or in memory if file is not specified.
`PDF_open_gif(pdfDoc, file)`	Integer	Opens the GIF file and returns an image for placement. This function is deprecated. Use `PDF_open_image()` instead.
`PDF_open_image(pdfDoc, type, source, data, length, width, height, components, bpc, params)`	Integer	Opens an image of the given type (JPEG, CCITT, or RAW) from the named source (file, memory, or URL) and returns an image for placement.
`PDF_open_image_file(pdf, type, file [, stringparam [, intparam]])`	Integer	Opens an image file of the specified type (GIF, JPEG, TIFF, and PNG) and returns an image for placement.
`PDF_open_jpeg(pdfDoc, file)`	Integer	Opens the JPEG file and returns an image for placement. This function is deprecated. Use `PDF_open_image()` instead.
`PDF_open_memory_image(pdf, image)`	Integer	Takes an image generated with the GD library and returns an image for placement.
`PDF_open_pdi(pdfDoc, file, stringparam, intparam)`	Integer	Opens the given input PDF file and prepares it for later use. It works only with PDFlib 4.0.
`PDF_open_pdi_page(pdfDoc, doc, page, label)`	Integer	Prepares the given page of the input PDF document for later use with `PDF_place_image()`. It works only with PDFlib 4.0.
`PDF_open_png(pdfDoc, file)`	Integer	Opens the PNG file and returns an image for placement. This function is deprecated. Use `PDF_open_image()` instead.

Function	Returns	Description
PDF_open_tiff(pdfDoc, file)	Integer	Opens the TIFF file and returns an image for placement.
		This function is deprecated. Use PDF_open_image() instead.
PDF_place_image(pdfDoc, pdfimage, x, y, scale)	Void	Places the given image at coordinates (x, y) at the given scale.
PDF_place_pdi_page(pdfDoc, page, x, y, sx, sy)	Void	Places the named PDI page into the PDF document with lower-left corner at (x, y) and scaled as specified by (sx, sy).
PDF_rect(pdfDoc, x, y, width, height)	Void	Draws a rectangle with given width and height from lower-left corner (x, y).
PDF_restore(dfDoc)	Void	Restores a previously saved graphics state and environment for the pdfDoc.
PDF_rotate(pdfDoc, angle)	Void	Rotates the coordinate system for the pdfDoc by angle degrees.
PDF_save(pdfDoc)	Void	Saves the current graphics state and environment.
PDF_scale(pdfDoc, xscale, yscale)	Void	Sets the horizontal and vertical scale values to xscale and yscale respectively.
PDF_set_border_color(pdfDoc, r, g, b)	Void	Sets the color of the boxes surrounding link areas.
PDF_set_border_dash(pdfDoc, black, white)	Void	Sets the border dash style for the boxes surrounding link areas.
PDF_set_border_style(pdfDoc, style, width)	Void	Sets the style for the boxes surrounding link areas.
PDF_set_char_spacing(pdfDoc, value)	Void	Sets the character spacing to value.
		This function is deprecated. Use PDF_set_value() instead.

Table continued on following page

507

Function	Returns	Description
PDF_setcolor(pdfDoc, type, colorspace, c, m, y, k)	Void	Sets the current color and colorspace to the given CMYK. It works only with PDFlib v4.0.
PDF_setdash(pdfDoc, numwhite, numblack)	Void	Sets the dash pattern to numwhite white pixels followed by numblack black pixels.
PDF_set_duration(pdfDoc, value)	Void	Sets the duration between pages to value. This function is deprecated. Use PDF_set_value() instead.
PDF_setflat(pdfDoc, value)	Void	Sets the flatness of pdfDoc to the given value.
PDF_set_font(pdfDoc, font, size, encoding [, embed])	Void	Sets the current font family, size, and encoding. This function is deprecated. Use PDF_findfont() or PDF_setfont() instead.
PDF_setfont(pdfDoc, font, fontsize)	Void	Sets the current font to the given font and size.
PDF_setgray	Void	Sets the document's greyscale fill and line color to value. This function is deprecated since PDFlib 4.0.
PDF_setgray_fill(pdfDoc, value)	Void	Sets the document's greyscale fill color to value. This function is deprecated since PDFlib 4.0.
PDF_setgray_stroke	Void	Sets the document's greyscale line color to value. This function is deprecated since PDFlib 4.0.
PDF_set_horiz_scaling(pdfDoc, value)	Void	Sets the horizontal text scaling to value. This function is deprecated. Use PDF_set_value() instead.

Function	Returns	Description
PDF_set_info(pdfDoc, field, value)	Boolean	Sets the named field in the PDF to the given value.
PDF_set_info_author(pdfDoc, value)	Boolean	Sets the author field of the PDF to value.
		This function is deprecated. Use PDF_set_value() instead.
PDF_set_info_creator(pdfDoc, value)	Boolean	Sets the creator field of the PDF to value.
		This function is deprecated. Use PDF_set_value() instead.
PDF_set_info_keywords(pdfDoc, value)	Boolean	Sets the keywords field of the PDF to value.
		This function is deprecated. Use PDF_set_value() instead.
PDF_set_info_subject(pdfDoc, value)	Boolean	Sets the subject field of the PDF to value.
		This function is deprecated. Use PDF_set_value() instead.
PDF_set_info_title(pdfDoc, value)	Boolean	Sets the title field of the PDF to value.
		This function is deprecated. Use PDF_set_value() instead.
PDF_set_leading	Boolean	Sets the current leading for the PDF to value.
		This function is deprecated. Use PDF_set_value() instead.
PDF_setlinecap(pdfDoc, value)	Void	Sets the linecap parameter to value.
PDF_setlinejoin(pdfDoc, value)	Void	Sets the linejoin parameter to value.
PDF_setlinewidth(pdfDoc, value)	Void	Sets the line width on the page to value.
PDF_setmatrix(pdfDoc, a, b, c, d, e, f)	Void	Explicitly sets the current transformation matrix for text and graphics.
		It works only with PDFlib 4.0.

Table continued on following page

Function	Returns	Description
PDF_setmiterlimit(pdfDoc, value)	Void	Sets the miter limit of pdfDoc to value.
PDF_set_parameter(pdfDoc, parameter, value)	Void	Sets a PDFlib parameter with the given value.
PDF_setpolydash(pdfDoc, dasharray)	Void	Sets a more complex dash pattern as given in the dasharray.
PDF_setrgbcolor(pdfDoc, r, g, b)	Void	Sets the document's RGB fill and line color to (r, g, b).
		This function is deprecated since PDFlib 4.0.
PDF_setrgbcolor_fill	Void	Sets the document's RGB fill color to (r, g, b).
		This function is deprecated since PDFlib 4.0.
PDF_setrgbcolor_stroke	Void	Sets the document's RGB line color to (r, g, b).
		Will be deprecated after the release of PDFlib v4.0.
PDF_set_text_pos(pdfDoc, x, y)	Void	Sets the (x, y) coordinates for the next time text needs to be placed in the document.
PDF_set_text_rendering(pdfDoc, mode)	Void	Sets how text will be rendered.
		This function is deprecated. Use PDF_set_value() instead.
PDF_set_text_rise(pdfDoc, value)	Void	Sets the text rise to value.
		This function is deprecated. Use PDF_set_value() instead.
PDF_set_transition(pdfDoc, transition)	Void	Sets the transition effect between the pages.
		This function is deprecated. Use PDF_set_value() instead.
PDF_set_value(pdfdoc, parameter, value)	Void	Sets a PDFlib parameter with the given value.

Function	Returns	Description
`PDF_set_word_spacing(pdfDoc, value)`	Void	Sets the spacing between words to value.
		This function is deprecated. Use `PDF_set_value()` instead.
`PDF_show(pdfDoc, text)`	Void	Displays the text at the current position on the page.
`PDF_show_boxed(pdfDoc, text, x, y, width, height, align [, feature])`	Integer	Displays the text at coordinates (x, y) on the page in a box of given height, width, and alignment.
`PDF_show_xy(pdfDoc, text, x, y)`	Void	Displays the text at coordinates (x, y) on the page.
`PDF_skew(pdfdoc, x, y)`	Void	Skews the coordinate system for the `pdfDoc` by x degrees horizontally and y degrees vertically.
`PDF_stringwidth(pdfDoc, text [, font, size])`	Double	Returns the width of the given text in the current `font` and `size` (or those specified).
`PDF_stroke(pdfDoc)`	Void	Draws a line along the current path.
`PDF_translate(pdfDoc, x, y)`	Void	Resets the origin of the page coordinates system to (x, y).

PHP FDF Language Reference

Forms Data Format (FDF) is a file format used for handling forms within PDF documents.

The general idea of FDF is similar to HTML forms. The difference is basically the format in which data is transmitted to the server when the submit button is pressed (that is, the Form Data Format) and the format of the form itself (which is the Portable Document Format).

We can take an existing PDF form and populate the input fields with data without modifying the form itself. In this case, we would create an FDF document (fdf_create()), set the values of each input field (fdf_set_value()), and associate it with a PDF form (fdf_set_file()). Finally it is sent to the browser with the Mime Type application/vnd.fdf. The Acrobat reader plug-in of the browser recognizes the MIME Type, reads the associated PDF form, and fills in the data from the FDF document.

If we look at an FDF document with a text editor, we will find a catalog object with the name FDF. Such an object may contain a number of entries like Fields, F, Status, and so on. The most commonly used entries are Fields which point to a list of input fields, and F which contains the filename of the PDF document this data belongs to. Those entries are referred to in the FDF documentation as the /F key or /STATUS key. These entries can be modified by using functions like fdf_set_file() and fdf_set_status(). The fields are modified with fdf_set_value(), fdf_set_opt(), and so on.

Here is a listing of the FDF functions:

Function	Returns	Description
`fdf_add_template(fdf_document, newpage, filename, template, rename)`	Boolean	Adds a template to the specified FDF document. This function is available in version 3.0.23 and later.
`fdf_close(fdf_document)`	Boolean	Closes the specified FDF document. This function is available from 3.0.6 and later.
`fdf_create()`	Integer	Creates a new FDF document. This function is available in version 3.0.3 and later.
`fdf_get_file(fdf_document)`	String	Returns the value of the /F key in the specified FDF document. This function is available in version 3.0.6 and later.
`fdf_get_status(fdf_document)`	String	Returns the value of the /STATUS key in the specified FDF document. This function is available in version 3.0.6 and later.
`fdf_get_value(fdf_document, fieldname)`	String	Returns the value of the named field in the specified FDF document. This function is available in version 3.0.6 and later.
`fdf_next_field_name(fdf_document [, fieldname])`	String	Returns the name of the field following the specified/current field.
`fdf_open(filename)`	Integer	Opens the specified FDF document with form data.
`fdf_save(filename)`	Boolean	Saves the FDF document to the specified file. This function is available in version 3.0.6 and later.

Function	Returns	Description
fdf_set_ap(fdf_document, field_name, face, filename, page_number)	Boolean	Sets the appearance of the named field in the specified FDF document. This function is available in version 3.0.6 and later.
fdf_set_encoding(fdf_document, string encoding)	Nothing	Sets the FDF character encoding. This function is available in PHP 4.1.0 and later.
fdf_set_file(fdf_document, filename)	Nothing	Sets the value of the /F key in the specified FDF document. This function is available in version 3.0.6 and later.
fdf_set_flags(fdf_document, fieldname, whichFlags, newFlags)	Boolean	Sets flags of the specified field. This function is available in version 4.0.2 and later.
fdf_set_javascript_action(fdf_document, fieldname, trigger, script)	Boolean	Sets a JavaScript action for the specified field. This function is available in version 4.0.2 and later.
fdf_set_opt(fdf_document, fieldname, element, value, name)	Boolean	Sets options of the specified field. This function is available in version 4.0.2 and later.
fdf_set_status(fdf_document, status)	Boolean	Sets the value of the /STATUS key in the specified FDF document. This function is available in version 3.0.6 and later.
fdf_set_submit_form_action(fdf_document, fieldname, trigger, url, flags)	Boolean	Sets a submit form action for the given field. This function is available in version 4.0.2 and later.
fdf_set_value(fdf_document, fieldname, value, is_name)	Nothing	Sets the value of the named field in the specified FDF document. This function is available in version 3.0.6 and later.

PHP and ImageMagick Language Reference

ImageMagick is a robust collection of tools and libraries to read, write, and manipulate an image in different formats. It supports over 68 major formats including popular formats like JPEG, PNG, PDF, and GIF. With ImageMagick we can create images dynamically, making them suitable for web applications. We can also resize, rotate, sharpen, add special effects, reduce the color of an image, and save our finished work in the same or in a different image format.

Here we will detail the basic ImageMagick functions and how we use them in our scripts:

imagick_create

```
resource imagick_create (void)
```

This function creates a new ImageMagick handle. It returns a handle on success and FALSE on error.

Here is an example:

```
<?php

$handle = imagick_create ()
or die ("Could not create handle");

print("Connected successfully");

imagick_free($handle);
?>
```

imagick_read

```
boolean imagick_read (resource imagick_handle, mixed filename)
```

This function reads an image. It returns TRUE on success and FALSE on error.

The filename parameter can be either a filename on our local filesystem, a URL (for example, http://my.server.com/picture.gif), or an array containing more than one string with filenames for multiple image support. The image format should be recognized automatically by imagick. If imagick_read() does not recognize the image format we can prefix the filename with the image format abbreviation plus a semicolon (for example, GIF:mygif.gif).

These are the image formats supported with ImageMagick 5.4.0:

In the table, r = read, w = write, and * = native blob support.

Image Type	Read/Write Support	Description
8BIM*	rw-	Photoshop resource format
AFM*	r--	TrueType font
APP1*	rw-	Photoshop resource format
ART*	r--	PF1: 1st Publisher
AVI*	r--	Audio/Visual Interleaved
AVS*	rw+	AVS X image
BIE*	rw-	Joint Bi-level Image experts Group interchange format
BMP*	rw+	Microsoft Windows bitmap image
CMYK*	rw+	Raw cyan, magenta, yellow, and black bytes
CMYKA*	rw+	Raw cyan, magenta, yellow, black, and matte bytes
CUT*	r--	DR Hallo
DCM*	r--	Digital Imaging and Communications in Medicine image
DCX*	rw+	ZSoft IBM PC multi-page Paintbrush
DIB*	rw+	Microsoft Windows bitmap image
DPX*	rw+	Digital Moving Picture Exchange
EPDF*	rw-	Encapsulated Portable Document Format
EPI*	rw-	Adobe Encapsulated PostScript Interchange format
EPS*	rw-	Adobe Encapsulated PostScript

Image Type	Read/Write Support	Description
EPS2*	-w-	Adobe Level II Encapsulated PostScript
EPS3*	-w+	Adobe Level III Encapsulated PostScript
EPSF*	rw-	Adobe Encapsulated PostScript
EPSI*	rw-	Adobe Encapsulated PostScript Interchange format
EPT*	rw-	Adobe Encapsulated PostScript with TIFF preview
FAX*	rw+	Group 3 FAX
FILE*	r--	Uniform Resource Locator
FITS*	rw-	Flexible Image Transport System
FPX*	rw-	FlashPix Format
FTP*	r--	Uniform Resource Locator
G3*	rw-	Group 3 FAX
GIF*	rw+	CompuServe graphics interchange format
GIF87*	rw-	CompuServe graphics interchange format (version 87a)
GRADIENT*	r--	Gradual passing from one shade to another
GRANITE*	r--	Granite texture
GRAY*	rw+	Raw Gray bytes
H*	rw-	Internal format
HDF	rw+	Hierarchical Data Format
HISTOGRAM*	-w-	Histogram of the image
HTM*	-w-	Hypertext Markup Language and a client-side image map
HTML*	-w-	Hypertext Markup Language and a client-side image map
HTTP*	r--	Uniform Resource Locator
ICB*	rw+	Truevision Targa image
ICM*	rw-	ICC Color Profile
ICO*	r--	Microsoft icon
ICON*	r--	Microsoft icon
IPTC*	rw-	IPTC Newsphoto
JBG*	rw+	Joint Bi-level Image experts Group interchange format

Table continued on following page

Image Type	Read/Write Support	Description
JBIG*	rw+	Joint Bi-level Image experts Group interchange format
JP2*	rw-	JPEG-2000 JP2 File Format Syntax
JPC*	rw-	JPEG-2000 Code Stream Syntax
JPEG*	rw-	Joint Photographic Experts Group JFIF format
JPG*	rw-	Joint Photographic Experts Group JFIF format
LABEL*	r--	Text image format
LOGO*	rw-	ImageMagick Logo
M2V*	rw+	MPEG Video Stream
MAP*	rw-	Colormap intensities and indices
MAT*	r--	MATLAB image format
MATTE*	-w+	MATTE format
MIFF*	rw+	Magick image format
MNG*	rw+	Multiple-image Network Graphics
MONO*	rw-	Bi-level bitmap in least-significant-byte-first order
MPC	rw-	Magick Persistent Cache image format
MPEG*	rw+	MPEG Video Stream
MPG*	rw+	MPEG Video Stream
MTV*	rw+	MTV Ray tracing image format
MVG*	rw-	Magick Vector Graphics
NETSCAPE*	r--	Netscape 216 color cube
NULL*	r--	Constant image of uniform color
OTB*	rw-	On-the-air bitmap
P7*	rw+	Xv thumbnail format
PAL*	rw+	16bit/pixel interleaved YUV
PBM*	rw+	Portable bitmap format (black and white)
PCD*	rw-	Photo CD
PCDS*	rw-	Photo CD
PCL*	-w-	Page Control Language

Image Type	Read/Write Support	Description
PCT*	rw-	Apple Macintosh QuickDraw/PICT
PCX*	rw-	ZSoft IBM PC Paintbrush
PDB*	r--	Pilot Image Format
PSD*	rw-	Adobe Photoshop bitmap
PTIF*	rw-	Pyramid-encoded TIFF
PWP*	r--	Seattle Film Works
RAS*	rw+	SUN Raster file
RGB*	rw+	Raw red, green, and blue bytes
RGBA*	rw+	Raw red, green, blue, and matte bytes
RLA*	r--	Alias/Wave front image
RLE*	r--	Utah Run length-encoded image
SCT*	r--	Scitex HandShake
SGI*	rw+	Irix RGB image
SHTML*	-w-	Hypertext Markup Language and a client-side image map
STEGANO*	r--	Steganographic image
SUN*	rw+	SUN Raster file
SVG*	rw+	Scalable Vector Graphics
TEXT*	rw+	Raw text
TGA*	rw+	Truevision Targa image
TIF*	rw+	Tagged Image File Format
TIFF*	rw+	Tagged Image File Format
TILE*	r--	Tile image with a texture
TIM*	r--	PSX TIM
TTF*	r--	TrueType font
TXT*	rw+	Raw text
UIL*	-w-	X-Motif UIL table
UYVY*	rw-	16bit/pixel interleaved YUV
VDA*	rw+	Truevision Targa image

Table continued on following page

Image Type	Read/Write Support	Description
VICAR*	rw-	VICAR Raster file format
VID*	rw+	Visual Image Directory
VIFF*	rw+	Khoros Visualization image
VST*	rw+	Truevision Targa image
WBMP*	rw-	Wireless Bitmap (level 0) image
WMF	r--	Windows Meta File
WPG*	r--	Word Perfect Graphics
X*	rw-	X Image
XBM*	rw-	X Windows system bitmap (black and white)
XC*	r--	Constant image uniform color
XML*	r--	Scalable Vector Graphics
XPM*	rw-	X Windows system pixmap (color)
XV*	rw+	Khoros Visualization image
XWD*	rw-	X Windows system window dump (color)
YUV*	rw-	CCIR 601 4:1:1

On some platforms, ImageMagick automatically processes these extensions – .gz for Zip compression, .Z for UNIX compression, .bz2 for block compression, and .pgp for PGP encryption. For example, a PNM image called image.pnm.gz is automatically uncompressed with the **gzip** program, and the image is subsequently read.

Here is an example:

```php
<?php

$handle = image_new()
or die ("Could not connect");

imagick_read($handle,"mypic.gif");

imagick_write($handle,"mypic.png");

imagick_free($handle);
?>
```

In this example, `imagick_read()` reads multiple images:

```php
<?php

$handle = image_new()
or die ("Could not connect");

imagick_read($handle,array("mypic.gif","http://my.server.com/mypic.png"));

imagick_write($handle,"PNG:mypic.myext");

imagick_free($handle);
?>
```

imagick_write

```
bool imagick_write (resource imagick_handle, string filename)
```

This function writes the image to a file. It returns TRUE on success and FALSE on error.

The `filename` parameter is a filename on our local filesystem. ImageMagick tries to find out the image format with the file extension we provide. If that fails or if we want another image format, we can prefix the filename with the image format code plus.

Refer `image_read()` for a detailed list of all supported image formats.

Here is an example:

```php
<?php

$handle = image_new()
or die ("Could not connect");

imagick_read($handle,"mypic.gif");

imagick_write($handle,"mypic.png","PNG");

imagick_free($handle);
?>
```

imagick_free

```
bool imagick_free (resource imagick_handle)
```

This function frees an `imagick_handle` and all the resources attached to it.

imagick_convert

```
bool imagick_convert (string input_file, string output_file [,string imageformat])
```

Converts a file to another file or dumps it to the browser. It returns TRUE on success and FALSE on error.

This is a wrapper function to create, read, write/dump, and free images. If $output_file is '-' or NULL it dumps the image to the output (mostly the browser). If we save it to an output file, then we can specify the format in which we want the image to be saved (if we want an image format different from the input image format).

imagick_copy_crop

```
resource imagick_copy_crop(resource imagick_handle,int width, int height,int x,
                            int y)
```

Crops an image and returns a new handle. It returns a new handle on success and FALSE on error.

imagick_copy_sample

```
resource imagick_copy_sample (resource imagick_handle, int width, int height)
```

Scales an image to the desired dimensions with pixel sampling and returns a new handle. It returns a new handle on success and FALSE on error.

Unlike other scaling methods, this method does not introduce any additional color into the scaled image.

imagick_copy_resize

```
resource imagick_copy_resize (resource imagick_handle, int width, int height,
                              int filter, int blur)
```

Scales an image to the desired dimensions with a filter and returns a new handle. It returns a new handle on success and FALSE on error. Also, $blur includes the blur factor where a value greater than 1 means blurry and a value lower than 1 means sharp.

The possible filters are:

Filter
IMAGICK_FILTER_UNDEFINED
IMAGICK_FILTER_POINT
IMAGICK_FILTER_BOX
IMAGICK_FILTER_HERMITE
IMAGICK_FILTER_HANNING
IMAGICK_FILTER_HAMMING
IMAGICK_FILTER_BLACKMAN
IMAGICK_FILTER_GAUSSIAN
IMAGICK_FILTER_QUADRATIC
IMAGICK_FILTER_CUBIC
IMAGICK_FILTER_CATROM
IMAGICK_FILTER_MITCHELL
IMAGICK_FILTER_LANCZOS
IMAGICK_FILTER_BESSEL
IMAGICK_FILTER_SINC

imagick_copy_rotate

```
resource imagick_copy_rotate (resource imagick_handle, double degrees)
```

Rotates a picture and returns a new handle.

Positive angles rotate anti clockwise (right-hand rule), while negative angles rotate clockwise. Rotated images are usually larger than the originals, and have 'empty' triangular corners. Empty triangles left over from rotating the image, are filled with the color defined by the pixel at the (0,0) location.

imagick_copy_shear

```
resource imagick_copy_shear (resource imagick_handle, double x_shear,
                             double y_shear)
```

Shears a picture, and returns a new handle.

An x direction shear slides an edge along the x axis, while a y direction shear slides an edge along the y axis. The amount of the shear is controlled by a shear angle. For x direction shears, x_shear is measured relative to the y axis, and similarly, for y direction shears y_shear is measured relative to the x axis. Empty triangles left over from shearing the image are filled with the color defined by the pixel at the (0, 0) location.

imagick_copy_morph

```
resource imagick_copy_morph (resource imagick_handle, long number_frames)
```

Morphs at least 2 pictures, and returns a new handle.

This function requires a minimum of two images. The first image is transformed into the second by a number of intervening images as specified by frames.

imagick_annotate

```
bool imagick_annotate (resource imagick_handle, array options)
```

This function annotates an image with text.

Here is an example:

```
<?php

imagick_annotate($handle,array("primitive"=>"text 150,150 hello
            world","pointsize"=>60,"antialias"=>1, "stroke"=>'green',
            "fill"=>'#ff7755', "font"=>"Arial.ttf","rotate"=>90));
?>
```

imagick_list-magickinfo

```
bool imagick_sample (string filename)
```

Lists the image formats to a file.

imagick_dump

```
bool imagick_dump (resource imagick_handle [, string imageformat])
```

This function dumps the picture to the output (mostly the browser).

imagick_set_attribute

```
bool imagick_set_attribute (resource imagick_handle, mixed attribute [, string
                            attribute_value])
```

Sets an image attribute.

This function either takes two strings with the attribute and the value, or an array with attributes as the key and the values as values. At the time of writing, the following attributes are supported:

Attribute Name
Adjoin
Delay
Format
Magick
Quality
Size

For more information about the attributes, refer to http://www.imagemagick.org/www/perl.html#seta.

Here is an example:

```php
<?php

$handle = imagick_create ()
or die ("Could not create handle");

imagick_read($handle,"mypic.gif");

imagick_set_attribue($handle,"quality",10);

imagick_write($handle,"mypic.jpg");

imagick_free($handle);
?>
```

In this example, imagick_set_attribue() takes more than one attribute at once:

```php
<?php

$handle = imagick_create ()
or die ("Could not create handle");

imagick_read($handle,"mypic.gif");

imagick_set_attribue($handle,array("quality"=>10,"format"=>"jpeg"));

imagick_write($handle,"mypic.jpg");

imagick_free($handle);
?>
```

imagick_get_attribute

```
bool imagick_sample (resource imagick_handle, string attribute_name)
```

Gets an image attribute.

At the time of writing, the following attributes are supported:

Attribute Name
Format
Magick
Quality
Height
Width

Color Screenshots Gallery

Ming

The following section showcases the color screenshots in Chapter 3.

Fig 3.1 – RGB color system representation

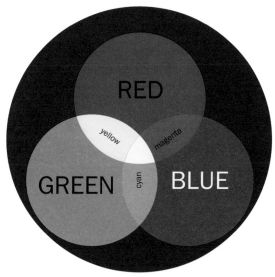

Fig 3.2 – SWFMovie

Fig 3.3 – SWFMovie-HTML

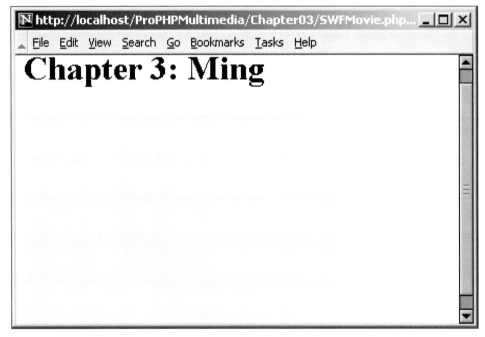

Fig 3.4 – SWFMovie-Flash

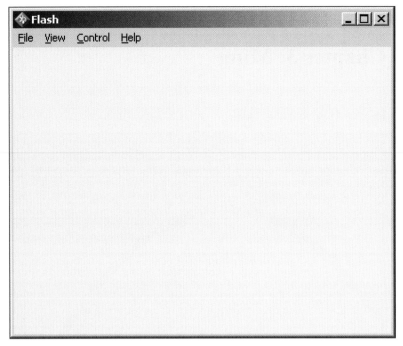

Fig 3.5 – SWFMovieLine

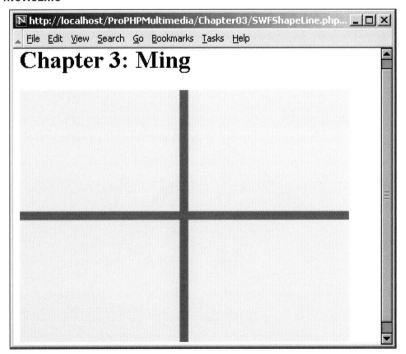

Fig 3.6 – SWFShapeCurve

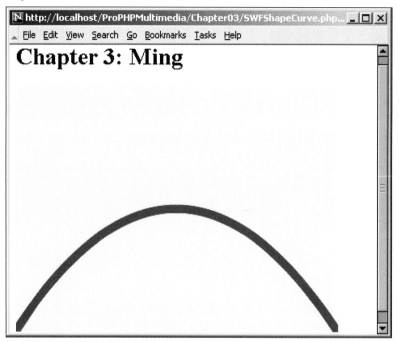

Fig 3.7 – SWFFill

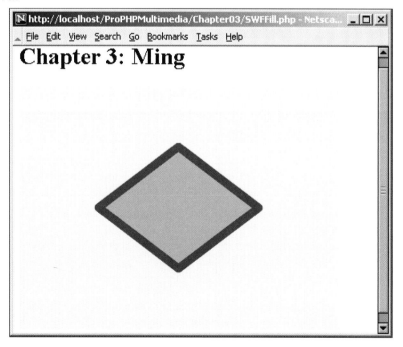

Fig 3.8 – SWFGradient

Fig 3.9 – SWFBitmap

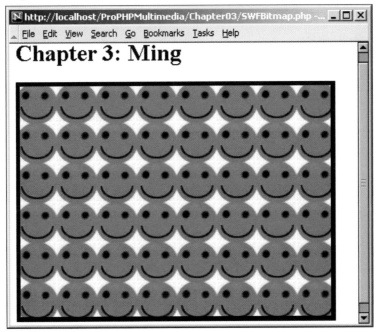

Fig 3.10 – SWFText

Fig 3.11 – SWFTextField1

Fig 3.12 – SWFDisplayItem1

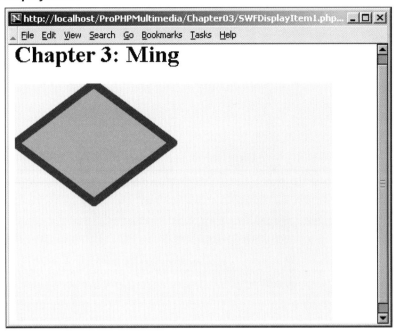

Fig 3.13 – SWFDisplayItem2

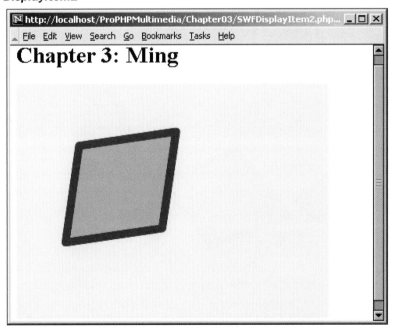

Fig 3.14 – SWFDisplayItem3

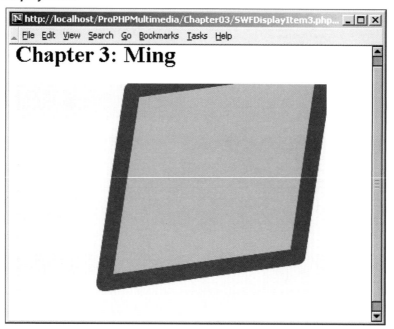

Fig 3.15 – Animation

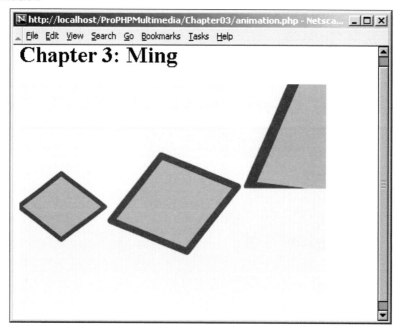

Fig 3.16 – SWFTextfield2

Fig 3.17 – SWFMorph

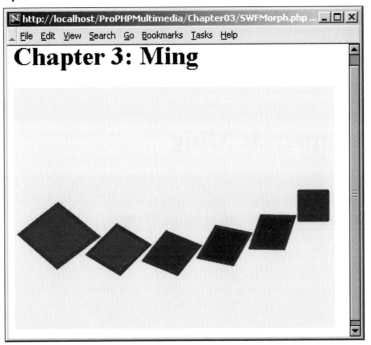

Fig 3.18 – SWFButton

This is the button, which we created:

The button's color changes when a mouse is placed over it:

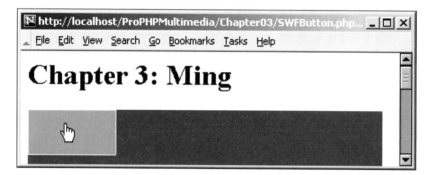

The button's color changes further when the mouse is clicked:

Ming with ActionScript

The following section showcases the color screenshots in Chapter 4.

Fig 4.1 – randomdots3.php

Fig 4.2 – randomdots4.php

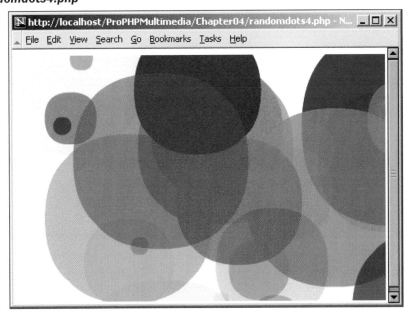

Manipulating Images with GD

The following section showcases the color screenshots in Chapter 5.

Fig 5.1 – ImageColorTransparent

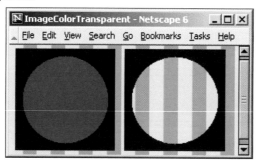

Fig 5.2 – ImageColorsTotal

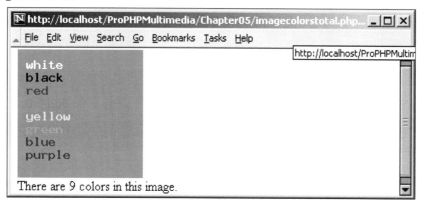

Fig 5.3 – ImageRectangle

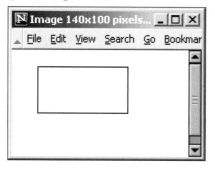

Fig 5.4 – ImageFilledRectangle

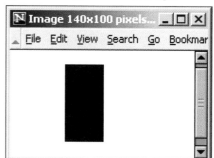

Fig 5.5 – ImageCopyMerge

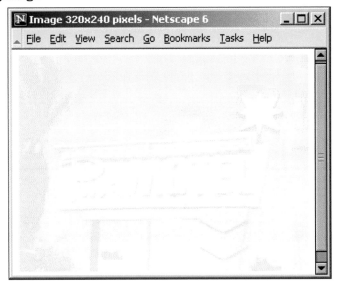

Fig 5.6 – Motels of the San Fernando Valley

ImageMagick

The following section showcases the color screenshots in Chapter 6.

Fig 6.1 – ImageMagick Manipulation Examples

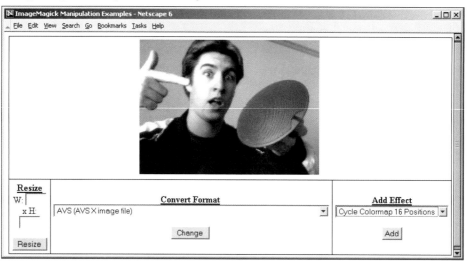

Fig 6.2 – ImageMagick Manipulation Examples

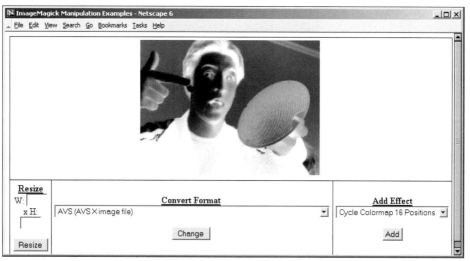

PDFlib

The following section showcases the color screenshots in Chapter 7.

Fig 7.1 – fill_stroke_clipping

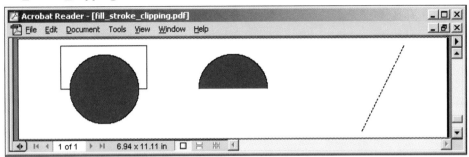

Fig 7.2 – class.PdfDoc

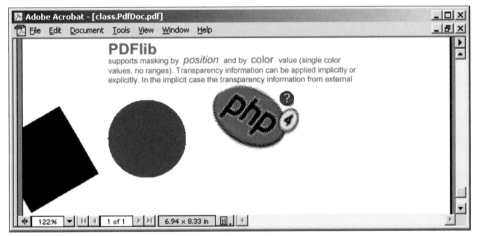

Case Study – Image Gallery

The following section showcases the color screenshots in Chapter 11.

Fig 11.1 – list.php

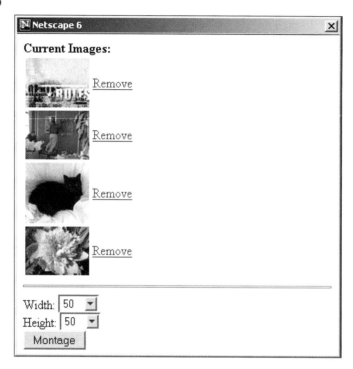

Fig 11.2 – montage.php

Setting Up Palm Desktop, POSE, and AvantGo on a Windows Desktop

Even if we don't own a PDA, with Internet connectivity we can see how our HAWHAW-based application will look on the users' PDA. PalmOS Emulator (POSE) is a program that emulates a PalmOS handheld on our desktop. With some extra configuration it can interact with the Palm Desktop software, which will allow us to install the AvantGo client on a virtual PDA.

Using POSE and AvantGo to View HAWHAW Pages

These are the steps involved in setting up POSE and AvantGo for HAWHAW development on the Windows desktop:

- ❑ Install the Palm Desktop software
- ❑ Configure Palm Desktop to allow Network HotSync
- ❑ Install POSE
- ❑ Set up a virtual PDA using a PalmOS ROM file
- ❑ Configure POSE to use Network HotSync
- ❑ Download and Install AvantGo on the virtual PDA
- ❑ Create a new AvantGo account and resync the POSE PDA

It looks like a lot of work, but it's really not hard to set up and it's definitely not as expensive as buying a PDA – all of the software we need is free.

Installing Palm Desktop

Palm Desktop is the software that lets PalmOS device users synchronize their calendar, address book, and other information between their computer and their handheld. It includes a program called **HotSync Manager**, which is the component that manages the actual transfer of data between the handheld and the desktop, including the installation of new software.

The Palm Desktop Software for Windows is available at http://www.palm.com/support/downloads/win_desktop.html.

Although we don't have a physical PalmOS device, we will be able to configure Palm Desktop and POSE, so that we can synchronize data and install new software too.

Installing AvantGo onto the emulated handheld is a straightforward task. When the setup wizard asks us for a username, we can enter pose. Further, the installation program will ask us if we want to register a Palm device and whether or not we want to set up mail. Since we're not setting up an actual Palm device and only setting up the Palm Desktop to run AvantGo, we should click Skip for registration and No for mail setup.

Once the installation is complete, we should see an icon for the HotSync Manager in the system tray, like this:

When we have an actual PalmOS device, it is usually connected to the desktop computer by a serial or USB connection. In our case since we don't have a physical device, we'll have to enable the Network HotSync feature to use HotSync with POSE.

To enable Network HotSync for the POSE handheld, click on the HotSync Manager icon and select Setup->Network. We should now see a window, like this:

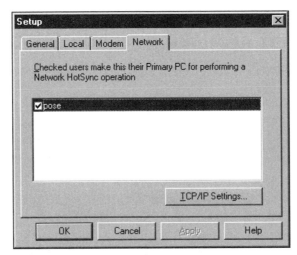

Now check the box next to the username (pose). Click on the TCP/IP Settings button and write down the following information:

❑ Primary PC Name

❑ Primary PC Address

Finally, click on the HotSync Manager icon and click Network. This tells the HotSync Manager to listen for HotSync requests over the network.

Installing POSE

POSE is available for download at http://www.palmos.com/dev/tools/emulator/. The Windows version comes as a .ZIP file called emulator-win.zip. Firstly, unzip this file into a directory of our choice, for example, C:\Program Files\pose.

> **Before we can run POSE, we have to sign up as a PalmOS developer and download the ROM image of a PalmOS device.**

Once we have installed POSE and downloaded a ROM image, we can start the POSE program by double-clicking on emulator.exe.

The following menu appears:

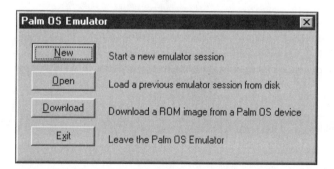

Once we click New another dialog box will pop up:

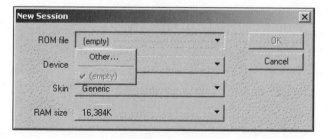

Select the ROM file from the list (use Other... to browse to the right directory if no ROM files show up in the list). Then click OK and the emulated PalmOS device will start to display a preferences screen:

As POSE is frequently used by software developers (while creating new programs); it has extensive debugging features that can give warnings about potential memory violations and other OS-level problems. Since we're using POSE only for checking our pages in AvantGo, we can turn debugging off. Right-click on the POSE window and select Settings->Debugging. Make sure all the boxes on the resulting pop-up window are unchecked and click OK:

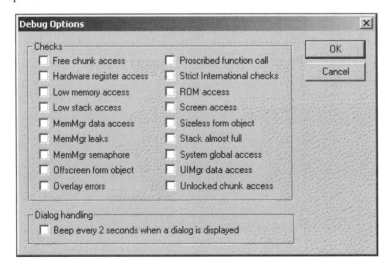

We have some more configurations to do in POSE to enable Network HotSyncing:

1. Click the Applications icon on the lower-left side of the POSE window, and then click on the HotSync icon.

2. Click the Menu icon on the lower-left side of the POSE window and select Modem Sync Prefs. Click on Network, then click OK:

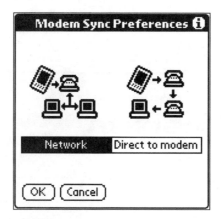

3. Select Modem on the HotSync screen:

4. Click Select Service and then click Done (we're not actually using a dialup service, but the software requires a value to be set for this option, so we'll just use whatever is there at the top of the list).

5. Click the Menu icon on the lower-left side of the POSE window and select Primary PC Setup. This is where we enter the Primary PC Name and Primary PC Address values that we wrote down earlier. Click OK when done.

6. Right-click on the POSE window and select Settings->Properties. Make sure the Redirect NetLib calls to host TCP/IP option is checked and click OK. This tells POSE to share our desktop computer's Internet connection.

We should now be able to HotSync our emulated PalmOS device with the Palm Desktop software. To try it out, click on the HotSync button in POSE:

The first time when we synchronize a PalmOS device (real or emulated) to the desktop, the HotSync Manager will pop up a window asking us to choose a profile to use for the device:

Select **pose** and click **OK**. The HotSync Manager will now synchronize our emulated PalmOS device with the Palm Desktop Software and ask us to reset the device (only when we synchronize our device to Palm Desktop for the first time).

Since we haven't entered any calendar items or addresses there isn't really much to synchronize, but the important thing is that our virtual PalmOS device is now recognized by Palm Desktop as one belonging to the user **pose** and we're ready to install AvantGo.

Installing AvantGo

AvantGo (https://ami.avantgo.com/setup/index.html) have streamlined their installation process to walk us through downloading and installing AvantGo and finally creating a new account for us. AvantGo is available for several different platforms, so we must make sure to specify PalmOS as our device type. After we download and run the installation wizard, we will be returned to the AvantGo web site where we see a message 'Place your device in its cradle and press the HotSync button'. Since we don't have a cradle for our virtual handheld, we need to click the HotSync button in POSE:

HotSync will run again and this time the AvantGo software will be installed on the POSE device. Click on the Applications button on the lower-left side of the POSE window. We should now see two new applications – AG Connect and AvantGo:

AG Connect handles our account and connection settings and AvantGo is the browser itself.

Before we continue setting up AvantGo on our virtual PDA, we need to go back to the AvantGo web site and click Next to create an account. Once we've filled out all the required fields and agreed to AvantGo's terms of service, click the button labeled Click Here to Configure. This will launch a wizard that will configure AvantGo to use our new username and password and subscribe us to a few sample channels based on the interests we have selected on the signup page.

Once the wizard is complete, go back to POSE and click the HotSync button. AvantGo will add our username and password settings on the virtual PalmOS device and automatically download the most recent pages from our sample channels.

Once HotSync finishes, we're ready to go. To use AvantGo, click the Applications icon on the lower-left side of the POSE screen and then click on the AvantGo icon. Our AvantGo home page will look like this:

The underlined words are clickable links to other pages while the navigation buttons at the top of the screen work just like a desktop browser.

How AvantGo Works

When we update our channels by pressing the HotSync button or open a URL directly in AvantGo, the requested pages are not downloaded directly from the target web server to our PDA. Instead, the pages are downloaded by an AvantGo proxy server. Then the AvantGo server attempts to optimize graphics and HTML for display on the tiny PDA screen by stripping out unsupported tags, compressing and resizing images, and converting the pages to PalmOS files that are readable by the AvantGo software, before delivering pages to our handheld.

Testing HAWHAW Applications with AvantGo

Being able to browse to a URL directly is an invaluable feature when it comes to testing HAWHAW applications to see how they look and perform on a PDA. What we have to remember is that since all AvantGo requests go through a proxy server, the web server we're using to build our mobile application must be accessible from the Internet; otherwise the AvantGo proxy server won't be able to download and convert our pages for use in the AvantGo browser.

Summary

These instructions provided a quick way to set up and run Palm Desktop, POSE, and AvantGo on our desktop. Here we touched on a number of tasks, including:

❑   Installing and configuring Palm Desktop

❑   Installing and configuring POSE

❑   Installing AvantGo and creating a new AvantGo account.

Here are a few resources that would be helpful in learning more about using PalmOS devices and AvantGo:

❑   **Palm Desktop**

   ❑   Palm Desktop and HotSync Support page – http://www.palm.com/support/palmdesktop.html

❑   **POSE**

   ❑   PalmOS Emulator page – http://www.palmos.com/dev/tools/emulator/

   ❑   Using the PalmOS Emulator – http://oasis.palm.com/dev/kb/papers/1311.cfm

❑   **AvantGo**

   ❑   Palm user guide – http://avantgo.com/doc/mobile/palm/

   ❑   Mobile Web Developer Guide – http://developer.avantgo.com/developers/web/index.html

Index

A Guide to the Index

The index is arranged in word-by-word order (so that *image resolution* would precede *ImageMagick*). Acronyms have been preferred to their expansions as main entries on the grounds that they are easier to remember. An asterisk (*) has been used to represent variant endings, so that readers seeking all references to the *PDF_set_text_pos() function*, for example, should also check for entries at *PDF_* functions*.

Symbols

$ *see variable name.*
$_SERVER array, determining browser type, 363
@ error control operator, ImageWbmp() function, 151
_rotation property, movie clips, 135
_xScale and _yScale properties, movie clips, 128
<% ... %>, <? ... ?>, <php ... ?> and <script> tags, 26

A

abstract methods, 58
Acrobat Forms *see* **PDF Forms.**
Acrobat
  electronic forms creation with FDF, 22
  forms tool, 291
  removing or hiding toolbars, 280
  requirements for using PDF forms, 289
  using Page Templates in, 305
ActionScript
  arrays, 120
  compared to JavaScript, 106
  data types
    Boolean, MovieClip and Number, 109
    Object, 110
    String, 108
  Flash movie dimensions, 107
  loops supported, 122
  OOP language for web site animation, 105
  operators, 121
  Ming library use with
    problems, 106
    color screenshots from, 541
  timelines, 105
  variable declaration
    HTML, 112
    loading external variables, 111
    TextField, 111
  versions, 106
    Arrays, 120
    supported in Ming, 72, 106
  writing, 107

ActionScript functions
  creating for buttons on interfaces, 343
  defining centrally, 342
  duplicateMovieClip() function, 125
  eval() function, 127
  getURL() function, 136, 353
  loadMovie() function, 335, 347, 353
  loadVariables() function, 111, 136, 335
  random() function, 127
  removeMovieClip() function, 129
  scrolling, 345
  setName() function, 108, 111, 112
  setRate() function, 107
  stop() function, 125, 134
ActionScript programming
  Eye Candy example, 123
  sending variables from Flash, 136
  Simple Clock example, 133
Add() method, Form class, 64, 68
add() method, SWFMovie class, 81, 92
addAction() method, SWFButton class, 342
addEntry() method, SWFGradient class, 85
addFill() method, SWFShape class, 84, 87
addShape() method, SWFButton class, 100, 101
addString() method, SWFText class, 89
administration scripts, Image Gallery Case Study, 404
Adobe Software Foundation *see* **Acrobat; Photoshop.**
AFM (Adobe Font Metrics) format, 239
Aladdin Free Public License and PDFlib, 218
angled text, 179
animation, 92
  animation.php script, 96
  Flash movie playing speed, 76
annotation notes
  see also **text.**
  PdfObjNote class and, 277
anti-aliasing and ImageTTFText() function, 177
app.alert() method, JavaScript, 302
architecture diagram, PHP4, 3
arcs, drawing, 169
arguments
  see also **variables, PHP.**
  passing by reference, 38
  passing by value, 47

arithmetic operators, PHP, 36
array data types, PHP, 32
Array object, ActionScript
    functions, 121
    length property, 120
array operator, PHP, 41
array() construct, PHP, 32
arrays
    splitting text into, PdfObjText class, 274
    storing SWFShape objects, 101
ASP tag syntax, PHP, 26
assignment operators, PHP, 40
ATM (Adobe Type Manager), 239
AvantGo
    browser for handheld devices, 361
    image sizes, formats and page size, 362
    installing, 552
    online resources, 554
    testing HAWHAW applications with, 554
    viewing HAWHAW pages with, 547
    with and without a PDA, 362

B

background colors, 154
backtick.php file, 198
bad_font.php script, 242
baseline JPEGs, 86
bc* family of math functions, 29
birthday tracking PDF Forms example, 290
    complementary application, 326
birthday.pdf form, 326
bitwise operators, PHP, 40
bold text, 249
bookmarks, PDFlib feature, 218
Boolean data type, ActionScript, 109
Boolean data type, PHP, 31
bouncing white dot, adding ActionScript with
    SWFAction class, 112
bounding boxes, 265
    rotating shapes, 94
    string text, 180, 181
Boutell.com, Inc. web site, 145
    see also GD Library.
broken image icons, 149
browser type, determining, 363
browsers
    see also AvantGo.
    can't display TIFF images, 400
    file formats supported by, 402
    fonts defined by, 88
    HAW_deck object and, 486
    images sent to, require MIME types, 149
    movies sent to, require MIME types, 77
    problems with using PDF in a frameset, 280
    scaling movies to fit browser windows, 76
bugs
    ImageCopyResampled() function, GD, 187
    ImageTTFText() function, 176
built-in character encoding, PDFlib, 241
built-in functions, PHP gettype() and settype(), 27
buttons
    adding ActionScript to, 342
    adding to interface, 341

adding to scroll headlines, 341
attaching sounds to, 72
creating, 344

C

C_Comment() function, imagemagick.php class, 206
C_Resize() function, imagemagick.php class, 207
callback functions, 336
case sensitivity, PHP keywords, 31
Case Studies see Coffee Shop Finder case study;
    Image Gallery Case Study; Ming Headline Grabber
    Case Study; PDF Template System Case Study;
Case Study, using GD on WAP sites and PDA
    Coffee Shop Finder case study, 366
    delivering custom content with PHP, 363
        determining user agent, 363
        HAWHAW, 364
        WML/HTML problems with generating dynamically, 363
    PDA web content - AvantGo, 361
    WAP, 359
casting operators, PHP, 28
catadmin.php script, Image Gallery Case Study, 405
Catalog object, FDF document body, 299
ceil() function, PHP, 29
CGI, PHP faster and more efficient than, 1
ChangeFormat() function, imagemagick.php
    class, 208, 212
character encoding
    FDF documents, 315
    glyph files, 240
    non-Latin character sets, 243
    PDFlib built-in encoding, 241
    vectors for text handling, 240
character width, PDF core fonts, 239
Chinese language support, 315
circles and ellipses, PdfObjCircle class, 270
class instantiation operator, PHP, 41
classes
    instantiation in PHP, 53
    subclasses and inheritance, 55
    objects and, in OOP, 51
class-method call operator, 59
client-side scripting, 3
    PDF Forms, 300
clipped PDF pages, 259
clipping operation, PDFlib, 231
closing tags, heredoc syntax, 31
CMYK encoding, PDF_setcolor() function, 233
code blocks, PHP, 42
code fragments, wrapper lines, 225
code reuse and subclassing, 56
Coffee Shop Finder case study
    application specification, 366
        components, 368
        MySQL database, 366
        tools, 367
        usability, 368
    common.php script, 369
        DbConnect function, 369
        DbInitDeck function, 371
        DbQuery function, 370
        ErrorPage function, 371
        FormatPhone function, 372
        ImageForceTwoColor function, 373
        ImageResize function, 375
        MakeRatingGraphic function, 375

Coffee Shop Finder case study (continued)
config.php, 377
details.php, 388
form.php, 380
hawhaw.inc, 369
index.php, 378
possible enhancements, 394
rate.php, 394
search.php, 384
color handling
color expression and the Ming library, 75
GD functions, 153
process and spot colors, 218
setting movie backgrounds, 77
color object, ActionScript
setRGB() function, 131
setTransform() function, 131
color picker script, 161
color screenshots gallery, 531
colorspaces
PDF_setcolor() function, 232
PdfColor class, PDF Template System Case Study, 434
PDFlib extension library feature, 218
ColorTransform object, ActionScript, 131
command-line scripting, 2
comments, C-style and Perl-style, 26
comparison operators, ActionScript, 122
comparison operators, PHP, 37
compound data types, PHP, 27, 31
compression
ImageJpeg() function, 150
LZW compression scheme, 145
concatenation operations, PHP, 36
conditional structures, PHP, 43
configuration scripts, Image Gallery Case Study, 402
constants, PHP, 35
ConstructParameterHtml() method, Form class, 63, 65
constructor methods in OOP, 52
control elements excluded from PDF pages, 279
control structures, PHP, 42
Convert utility, ImageMagick, 196
Image Gallery Case Study, 408, 414
online image manipulation functions, 197
Convert() function, imagemagick.php class, 205
convert.exe files, Windows 2000, 18, 196
coordinate system, PDFlib, 226
coordinates, GD images, 162
ImageCopy() function, 184
ImageTTFText() and ImageString() functions differ, 177
core fonts, PDF, 238
count() function (PHP), 120
cropping images, 184
cross-platform operation
FDF scripts, 287
GD library scripts, 145
Ming library scripts, 73
PDFlib extension, 220
CSV (Comma Separated Values) files
storing headline data, 337, 355
updating headline data, 356
current point, PDFlib, 231

D

data accessor methods, 57
data compression *see* **compression.**
data merging, PDF Template System Case Study, 425
data types, PHP, 26
casting, 28
returning values from functions, 48
databases
Image Gallery Case Study, 399, 401
PDF Template System Case Study
table definition, 456
Date object, ActionScript, 135
DBL (Define Bits Lossless) files, 86
default blocks, switch...case... statements, 44
default coordinates, PDFlib, 226
default variables, PHP functions, 48
define() function, PHP constant identifier, 35
Delete() method, PdfDoc class, 262
Delete() method, PdfDocument class, 432
demo stamp, PDFlib, 219
deprecated functions, 231
depth dimension, 107
design mode, PDF Form creation, 297
Display() method, Form class, 67, 68
displays, ImageMagick colors adjust for, 18
DisplaySubmitButton() method, Form class, 66
DisplayTextField() method, Form class, 66
dithering, ImageTrueColorToPalette() function, 155
DLL file prefixes, 16
do...while loops
PHP, 45
supported by ActionScript, 122
document formats supported by ImageMagick, 193
document scope, PDFlib, 223
patterns defined within, 236
templates defined within, 234
documentation errors, ImageArc() function, 169
DOM (Document Object Model) and PDF documents, 300
dot notation method, compared to JavaScript's HTML DOM, 107
Draw() function, PdfObj class, 265, 268
Draw() function, PDFObjBookmark class, 454
Draw() function, PdfObjCircle class, 270, 447
Draw() function, PdfObjline class, 269
Draw() function, PdfObjNote class, 278, 454
Draw() function, PdfObjPDF class, 276, 455
Draw() function, PdfObjPict class, 271, 447
Draw() function, PdfObjRect class, 269, 446
Draw() function, PdfObjText class, 273, 448
Draw() function, PdfPage class, 440
Draw() method, PdfDoc class, 263
Draw() method, PdfDocument class, 427
drawCurve() function, SWFShape class, 82
drawCurveTo() function, SWFShape class, 124
drawing, Ming classes for, 79
drawLine() and drawLineTo() methods, SWFShape class, 80
drop down list boxes, 322
duplicateMovieClip() function, ActionScript, 125

dynamic generation
Flash movies, 71
image generation, 143
information in PDFs, 279
WML/HTML, 363

E

EBCDIC (Extended Binary Coded Decimal Interchange Code) and PDFlib, 218, 241
effects.php script, Image Gallery Case Study, 413, 414
ellipses, creating using the GD Library, 173
filled ellipses, 175
<embed> tags, including PDF in HTML, 280
embedding bitmap images, 252
embedding SWF movies, 338
embossed text, using the ImageTTFText() function, 179
empty bracket syntax, 32
encoding see **character-encoding; CMYK; RGB; URL-encoding.**
Encoding resource category, 246
encryption limitations of PDFlib, 219
envelope_merged.php script, 458
envelope_template.php script, 458
environment variables
enabling for PDF forms support, 289
modifying PATH for ImageMagick, 194
EPS (Encapsulated PostScript) files, 219
error control reporting operator, PHP, 41
error() function, imagemagick class, 203
escape sequences, PHP double quoted strings, 30
eval() function, ActionScript, 127
examples, see **birthday tracking; Coffee Shop Finder case study; Eye Candy; Simple Clock.**
Excel, Microsoft see **CSV files.**
Exec() function, imagemagick.php class, 206, 210
execution operator, PHP, 41
explode() function, PdfObjText class, 275, 451
Export Format
Adobe Acrobat form tool, 293, 296
fdf_save() function alternative, 313
Export Value, radio buttons in PDF forms, 298
extends keyword, 59
extension libraries see **PHP extension libraries**
extension_loaded() function, 73, 145, 221, 288
external character encoding, PDFlib, 241
eXtreme PHP Form Framework, 55, 62
checking control types, 64
Eye Candy example
color and color transform, 131
creating a circle, 124
duplicateMovieClip() function, 125
eval() function, 127
removeMovieClip() function, 129
scenario, creating a PHP/Ming movie that outputs random dots, 123

F

FastTemplate HTML template system, 421
FDB (Font Definition Block), 88

FDF (Forms Data Format), 285
advantages over HTML, 286
API functions, 304
classic and template-based FDF, 304
document structures, 298
installation, 22
introduced, 283
language reference (Appendix), 513
testing the installation, 22
using with PHP, 290
API functions, 299, 304
fdf_* functions, full list (Appendix), 513
fdf_add_template() function, 304
fdf_close() function, 305
fdf_create() function, 306
fdf_get_file() function, 307
fdf_get_status() function, 308
fdf_get_value() function, 309
fdf_next_fied_name() function, 310
fdf_open() function, 295, 311
fdf_save() function, 312
fdf_set_ap() function, 313
fdf_set_encoding() function, 315
fdf_set_file() function, 316
fdf_set_flags() function, 317
fdf_set_javascript_action() function, 319
fdf_set_opt() function, 320
fdf_set_status() function, 322
fdf_set_submit_form_action() function, 323
fdf_set_value() function, 324
features, ImageMagick see **ImageMagick.**
file extensions
extracting, 403
ImageMagick automatic processing and, 522
PHP, 25
file formats
see also **document formats; image formats.**
array in imagemagick.php class, 200
converting in ImageMagick, 213
ImageMagick Convert utility, 196
ImageMagick Mogrify utility, 197
supported by web browsers, 402
file names, extracting, 403
file size
advantages of PDF, 218
saving PDF forms and, 298
fill operation, PDFlib, 231
fill_stroke_clipping.php script, 233
FillStroke() function, PdfObj class, 268, 445
filters, imagic_copy_resize() function, 525
fixed layout, template systems, 422
flags, setting in PDF forms, 318
Flash, Macromedia
ActionScript as tool within, 105
version output by the Ming library, 72
Flash movies
see also **SWF movies.**
accessing movie clip properties, 113
adding text, 88
adding variables
ActionScript, 111
HTML, 112
loading external variables, 111
TextField, 111
using <embed> and <param> tags, 118

Flash movies (continued)
animation, 92
creating external variables, 116
creation process, 112
dimensions
depth, 107
dot notation, 107
nesting of objects, 107
specifying display sizes, 76
time, 107
dynamic generation with Ming, 71
interaction, 100
nesting objects, 112
playing speed, 76
sending variables from, 136
terminology, decreasing the _y value, 346
Flash player, 76
floating frames, 280
floating layout, template systems, 422, 436
floating point data type, PHP, 29
flood fills, ImageFill() function, 154
floor() function, PHP, 29
font embedding, PDFlib, 243
font_resource.php script, 244, 259
FontAFM resource category, 246
FontOutline section, Resource Configuration file, 240, 246
FontPFM resource category, 246
fonts
browser-defined and FDB, 88
defining defaults, PDF Template System Case Study, 428
PDF support, 238
font names, 239
subsetting not supported, 245
setting sizes in PDF form fields, 298
fopen() and fwrite() functions, 312
for in loop, ActionScript support, 122
for loop, ActionScript support, 122
for loops, PHP, 45
foreach loops, PHP, 46
foreground colors, ImageWbmp() function, 151
Form class creating, 62
formats, image, supported by ImageMagick 5.4.0, 18, 518
image and document formats, 193
FormControl class
HiddenField subclass, 61
inheritance example using, 56
SubmitButton subclass, 60
TextField subclass, 59
forms
see also **PDF Forms.**
general design aims, 330
framesets, using PDF in, 280
FreeType
annotating images with ImageMagick Mogrify, 197
using GD text functions under UNIX, 176
front end scripts, Image Gallery Case Study, 411
fully-formatted text, PDFlib library feature, 219
function overloading, 47
function references, PHP (Appendices)
FDF language reference, 513
GD language reference, 475
HAWHAW reference, 483
ImageMagick language reference, 517
Ming language reference, 463
PDF language reference, 501

functional programming compared to OOP, 50
functions, PHP
built-in functions, 46
calling by reference, 39
calling dynamically, 38
default variables, 48
passing arguments by reference, 38
returning values, 48
user-defined functions, 47

G

gallery database, 401
garbage collector, PHP4, 33
GD Library
see also **Case Study, using GD on WAP sites and PDA.**
color screenshots from, 542
editing images using, 147
copying, resizing and merging, 183
existing images, 183
functions, 475
color handling functions, 153
ImageColor*() and ImageWbmp() functions, 373
overview of basic functions, 147
text manipulation functions, 176
geometric drawing, 162
ellipses, 173
including in PHP, 17
introduction and supported formats, 144
introduction and versions, 16
language reference (Appendix), 475
testing the installation, 17
UNIX installation, 16
Windows installation, 16
general code flow, PDFlib, 223, 231
geometric drawing, 79, 162
get_class() function, PHP, 64
GetFooterHtml() and GetHeaderHtml() methods, FormControl class, 58, 60
getHours() function, Date object, ActionScript, 135
GetImageSize() function, GD Library, 475
GetParameters() method, Form class, 63
getShape1() and GetShape2() methods, SWFMorph class, 98, 99
GetTagHeader() method, Form class, 65
getter methods, 57
gettype() function, PHP, 27
getURL() function, ActionScript, 136
getValue() method, FormControl class, 57
Ghostscript
annotating images with ImageMagick Mogrify, 197
font subsetting workaround, 245
GIF Format, GD Library support, 144
gif2dbl utility, Ming library, 86
GIMP, GD library as alternative, 143
GiveHandle() function, PdfColor class, 435
GiveHandle() function, PdfFont class, 433, 434
glyph files, 240
graphics see **images.**
GUI programs
see also **GIMP; Photoshop.**
editing images using the GD Library, 147
Gutmans, Andi, PHP developer, 3

H

HAW_banner class methods, 484
HAW_checkbox class methods, 485
HAW_deck class methods, 486
HAW_deck object properties and methods, 364
HAW_form class methods, 488
HAW_hidden class methods, 489
HAW_image class methods, 490
HAW_input class methods, 491
HAW_link class methods, 493
HAW_linkset class methods, 493
HAW_phone class methods, 494
HAW_radio class methods, 495
HAW_row class methods, 496
HAW_rule class methods, 496
HAW_select class methods, 497
HAW_submit class methods, 498
HAW_table class methods, 498
HAW_text class methods, 499
HAWHAW (HTML and WML Hybrid Adapted
    Webserver), 364
    platforms supported, 364
    reference Appendix, 483
    testing applications using AvantGo, 554
    visualizing applications on PDAs, 547
HAWHAW PHP class, 364
    determining the user agent, 365
    HAWHAW toolkit component, 364
HAWHAW toolkit components, 364
HAWHAW XML, 364, 483
HAWXY proxy, 364, 484
Hayden, Dave, creator of the Ming library, 72
HDML (Handheld Device Markup Language)
    supported by HAWHAW, 364, 483
header() function and HTTP Content-type headers, 149
helloworld.php script, 224
heredoc syntax, 30
hexadecimal color values, 153
HiddenField class, 61
host encoding, PDFlib, 241, 242
HotSync Manager, Palm Desktop, 548
    enabling in POSE, 551
HTML
    adding variables to Flash movies
        using <embed> and <param> tags, 118
    embedding SWF movie output, 78, 338
    FDF advantages over, 286
    forms, PDF Forms compared to, 284
    imagemagick.php script, 212
    including PDF in, 279
    problems with dynamic generation, 363
    removing or hiding Acrobat toolbars, 280
    submitting PDF Forms data as, 285
HTML and WML Hybrid Adapted Webserver see
    HAWHAW.
HTML editors and <script> tags, 26
HTML Template System compared to PDF Template
    System, 421
$HTTP_RAW_POST_DATA variable
    creating a PDF form manually, 312
    enabling for PDF forms support, 289
    FDF data stored by PHP in, 294
httpd.conf file and variant PHP extensions, 25

hypertext
    hyperlinks as PDFlib extension library feature, 218
    hypertext functions use default coordinate
        system, 227
    PdfObjNote class and hypertext functions, 277
    PDI won't import, 258

I

icons, PDF_add_note() function, 277
Identify utility, ImageMagick, 197, 205
Identify() function, imagemagick.php class, 209
IdentifyPing() and IdentifyVerbose() functions,
    imagemagick.php class, 210
if condition, ActionScript support, 122
if...elseif...else statements, PHP, 43
<iframe> element, 280
image categories
    managing in Image Gallery Case Study, 405
    selecting in Image Gallery Case Study, 411
image creation, dynamically with ImageMagick, 18
image formats supported by ImageMagick 5.4.0, 18,
    193, 518
Image Gallery Case Study, 399
    application components, 401
    application specification, 399
    color screenshots from, 546
    possible enhancements, 418
    program listings, 402
image geometries
    cropping images, PDF Template System, 438
    PDF Template System Case Study enhancement, 459
    resizing and thumbnail generation, 409
    resizing with imagic_copy_resize() function, 525
    specifying with ImageMagick Identify, 197
image handlers, PHP, 147
image handling, PDFlib, 252
    forcing printed image size, 255
    image masks and transparency, 256
    placing images using top-down coordinates, 229
    supported formats, 252
image manipulation with GD, 143
    changing existing images, 183
        copying, resizing and merging, 183
    creating new images, 148
    geometric drawing, 162
    saving or sending images to the browser, 149
image resolution, PDFlib, 253
image resource variables, 147, 154
    copying text, 184
Image* functions, GD Library, 475
$image* variables, imagemagick.php class, 202
IMAGE_ARC_* constants, ImageFilledArc()
    function, 170
    IMAGE_ARC_CHORD style, 172
    IMAGE_ARC_EDGED style, 173
    IMAGE_ARC_NOFILL style, 172
    IMAGE_ARC_PIE style, 171
image_res.php script, 253
image_size.php script, 255
image_unproportional.php script, 256
ImageArc() function, GD, 169
ImageColor*() functions, image manipulation, 148
ImageColorAllocate() function, GD, 153, 373
ImageColorAt() function, GD, 159, 373

ImageColorSet() function, GD, 161
ImageColorsForIndex() function, GD, 161, 373
  using ImageColorAt() function with, 159
ImageColorsTotal() function, GD, 158
ImageColorTransparent() function, GD, 154
ImageCopy() function, GD, 183
ImageCopyMerge() function, GD, 188
ImageCopyResampled() function, GD, 187
  known bug, 187
ImageCopyResized() function, GD, 185
  ImageCopyResampled() results compared to, 187
ImageCreate() function, GD, 148
ImageCreateFromJpeg() function, GD, 183
ImageCreateFromPng() function, GD, 183
ImageCreateTrueColor() function, GD, 148
ImageFill() function, GD, 154
ImageFilledArc() function, GD, 170
ImageFilledPolygon() function, GD, 167
ImageFilledRectangle() function, GD, 165
ImageJpeg() function, GD, 150
ImageLine() function, GD, 162
ImageMagick, 193
  automatic processing of files by extension, 522
  class library, 199
    implementing the class library functions, 211
  color screenshots from, 544
  features, Image Gallery Case Study, 402, 414
  formats supported by ImageMagick 5.4.0, 18,
    193, 518
  installation on UNIX, 19, 194
  installation on Windows, 18, 194
  introduced, 18
  language reference (Appendix), 517
  macros tabulated, 206
  testing the installation, 19
  tools introduced, 193
  using with PHP, 198
imagemagick.php class, 199
  ImageMagick() function, 202
  ImageProperties() function, 203, 204
  use in Image Gallery Case Study, 401
imagemagick.php script, 211
ImagePng() function, GD, 149
ImagePolygon() function, GD, 166
ImageProperties() function, imagemagick class, 203, 204
ImageRectangle() function, GD, 163
images
  applying effects in ImageMagick, 214
  converting in ImageMagick
    imagemagick.php script, 212, 213
  filtering with ImageMagick, 196
  formats supported by ImageMagick 5.4.0, 518
  opening in a new window, 413
  resizing in ImageMagick, 196, 208
    imagemagick.php script, 211, 213
    specifying maximum size in pixels and as a
      percentage, 209
  variables describing, in ImageMagick, 202
ImageSetPixel() function, GD, 162
ImageString() function, GD, 176
ImageTrueColorToPalette() function, GD, 155
ImageTTFBBox() function, 180
ImageTTFText() function, GD, 176
ImageWbmp() function, GD, 151, 373
imagick_* functions (Appendix), 517, 523
i-Mode supported by HAWHAW, 364, 483
importing files, limitations of PDFlib, 219

indenting and heredoc syntax, 31
index.php script, Image Gallery Case Study, 411
indexed-color graphics, 144
  converting true-color to, 155
  ImageColorAllocate() function, GD, 154
  ImageColorsTotal() function, 158
  ImageCreate() function, 148
infinite loops, 45
inheritance and subclasses, 55
Init() function, PdfColor class, 435
Init() function, PdfFont class, 433
InitColors() function, PdfDocument class, 429
InitFonts() function, PdfDocument class, 429
input field retrieval with fdf_get_value(), 310
instantiating classes in PHP, 53
integer data type, PHP, 29
interaction and Flash movies, 100
is_int() function, PHP, 29
italic text, 249
iterators, PHP, 62

J

Japanese language support, 315
JavaScript
  associating with PDF form fields, 320
  client-side input validation and, 300
JPEG (Joint Photographic Experts Group) graphics
  ImageCreateFromJpeg() function, 183
  ImageJpeg() function, 150

K

keyword searches, Image Gallery Case Study, 412

L

layout design
  page layout, PDF, 226, 231
  PDF Template System Case Study, 456
layout tools, pdfTex publishing tool, 422
layout types, template systems, 422
length property, Array object, ActionScript, 120
Lerdorf, Rasmus, PHP creator, 3
LGPL (Lesser General Public License) and Ming library, 72
libc rand() function, 408
LibSWF library deficiencies compared with Ming, 72
licensing
  Ming library, 72
  PDFlib library, 218
line breaks, PDF Template System Case Study, 451
line drawing, 162
line terminators and heredoc syntax, 31
list.php script, Image Gallery Case Study, 413, 415
loadMovie() function, 347
  inherits position, rotation and scale of target clip, 353
  testing, 347
loadVariables() function, ActionScript, 335
  creating external variables, 116
  loading external variables, 111
  sending variables from Flash movies, 136
local storage, implementing with flat text files, 354

logical operators, ActionScript, 121
logical operators, PHP, 38
looping structures, PHP, 44
LZW compression scheme, 145, 259

M

Macintosh, ImageMagick binaries, 194
macroman encoding, PDFlib, 241
Macromedia see ActionScript; Flash.
makepsres utility, 246
mask-explicit.php script, 258
mask-implicit.php script, 257
masking by position and color, 256
Math class, ActionScript, random() function, 127
math functions, PHP, 29
members of classes in OOP, 51
MergeData() function, PdfDocument class, 431, 456
method calls
    class-method call operator, 59
    instance methods in PHP, 54
methods in OOP, 51, 52
metric coordinates, PDFlib, 227
metrics information, PDF core fonts, 239
MIME (Multipurpose Internet Mail Extensions) type
    Flash movies, 77
    images, 149
Ming Headline Grabber Case Study, 333
    application development, 337
        adding local storage, 354
        completing the interface, 342
        creating the basic interface, 337
        enhancements, 353
        grabbing and using the data, 348
    application specification, 333
        components, 337
        data retrieval and manipulation, 334
        interface, 334
        local storage, 337
        PHP XML functions, 336
        RSS, 335
        tools, 337
        usability, 334
Ming library, 71
    ActionScript versions supported, 106
    adding text to movies, 88
    advantages over LibSWF, 72
    animation, 92
    color expression, 75
    color screenshots from, 531
        using with ActionScript with, 541
    drawing classes, 79
    including support with PHP, 15
    inconsistent documentation, 88
    installing on UNIX, 15, 72
    installing on Windows, 14, 73
    interaction, 100
    introduced, 14
    language reference (Appendix), 463
    PHP/Ming's thirteen classes tabulated, 74
    problems with SWFFont and SWFText classes from
        using ActionScript and, 106
    SWH movies and, 75
    testing the installation, 16, 74
    web site, 102
ming_* miscellaneous functions, 472

Ming with ActionScript, 105
    see also ActionScript.
mirroring text, 228
MML (Multimedia Markup Language) HAWHAW
    support, 364, 483
Mogrify utility, ImageMagick, 197
Mogrify() function, imagemagick.php class, 207
montage.php script, Image Gallery Case Study, 417
move() method, SWFDisplayItem class, 93
movePen() and movePenTo() methods, SWFShape
    class, 80
moveTo() method, SWFDisplayItem class, 93, 97
moveTo() method, SWFText class, 89
    animation, 92
MoveUploadedFile() function, 408
movie clip creation, 340
    containing a multi-line text box, 345
    decreasing the _y value, 346
movie clip properties, 128
    _rotation property, 135
MovieClip data type, ActionScript, 109
mt_rand() function, 408
multidimensional arrays, 33
multimedia introduced, 4
MyRectangle() function, 164
    filled rectangles, 165
MySQL database, Image Gallery Case Study and, 400
mysql_connect() function, 369
mysql_query() function, 370

N

naming conventions
    PDF Forms variables, 298
    PHP constants, 35
    PHP variables, 26
nextFrame() method, SWFDisplayItem class, 96
non-progressive JPEGs, 86
non-proportional scaling, 256
notice warnings, HAWHAW output, 484
NULL data type, PHP4, 34
Null scope, PDFlib, 223
Number data type, ActionScript, 109
numeric operators, ActionScript, 121

O

Object data type, ActionScript, 110
object data type, PHP, 33
object member access operator, PHP, 41
object scope, PDFlib, 223
<object> tags, including PDF in HTML, 280
object-orientation
    creating object-oriented web pages, 364
    defining PDFlib page layout, 261
        implementation, 278
    PDF Template System Case Study model, 423
objects and classes in OOP, 51
on the fly see dynamic generation.
online resources see web site references.
OOP (Object-Oriented Programming)
    PHP and, 2
    PHP4 support, 4
    variable functions, PHP, 49

open_image.php script, 252
OpenOffice suite, PDF Template System Case Study
  enhancement, 459
Openwave SDK, 361
operators, PHP, 36
  assignment operators, 40
  bitwise operators, 40
  miscellaneous operators, 41
  operator precedence, PHP, 41
Output() function, PdfDocument class, 432
Output() method, PdfDoc class, 263
output() method, SWFMovie class, 77
overloading, 4, 52
overriding methods, 58
  parser bahavior and, 60

P

page layout
  PDF page size limits, 231
  PDFlib coordinate system, 226
page scope, PDFlib, 223
PageFromTemplate() method, PdfDocument class, 429
painttype paramter, PDF_begin_pattern()
  function, 236
Palm Desktop software, 548
  online resources, 554
Palm Operating System Emulator *see* POSE.
PalmOS devices, ROM images, 362
parallelograms, drawing with ImagePolygon(), 167
parent class example, 56
parentheses
  overriding operator precedence, 42
  variable functions, PHP, 49
parsers
  improvements to PHP parsers, 3
  treatment of overridden methods, 60
party.html form, 290
party.pdf form, 296
  complementary application, 326
party.php script, 294
  fdf_get_value() function and, 309
PATH environment variable, ImageMagick on Windows
  2000 or NT, 194, 195
path information, PDF forms, 307
path scope, PDFlib, 223
paths, PDFlib, 231
pattern colorspace, PDF_setcolor() function, 233
pattern scope, PDFlib, 223
patterns, PDFlib, 236
  defined within document scope, 236
  extension library feature, 219
patterns.php script, 237
PDA web content
  AvantGo browser suitability for, 361
  viewing HAWHAW pages with AvantGo and POSE, 547
PDF (Portable Document Format), 217
  enabling support on UNIX and Windows, 220
  font support, 238
  import with PDI, 258
  including in HTML, 279
  PHP PDF language reference (Appendix), 501
  programming concepts of PDF creation, 222
  testing an installation for support, 221

PDF Forms, 283
  Adobe Acrobat requirements, 289
  client-side input validation, 300
  compared to HTML forms, 284
  creating a basic form, 290
  creating a complementary application, 326
  creation strategies, 297
  naming global variables, 298
  populating another document with processed
    data, 327
  setting field values programmatically, 326
  specifying action on submitting, 323
  submitting data as HTML or FDF, 285
PDF Template System Case Study, 421
  application components, 423
  application specification, 423
  class description, 423
  class relationship diagram, 424
  database table definition, 456
  example template, 458
  layout design, 456
  linking with the database, 458
  possible enhancements, 459
  program listing, 426
  testing, 456
PDF_* functions (Appendix), 501
PDF_add_note() function, 277
PDF_begin_page() function, 263
  general code flow, PDFlib, 224
PDF_begin_pattern() function, 236
PDF_begin_template() function, 234
PDF_circle() function, 270
PDF_close() function, 263
  general code flow, PDFlib, 224
  PDF_close_image() and, 253
PDF_close_image() function, 253, 271
PDF_close_pdi_page() function, 259
PDF_delete() function, 262
  general code flow, PDFlib, 224
PDF_end_page() function, 263
  coordinate system and, 227
  general code flow, PDFlib, 224
PDF_endpath() function, 268
PDF_fill() function, 268
PDF_fill_stroke() function, 268
PDF_findfont() function, 240, 242
  setting text as bold or italic, 249
PDF_get_buffer() function, 263
  general code flow, PDFlib, 224
PDF_get_pdi_value() function, 259
pdf_import.php script, 259
PDF_lineto() function, 269
PDF_linewidth() function, general code flow,
  PDFlib, 232
PDF_moveto() function, 269
PDF_new() function, 262
  general code flow, PDFlib, 224
PDF_open_file() function, 262
  general code flow, PDFlib, 224
PDF_open_image_file() function., 252, 271
PDF_open_pdi() and PDF_open_pdi_page()
  functions, 259
PDF_place_image() function, 234, 252, 271
PDF_place_pdi() and PDF_place_pdi_page() functions,
  259

PDF_rect() function, 268
  scopes, 223
PDF_rotate() function, translating, 266
PDF_scale() function
  correcting mirrored images, 230
  metric coordinates and, 227
PDF_set_border_color() function, 277
PDF_set_info() function, general code flow, PDFlib, 224
PDF_set_parameter() function, 240
  setting resources with, 248
  specifying external code page files, 242, 245
  underlined text, 249
PDF_set_text_pos() function, 273, 275
  PdfObjText class, 452
PDF_set_value() function, correcting mirrored text, 229
PDF_setcolor() function, 232, 267
  general code flow, PDFlib, 231
  path finishing commands and, 232
  patterns, 236
  scopes, 223
PDF_setfont() function, 273, 276
  PdfObjText class, 452
  scopes, 223
  setting text as bold or italic, 249
  underlined text, 249
PDF_setlinewidth() function, 267
PDF_show() function, 273, 275
  PdfObjText class, 452
  scopes, 223
PDF_show_boxed() function, 250
PDF_skew() function, translating, 266
PDF_stringwidth() function, 273, 275
PDF_stroke() function, 268
PdfColor class, PDF Template System Case Study, 434
PdfDoc class, 261
  implementing the functions, 278
PdfDocument class, PDF Template System Case Study, 427
PdfDocument.php script, 426
PdfFont class, PDF Template System Case Study, 433
PDFlib extension library, 217
  color screenshots from, 545
  coordinate system, 226
  cross-platform operation, 220
  image handling, 252
  implementing the PDFlib functions, 261
  including PDI, 258
  installing on UNIX, 20
  installing on Windows, 20
  limitations, 219
  packages, 219
  platforms supported, 218
  templates, 234
  testing the installation, 21
  text handling, 238
  use in PDF Template System Case Study, 423
pdflib.upr file, 247
PdfObj class, 264
  constructor, 443
  Draw() method, 265, 268
  FillStroke() method, 268
  parameters defining, 442
  PDF Template System Case Study, 442
  SaveSpace() method, 265
  SetFillStroke() method, 267
  Transform() method, 266

PdfObjBookmark class, PDF Template System Case Study, 454
PdfObjCircle class, 270, 447
PdfObjLine class, 269, 446
PdfObjNote class, 277, 454
PdfObjPDF class, 276, 455
PdfObjPict class, 271, 447
PdfObjRect class, 268, 446
PdfObjText class, 272
  explode() function, 275
  PDF Template System Case Study, 448
  possible enhancements, 459
PdfPage class, PDF Template System Case Study, 439
PdfPageTemplate class, PDF Template System Case Study, 441
PdfRel class, PDF Template System Case Study, 436
PdfRelBoxAround class, PDF Template System Case Study, 437
PdfRelClip class, PDF Template System Case Study, 438
PDFTemplates class, PDF Template System Case Study enhancement, 459
pdfTex publishing tool, 422
PDI (PDF Import Library), 258
  availability for UNIX, 20
  placing PDF pages, 455
PECL (PHP Extension C Layer) and ImageMagic, 18, 198
personalization of PDF forms, 307
PFB (PostScript Font Binary) format, 239
PFM (PostScript Font Metrics) format, 239
photomontage
  form for creating, 416
  ImageMagick effect, 402
  shopping cart analogy, 413
Photoshop, GD graphics library alternative, 143, 182
  text updating, 176
PHP, 25
  delivering custom content, 363
  editing images using the GD Library, 147
  GD functions, image manipulation, 367
  PHP4 architecture diagram, 3
  PHP4 improvements over previous versions, 3
  PHP4 OOP support, 4
  script creation, outputting SWF files, 340
  XML callback functions, 336
PHP Extension libraries, 13
  see also FDF; GD Library; ImageMagick; Ming library; PDFlib.
  self-contained in PHP4, 3
php.ini file
  enabling the $HTTP_RAW_POST_DATA variable, 289
  specifying tag styles, 26
  suppressing notice warnings, 484
php_gd2.dll file, bug affecting ImageTTFText() function, 176
php_ming.dll file, 14
PHP_OS constant variable, 73, 145, 221, 287
php_pdf.dll file, 220
PHP-GTK extension, 3
phpinfo.php script
  FDF detection and, 22, 288, 289
  GD Library detection and, 17, 146
  ImageMagick detection and, 19
  Ming Library detection and, 16, 74
  PDF support detection and, 221
  PDFlib detection and, 21

PHPLib Template, 421
placeholders, PDF template data merging, 425
platform-independence, PDFlib scripts, 246
PNG (Portable Network Graphics)
    ImageCreateFromPng() function, 183
    ImagePng() function, 149
    preferred GD Library format, 144
png2dbl utility, Ming library, 86
polygons, drawing with ImageFilledPolygon(), 167
polymorphism, 66
pop function, Array class, ActionScript, 121
POSE (Palm Operating System Emulator)
    installing, 549
    online resources, 554
    using, 362
    viewing HAWHAW pages with, 547
$_POST variable, 211
PostScript fonts, PDF support, 239
prefixes, .dll files, 16
preg_match() function, 205
preg_split() function, PdfObjText class, 450
primitive varaible types, PHP, 27
procedural programming compared to OOP, 50
process colors
    PdfColor class, PDF Template System Case
        Study, 434
    PDFlib extension library feature, 218
ProcessBirthday.php script, 327
ProcessBirthdayAdvanced.php script, 328
ps2pdf utility, Ghostscript, 246
push function, Array class, ActionScript, 121

R

radio buttons
    customizing the Export Value in PDF forms, 298
random numbers, libc rand() function and
    mt_rand(), 408
random() function, Math class, ActionScript, 127
Read_Comments() function, imagemagick.php
    class, 210
rectangles, drawing, 163
    filled rectangles, 165
    with supplied width and height, 164
reference operator, PHP, 38
register_globals variables
    $_POST alternative, 211
    security issues, 138
regular expression matching, ImageMagick Identify
    output, 205
removeMovieClip() function, ActionScript, 129
repeated elements, PDF, templates for, 234
Replace() function, PdfObj class, 445
Replace() function, PdfObjText class, 454
Replace() method, PdfDocument class, 430
Resize() function, imagemagick.php class, 208
$resizerFlag variable, imagemagick.php class, 201, 208
resource categories, PDFlib, 246
resource configuration file
    alternatives for setting resources, 248
    defining, 246
    PDFlib searching for, 248
    PDFlib text handling, 246

resources data type, PHP4, 33
RestoreSpace() function, PdfObj class, 444
return keyword, PHP, 48
reverse function, Array class, ActionScript, 121
RGB (Red, Green, Blue) encoding
    color screenshot, 531
    ImageColorAllocate() function, 153
    Ming library, 75
    PDF_setcolor() function, 232
    retrieving values for a given pixel, 159
ROM files from PalmOS devices, 363
rotation
    see also transformation.
    moveTo() method, SWFDisplayItem class, 94
    Transform() method, PdfObj class, 266
RSS (RDF Site Summary) files
    description and sample, 335
    headlines provided as, 335
    writing a class to process, 348
runtime mode, PDF Form creation, 297

S

SAPI web server abstraction layer, 3
save() method, SWFMovie class, 79
SaveSpace() function, PdfObj class, 265, 444
saving files and PDF form file sizes, 298
scalar data types, PHP, 27, 28
scale() method, SWFDisplayItem class, 95
scaling
    see also transformation.
    dpi calculations and, 253
    images to fit page area, 255
    non-proportional scaling, 256
scoping system, PDFlib, 222
screenshot gallery (Appendix), 531
script example
    finding text string bounding box coordinates, 180
    finding text string dimensions, 181
scripts
    Image Gallery Case Study, 402
    manually loading the Ming DLL, 73
    PDF Template System Case Study, 426
    scripting engine redesign for PHP4, 3
    suitability of PHP for command-line scripting, 2
select boxes, setting values dynamically, 322
semicolon line terminators and heredoc syntax, 31
servers supported in PHP4, 3
server-side scripting, PDF Forms, 290
session management, Image Gallery Case Study, 415
Set() function, PdfColor class, 435
setAction() method, SWFButton class, 342
setBackground() method, SWFMovie class, 77
setColor() method, SWFText class, 89
SetConstraint() method, FormControl class, 57
setDimension() method, SWFMovie class, 76
SetFillStroke() function, PdfObj class, 267, 444
SetFillStroke() function, PdfObjText class, 453
setHeight() method, SWFText class, 89
setHeight() method, SWFTextField class, 97
setLine() method, SWFShape class, 80
setName() function, ActionScript, 108, 111, 112
    naming movie clips, 113
SetParameters() method, Form class, 63

setRate() function, ActionScript, 107
setRate() method, SWFMovie class, 76
setRatio() method, SWFMorph class, 98, 99
setRGB() function, color object, ActionScript, 131
setter methods, 56
setTransform() function, color object, ActionScript, 131
settype() function, PHP, 27
setValue() method, FormControl class, 57
shape drawing
    see also paths, PDFlib.
    geometric drawing, 79, 162.
shape tweens, 98
shell_exec() function, PHP, 198
Shockwave see Flash; SWF.
shopping cart analogy for photomontage creation, 413
short tag syntax, PHP, 26
Simple Clock example, rotating objects with
    ActionScript, 133
skewing
    see also transformation.
    Transform() method, PdfObj class, 266
Smarty HTML Template, 421
sounds, attaching to buttons, 72
SourceForge.net web site, 15, 102, 459
special data types, PHP4, 27, 33
spot color
    PDF_setcolor() function, 233
    PdfColor class, PDF Template System Case
        Study, 434
    PDFlib extension library feature, 218
square bracket syntax, 32
squares, PDFlib example to generate, 226
stage, Flash movies, specifying display sizes, 76
/Status key, FDF, 322
/status keys, PDF forms, 308
stop() function, ActionScript, 125, 134
String data type, ActionScript, 108
string data type, PHP, 30
    see also text.
string operator, ActionScript, 121
string operators, PHP, 36
stroke operation, PDFlib, 231
subclasses, 55
submit buttons, adding with the Acrobat forms
    tool, 292
SubmitButton class, 60
substr() function and hexadecimal color values, 153
Suraski, Zeev, PHP developer, 3
SVG (Scalable Vector Graphics), 459
SWF file output, 340
SWF movies
    see also Flash movies.
    building with PHP/Ming, 353
    embedding in HTML file, 338
    Ming library for, 71
swf_placeobject() function, 107, 473
SWFAction class, PHP/Ming
    adding ActionScript to a bouncing white dot, 112
    init() method, 472
    introduced, 102
SWFBitmap class, PHP/Ming, 86
    full list of members, 470
    inconsistent documentation, 88
SWFBitmap() function, Ming, 144

SWFBitmap.php script, 87
SWFButton class, PHP/Ming, 100
    addAction() method, 342
    adding labels, 339
    adding shapes for button state, 338
    full list of members, 467
    setAction() method, 342
SWFButton.php script, 100
SWFDisplayItem class, PHP/Ming, 92
    full list of members, 468
    move() and moveTo() methods, 93
    nextFrame() method, 96
    scale() method, 95
SWFDisplayItem1.php script, 92
SWFDisplayItem2.php script, 93
SWFDisplayItem3.php script, 95
SWFFill class, PHP/Ming, 84, 469
SWFFont class, PHP/Ming, 88, 466
SWFGradient class, PHP/Ming, 85, 470
SWFGradient.php script, 85
SWFMorph class, PHP/Ming, 98, 470
SWFMorph.php script, 98
SWFMovie class, PHP/Ming, 75
    add() method, 81, 92
    full list of members, 463, 464
    output() method, 77
    save() method, 79
    setBackground() method, 77
    setDimension() method, 76
    setRate() method, 76
SWFMovie.php script, 77
SWFShape class, PHP/Ming, 79
    addFill() method, 84, 87
    creating, 113
    drawCurve() function, 82
    drawCurveTo() function, 82, 124
    drawLine() and drawLineTo() methods, 80
    full list of members, 464
    movePen() and movePenTo() methods, 80
    objects, storing in an array, 101
    setLeftFill() and setRightFill() methods, 84
    setLine() method, 80
SWFShapeCurve.php script, 83
SWFShapeLine.php script, 82
SWFSprite class, PHP/Ming
    adding shape to, 125
    adding to main movie timeline, 125
    full list of members, 472
    movie clip creation, 98, 113, 335
SWFText class, PHP/Ming, 88
    full list of members, 466
    moveTo() method, 92
    Windows instability, 90
SWFText.php script, 89
SWFTextField class, PHP/Ming, 90
    adding text box to movie, 111, 112
    creating text label, 340
    does not have moveTo() function, 114
    full list of members, 470
    optional arguments, 471
    setHeight() method, 97
    SWFTEXTFIELD_DRAWBOX argument, 113
SWFTextField1.php script, 91
SWFTextField2.php script, 97
switch...case...default statements, PHP, 44

T

tags
closing, heredoc syntax, 31
distinguishing PHP, 25
formatting, PdfObjText class, 448
text formatting, PdfObjText class, 272
templates
adding to PDF forms, 304
HTML and PDF Template Systems compared, 421
subclasses as, 58
PDFlib, 234
template scope, 223
templates.php script, 234
text
adding to Flash movies, 88
annotations in PDFlib can't be rotated or
skewed, 227
drawing text strings, 177, 182
string data type, ActionScript, 108
string data type, PHP, 30
text label creation, SWFTextField class, 340
text handling, PDFlib, 238
character encoding, 240
resource configuration file, 246
text formatting, 249
PdfObjText class, 272
setting font sizes in PDF Forms, 298
text layout
blocks of text, 250
limitations of PDFlib, 219
mirroring text, 228
placing text with PDFlib top-down coordinates, 227
text manipulation, GD Library functions, 176
text strings, drawing
changing site text graphics with GD, 182
positioning, using the ImageTTFBBox() function, 182
using the ImageTTFText() function, 177
angled text, 179
embossed text, 179
relief effects, 180
text_layout.php script, 251
textboxes
adding to Flash movies, 111
adding with the Adobe Acrobat forms tool, 291
TextField class, subclass of FormControl, 59
textfomatting.php script, 249
$this keyword, 53
polymorphism and, 67
thumbnailed images, 185, 187
generating, Image Gallery Case Study, 409
sizing, Image Gallery Case Study, 402
TIFF (Tag Image File Format), 400
time dimension, setting, 107
timelines, Flash, 105
ToArray() method, Form class, 63
ToHTML() method, Form class, 67
ToHTML() method, FormControl class, 58
toolbars, Acrobat, removing or hiding, 280
tools.php script, Image Gallery Case Study, 403
top-down coordinates, PDFlib, 227
correcting by subtraction, 231
placing images, 229
placing text, 227
top-down_1.php script, 227
top-down_2.php script, 228

top-down_3.php script, 229
top-down_image_mirrored.php script, 229
top-down_image_ok.php script, 230
Transform() function, PdfObj class, 266, 443
transformation
objects with classes derived from PdfObj, 264
PDF output pages, 258
rotation, 94, 266
scaling, 253, 255, 256
skewing, 266
templates, 234
transparency
Acrobat support, 258
image handling, PDFlib, 256
specifying with PHP/Ming, 75
triangles, drawing with ImagePolygon(), 166
true-color graphics
ImageColorAt() function, 159
ImageTTFText() function and bug in php_gd2.dll
file, 176
indexed-color compared with, 148
TrueType fonts, 176
PDF support for, 239, 240
tweening, 98

U

UML diagrams, PDF Template System Case Study, 424
undefined type casts, 28
underlined text, 249
Unisys, GIF licensing issues, 144
UNIX platforms
enabling FDF support on, 287
enabling Ming on, 72
enabling PDF support on, 220
installing FDF, 22
installing ImageMagick, 19
installing PDFlib, 20
installing PHP extension libraries, 14
installing the GD library, 16, 145
upload.php script, Image Gallery Case Study, 407
**URL-encoding alternative to FDF for PDF Forms,
286, 296**
URLs, PDF forms, specifying with fdf_set_file(), 317
user space, translating, 266
scaling and, 256
user-defined functions, PHP, 47
**UTF-8 character encoding, ImageTTFText()
function, 177**

V

Validate() method, Form class, 54
Validate() method, FormControl class, 57
variable declaration, 52
variable functions, PHP, 49
variable variable operator, PHP, 41
variable variables, 35
variables, PHP
assigning by reference, 35
assigning by value, 34
naming convention, 26
passing by value and by reference, 47

vector graphics importing, limitations of PDFlib, 219
Vector utility class, 62
version_compare() function, 408
VMS, ImageMagick binaries for, 194

W

WAP (Wireless Application Protocol), 359
  see also HAWHAW.
  Deckit, 361
  development, 359
  Openwave SDK, 361
  WBMP graphics, ImageWbmp() function, 151
  WML, 360
watermark images, ImageCopyMerge() function, 188
WBMP (Wireless Bitmap) graphics, ImageWbmp()
  function, 151
web applications, suitability of PHP for, 2
web site references
  ActionScript features, 105
  AvantGo browser, 554
  Boutell.com for GD library, 145
  ECMA specifications, 106
  Macromedia Flash Support Center, 121
  Ming library, 15, 102
  Palm developers web site, 363
  Palm Desktop, 554
  PDFTemplates class, 459
  PEAR, 348
  PHP documentation, 106
  POSE, 554
  RSS-DEV working group, 335
  SourceForge.net, 15, 102, 459
while loop ActionScript support, 122
while loops, PHP, 45
winansi encoding, PDFlib, 241
window.open method, JavaScript, 413
Windows platforms

enabling FDF support on, 287
enabling Ming on, 73
enabling PDF support on, 220
font names, PDF names and, 239
HAWHAW output destroyed by notice warnings, 484
instability of the SWFText class, 90
  faking an SWFText object with SWFTextField, 97
installing FDF, 22
installing ImageMagick, 18
installing PDFlib, 20
installing PHP extension libraries, 13
installing the GD library, 16, 145
viewing HAWHAW pages with AvantGo and POSE, 547
WMF (Windows Metafile Format) files, 219
WML (Wireless Markup Language)
  problems with dynamic generation, 363
  compared to HTML, 360
  HAW_deck objects and, 486
  problems with dynamic generation, 363
  sample of basic deck, 361
  tags, 360
  XML and, 360
WML deck, sample of basic deck, 361
wrapper lines, code fragments, 225

X

XML
  PHP callback functions, 336
  tag syntax, PHP, 26
  XML-to-PDF translator, 251
XObjects see templates.

Z

Zend scripting engine, 3

wrox
Programmer to Programmer™

p2p.wrox.com
The programmer's resource centre

A unique free service from Wrox Press
With the aim of helping programmers to help each other

Wrox Press aims to provide timely and practical information to today's programmer. P2P is a list server offering a host of targeted mailing lists where you can share knowledge with four fellow programmers and find solutions to your problems. Whatever the level of your programming knowledge, and whatever technology you use P2P can provide you with the information you need.

ASP Support for beginners and professionals, including a resource page with hundreds of links, and a popular ASP.NET mailing list.

DATABASES For database programmers, offering support on SQL Server, mySQL, and Oracle.

MOBILE Software development for the mobile market is growing rapidly. We provide lists for the several current standards, including WAP, Windows CE, and Symbian.

JAVA A complete set of Java lists, covering beginners, professionals, and server-side programmers (including JSP, servlets and EJBs)

.NET Microsoft's new OS platform, covering topics such as ASP.NET, C#, and general .NET discussion.

VISUAL BASIC Covers all aspects of VB programming, from programming Office macros to creating components for the .NET platform.

WEB DESIGN As web page requirements become more complex, programmer's are taking a more important role in creating web sites. For these programmers, we offer lists covering technologies such as Flash, Coldfusion, and JavaScript.

XML Covering all aspects of XML, including XSLT and schemas.

OPEN SOURCE Many Open Source topics covered including PHP, Apache, Perl, Linux, Python and more.

FOREIGN LANGUAGE Several lists dedicated to Spanish and German speaking programmers, categories include. NET, Java, XML, PHP and XML

How to subscribe
Simply visit the P2P site, at http://p2p.wrox.com/

wrox

Programmer to Programmer™

Registration Code : 76475V5L1U4D7AK01

Wrox writes books for you. Any suggestions, or ideas about how you want information given in your ideal book will be studied by our team. Your comments are always valued at Wrox.

Free phone in USA 800-USE-WROX
Fax (312) 893 8001

UK Tel.: (0121) 687 4100   Fax: (0121) 687 4101

Professional PHP4 Multimedia Programming – Registration Card

Name _____

Address _____

_____

_____

City _____ State/Region _____

Country _____ Postcode/Zip _____

E-Mail _____

Occupation _____

How did you hear about this book?

❏ Book review (name) _____

❏ Advertisement (name) _____

❏ Recommendation _____

❏ Catalog _____

❏ Other _____

Where did you buy this book?

❏ Bookstore (name) _____ City _____

❏ Computer store (name) _____

❏ Mail order _____

❏ Other _____

What influenced you in the purchase of this book?

❏ Cover Design ❏ Contents ❏ Other (please specify):

_____

How did you rate the overall content of this book?

❏ Excellent ❏ Good ❏ Average ❏ Poor

What did you find most useful about this book? _____

_____

What did you find least useful about this book? _____

_____

_____

Please add any additional comments. _____

_____

_____

What other subjects will you buy a computer book on soon?

_____

What is the best computer book you have used this year?

_____

Note: This information will only be used to keep you updated about new Wrox Press titles and will not be used for any other purpose or passed to any other third party.

wrox

Programmer to Programmer™

Note: If you post the bounce back card below in the UK, please send it to:

Wrox Press Limited, Arden House, 1102 Warwick Road,
Acocks Green, Birmingham B27 6HB. UK.

Computer Book Publishers